JEWISH VALUES IN OUR OPEN SOCIETY

[Handwritten inscription:]

ב"ה מנחם אב תשס"א

To Sam

בברכת כוחך וחילך

Thanks for your good humor and the best "Torah" which can only come from a heart as deep as yours!

Josh

JEWISH VALUES IN OUR OPEN SOCIETY

A WEEKLY TORAH COMMENTARY

MEIR TAMARI

JASON ARONSON INC.
Northvale, New Jersey
Jerusalem

This book was set in 11 pt. Berkeley Book by Pageworks of Old Saybrook, CT and printed and bound by Book-mart Press, Inc. of North Bergen, NJ.

Copyright © 2000 by Meir Tamari

10 9 8 7 6 5 4 3 2 1

All rights reserved. No part of this book may be used or reproduced in any manner whatsoever without written permission from Jason Aronson Inc. except in the case of brief quotations in reviews for inclusion in a magazine, newspaper, or broadcast.

Library of Congress Cataloging-in-Publication Data

Tamari, Meir.
    Jewish values in our open society: a weekly Torah commentary / by Meir Tamari.
       p.   cm.
    Includes index.
    ISBN 0-7657-6122-X
    1. Bible O.T. Pentateuch Commentaries. I. Title.
BS1225.3.T236 2000
222'.107—dc21   99-41843
                                                                                 CIP

Printed in the United States of America on acid-free paper. For information and catalog write to Jason Aronson Inc., 230 Livingston Street, Northvale, NJ 07647-1726, or visit our website: www.aronson.com.

CONTENTS

Introduction	ix

SONG OF THE JUST — 1

SEFER HAYASHAR — 3
  Introduction of HaEmek Davar — 3

BEREISHIT — 5
  Adam in the World

NOACH — 11
  His Lovingkindness

LECH LECHAH — 18
  The Land of Israel

VAYEIRAH — 24
  Economic Egoism

CHAYEI SARAH — 31
  A Woman of Valor

TOLDOT — 37
  Spiritual Turmoil

VAYEIZEI Bread and Clothing	42
VAYISHLACH Ya'akov, Yisrael, and Yeshurun	47
VAYEISHEV All Were without Sin	53
MIKETZ The Interpretation Is the Lord's	58
VAYIGASH Two Sons of Rachel and Leah	63
VAYECHI Sur Mirah–Asei Tov	69

SONG OF THE NATION   75

SHMOT Introduction	77
SHMOT Exile and Redemption	80
VAEIRAH Ten Plagues	87
BO To Walk in the Way	93
BESHALACH Generation of the Wilderness	99
YITRO Ten Commandments	106
MISHPATIM You Shall Not Take Interest	114

CONTENTS

TERUMAH To Dwell in Their Midst	121
TETZAVEH Levels of Holiness	127
KI TISAH Attributes of Mercy	133
VAYAKHEL The Gift of Knowledge	139
PEKUDEI Transparency	145

SONG OF HOLINESS — 153

INTRODUCTION OF DAVID TZVI HOFFMAN Based on the *Sefer HaMitzvot* of the *Ramban*	155
VAYIKRA Korban—An Invitation	158
TZAV Law and Religiosity	164
SHEMINI Limits of Spirituality and Ecstasy	170
TAZRIAH Taharah and Tumah	176
METZORAH Physical Ills and Social Immorality	181
ACHREI MOT Repentance, Confession, and Atonement	187
KEDOSHIM To Be Holy	193

EMOR — 199
    The Balance of Material and Spiritual

BEHAR — 205
    The World Is Built by *Chesed*

BECHUKOTAI — 213
    That Which Brings National Prosperity, Peace, and Happiness

SONG OF THE WANDERINGS — 221

INTRODUCTION TO BAMIDBAR — 223
    Ramban

BAMIDBAR — 225
    To Be Counted

NASO — 231
    Ascetism is Holiness?

BEHA'ALOTCHA — 236
    Prayer in Trembling and Prayer in Joy

SHELACH — 241
    Sanctifying His Name

KORACH — 247
    For the Sake of Heaven

CHUKKAT — 252
    Permitted and Forbidden War

BALAK — 259
    To Achieve the Spiritual Potential

PINCHAS — 266
    The Cycle of the Jewish Year

MATTOT — 274
    The Power of Speech

MASA'EI	281
National Reward and Punishment	281

SONG OF THE HOLY COMMONWEALTH — 285

DEVARIM	287
Introduction: S. R. Hirsch	
DEVARIM	290
The Pursuit of Justice	
VE'ETCHANAN	296
Love of the One God	
EIKEV	302
The Yoke of *Mitzvot*	
RE'EH	309
Pesach Questions of the Four Sons	
SHOFTIM	315
Kingship, Statehood, and Government	
KI TEITZEI	322
The Torah Spoke Only Regarding the Yetzer Harah	
KI TAVO	326
Fruits of the Land	
NITZAVIM	334
Eternal Covenant	
VAYELECH	339
The Hidden Face of God	
HA'AZINU	345
Stages of Redemption	
VEZOT HABERACHA	349
Tribes, Months, and the Signs of the Zodiac	

INTRODUCTION

This is neither a commentary, nor an anthology, nor a translation of the work of a great Torah scholar. Rather, it is an attempt to provide perspectives on living in the benevolent open societies, that is, the spiritual and religious challenge to our Judaism. These perspectives reflect personal experiences and involvement in many of the events and phenomena of the past seventy years of Jewish living in that open society.

 The South African Jewish community in which I grew up prior to World War II knew little if any economic difficulty or anti-Semitic persecution, yet at the same time was faced with the struggle to develop and maintain a specific Jewish character, both collectively and individually. The answer for me was involvement in what was the first outreach in any country to the uncommitted or marginally religious through *HaShomer Hadati*, later *Bnei Akiva*. So the 1940s were spent in actively helping to innovate many of the techniques, concepts, and attitudes used today in working for Jewish Continuity, what is today called "outreach." However, there was also the ever-present moral challenge of the anti-black racism that was both socially and legally accepted. For some of us this meant identification with the primarily communist left. For others, in later years, the answer was emigration. Like many of my generation, I chose *aliya* to the new State of Israel. From 1950 until today I have experienced Israel in all its facets and developments. The period of national rebirth, a decade in a religious left-wing kibbutz, and the military service of a religious pacifist were aspects of that experience, as was my professional life after leaving kibbutz. Many years of academic and professional work as a research economist in Israel's central bank not only meant awareness of the moral, ethical, and social challenges posed by methods of acquiring, investing, and spending wealth, but also the Jewish reply to these challenges. These were also years of a cultural and social interaction with secular Israelis; international travel involving consulting to public bodies; academic teaching and research regarding corporate finance, small firms, and entrepreneurs; and risk evaluation. All this and at the same time, the pattern of everyday living was retained, enjoined by careful halakhic standards in all areas. Professional achievement, cultural impact, and the diversified global village all posed their challenges to religion, Jewish lifestyle, and Torah philosophy.

This book reflects the knowledge gained from four main sources that provided the Torah perspectives and halakhic wherewithal necessary to meet the religious and spiritual challenges of all these phenomena and experiences. These four were my infrastructure built on the basis of the classical commentators; *halakhic* codes and responsa and homilitical literature. First there was Abarbanel, living in an open society, involved in commerce and statecraft and at the same time a Torah scholar, religious thinker, and biblical commentator. He provided answers of an independent mind beyond that of the classical commentators: Rashi, Ibn Ezra, and the Ramban, but also his own perspectives on the ideas of Greek philosophers or the Guide to the Perplexed of Maimonides. This acquaintance was made during my undergraduate years, while studying *Gemara* with Rabbi E. W. Kirzner, whose arrival in South Africa was a major catalyst for me from my bar mitzvah year until my going on *aliya* eight years later.

In kibbutz there was a meeting with Rav Tzvi Yehuda Kook, and then there was the consequent studying of his own ideas and those of his father, Avraham HaCohen Kook. The integration of Land, People, and Torah, the perspective of *galut* and redemption and the importance

INTRODUCTION

of *K'lal Yisrael*, the Jewish communal entity, were now an additional perspective of Torah study and knowledge. Above all, there was now the understanding that there are Jewish spectacles for all personal, social, and political issues, and, therefore, the necessity to look at these issues through these spectacles. Even though we parted ways regarding the linear nature of redemption and the existence of a Judaism in which there is the single issue of nationalism, borders, or political state, nevertheless, there was an acceptance by me of the importance of all of these in my Torah thinking.

Then there was the move to Jerusalem and the *Shem MiShmuel*, Chassidic Master of Sochachow, whose ideas and teachings so changed much of my religious outlook and life. Here was a well-constructed and well-written text, in which talmudic discussion, seemingly ritualistic or legal, reflects spiritual perspectives, while being interwoven with mysticism of the *Zohar* and with the teachings of the *Maharal*, Rabbi Lowe of Prague. The *Midrashim* are further vehicles for understanding different concepts and teachings of religiosity, worship, and Man-Divine relationships. Body, *nefesh* and *neshama*; Wisdom, knowledge, and understanding; Time, the cycle of the Festivals and the *Shabbat* all became part of that which is taught in this Torah. This is a Torah that rests on Menachem Mendel of Kotzk, Simcha Bunem of Physcha, the *Yehudi HaKadosh* and the *Avnei Nezer* with their specific school of Chassidism based on intensive study of the Written and Oral Laws.

Later came, quite by accident, the writings of S. R. Hirsch, so powerfully solving the spiritual and religious challenges of modernity and the open society. Here was a comprehensive and elegant tapestry of the immutable and eternal Torah, morality, and integrity, and the mission of the Jew to achieve and demonstrate holiness in all facets of behavior. I can always see in these pages, the educator of average men and women, constantly striving to create a Jewish role model able to live fully, positively, and independently within the material, cultural, and ideological effects of the real world; that is, a world open and tolerant, yet at the same time full of ethical and spiritual pitfalls and corruption.

I would like to imagine that this book of weekly *parshiot* is a parallel to the fourfold song of A. I. HaCohen Kook:

There is one who sings the song of his own life, and in himself he finds everything, his full spiritual satisfaction.

There is another who sings the song of his people. He leaves the circle of his own individual self, because he finds it without sufficient breadth, without an idealistic basis. He aspires toward the heights, and he attaches himself with a gentle love to the whole community of Israel. Together with her he sings her songs. He feels grieved in her afflictions and delights in her hopes. He contemplates noble and pure thoughts about her past and her future, and probes with love and wisdom her inner spiritual essence.

There is another who reaches toward more distant realms, and he goes beyond the boundary of Israel to sing the song of man. His spirit extends to the wider vistas of the majesty of man generally, and his noble essence. He aspires toward man's general goal and looks forward toward his higher perfection. From this source of life he draws the subjects of his meditation and study, his aspirations and his visions.

Then there is one who rises toward wider horizons, until he links himself with all existence, with all God's creatures, with all worlds, and he sings his song with all of them. It is of one such as this that tradition has said that whoever sings a portion of song each day is assured of having a share in the world to come.

And then there is one who rises with all these songs in one ensemble, and they all join their voices. Together they sing their songs with beauty, each one lends vitality and life to the other. They are sounds of joy and gladness, sounds of jubilation and celebration, sounds of ecstasy and holiness.

The song of the self, the song of the people, the song of man, the song of the world all merge in him at all times, in every hour.

And this full comprehensiveness rises to become the song of holiness, the song of God, the song of Israel, in its full strength and beauty, in its full authenticity and greatness. The name "Israel" stands for *shir El*, the song of God. It is a simple song, a twofold song, a threefold song, and a fourfold song. It is the Song of Songs of Solomon, *Shlomo*, which means peace or wholeness. It is the song of the King in whom is wholeness. (*Orot HaKodesh*—Light of Holiness, Vol. II, pp. 458–459)

SONG OF THE JUST

SEFER HAYASHAR

Introduction of HaEmek Davar

"This book of Bereishit called by the prophets, the book of the just [or the righteous] (*Talmud Bavli, Avoda Zarah* 25a)," said Rabbi Jochanan. "This is the book of Avraham, Yitzchak and Ya'akov who are called Yesharim—just, or righteous—as it is written: 'I myself would like to die the death of the righteous' (*Devarim* 23:10)." We need to understand why Bilam in that verse should have chosen particularly to use just-righteous for the Patriarchs rather than saintly or pious or any other religious term of praise. Furthermore, why should Bereishit be called by this name?

The issue becomes clear when we read "Righteous and Justice" (*Devarim* 35:4). This we understand to justify the Divine Judgment that decreed the destruction of the Second Temple, even as the next verse describes that generation as "a generation obstinate in its crookedness." They were a saintly and pious generation, busily engaged in Torah study. However, they were not straight or just in their interpersonal relationships so that needless hatred typified them. This led them even to bloodshed, internal strife [between the Zealots, the Sicarii, and the peace parties of the last days of the Second Temple], and all imaginable evils. So the Temple itself was destroyed, just retribution [for their needless hatred]. *HaKadosh Baruch Hu* is straight (just-righteous) and does not tolerate such kinds of saints. Rather, he requires that they pursue a straight and just path also in their worldy behavior and avoid deviousness or crookedness therein, even when their actions are motivated for the sake of Heaven. [The lack of a straight path] brings in its wake the destruction of the Creation and the breakdown of human society [as in the case of the Second Temple].

The Patriarchs were saintly, pious, and lovers of God to the utmost extent. They are praised [in that Genesis is called the Book of the Just]. Furthermore, they were also praised because they were straight and just. This means that they behaved toward the nations of the world, even the idolators among them, righteously and justly. They showed a love toward them [without in any way condoning idolatry or compromising their faith] and were concerned for their welfare because this represents the continued existence of the world. So we see how Avraham prays and prostates himself for the people of S'dom—even as it is written (*Bereishit Rabbah VaYeirah* 49): "He said to Avraham *Avinu*, 'You love justice and hate evil—you love to justify My creatures and hate to find them guilty.'" This is fitting for Avraham, who is the father of many nations. Even when the sons do not always follow straight and just paths, nevertheless, the father endeavors to offer them peace and welfare. So, too, we see that Yitzchak carefully appeases Avimelech and his allies, far beyond that which was necessary (*Bereishit* 26). Ya'akov, even though he was oppressed by Laban and knew that only Divine intervention prevented Laban from destroying him, nevertheless, spoke only words of peace and goodwill (Gen. 31). This led our sages to teach "Better to suffer the slavery of the Fathers than the modesty of the sons" (*Bereishit Rabbah* 74).

We are taught many similar lessons concerning the Patriarchs in relation to the existence of the world, especially in this book which is the story of Creation. Therefore *Bereishit* is called the Book of the Just and Righteous.

BEREISHIT

Adam in the World

The beginnings of all other religions lie in the birth of the gods as in pagan Greece and Rome or in the birth of the founder of the faith as in Christianity and Buddhism or in divine revelation as in the case of Islam. The Torah, however, has nothing to say about God beyond His creation of the world, but everything to say about Mankind who stand forever after at the center of our religion.

"So God created Man in His Image, in the image of God, He created him, Male and Female He created them, and God blessed them and said to them, be fruitful and multiply and fill the earth, and conquer it, and rule over the fish of the sea and the birds of the heavens and over every living thing that moves upon the earth" (*Bereishit* 1:27–28). In our prayers on Rosh Hashanah, we call this New Year, the day of the conception of the World. However, it is a conception that actually marks the creation of Man since the six days of creation started on the 25th of Ellul. In such a human-centered religion, the very nature and order of creation must be spiritually related to Man and Woman, Adam and Chava.

This relationship is expressed in the *Midrash* of the controversy among the Sages regarding the sequence of the creation. It was crucial for their understanding of human religiosity to learn what was created first, the Heavens or the Earth. Their dilemma was sparked by the two versions in *Bereishit* 1:1 and 2:4. From the first verse we know that "in the beginning God created the Heavens and the Earth," but further on we read, "on the day the Lord God made Earth and Heaven."

Beit Shammai maintain that first the Heavens were created and then the Earth. They sought to prove their viewpoint by means of a parable—a king once made himself a throne, and then, when it was completed, he made a footstool—as it is written, "The Heavens are My throne and the Earth is My footstool" (Isa. 60:1).

It is the opinion of Beit Hillel, however, that first the Earth was created. They used the example of a king who built a palace for himself to support their view. First he built the foundations and the walls thereof, then he completed the upper portions and the roof; even as it is written, "In the day that the Lord God created Earth and Heavens" (*Bereishit* 2:4).

Rabbi Yochanan, in the name of the Sages, holds that the Heavens took precedence in creation but that the Earth took precedence in completion. He differentiates between the concept of Creation and the completion thereof. This is similar to the idea of the *Midrash* that everything created in the six days needs completion or improvement, like the mustard that needs to be sweetened.

Rabbi Shimon bar Yochai said, "Both Heaven and Earth were created simultaneously just like a vessel and its lid." This is a reference to ancient clay vessels made as one entity.

The above discussion of our Sages is concerned with the value of human actions relative to Divine mercy or grace. Do such actions have as their own intrinsic value or are they only derived from the prior granting of God's mercy? Is mankind a participant in the world or only a reactor to God's mercy?

Perhaps the question may be concretasized by the explanation of the master, Shmuel of Sochochow, regarding a halachah of *Shabbat*. This centers on the status of one stranded in the desert, who had lost track of time, so did not know when *Shabbat* should be observed. Beit Shammai held that he should observe *Shabbat* immediately and then count six days to the next *Shabbat*. Beit Hillel maintains, count six days and then observe *Shabbat*. The halachah is like Beit Hillel. It is often forgotten that the legal and technical discussions of the rabbis are inherently reflections of important theological and ideological trends. This discussion is no exception, as the Sochochower's commentary, *Shem MiShmuel*, explains.

There are two aspects to the *Shabbat*. On the one hand *Shabbat* comes after six days of Creation; on the other hand, it is a prelude to the six days of activity that follow. These two aspects are both reflected in the Creation of the World. From the Talmud, we learn that Adam was created on the eve of the first *Shabbat* so that he should immediately enter the world of *mitzvot*—more specifically, as Rashi says, the mitzvah of *Shabbat* (*Bavli*, *Sanhedrin* 38a). The same source tells us that Adam was created a few hours earlier in the sixth day of Creation so that he would still be able to be a part of the period of creativity. Before the sin of Adam, the work and service of man during the six days of the week, that is, removing himself from evil, pursuing good, and separating the good from the bad, would have enabled him to enter into the sanctity of the *Shabbat*. After the sin, however, there is room to suppose that man may not have the same inherent ability to serve God in the mundane affairs of the ordinary weekdays. In that case, the *Shabbat* would have to somehow present itself in greater sanctity so as to provide the additional spiritual power needed for the following week.

So the cycle of the year reflects in time the sequence of creation. The *Shabbat* and festivals are a reflection of the Heavens, whereas the weekdays are a reflection of the Earth. Just as the Heavens affect the Earth, so the Holy Days guide and transform the weekdays.

Beit Shammai hold that the Heavens were created first, as their basic trait and philosophy is *Din*, Justice. Because one could not imagine that human actions by themselves would merit the existence of the sanctity of the *Shabbat*, that sanctity had to be created first by the *Kodosh Baruch Hu*. Only after this act of Divine mercy could one perform their pursuits in service of God in the weekdays. In the case discussed, first one has to keep a *Shabbat* and then count six days to the next *Shabbat*.

Beit Hillel, however, whose central feature and trait is that of *Chesed*, hold differently. They say that the actions in this world, which, even though they may not merit a great sanctity like that of the *Shabbat*, are rewarded through God's mercy with that sanctity. God's mercy rewards our actions, and, therefore, the *Shabbat* and all the spirituality that flows from it are a result of the pursuit of sanctity during the week. So Beit Hillel maintain the Earth was created first, and one counts six days and keeps the seventh as *Shabbat*.

Neither Hillel nor Shammai denied the value of human action nor the fructifying effect of God's mercy; the issue is solely one of precedence. Support for the view of Hillel may be found in the *Midrash Rabbah* on the verses in Genesis quoted above. The first verse uses *Elohim*, God in His attribute of *Din*, but the second reads "in the day they were created by *HaShem Elohim*" Justice, the attribute of mercy. "God first thought to create the world in His attribute of Justice; however, knowing that this creation would not survive, He added His attribute of mercy." This mercy gives credence and value to the actions of mankind, petty, trivial, and imperfect as they are, so that the world may continue to exist.

Rabbi Yochanan, who makes a distinction between creation and fulfillment, says that first God created a *Shabbat*, paralleling the opinion of Beit Shammai. However, the *Shabbat* alone does not produce the next *Shabbat*, but rather the following *Shabbat* comes as a result of man's perfection or of man's improvements, so to speak, of God's world during the subsequent six days of labor. This cycle continues until we enter a world which, as a result of our actions and our improvements, is one of a complete *Shabbat*.

Shimon bar Yochai, who taught that Heaven and Earth were created simultaneously and fitted together like a lid and a vessel, holds that all action is the fruit of thought, and, therefore, the actions of man during the six days of Creation find their inspiration or source in the original perfect *Shabbat*, so that, in effect, they are created together. As the *Lecha Dodi*, we recite on the *Shabbat* Eve, sings, "Observe (Ten Commandments, *Devarim* 5:13) and Remember (*Shmot* 20:8) . . . in a single sentence."

Heaven or Earth? Duality of Mankind

The duality of the image of God encased in the mortal, material, and physical human body has lain at the essence of all religions and philosophies. The gap between these two images led to paganism's emphasis on the reality, pleasure, and power of human intelligence and ability to the exclusion of all else. Christianity, basically following the same path of despair, saw salvation through grace and the love of God, relegating acts to a marginal role, if any. Judaism, too, has to face up to this duality but seems to have done so through a perpetual balance between the contradicting components.

"These are the *Toldot* [usually translated as generations but more accurately as] the developments of Adam . . . on the day that God created Adam He formed him in the likeness of God, Male and Female He created them" (*Bereishit* 5:1–2).

The *Midrash* tells us that when the Holy One, blessed be He, came to create Adam, the ministering angels were divided into conflicting groups, some favoring the Creation and others opposing it. It was this controversy that led the psalmist to sing (Ps. 5:11) "Righteousness and Truth met together, Justice and Peace embraced."

The Angel of Righteousness argued, "Let man be created since it is his nature to do *chesed* and acts of charity." Opposed to man's creation was the Angel of Truth. "It is not fitting," he argued, "for the Master of Truth to create something whose whole personality is permeated with falsehood and lies." To this the Angel of Justice replied that man has a natural urge to pursue justice. "What purpose does this pursuit of Justice serve," countered the Angel of Peace, "when men are constantly embroiled in quarrels, strife, and conflict?"

The angels' controversy over the creation of Adam is a reflection of the conflict that exists in mankind, that is, the pinnacle of Creation and, at the same time, frail, mortal, and morally ambivalent.

So what did the Holy One do? He threw down to Earth the Angel of Truth even as it is written "and Truth was cast down to Earth" (Dan. 8:12). It is truth, not Satan, that is sent down to Earth. It is that truth that Adam is required to use to restore, through actions and efforts, the unity of being created through the merger of Heaven and Earth, and to reflect the divinity in which Adam was created.

Rabbi Simcha Bunem of Psycha physically demonstrated the nature of duality. He made himself a pair of trousers with two pockets. Then he wrote on two slips of paper the contradictory opinions regarding the creation of Adam. On one he wrote, "Every one should always say for me the world was created" (*Talmud Bavli, Sanhedrin* 36a). The other slip contained Abraham's estimate of himself: "And I am only dust and ashes." Each slip was deposited in a separate pocket and then Reb Bunem taught, "The true wisdom is to know which pocket to use and when one should read which slip and many err in this matter."

Another aspect of this same duality was noticed by the *Chidushei HaRim*. The Talmud tells us in *Shabbat* that "King Solomon laid down the laws of Eruvim [which legally join together separate domains so that one may carry between them on *Shabbat*] and the laws of ritually washing the hands before meals. Then a *Bat Kol*, a Divine voice, said, 'My son, if your heart is wise, then my heart will rejoice too'" (14b).

The *Chidushei HaRim* found it difficult to understand what special wisdom is involved in these two laws which should have prompted such Divine praise. He found his answer in the contradictory character of the laws. *Eruvim* teach us that a man should be involved and integrated into everything that is happening about him in the world. On the other hand, the washing of the hands comes to separate and divide one from the impurity of the world.

So the *Chidushei HaRim* taught, "It is a great wisdom to separate oneself from the world and to integrate oneself with it at the same time."

NOACH

His Lovingkindness

Before creating Adam, God had consulted with all of creation saying, "Let us make Man." All the creatures felt themselves cut off from God after their Creation having no one who could connect them back to the Divine Source. Now each of them gave some of their strengths and intrinsic power toward the Creation of man so that their welfare and his would be intertwined. When mankind was good, just, and kind, then all Creation would benefit. However, Man's evil and punishment would also be reflected in the evil and punishment of the world (Mordechai Meizbitza).

Now ten generations had passed since the Creation, and each generation of mankind added its measure of sin and evil. During these ten generations, Divine patience waited for them to repent and avert destruction. Yet God's patience did not avail, and finally, "and the Earth was filled with wrongdoing . . . and behold it was corrupted for all flesh [not only men and women] had corrupted its way . . . and God said to Noah, the end of all flesh is come before Me" (Gen. 6:11–13). All these generations lived in benign climatic conditions and enjoyed God's bounty with little effort. The world revolved on an upright axis so that there was little difference between the seasons. Mankind should have been able to realize their great spiritual potential, but rather chose moral decadence as the basis for human society.

As human beings after Adam and Eve multiplied, so did the animals and the birds. People began to worry that there would not be enough natural resources to support them in their accustomed standard of living. They feared having to share their wealth with others. There was an increase in the proportion of weak and unproductive men and women and a suspected degeneration of the animal species now called on to provide for an increased population. So, means were sought to prevent economic catastrophe. Limitations were placed on population growth, and only the finest and strongest of all species were allowed to procreate. Alternative life styles, homosexuality and bestiality—both nonproductive sexual relations—became rampant. Man taught the rest of Creation to follow in his footsteps and "the whole world became depraved" (*Zohar Ber.* 56; see also *Ber. Rabbah* 34).

When this was considered insufficient to save their wealth, robbery and theft became the norms. The crimes against property led to bloodshed and murder so that the social harmony that had existed despite sexual immorality and idolatry was destroyed. In the Talmud (*Bavli Sanhedrin* 108a), the Sages taught, "the destruction of the Flood was decreed only because of theft." We know that they sinned in idolatry, sexual immorality, and murder, all of which are punished by death, but it was theft—for which there is no death penalty—that started to unravel their whole fabric (*Shem MiShmuel*).

Yet robbery and theft do not bring about the downfall of society, which can protect itself by police, prisons, and penalties. What brought about the downfall of that generation was *chamas*. Halachically, *chamas* is the theft of something whose value is less than a prutah, the smallest coin of legal tender—marginal, trivial, and for which there is no legal recourse. "One had a bag of beans, men, women and children came and each one took one bean, less than a prutah. The owner lost all his property, yet nobody was legally liable" (*Talmud Yerushalmi, Baba Metzia,* Chapter 4, *Halakhah* 2). It was this petty thievery, the underhand dealing, cunningly keeping within the letter of the law, that undermined their morality.

Because they stole those things for which there was no legal protection or recourse, the people of the flood showed that they had neither fear of the retribution of a God before whom there are no secret crimes nor faith in Him to provide all their needs. Their actions were prototypes of commercial methods and economic behavior, found in all ages, that like *chamas* are not redeemable in a court of law. The rabbis created a halakhic instrument which by public disapproval and protest would limit such immoral actions, wherein nobody was legally liable. Social approval or displeasure are powerful factors in determining the moral parameters of the market place, existing as they do beyond the legal framework of that market place. One of these is the *mi sheparah* (literally, he who claimed payment) text that is read in the synagogue at the demand of the injured party in such cases. The text recalls God's payment extracted from the generation of the Flood, from the people of S'dom and from Pharaoh of Egypt. For example, *mi sheparah* is the public rebuke of one who does not keep his contract, even in those cases where no monetary loss occurs, and therefore no legal action is possible. "He who demanded payment from the generation of the Flood . . . will surely punish one who does not keep his word" (*Talmud Bavli, Baba Metzia* 48a).

The destruction of the world through the Flood, indeed, all the scenes of punishment in the Bible, make it easy to understand the idea of the angry, zealous God of the Old Testament. Nevertheless, it is a false idea, flowing from a need to justify the emergence of Christianity, stressing mercy and love. This same idea is also falsely used to explain *Chassidism* as a rebellion against normative rabbinical Judaism. In truth, the God of Judaism balances justice and mercy. He is King but also Father, and mankind are both subjects and children. "His mercy extends to all His creatures."

"The Lord is gracious and compassionate, slow to anger and He shows His greatness primarily in His loving-kindness" (Ps. 145:8; S. R. Hirsch translation and commentary).

"The process of repentance is a great mercy which the Almighty has given to His creatures. He has prepared a way for them out of the guilt-filled pit and an escape out of the conscience-racked trap of their offenses. Even if they have offended, rebelled, and corrupted, He has not closed before them the gates of repentance (R. Jonah of Gerondi, Italy, *Sha'arei T'shuva*, First Gate, Section A). When Israel erred with the Golden Calf, Moshe prayed for forgiveness, and the Lord not only forgave but Himself taught Moshe and Israel of the Divine Attributes of mercy, forgiveness, and loving kindness (Exod. 34:6–7)—the key to calls of forgiveness throughout the centuries. When Adam and Eve sinned in Eden, Justice demanded that they be punished and expelled. His Mercy, however, clothed them "and He made for them clothes of skin" (*Bereishit* 3:21). Rabbi Meir taught in the Midrash: not *or* skin but *or* (spelt with an *Aleph*), namely, clothes of light. When Cain sinned, he became a wanderer, fearful for his life, so God, in His Mercy, placed His mark on him to protect Cain against injury and death.

This is evident in the whole Creation. He causes plants to spring from the soil, fish to swarm in the water, animals to wander on the earth, birds to fly in the sky, and then Adam and Eve to populate and guard all He created. Divine mercy provides all living things with their care and sustenance—"To give drink to every beast of the fields, to quench the thirst of all wild creatures . . . the earth is satiated by the fruits of Your works. He makes fodder grow for the cattle and . . . brings forth bread from the earth and wine that gladdens the heart of people . . . the trees of the land also have their fill" (Ps. 84:11–16): "For there is nothing missing in their Universe, and He created in it good creatures and good trees to cause mankind pleasure with them"; "He Who clothes the naked": "He Who is good and does good"; "Who creates numerous living things with all their needs [but] for all that You have created with which to maintain the life of every being" (blessings for various benefits).

Not only material gifts flow from God's goodness—"You graciously bestow knowledge upon Man" (daily *Amidah*). *Chonen* means to give undeserved or even unrequited gifts. The knowledge and intelligence people have flows from God's grace. So we recite a blessing on seeing scholars, scientists, and wise people of all faiths and nations—"He Who has given of His knowledge to human beings . . . And they taught in the name of Shimon bar Yochai, He [God] adorned her [Eve] like a bride and He braided her hair as a crown. It was a great honor [to Adam and Eve] that God Himself led them to the marriage canopy . . ." (*Midrash Bereishit Rabbah* 18:1–3).

So "the eyes of all (creation) look to You with hope and You give them their food in its proper time. You open Your hand and satisfy the desires and needs of all living things" (Ps. 145:15–16). This declaration of God's mercy and kindness for all creatures is one of the reasons why this psalm is recited three times a day, every day. If one did not fully understand or take cognizance of God's *chesed*, the *Shulchan Arukh* (Yosef Karo's normative code of Jewish law, compiled sixteenth century, Land of Israel) rules that one needs to repeat the psalm (*Orech Chaim*, Section 51, Subsection 7).

Recognition of Divine Mercy and *chesed* is meant to be translated into human actions of righteousness and charity. Rabbi Yaakov Yoseph, the chronicler of the *Ba'al Shem Tov*, founder of Chassidism, writes in his *Toldot Yaakov Yoseph* that if the world would have been created only in justice, then all would have been equal in wealth and in intelligence, but then how would truth and righteousness be practiced? Now that this attribute of mercy also created the world, the inequality of people provides an opportunity to emulate Him and share their wealth and their capabilities ("Treasury of Chassidic Thought," Shubba Weiss, Tel Aviv, 1960).

"Lord, Who is like You: Who saves the poor from one stronger than him, the poor and the destitute from those who would rob him" (Ps. 35:10). Just as God is all-merciful, so man should be merciful; just as God is kind and righteous, so man should be kind and righteous; just as God is careful to look after all the creatures in His world, so should man be. Rabbi Simlai taught that the Torah begins and ends with an act of *chesed*. At the beginning, it is written, "And the Lord God made garments of skin for Adam and Eve and clothed them" (*Bereishit* 3:21), and at the conclusion is written, "He [God] buried him [Moshe] in the valley in the land of Moab" (*Devarim* 34:6; *Talmud Bavli, Sota* 14a). The world is built on *chesed*, mercy and righteousness.

So, too, in the time of the Flood when ten generations of sinners lived and only then was the punishment inflicted. Yet even here mercy exists. The Torah does not write (*Bereishit* 7:21) *Vayamoto*—and they died—but *Vayigvah*. This is a phrase reserved for the passing of great and pious people. *Vayigvah* in our text is correctly translated by Isaac Levy (The Pentateuch, London, 1959) as "became torpid, unconscious, unresponsive," and he writes that he would like to translate it as euthanasia. When Noah and his family entered the ark, God Himself in His mercy, closed the entrance. This mercy came also to provide mankind with the spiritual guidelines that could prevent corruption and, therefore, destruction, so God made a covenant with Noah and his descendants. With this covenant, mankind was given seven commandments, an act of Divine Grace, creating basic parameters for human coexistence and happiness. These "Noachide Laws," are part of the ethical and moral inheritance of all peoples on earth and one who lives contrary to them, places himself beyond the pale of civilization (*Torah Temimah*, *Shmot* 21:35).

"Six *mitzvot* were given to Adam, forbidding idolatry, cursing God, murder, adultery, and theft and making the appointment of judges and a judicial system obligatory" (*Midrash Rabbah*, Chapter 16, Section 6, based on *Bereishit* 2:16). In His covenant with Noah, God added the injunction against eating the flesh of living animals (*Mishneh Torah*, *Hilkhot Melakhim*, Chapter 9, Halakhah 1). Nachmanides (*Bereishit* 34:13) sees the requirement to establish a judicial system as obligating non-Jews with all the commercial and business *mitzvot* obligatory on Jews. These include the laws of bailees, theft, oppression, protecting wages, infringing property rights, the obligation to pay workers on time, *ona'ah* (price oppression), truth in trading, money lending and trading, and the prevention of damages. Maimonides sees these obligations as flowing from the injunction against theft. Where Jews have sovereignty on non-Jews, they are obligated to force them to abide by the Noachide Laws. Rabbi Menachem Mendel Schneersohn of Lubavitch holds that Jews always have a moral obligation to educate non-Jews to keep these laws.

These would logically apply to providing for the stranger, the needy, and the weak. Indeed, many authorities rule that Noachides are also obligated to give charity as part of an equitable judicial system. It was the failure of Sodom and Gomorra to do just that that led to their destruction.

"One who keeps the Seven Noachide Laws as part of a Divinely ordained framework for society is considered to be one of the righteous of the nations and has a share in the world to come" (*Mishneh Torah, Hilkhot Melakhim*, Chapter 8, Halakhah 11).

LECH LECHAH

The Land of Israel

This *sedrah*, which is the beginning of the story of the Jewish people, does not start with a revelation of a new religion nor with a spiritual message to a prophet. Rather, there is the command to go to a foreign land in which a nation will be forged. The generations that preceded Abraham were great spiritual figures, but Cain and Abel, Noah, Shem, Japhet and Ham, and all the others were not Jewish. Abraham is the first Jew, and the land is chosen together with him.

"To the Land that I will show [to] you," said Rabbi Yitzchak, "The Torah should have begun with 'this month' (*Shmot* 12:2), which is the first mitzvah given to Israel [that of the lunar calendar beginning with Nissan, the month of Exodus]. Why then does it commence with the story of Creation? The answer is in order to morally justify the claims of Israel to the Land of Israel, since the Lord who created all the world takes and gives countries to whom He desires" (*Tanchuma, Bereishit* 11).

These twin strands of nation and land constitute the very beginning of Judaism, and their development parallels each revelation and covenant between God and Abraham.

At first, the message is short and vague; no mention of which land Abraham is to go to nor of boundaries nor of time of possession. Only a promise "that I will show you," which is accepted with the perfect trust

LECH LECHAH

and faith that is the Abrahamic hallmark. Then, on the return from Egypt, Lot separates himself and his flocks from Abraham and from the still vague Promised Land, to settle in the wealthy but evil city of Sodom. Lot is a nephew and a disciple, both family and potential spiritual heir, but he is not destined to fulfill the Abrahamic covenant. Later, through Ruth the Moabite, ancestress of David and Na'amah the Amonite, wife of his grandson, the sparks of holiness residing in Lot would come back to rejoin the Abrahamic family.

With Lot's departure, an expanded promise is given to Abraham, ". . . look from the place where you stand, northward, southward, eastward and westward, for all the land you see to you do I give it and to your seed for ever." This is the Promised Land, however, the covenant has a new dimension. Not only the scope of the land is made more specific but also for the first time there is the promise to an old man of children; not only of a child but of countless generations of many nations (*Bereishit* 13:14–16).

Years pass, yet Abraham and Sarah are still childless. Another revelation comes to Abraham, a promise of God's protection and great reward despite great sacrifice. A revelation that comes to show Abraham that his mission and role in the world will not devolve on a disciple, as has been common to many religions and faiths, but on a son. Eliezer of Damascus, servant, apostle, and disciple, will not inherit the promise of the Land. Together, with the promise of sons, the vague land now acquires physical boundaries, as well as a date of fulfillment.

On that day God made a covenant with Abraham to give him the land between the river of Egypt and the river Prat, all the land of the Seven Nations. Yet four hundred years had to elapse before this would occur, years of enslavement in a foreign land. The sin of the Emorites, now living in this Holy Land, had not reached the limits that would justify their expulsion, and, therefore, his heirs would yet not be able to inherit.

After this covenant, Sarah gives Hagar, the daughter of Pharaoh, king of Egypt, as a wife to Abraham. Now that the covenant has become explicit, perhaps the promised son would be born to Abraham by Hagar, yet raised by Sarah in the spiritual qualities needed to inherit Abraham. Yet Ishmael is not destined to inherit and so another covenant heralding the birth of a son to Sarah and to Abraham is made. This son to whose descendants will be given the Promised Land is also the inheritor of a special spiritual relationship with God. This relationship of a religion is introduced here for the first time in the Abrahamic story: "and I will give to . . . to your descendants . . . all the Land of Canaan for an everlasting possession and I will be a God unto them" (*Bereishit* 17:8).

This covenant of Land, people, and Divine relationship is marked by the changing of the names of Abraham and Sarah to denote their new personality, by the injunction of circumcision—the memorial of the covenant—and the announcement of Yitzchak, son and heir.

Many years later, this covenant is reestablished when Sarah demands the expulsion of Hagar and Ishmael. "Sarah saw the son of Hagar, the Egyptian, born to Abraham *metzachek*, mocking" (*Bereishit* 21:10).

"Rabbi Shimon bar Yochai says, *metzachek* is idolatry. Rabbi Eliezer says this is sexual immorality, Rabbi Yehoshua says this is murder, and I say, God forbid that these things should occur in the house of that tzaddik. Rather, Ishmael mocked Yitzchak, saying, "I am the first born and therefore I will inherit the double portion [of the Divine promise of the Land and the Law]" (*Tosephta Sota*, Chapter 6).

Sarah does not wish to send Hagar away because of any jealousy, neither it would seem from the *Tosephta* it is the reason for Ishmael's errant behavior. After all, God made him a great nation. Her reason is solely the issue of who is to inherit the Promised Land. The text itself bears this out. Sarah says clearly, "Her son will not inherit with my son, with Yitzchak." God Himself makes this the issue when He tells Abraham, "In Yitzchak will be called your seed."

The issue of inheritance of the Promised Land is not marginal but is parallel to the whole development of the Abrahamic family and their spiritual destiny. This Holy Land is intrinsically unlike any other land. It possesses its own spiritual value, so that Moses warns Israel not to behave as did the Canaanites, otherwise the Land will vomit them out as it did their predecessors; this Land is unable to stomach, as it were, evil,

LECH LECHAH

immorality, and idolatry (*VaYikrah* 18:26–28). It is a Land from which Israel is exiled for seventy years because of its social sins of not releasing the bondsman on the *shmittah* year (Chronicles II 36:21).

"Eretz, land, has its roots in *ratz*, to run, because the earth hastened to God's desire at the time of creation. One runs after those things that one loves and wishes to gain. So the earth runs after the heavens. The heavens, however, fearing a tainting of their spirituality reject the earth. This tension of attraction and rejection keeps heaven and earth separate. The Land of Israel, however, is different, because, being chosen, just as Israel is chosen, it is able to remain close to heaven, being "a Land that God cares for, on which the eyes of the Lord dwell always" (*Devarim* 11:12; *Shem MiShmuel*, Lech Lecha).

"Why should the people of Sodom and Gomorra be destroyed when many other nations and cities were just as evil," asked Nachmanides. "It was because the Land of Israel is intrinsically unable to bear corruption and evil" (commentary on *Bereishit* 13:13).

The spirituality of the Land is such, that even *mitzvot* practiced in the *Golah* have a different dimension when practiced in *Eretz Yisrael*. *Mezuzah* is linked to "longevity on the Land which God promised to your fathers" (*Devarim* 11:20–21). Rashi queries the linkage because these are not *mitzvot* specific to *Eretz Yisrael*. He says that outside the Land one should observe these *mitzvot* in order that they should not be strange to us when we return from the *Golah*.

Severance with *Eretz Yisrael* produces severe spiritual dislocation, perhaps even similar to severance with the people of Israel. "One who dwells outside the land of Israel, it is as though he worships idols" (*Mishneh Torah, Hilkhot Melakhim*, Chapter 5, Halakhah 12). The opposite is also true. The land is flowing with milk and honey, both of them kosher food that have their source either in a forbidden mixture—meat and milk, or produced in the body of a non-kosher creature. The Land has the spiritual power of transforming material things into kosher food, but it also has the power to cure and refine the nature of people (A. I. HaCohen Kook).

The triple thread interweaving the spiritual values of Land, People, and Torah shows that the Promised Land is not meant to be a place of pilgrimage, nor merely a center of ritual. Rather, the Land is place in the real world where the Israelite nation can, in its everyday activities, concretize through the Divine Law, its spiritual striving. It is, however, also not merely ground for nationalist identification nor for political aggrandizement. Hirsch points out that both honey and leavened bread, two of the products with which the Land is blessed, may not be offered on the altar. Only on Shavuot, Festival of the Giving of the Law, is leavened bread offered, specifically to teach of the triple thread of Land, People, and Law. Poised before entering the land, Moses sent twelve princes to spy out the country. When they returned, they spread false reports, prevented Israel from entering the land, and doomed themselves to forty years of wandering (*Bamidbar* 13). "What," asked the *Shem MiShmuel*,

> prevented these great men from having faith in God's ability to give them possession of the Land, especially in view of the miracles of the Exodus and of the desert? As long as they were in the desert, all their material needs were taken care of from Heaven—*manna*, water from the Well of Miriam, and Clouds of Glory for shade and protection. They knew that when they crossed the Jordan they would have to earn a livelihood, build cities and organize their public lives in a normal, material way, but yet within the demands of God's law and teachings. They feared that they were not of a spiritual level to combine the material and spiritual in the Promised Land.

This combination that is so specific to Judaism in all spheres is also expressed halachically. "One who lives in *Eretz Yisrael* but does not earn a livelihood there, does not really fulfill the *mitzva* of *Yishuv Eretz Yisrael*" (*Avnei Nezer*). The *Chatam Sofer* taught that "six days you shall labor" is not an obligation in *chutz la'aretz* but is in *Eretz Yisrael*. This Jewish view of the combination of the material and spiritual is not surprising. After all, so much of Judaism is expressed just in that combination regarding food, sex, wealth, war, ecology, and every other aspect of life. It is only natural, therefore, that there should be a Land that expresses this spiritualism in the mundane, everyday aspects of a national group.

Just as the non-Jewish world always had great difficulty in understanding or accepting the expression of holiness in material and human actions, so, too, there was a difficulty in accepting this role of the Land. Balak, king of Moab, brought Bilam to curse Israel, but his motives are not clear. He is in no way threatened materially or politically by the entry of Israel to its Land. He also does not ask Bilam to cause Israel to be defeated in war, only to prevent their entry. The *Shem MiShmuel* explains that their entry would both obligate Israel to conduct its economy, its social structure, and its policies according to the Law of God and to show that this is possible. Then the nations of the world would have to do the same. This was a religion contrary to all others that dealt only with God, spirituality, or things of another world. Balak could neither understand nor accept this concept.

VAYEIRAH

Economic Egoism

The past fifty years have witnessed an explosion of wealth, unparalleled in world history, one that has been shared, even if unequally, by all countries. It may have been expected that this great increase in economic wealth would solve all problems, ushering in an almost messianic period of human happiness and mutual assistance. After all, the pressure of competition for scarce resources, the cause of so much hate, war, and misery, has been dramatically reduced. Yet our Sages taught that "one has a hundred but wants 200"; economic wants as distinct from needs are seen to be unlimited. More is always deemed better than less. This *yetzer harah* is unlike any other need of mankind, for example, with sex, the less one has the less one wants, the more one has, the need is never satiated (Talmud, *Sukkah* 52b). In the case of food, the less one has the more one wants, but the more one has the less one wants. Money, the less one has, the more one wants and the more one has, the more one wants. "You shall love the Lord . . . with all your might" is understood (*Rashi, Devarim* 6:5), as "with all your possessions" as there are people who value their wealth more than their lives. So, increased wealth fuels an illogical fear of never having enough; self-indulgence made possible by the wealth paradoxically blinds us to the needs of others; and the insatiable wants blind us to the morality of the methods used to increase wealth.

Torah, however, provides a spiritual, educational, and legal religious framework that enables us to separate needs from wants and to use our wealth morally, kindly, and justly. The Talmud (*Shabbat* 10a) teaches that one who eats within the first hour of the day is a potential murderer, within the second is a robber, within the third has inherited wealth, the fourth is that of the workers, the fifth ordinary people, and the sixth hour is that of the Torah scholars. This is understood by the *Maharal* to reflect the ability of these types to limit their material desires or to postpone gratification, both indicators of spiritual control. One who cannot postpone his wants even for an hour could murder if these wants cannot be instantly met. Denied, this one will steal, or waste the wealth for which no work nor labor was entailed. Workers who have earned their wages will have the strength to partake early of its fruits, whereas ordinary people possess an ethical framework that enables saving, investment, or other forms of delaying choices of wealth. Torah scholars, able to place their needs and wants beneath God's ethical and spiritual teachings, use their wealth in the moral and just ways. The people of S'dom and her sister cities were wealthy, for it was as well watered as the Garden of the Lord. It is in the perspective of the challenge of wealth that the story of S'dom needs to be seen.

"Hear the word of the Lord, you rulers of S'dom" (Isa. 1:10). "And the people of S'dom were exceedingly evil and sinful before the Lord" (Gen. 13:13). Said Rabbi Yehudah,

> Evil in the use of their bodies, as it is written [in the response of Joseph to Potiphar's wife] "How will I do this evil?" and sinful in the use of their money, as it is written [in regard to delayed payment of wages (Deut. 24:15)] "and it shall be considered a sin for you" (*Sanhedrin* 109a). [However] we have learnt an alternative view in a *beraita* [opinions of rabbis of the Mishnaic period not included in the *Mishnah*]: evil with their wealth, as it is written, "and your eyes will look in evil

towards your needy brother" (*Devarim* 15:9) and sinful, as it is written [in the case of Joseph] "and I will have sinned before God."

The *Ein Yaakov* (a collection of talmudic *aggadot*) explains that Rabbi Yehudah maintains that monetary sins are worse because they are evil for human beings and evil toward God Who forbids them. The *Tanna* of the *beraita*, however, maintains that because monetary crimes can be rectified by returning the fraudulent or stolen wealth, sexual immorality cannot be rectified and therefore is a greater sin.

It would seem that the halakhic codes would agree with Rabbi Yehudah as to the severity of the punishment for theft. "The punishment for defective weights and measures is greater than for the forbidden sexual relations [adultery, close kin, etc.] because the latter are [sins] between Man and God [Who forbade them] while the former are [sins] between Man and his fellow [being a double evil both social and against God Who forbade theft]" (*Mishneh Torah, Hilkhot Geneivah*, Chapter 7, Halakhah 12). A gloss on the *Tur* (the Code of Yechiel ben Asher, Spain, thirteenth century) argued that whereas repentance for sexual immorality was viable, in the case where fraud of weights affected many people, perhaps like stock fraud or pyramid schemes, atonement was not really possible as the fraud could not be returned to all those affected; public works are proposed as an inferior penance (*Panim Meirot, Choshen Mishpat*).

The greater punishment for false weights and measures should not blind us to the rejection by Judaism of all forms of immorality, arguing that a society immoral in one aspect will ultimately degenerate completely. This is clearly shown by the *Midrash Bereishit Rabba* (Section 41, Subsection 6) regarding our verse in *Bereishit* 13:13: "evil" to each other, "sinful" in sexual relations, "before the Lord" denoting idolatry, and "exceedingly" through murder. The people of S'dom not only protested Lot's concern for the strangers, but also demanded that he hand them over to the S'domites "that we may know them [sexually]." In this, they resembled the generation of the Flood, and like that generation caused their own annihilation. "[With regard to S'dom] it is written (*Bereishit* 18:20): 'The outcry of S'dom and Gomorra is exceedingly great' and with regard to the Flood it is written: 'for the evil of Mankind is exceedingly great' (*Bereishit* 6:5) to teach us that their evil deeds were the same" (Jerusalem Talmud, *Baba Metziah*, Chapter 4, Halakhah 2).

So S'dom became a synonym for sexual immorality, stinginess, and economic injustice. It became a symbol of the incongruity of trying to differentiate between these different types of evil, a rejection of a society that imagines that it can be moral in one respect and at the same time immoral in other respects. Lot, true to his upbringing in the home of Abraham and Sarah, is dedicated to providing board and lodging for the strangers; the angels, who came to S'dom, are representatives of the weak, the marginal people of society, and those whom it is easy to exploit. Yet the same verses that tell of this socially admirable trait also disclose Lot's depravity. "In his desire to protect his guests he is willing to appease the S'domites by allowing them to rape his daughters. This is because sexual immorality was tolerated by him [another source mentions that Lot himself was not averse to incest]. Therefore, our rabbis said, 'it is the custom of the world that a man is prepared kill or be killed in order to protect his wife and daughters, yet this one [Lot] is willing to give his daughters over to sexual abuse,'" (Tanchuma *Bereishit* 36).

Because God is not only the Creator omnipresent and universal but also oversees and intervenes in the affairs of every person, the rabbis connected the sin and punishment of S'dom to the personal fates of individuals. The feminine form used in *Bereishit* 18:21 regarding the outcry that came before the Lord, *haketsakata*, may grammatically seem to refer to the city of S'dom because cities are always feminine in Hebrew. However, the *Midrash* in *Pirkei Eliezer* (*Vayirah*) (a homiletical collection made in *Eretz Yisrael* in the post-*Mishnaic* period) sees in the feminine form a reference to the typical sins of S'dom exemplified in the story of Plotit, the daughter of Lot.

> In S'dom they passed a law that anybody found guilty of keeping the poor or the strangers alive by giving them bread, will be burnt to death. Plotit was married to one of the noblemen of S'dom. Once she had

mercy on a very poor person and each time she went to draw water from the city well she placed food in her empty jar and fed him. Curious as to how the poor person managed to stay alive despite their law, the city fathers investigated and found Plotit guilty. When they started to punish her, her outcry reached the Heavenly throne. Then said God, I will go and see if the evil is as great as her outcry.

It is pertinent in view of the many similar *Midrashim* to point out that the crime of S'dom was not primarily a lack of hospitality but rather greed and selfishness. Only poor strangers were not welcome in S'dom. The wealthy, like Lot, were welcome; a forebear, perhaps, of our own distinction between poor immigrants and those entitled to capitalist visas. One who lives according to rules of unlimited private property who says, "What's mine is mine, what's yours is yours," is considered by our sages to live according to the ethics of S'dom (*Mishnah*, Chapters of the Fathers, Chapter 5, *Mishnah* 11). Situated in "the garden of the Lord in the land of Egypt" (*Bereishit* 13:10) made the people of S'dom and her neighboring cities extremely wealthy. It was the fear that the nomadic tribes or the peasants surrounding them would come and try and share in their wealth that led to the evil of S'dom (*Malbim*). It was that same wealth that prevented them from seeing the surrounding immorality and even trying to rectify their behavior. As has happened throughout history, this wealth led them to mock Lot, saying, "You stupid man, there is only merry making and the sounds of flutes, harps and lyres in the streets of the city, and you insist that S'dom is about to be destroyed."

It is possible to distinguish between different types of economic immorality. There is crime like theft and robbery, practiced by individuals but condemned and punished by society. There is social injustice rectified by legislation. There is corruption when immorality becomes a normal way to earn and retain wealth, considered and accepted by society. The destruction of S'dom, like the other national or global disasters described in the *Tanach*, never comes to punish the wrongdoing and crimes of individuals. It is only when economic crime becomes an acceptable civil norm, is allowed to be perpetrated publicly without shame, and to graduate from the spur-of-the-moment acts of an individual or a mob that it becomes a way of life, then that society becomes corrupt and destined for Divine Punishment. Perhaps that is why Abraham's plea for S'dom went no further than the existence of ten righteous people, it being the minimum of a community. In S'dom, like other societies both of the ancient world and of latter centuries, this corruption permeated the whole society. "And the people of S'dom surrounded the house [of Lot] from the youngest to the oldest, all of the people, from one corner of the city to the other" (*Bereishit* 19:4). There was not a single one who protested, not even one single righteous man in S'dom (*Rashi*). The best expression of their corruption is the fact described in the *Pirkei de R. Eliezer* cited previously: it became enshrined in their legal system. Selfishness, and according to another source homosexuality, became accepted patterns of behavior.

A parallel to this understanding of corruption through the legal system may be found in the comment of Rashi to the verse in Amos (2:6), "sold the poor for a pair of shoes." The Hebrew word for shoe, *na'al*, has the same root as the word lock, because the shoe is distinct from the sandal which is open, and locks as if it were the foot. Rashi sees the sin being the purchase by the rich of the fields surrounding the poor farmer and then forcing him to sell his property. Legal but corrupt is one of the causes for the destruction of the kingdom of Israel.

It was because they were the antithesis of the Abrahamic mission that God revealed the imminent destruction of S'dom to Abraham. "For I know him intimately, that he will command his children and his household after him that they shall keep the way of God to do *chesed* as an obligation and justice" (*Bereishit* 18:19). This characteristic of righteousness and charity, of acts beyond the letter of the law, and of the willingness to forego legal property, rights for the benefit of others, has been the hallmark of the Jewish nation throughout the centuries. "One who does not do a favor with his money for his fellow, we may suspect that he is not of the Jewish people" (*Pesachim* 112b–113a). This *chesed* was never allowed to remain dependent only on the individual's choice, but, like all other aspects of life in Judaism, was formalized by the halakhah and made legally enforceable. "[A *bet din*] may coerce one not to act in the ways of the people of S'dom" (*Bach*, Section 12). "Even those authorities who hold that we cannot enforce this, nevertheless maintain that the courts are obligated to use social and verbal pressure to dissuade people from acting selfishly" (*Teshuvot—HaTzemach Tzedek, Choshen Mishpat,* Section 23).

However, even *chesed* is not unlimited, and unrestricted charity can become corrupt. This is why the destruction of S'dom was revealed to Abraham, whose characteristic relative to the other Patriarchs is that of *chesed*. To destroy S'dom in the presence of Isaac, the epitome of justice, would have simply been a reinforcement of an accepted concept. In Abraham's case, however, both the revelation and the destruction come to reaffirm the balance between justice and mercy (*Shem MiShmuel*).

CHAYEI SARAH

A Woman of Valor

A woman of valor, who shall find.
—Michlei 31:10

If Judaism is the framework of the Mosaic Torah, then it is expressed with the families that make up the nation of Israel. These families of husbands, wives, children, and grandchildren form a living tree rooted in Abraham and Sarah, Yitzchak and Rivkah, and Yaakov, Rachel, and Leah, Patriarchs and Matriarchs. These roots are both physical and spiritual. So the death of the first Matriarch, Sarah, reechoes in Jewish homes down to today.

> All the years that Sarah was alive, there was a cloud at the entrance of her tent . . . the doors of the tent stood wide open . . . there was blessing in the dough of the bread . . . there was a light burning from one *Shabbat* eve to the next *Shabbat* eve. (*Midrash Rabbah, Bereishit* 60:10)

All these things the *Midrash* learns from the verse "and Yitzchak brought Rivkah to the tent of Sarah his mother" (*Bereishit* 24:67). The tent that Sarah had made into a place of sanctity so that the *Shechinah* rested on it even as "and when Moses came to the tent [the *Mishkan*] to speak with God, the cloud of glory [*Shechinah*] stood at the entrance" (Exod. 33:9). They both were expressions of a religious dialogue between human beings and God. The tent stood open on all four sides to provide easy entrance for wayfarers. This hospitality is often considered a characteristic of Abraham. Yet, it was to her tent, to Sarah, that Abraham hurried and said, "Make ready quickly three measures of fine meal, knead it, and make cakes" (*Bereishit* 18:6). So it was her zealousness in feeding the hungry and the strangers that brought the blessing in the dough. "She spreads out her palms to the poor and her hands stretch out to the needy" (Mishlei 31:20). So the Sages taught, "Every man who is not married lives without a [this] blessing" (*Talmud Bavli, Yevamot* 62b).

When Rivkah came, all these blessings returned, and the next link in the chain of the Matriarchs was forged. This link exemplified all the values by which Sarah had lived, and was shared by all those who followed her. The first time that anybody praised God for His gifts was at the birth of Yehudah. Leah saw that she had borne a fourth son, an added gift since the twelve sons could have been borne equally to the four wives. So she called him "Yehudah"—I will praise God. Mother Rachel in her tomb comforted the exiles, and it was her tears that brought God's promise of return.

"Her candle is not extinguished in the night" and the verses in Mishlei balance spirituality and charity with the material achievements of the *Eishet Chayil*. Never idle, rising early to see to the material needs of her household, creating economic goods, engaged in commerce and overseeing the behavior of her family, she is wise and versed in righteousness as she busies herself even buying fields and vineyards. Our Sages ascribed to Sarah the idea of buying the Cave of Machpelah in Hebron. This was the burial place of Adam and Eve, Abraham and Sarah, Yitzchak and Rivkah, and Yaakov and Leah. It is the entrance to Gan Eden. However, it is also together with Shechem (present day Nablus) and the Temple Mount, sites bought for full money, rather than obtained by Israelite conquest. So these three sites remained eternally the possessions of the sons of Sarah and Abraham (*Bereishit Rabbah* 79:7).

CHAYEI SARAH

This *Eishet Chayil* served as a model for the prophetesses, pious women, and matriarchs descended from Sarah who are represented in the verses from Mishlei.

"She stretched out her hand to the distaff," this is Yael who killed Siserah with a tent peg instead of with a sword because of her modesty, refusing to bear weapons characteristically belonging to men (Judges). "Her palm she spread out to the poor," this is the widow from Tzorfat (close to present-day Lebanon) who fed Elijah (Kings I 17:9–15). "She fears not snow for her household," this is Rahab who had no fear of the Israelite conquest of Jericho because she trusted in the promised sign of the scarlet thread (Jos. 2:18–19). "Her husband is well known in the city councils," this is Michal who saved her husband, David, from the anger of her father, King Saul. "She makes a cloak to sell," this is Tzellafonit who gave birth to Samson who judged Israel for twenty years. "She opens her mouth with wisdom," this is Serach bat Asher who was the wise woman who counseled Joab to bring about the reconciliation between David and Absalom (2 Sam. 14:1–20). "She anticipates the ways of her household," this is the wife of Ovadiah who saved her children from the idolatry of Ahab (1 Kings 18:3–4). "Her sons rise up to praise her," this is the Shunemite whose son was brought back from the dead by Elisha [by merit of her acts of charity] (2 Kings 4:8–37). "Many daughters achieved greatness but you have outdone them," this is Ruth of Moab who brought herself to nestle beneath the wings of the *Shechinah* [through acts of *chesed*] and was the ancestress of David and Solomon who sang songs of praise to God (*Yalkut Shimoni, Mishlei* 31).

Sarah shares equally in Abraham's spiritual mission. Abraham converts the men to belief in monotheism, and Sarah converts the women so that when they leave for Canaan they take "the souls that they created in Haran" (*Bereishit* 12:5). It is interesting that our sages commented that these converts left after the deaths of Sarah and Abraham; perhaps Yitzchak's merit of justice was too powerful. Sarah is greater than Abraham in prophecy as God tells Abraham to do "Everything that Sarah tells him" (*Bereishit* 21:12). The *Neziv*, Naftali Zvi Berlin of Volozin, innovator of the present-day *yeshivot* in nineteenth-century Lithuania, sees an added dimension in this oft quoted idea. He finds it strange to place Sarah above Abraham in prophecy, because the text tells us of numerous revelations made to him but only one made to Sarah. Akin to prophecy is receiving *Ruach HaKodesh*, the holy spirit of God, and it was in this that Sarah was superior. This spirit only dwells among those who live, rejoicing in their lot and with perfect trust in God. Sarah leaves Charan and makes her way to the Promised Land without a direct revelation but with faith and trust. In the same way, she wanders with Avraham through the Land, down to Egypt and back, and suffers the trials of Pharaoh and Avimelech, king of the Philistines. In this combination of joy and faith, she gives Hagar to Avraham, hoping that this may bring to fruition the prophecy he received. Dwelling in modesty and in purity she trusts the message of a great nation even though she is barren until her ninetieth year. "You live with the revealed promise but I do so with my faith," she tells Avraham (*Bereishit Rabbah*). For the righteous, this faith is superior to the promise that may or may not materialize if one is found to be unworthy (*HaEmek Davar Bereishit* 23:1).

It is to the tent of this Sarah that Rivkah is brought, and it was because of this tent and all it stood for that Abraham sent Eliezer to Aram Naharim, to the city of Nahor, brother of Avraham, to find a wife for Yitzchak. The family of Nahor were idolaters just as were the Canaanites, so why did Avraham not choose a wife from his neighbors or his allies? Idolatry, however, is only an error of the intellect, and can be easily corrected through study and logic. Moral and ethical qualities are an integral part of a person's personality and are acquired from values and a long educational birth-family tradition. The idolatry of Nahor could relatively easily be eradicated from members of his family, but the lack of righteousness and mercy of the Canaanites could almost never be corrected. So Eliezer was sent to Nahor because it was there these Abrahamic qualities existed, making the test of the water a feasible measure of the future bride (*Shem MiShmuel*).

The mission of Eliezer to find a wife for Yitzchak is shown in our text to be a task of great importance, one deserving of much preparation and consideration. Sixty-seven verses are devoted by the Torah to the nuptials of Yitzchak and Rivkah. This is equal to all the verses describing the days of Creation, the Creation of Adam and Eve, and the Garden of Eden and *Matan Torah*, both the first and the second tablets. The comparison is stark in Torah, where every letter and word is considered holy and where superfluous ones or unusual usage are the basis of halakhic rulings or homiletical teachings. Of what importance is Avraham's instructions and the oath administered to Eliezer, the loading of the camels, the test prepared by Eliezer, the story of Rivkah's watering of the people and the animals and the detailed repetition for the benefit of her family?

At first glance, this textual emphasis may be explained by the importance of the marriage of the heir of the three-sided Abrahamic covenant—Land, Nation, and Torah—to the mother of the future inheritors. Two saints marry and create a second foundation stone for the children of Sarah and Avraham; this indeed merits these sixty-seven verses. There is, however, perhaps another dimension, far closer to us. All persons, men and women, are a world in themselves, a replica of the Heavens and Earth, and their unity in marriage has far-reaching and important consequences. To this must be added the specifics of a Jewish world. We are an ancient people who have enriched the world and all its people in innumerable ways, moral, spiritual, and material. Our historical experiences, both as individuals and as a collective, have taught us that the continuation of this enrichment requires first and foremost the creation of Jewish families. Judaism is not a religion aimed primarily at the spiritual salvation of individuals but at the creation of a holy nation whose basic unit is a family. The components of each family are therefore not only of personal importance but also of historical, communal, and spiritual significance because they add up to the continuation of the Jewish march through history.

Isaac is the embodiment of justice. He is prepared to sacrifice himself on God's commandment, and models himself in the traditions of his father. Rivkah taxes her physical strength to do charity to stranger and animal, is prepared to leave her home and family to join the Abrahamic people, has sensitivity so that she does not give humans the same jar of water poured for animals, and also does not waste but pours the remaining water back into the trough. These are the qualities that contribute to the Jewish home, the continuation of Jewish being. This concept of a home spirituality as expressed in the mundane, everyday acts of normal living that is special to Judaism. The closeness of man and wife creates a spiritual dimension perhaps unknown in any other faith.

"Said Rabbi Eliezer," the verse [Isa. 2:3] 'and many nations went and said, let us go up to the mountain of the Lord, to the House of the God of Yaakov.' "Why not of Avraham or of Yitzchak? To Avraham, the God experience is a mountain. 'On the Mount of God one is seen' (*Bereishit* 22:14). To Yitzchak, this experience is a field, 'and Yitzchak went out to meditate' (*Bereishit* 24:63), but to Yaakov, the father of the twelve tribes, and the merger of the Abrahamic quality of *chesed* with the justice of Yitzchak, this experience is a house. 'This is none other but the house of God and this is the gate to heaven' (*Bereishit* 28:17; *Talmud Bavli, Pesachim* 88a)."

"The sun rises and the sun sets" (*Kohelet* 1:5). R. Aba bar Kahane said, "Do we not know that the sun rises and sets? However, this is to teach us that the sun of one *tzadik* does not set until the Holy One blessed be He causes the sun of another *tzadik* to rise, as it is written (*Bereishit* 22:20–23) "and Milkah also bore sons . . . and Bethuel bore Rivkah." Then the text tells us, "and the life of Sarah was one hundred years and twenty years and seven years" (*Bereishit* 23:1). One sun rises, then the other sets (*Ber. Rabbah* 48:2).

TOLDOT

Spiritual Turmoil

Ya'akov and Eisav! What a torrent of images, concepts, and interpretations is released by the story of these twin brothers. The very name Ya'akov, literally to supplant, fed and feeds the anti-Semitic stereotype of the Jew, cheating and exploiting the naive, hardworking, and hungry gentile. The dictionaries of modern civilized countries continued for many years to include "jewing" as being just that. Our own Sages linked the bitter cry of Eisav at his loss of Yitzchak's blessing to the great cry of Mordechai in Shushan, at the decree of Haman, the descendant of Eisav—Jewish anguish as payment for the tears shed by Eisav. Identical twins, sibling rivalry, and parental favoritism are the ingredients in our story for a welter of modern psychological insights; echoed perhaps by Rabbi Samson Raphael Hirsch's comment that, had Yitzchak and Rivkah given them the education specially suited to them, each son would have achieved his proper spiritual development. Menachem Mendel of Kotsk wryly remarked, however, "We have so much trouble with Eisav as evil, imagine how much more we would have suffered had he been a *tzaddik*."

In reality, however, the conflict between Ya'akov and Eisav goes far beyond these concerns. It is an eternal one of differing ideologies and weltanschauung: a conflict that continues to affect the spiritual development, not only of Jew but of mankind, a conflict in which there can be neither equilibrium nor compromise. "You may believe it when you are told 'Ceasarea [seat of the Roman governors after the destruction of the Temple] Edom, ascends and Jerusalem descends, [or] Jerusalem is at the zenith and Ceasarea at the bottom. [However] Jerusalem and Ceasarea are in equilibrium' cannot be true" (*Talmud Bavli, Megillah* 6a). Physically and spiritually, the conflict is epitomized by Amalek, Eisav's grandson, and paralleled by Edom, the rabbinic designation for all the enemies of Israel. Physically, Amalek launches the first attack in history on Jews, unawed by the divine redemption from Egypt and the destruction of Pharaoh. His descendant, Haman, conspires to destroy the Jews; their descendants have done so down to present days. Spiritually, Amalek separates Jews from each other and then attacks the stragglers, the weak, and those on the margin. However, Amalek also separates the Jews from their Father in Heaven, so that His throne is not complete until the very memory of Amalek is wiped out (*Shmot* 17:16). Literally, *asher karkha* describing Amalek's attack, means who "chanced upon you," but *Chassidic* sources seeing *kar* referring to cold, teach that Amalek cooled the Jewish service of God by making it a mechanical service, one bereft of fervor and love.

The true nature of this eternal struggle is highlighted by the fact that it is played out not between Jews and anti-Semites but rather within the Abrahamic family—more specifically, not even between the sons of Ishmael and Yitzchak but specifically between the grandsons of Abraham and Sarah and Yitzchak and Rivkah, the descendants of the twins, Ya'akov and Eisav. It goes far beyond simple enmity so that to see every persecutor or enemy of the Jews as Eisav or as Amalek is to minimize the importance of the struggle and to diminish the stature of Eisav.

The twinship of Ya'akov and Eisav was not accidental but rather a physical reflection of their spiritual similarities. The *Midrash* tells us that when the sons of Ya'akov slew Eisav at their father's funeral, they stabbed his back so they would not have to see his face which was identical to that of Ya'akov; this despite Eisav's being *seir*, hairy and Ya'akov *chalak*, smooth. Yitzchak thought that being twins, unlike himself and Ishmael with different mothers, the sons would divide the Abrahamic covenant,

TOLDOT

each having six of the twelve tribes: Eisav to inherit this world and Ya'akov, the world to come. Rivkah, knowing that Judaism cannot separate the two worlds, and that the ethnic nature of the Jewish people is indivisible, saw the futility of separating Yitzchak's blessing. Above all, she understood that beneath the spiritual similarities lay serious and intrinsic differences reflected in God's promise that the "elder would serve the younger."

The Kotsker said that Eisav was not an ignorant peasant nor a cloddish gentile, but an *Admor*, spiritual leader, who taught Torah to his followers even as did Ya'akov. This is because both possessed a *t'shukah*, a lust for God and religiosity. Their passion for spirituality, inherited from their saintly forebears had, however, found different channels in the twins. Just as sometimes grapes from the same vine, even after the same physical care and treatment, give excellent wine but also vinegar, so, too, Eisav had become the vinegar of Yitzchak's wine. He is actually Ya'akov distorted. *Akalkal*, the root of the name Amalek, is to bend or to distort. Both Ya'akov and Eisav wished to unite Heaven and Earth. Ya'akov sought to join Heaven and Earth by sanctifying the material, making the mundane holy and refining human animal traits. Eisav's connection was to be achieved by debasing the Heavens, so that they become mere reflections of the Earth. He saw only the existence of the "here and now," the satisfaction of unrestrained wants, and the centrality of his physical appetites. He does not wish to be fed in his hunger but asks "*Haleirreni*, let me gulp for I am faint." He despises the Abrahamic covenant, selling it for a mere mess of pottage, available and edible now. After all, it is a covenant devoid of material goods, only a spiritual covenant of a promised Holy Land to be realized in 400 years, long after he is dead. Meanwhile he is hungry and cannot wait, even though they are not in a desert where Ya'akov is the only source of food, but rather in a family encampment with servants to prepare food, readily available. Only this takes time and Eisav wants now.

"*Ki tz'aid befiv*" literally "for there is hunting in his mouth." The Midrash saw this as referring to Eisav's question, "How does one tithe straw and how do we tithe salt?" Yitzchak is impressed by this piety, but the sages heard the son ensnaring his father, hunting him with his mouth. The *Admor* Shmuel of Sochochow describes this as one of the basic traits of Eisav. Tithing, separating that which remains our own property from that part of our wealth that needs to be given to the poor, the priest, and the Levite or to be eaten in sanctity in Jerusalem, applies only to those things that are primary and important. Straw, however, is marginal to wheat so only the latter is tithed; salt is secondary to meat and so need not be tithed. It is Eisav's inability to distinguish between primary and secondary, holy and profane, restraint and asceticism, and limited satisfaction and gluttony that lies at the source of his perversion of Judaism.

His grandson, Amalek, is Eisav's primary heir, and he repeats the image of the perverted twins. Throughout the centuries, other enemies killed, raped, and plundered Jews for economic gain, or political power. Only Amalek, possessing his ancestors' spiritual lust attacks without consideration of gain or pleasure. The anti-Jewish attack and the battle are in themselves the reward and the pleasure. In the ownerless desert, when Israel's passage to the Holy Land is no threat to his own geographic existence nor is there any damage to be prevented, he is the first to attack. Other nations stand in awe of God's power and of His intervention in the affairs of mankind as shown by the redemption from Egypt. Amalek stands only in awe of his own spiritual conflict with God and Israel. To reject the liberation of enslaved people, to oppose the elevation of mankind through a divinely revealed message, and to venerate only the physical power and appetites is the war of Amalek. His descendants burn Israel's books, exile him, and try to destroy him because Israel's very existence threatens the world of Eisav and Amalek.

This destruction is always planned in secrecy and with cunning. Eisav and Amalek knew that the civilized and moral world will not allow open and undisguised war against the ideals and teachings of Israel. Eisav says in his heart, "When mourning for my father is over, I will kill Ya'akov." Haman, his descendant, hides his hatred beneath a cloak of concern for the welfare of the empire of Achashverosh: "There is a people . . . and their laws are diverse from those of every other people, neither do they keep the laws of the king" (Esther 3:8). In every generation, poverty, misfortune, nationalism, ethnic purity, indeed, every social or national phenomenon is used to cloak the real design, the destruction of Israel and its Torah.

Justice in Judaism is symmetrical so that Ya'akov's spiritual supremacy is only valid when he fulfills his own spiritual role. When he ignores or perverts this role, Eisav's rule becomes paramount and Ya'akov is persecuted and enslaved. The injunction to remember the evil of Amalek and to destroy his memory is read every year before Purim. *Devarim* 25:17–19 follows the Torah's demand for just weights and measures. Rashi explains the proximity of these verses, saying, "Because the Jews were lax in the social *mitzvot* of weights and measures, God sent Amalek to punish them." This vision of punishment for social malaise is repeated in the *Admor* of Lubavitch's observation that Amalek attacked the *nechsalim*, the failures, a punishment of Israel's allowing there to be failed people in their midst.

Eisav remains eternally the twin. His roots in the Abrahamic family, the lust for spirituality, and the desire to link Heaven and Earth can be made to yield excellent wine. They provide the sources with which the perversion can be cured. When the older serves the younger so that Eisav acknowledges Ya'akov's Torah, the twins can become one. Our sages saw the grandsons of Haman studying Torah in the academies of B'nei Brak.

VAYEIZEI

Bread and Clothing

"Give me bread to eat and clothes to wear" (*Bereishit* 28:20). Akilos, the convert said to R. Eliezer, "Is all the reward granted to a convert summed up in the verse (*Devarim* 10:18) God knows the stranger [convert] and gives him bread and clothing?" R. Eliezer answered, "Let this not be trivial in your eyes. After all, our father Ya'akov, beseeched God in his first revelation for exactly that" (*Bereishit Rabbah*).

The convert found it difficult to conceive of a religion where the "rewards" were expressed in materialistic terms. Indeed, it sounds strange, especially in view of all the promises contained in the revelation made while Ya'akov slept. The angels ascended and descended the ladder and God stood over him. "The land upon which you lie will I give to you and your children . . . they will be as the dust of the earth, and you will spread out [because of their numbers] west, east, north and south. All the families of the earth shall be blessed through you and your seed. I am with you and will guard you wherever you go and will bring you back to this land."

In this was repeated the promise given to Avraham and to Yitzchok of Eretz Yisrael, generations of sons and daughters afforded Divine Protection. Nevertheless, Ya'akov asks for Divine Providence in assuring him food and clothing. It is this contradiction between the grandeur of the Divine Promise and Ya'akov's seemingly prosaic prayer that bothers Akilos.

Akilos's difficulty with a religion whose rewards are reflected in materialistic goods and economic possessions finds expression in many parts of the *Tanach*. In the second paragraph of the *Shema Yisrael* (*Devarim* 11:1–17), the reward for keeping His Covenant is "rain in its season . . ., grass and fodder for the flocks . . ., and you shall eat and be satisfied." In the chapters dealing in graphic detail with the results of human spiritual and moral behavior (*VaYikrah* 26:3–41 and *Devarim* 28:1–68) economic prosperity is clearly the reward and scarcity, hunger, and physical suffering clearly the punishment. A pious person is compared by the psalmist to a fruitful tree planted besides a perpetually flowing stream (Ps. 1:1–3). Furthermore, the spiritual challenges of Judaism are, as often as not, seen to revolve precisely around the acquisition of wealth and power and the use of that same wealth and power.

So there is no contradiction between the spiritual blessings given to Ya'akov, nor is the trivial request relevant to the promises. Wealth symbolized by food and clothing, is essential for human existence and development. Furthermore, it is true that God ordered the world in such a way that people's material needs are satisfied through normal, nonmiraculous ways.

In his prayer, Ya'akov acknowledges that in reality God is the source of all wealth and that it is Divine *Chesed* that allocates it. God's grace, mercy, and love for His creatures is primarily shown by His satisfaction of their material wants and needs. Every benefit, material or otherwise, that we enjoy is therefore preceded and followed by a blessing, recognizing God as our God and as King of the Universe. Thereby, we acknowledge the source of the blessing and express our thanks for receiving it. Not to acknowledge the source would in effect be stealing; by not expressing our thanks, we show a lack of gratitude. People who see only their own hard work, luck, or intelligence as the source of their material success are in fact showing their lack of belief in a Divine Provider. This lack of belief must sooner or later lead to a pattern of behavior contrary to the laws of the God Who provides the wealth in the first place. In turn, this is followed by a withdrawal of the Divine Bounty.

This concept that wealth comes from God and is dependent on people's moral and spiritual behavior is repeated in many aspects of Judaism. After completing the atonement service on Yom Kippur, the high priest prays for economic well-being and communal prosperity. There is a book of *Parnasah* that is opened and sealed during the days of Rosh Hashanah and Yom Kippur, just as there are books of life, atonement, and redemption.

In matters of wealth and livelihood, the Divine Presence implicates people in a certain pattern of behavior regarding creating and spending. Wealth in all its forms is a means of satisfying the material needs of people. The distinction between needs and wants is all too often not very clear nor easily maintained. Because wants are unlimited, so, too, is our desire for wealth. More is better than less is a maxim that underlies modern merchandising and often figures on the introductory pages of economic textbooks. The more one has, however, the more one wants, so that rabbis of the Talmud taught "one has a hundred coins but then wants two hundred."

There are the blessings before meals or the partaking of any food or drink to acknowledge thanks for them. In the *shmittah* year, land lays fallow, but, more importantly, all the agricultural yields become ownerless to be enjoyed by the poor, weak, and strangers. When this is not observed, seventy years of exile bring to an end the First Temple period, so that the land may enjoy its *Shabbat*. In reply to our uncertainty as to what we would eat in the *shmittah* year and also in the following year, we are told that the Divine Bounty in the sixth will suffice for all three years. Every day there is a prayer for a livelihood that is earned ethically.

The *Maharal*, Rabbi Loew of Prague, explained that this had to be so because God created only one man and woman, and each of their descendants imagines that they are the only people in the world, entitled to all of the material blessings that God put into this world. Therefore, wealth is also the cause of jealousy, strife, war, oppression, exploitation, and crime.

Commenting on the ladder on which the angels ascended and descended, the *Ba'al HaTurim* points out that *sulam* (ladder) has the same numerical value of the letters in *mamon* (money). Money is like the ladder: Some people rise ennobled by the way they earn and use their money; others descend, becoming corrupt and depraved. When Ya'akov prays for *parnasah*, he acknowledges that the Divine Source of material wealth denies the recipients use of nonkosher ways of earning money and demands from them a certain pattern of behavior in their use of it.

Rabbi Samson Raphael Hirsch links the promise to Avraham that the Jews would leave Egypt with great wealth, to the promise to Moses that when they left Egypt they would worship God at Mount Sinai. God would give them great wealth at the Exodus and then give them a Torah at Sinai that would teach them how to use it (*Shmot* 3:12). Perhaps this is what the Sages meant when they said that earning a livelihood is a greater miracle than the splitting of the Red Sea, that is, the acceptance of a Torah way of earning and spending money.

In *Bereishit* 28:20, the prayer for protection precedes that for food and clothing and must therefore refer to spiritual and moral possessions. The greater the struggle for material wealth, the greater the need for this spiritual and moral protection. Having upset the harmony between himself and the forces of nature, Adam and his descendants have been engaged in a struggle to wrest their livelihood from those forces; this is regardless of whether it is the elementary level of land, water, wind, and so on but also at the most sophisticated level of modern scientific use of natural resources. At the same time, we struggle against other humans to protect or enlarge our economic stake. To succeed in this struggle, morally and without harming others, requires this prayer for integrity and morality (Hirsch, *Bereishit* 28:20).

Victory in this struggle is possible despite the greed that prompts economic endeavor and despite the uncertainty that is an integral part of market activity. Both of these lead, over and above legitimate business and commerce, also to unethical market behavior. Nevertheless, operating with integrity and morality is our own decision. There is a Divine Promise to Ya'akov that He will bring him back home. Still, Ya'akov says,

"If I will return in peace," actually *shalem*, complete. This spiritual peace is dependent only on his own free will; "everything is in the hands of Heaven except for the Fear of Heaven."

Wealth is provided for two main purposes: the satisfaction of one's needs and those of their families but also for assistance to the needy, the poor, the aged, the sick, and the stranger. So Ya'akov pledges, "Of all that You will give me, I will repeatedly tithe" (*Bereishit* 28:22). During Temple days, his descendants tithed all their income, annually, *Terumah* to the priests, *ma'aser* to the Levites, in the third and sixth year of the *Shmittah* cycle, *ma'aser ani*, and in the other years *ma'aser sheni* to be eaten during their pilgrimage to the Temple. In all these cases, the poor, the landless, benefited.

> God wanted that His creatures should become versed in and accustomed to acts of mercy and righteousness for these are desirable human traits. The perfection of their bodies (that is their material wealth) through these traits, makes them eligible to receive prosperity from God, since blessings and goodness always accrue to the good. In this way God's bounty to the merciful will achieve His desire to benefit the world. It is possible for Him to provide the poor and the needy with all their needs, but in this way His mercy enables us to be His emissaries. (*Sefer HaChinuch, Mitzvah* 66)

In our own day, there is an obligation to similarly tithe ten percent as a minimum level or a more generous twenty-percent level for people of average means. Irrespective of whether we accept the opinions of those authorities who see our tithing as a continuation of the biblical commandments or those who see it only as a binding custom sanctioned by age-old behavior, this obligatory tithing is to be made from all incomes after deducting the costs of earning that income, after paying taxes, but not from insurance-like taxes such as social security. In the present day absence of communal taxation, *ma'aser*, is perhaps the primary coercive way of funding communal service and religious needs. As important, however, it is the acknowledgment of the Divine Source of our wealth. After all, Ya'akov undertook to tithe after praying for food and clothing.

VAYISHLACH

Ya'akov, Yisrael, and Yeshurun

For you have power with God and with men, you have been able to prevail.
—*Bereishit 32:29*

> Bar Kapparah said, Everyone who refers to Avraham as Avram, transgresses a positive mitzvah. R. Levi said, Transgresses a negative mitzvah, as it is written: "And your name shall no longer be called Avram" and a positive mitzvah: "But Avraham will be your name" (*Bereishit* 17:5). Shall we then say also that one who refers to Israel as Ya'akov similarly transgresses a negative mitzvah? No, because "Not only Ya'akov, *ki im*, rather Israel will be your name" (*Bereishit* 35:10), showing that the name Israel will be the primary name and Ya'akov secondary. (*Bereishit Rabbah* 78:3)

The names people are called not only identify them technically but also reflect their spiritual, social, and cultural awareness. Avraham, after the promise of an heir, the promise of the God-Nation relationship, and the mitzvah of circumcision, represents a spiritual stature and a religious personality, radically and intrinsically different from Avram of before. So, too, after the same promises Sarah is no longer identifiable with Sarai who left Haran. Although his parents and his family called Moshe various names, he is only known by the name the daughter of Pharaoh who saved him, gave him. In return for her righteousness, God called her Bityah, daughter of God. Hoshea bin Nun, when sent together with the spies had his name changed by Moses to Yehoshua to protect him from their evil counsel. Some have seen the name change as coming from the *Yud* of Sarai. The *Admor* of Sochochow taught that the word *anav*, humble, is spelt in reference to Moshe without a *Yud*, which was transferred to Yehoshua. This was to teach Yehoshua that leaders and kings in Israel need to learn from the most humble of all men, Moses. So, too, the additional name of Israel represents a new dimension in Ya'akov.

Our Sages taught that the actions of the Patriarchs are guidelines for their descendants, and Ya'akov's preparations for his meeting with Eisav and his four hundred followers has set a model followed by generations of Jews. The preparation is threefold. He sends a large gift of flocks and herds either to appease Eisav for the birthright or to show him that he, Ya'akov, never benefitted materially from the blessing of Yitzchak. Rather, all he has is what he earned from working with Lavan. He prays to God (*Bereishit* 32:10–13), expressing his gratitude at God's benevolence and asking for deliverance. He also prepares himself for war—dividing his camp in two so that in case of attack at least the weaker camp (perhaps shown by the feminine number *achat* in verse 9 for camp which is masculine) will escape.

The Sages expressed two conflicting appraisals of Ya'akov's behavior, both still relevant approaches of how Jews should behave in *Galut*. Rabbi Yehuda HaNasi (Redactor of the Mishnah, circa 250 C.E.) sent a message to Marcus Aurelius, emperor of Rome, addressing him as the exalted king and signing himself as "your servant Yehudah." When criticized for demeaning himself, he answered, "Am I then better than our father, Ya'akov, who told his messengers, So says your servant Ya'akov (*Bereishit* Rabbah 75:5)?" Yet in the same order but section 11, we find in the *Midrash:* God said to Ya'akov, "You humbled yourself before Eisav and called him your master eight times; by your life I will raise up eight kings from his sons before there will be a king in Israel."

There is no disagreement regarding the spiritual preparation shown

VAYISHLACH

in his prayer, a prayer to which the answer only came that night after he had led his family, flocks, and herds and his servants across the ford of the Yabbok, the rift between the mountains of Moav and those of the Gilead, that provides a path over the Jordan leading to Shechem. Then he remained alone to examine and perfect himself spiritually. That same night before meeting Eisav physically, Ya'akov is involved in a titanic struggle with the angel of Eisav. Irrespective of whether one follows the opinion of Maimonides that this struggle took place in a dream-revelation or whether one follows the Ramban (Nachmanides) in seeing this as an actual physical struggle, the spiritual significance of the event remains.

R. Meir Leibush Malbim sees the struggle as having two dimensions, one relating to the conflict of the *Yetzer HaRah* and *Yetzer HaTov* in the individual and the other the spiritual differences between the Jewish people and the descendants of Eisav.

> In the world God created good and evil. Every person has the freedom and the power to decide between these two inclinations. So too, He created two nations, Edom (Eisav) and Israel . . . collectively each of them has the ability to tilt the balance between good and evil. If the collective, Israel observes God's Torah and *mitzvot* then Edom will be subservient. If, however, Israel does not do so then Edom will dominate . . . . So before meeting Eisav in the flesh, either for peace or for war, Ya'akov fought both with his own *Yetzer HaRah* and with the collective evil of Eisav dedicated to make Israel disobey God's Torah. (*Malbim, Bereishit* 32:answer 25)

All night long, Ya'akov and the angel of Eisav wrestled. Unable to overcome him, the angel gripped the joint of Ya'akov's thigh and dislocated it; nevertheless, he was unable to throw Ya'akov down or escape from him. Seeing this he said, "Not Ya'akov shall express your name but Yisrael, for you have been a prince with God, and with men" (*Bereishit* 32:29).

"Your name shall no longer have the meaning of Ya'akov—one who holds onto the heel" but shall be understood as Israel. Israel means, literally, God is the all-conquering One. Only when a Ya'akov, one who, to all outward appearances, is under the heel of all others, obtains the victory over the vicious attacks of enemies fully equipped with all material means, does the victory show the existence of a spiritual power. It shows the existence of an Almighty God Who reveals Himself just in the victorious embrace of this outwardly weak opponent. In politics and religion, Eisav says: "Apart from me there is no salvation"—Ya'akov concedes all pure human beings with the right to be left untouched . . . all have the highest meaning and destiny if they accept the basic principles of human life which he [Ya'akov] brings them. "Blessing acknowledgment (verse 30) is all that Ya'akov fights Eisav for" (Hirsch, *Bereishit* 32:29).

Ya'akov may be seen as the individual and Israel as the group. Alternatively, Ya'akov, who held onto the *akeiv*, the heel of Eisav at birth, may refer to the Jew trying to prevent being crushed physically or spiritually by Eisav, while Israel describes the rule over Eisav. Parallel to this, Ya'akov may be the Jew in *Galut*, and Israel, the Jew in the Promised Land.

He had defeated the embodiment of Eisav, who was unable to throw him down, so the angel changed his name from Ya'akov, "One who grasps the heel" to Israel, who has defeated gods and men. The defeat of the gods refers to the angel and the men refer to Eisav who will be unable to crush Ya'akov (Abarbanel). The real name change, however, is made by God Himself further on in our *sedrah*: "shall not only be called Ya'akov but Israel shall be your name" (*Rashi*), not one who comes cunningly and slyly (35:10). Here the name change denotes the sanction of a different perspective of Ya'akov. The Divine Approval comes only after he had appeased Eisav by his gifts for the wrong he had done to him. So in all matters between man and man, appeasement of the wronged party must come before Divine Forgiveness. There is in the future another name change for Ya'akov, beyond the name of Israel. In *Devarim* 35:15, we find the name Jeshurun, from *yashar*, straight, without deviating from the correct path. For Hirsch, this name reflects the ideal of Israel's moral mission. It is a demand that Israel show that the highest degree of morality may be achieved without renouncing material well-being and that wealth can be transformed into moral deeds.

In its usual pattern, the Torah cannot let spiritual truths and moral strivings remain only in the sphere of philosophy or pious musing. Rather, the former are always transformed into practical forms of conduct and coerced ways of behavior. So, too, the spiritual message of the ability of Ya'akov to withstand the physical and spiritual power of Eisav and other enemies and the possible victory within the individual of good over evil finds expression in the *halakhah*. "Therefore the children of Israel do not eat sinew which is on the joint of the thigh, because he (the angel) gripped the tendon of weakness" (*Bereishit* 32:33). We do not eat of the hindquarters of a kosher animal, ritually slaughtered, unless the many sinews are removed (Shulchan Arukh, *Yoreh De'ah*, Section 64). In some places, however, the removal of these sinews is so costly that the whole hindquarters are sold to non-Jews.

This halakhah of *kashrut* is conceptually of a different value than the injunction against eating blood, mixing milk and meat, or the differentiation between kosher and nonkosher animals. These may be seen as educating us to restraint, to purifying the satisfaction of our material needs, or to separating us from the non-Jews of the world. The injunction against eating the *Gid HaNasheh*, the sinew of submission, is a sign for the history of the Jews.

> The root of this mitzvah lies in the sign to Israel that they will suffer persecution and oppression at the hands of the nations and at the hands of the children of Eisav. [In *parshat* Toldot we discussed the importance of distinguishing between these two types of enemies.] Nevertheless this suffering will never lead to Israel's destruction, rather they, their descendants and their name will remain for ever. [At the end of the night, as in the case of Ya'akov, light will dawn and] a savior will come to them and redeem them. This mitzvah is a memorial to us to hold steadfast to our faith. (*Sefer HaChinuch*, Mitzvah 3)

Hirsch sees the *Gid HaNasheh* as a reminder that the cause of our calamities lies not in the lack of military might or material power or even in the prowess of our enemies but rather our own desertion of God. In such circumstances, Eisav can hamstring Ya'akov so that he cannot stand or walk steadily. The sinew is one of submission to Eisav and redemption lies only in the hands of God.

The *Gid HaNasheh* has also been seen as referring to the male sex organ. *Yerekh* are offspring, literally, a coming out of the father's loins, thigh. Avraham made Eliezer place his hand on the circumcision when making his oath because this was the first mitzvah given to Avraham (*Bereishit* 24:2). Later Yoseph did the same in his oath to Ya'akov (*Bereishit* 46:26). Even though Ya'akov had spent the night of the struggle purifying himself, this part of man can never be completely deanimalized and purified. Here the injunction comes to remind us of the attack of our enemies on our seed, our children (Malbim and Abarbanel).

Recognizing the awesomeness of his struggle and the spiritual significance of the inability of the angel of Eisav to destroy him, Ya'akov names the place of the struggle Pniel. He has seen God, *El*, not in a dream like all his other revelations, but face to face. He had been in danger of losing his life to the angel and saw the threat to his descendants. Yet in the words of the prophet Micah "In that day, said the Lord, I will collect the lame and gather in the castaways . . . and I will set up the lame to be a beginning and despised ones as a mighty people, and God will rule over them in Zion for evermore" (4:6). Indeed, Pniel is a fitting name for this place.

VAYEISHEV

All Were without Sin

So the sons of Ya'akov were twelve—to teach us that all were without sin.
—Rashi, Bereishit 35:22

The sale of Yoseph had far-reaching, almost traumatic, effects on our history. In the Covenant of the Pieces, Brit bein HaBetarim (*Bereishit* 15:13-14), exile and oppression were clearly to precede the gift of the Promised Land. However, in which country and in which society this exile was to occur is not revealed. It may have been possible for them to remain in the Land of Israel as strangers and noncitizens, subject to discrimination and persecution, but nevertheless still attached to the sanctity of the Holy Land. This was the situation of Yitschak, from whose birth the four hundred years of *galut* are numbered. Instead, because of the sale of Yoseph, the tribes of Israel are forced down into Egypt, a harsh country ruled by a harsh king, which was the epitome of immorality and idolatry.

Ya'akov suffered great anguish, and Yoseph was forced at the age of seventeen to face great physical and spiritual temptation over and above his suffering. Centuries later, because of this sale, the spiritual leadership of a whole generation, including Rabbi Akiva, was destroyed in cruel and terrible deaths. There is a tradition that the sale of Yoseph took place on Yom Kippur, and the *mussaf* prayers of that day describe these ten martyrs and their connection with the acts of the ten brothers.

The responsibility for the sale is clearly laid at the feet of Yehuda, and our Sages offer two perspectives of his advice. And Yehuda said to his brothers: "What profit is there if we kill our brother and cover his blood? Come let us sell him to the Ishmaelites" (*Bereishit* 36:26–27). "Rabbi Meir said, one who blesses Yehuda [expressing support for his advice in the above verses] is a blasphemer" (*Talmud Bavli, Sanhedrin* 6b). "Rabbi Yehuda, the son of R. Illai said, This verse speaks in praise of Yehuda" (*Midrash Bereishit Rabbah* 84:26). For R. Meir, Yehuda's advice was blemished because he, being the authority among the brothers, should have told them to return Yoseph to his father. The *midrash*, however, sees Yehuda in a positive light because in reality this was the only way to save Yoseph. So, too, does the Talmud, when it uses Yehuda as an example of one who performs the praiseworthy act of arbitration rather than insisting on justice.

These two sources highlight a problem far beyond the issue of the sale of Yoseph. It is one that is expressed in the many cases in the Torah, where personalities act in ways that seem at variance with our expectations of the behavior of those who are the foundations of Judaism and the Jewish people. Much of the popular Torah literature that has flourished in recent years, has broadly speaking, been divided between two approaches to this problem. One school of writers and teachers seems to insist and emphasize that the patriarchs and other biblical personalities were simply human beings with the perspectives, personality traits, and reactions of ordinary men and women. To wean us away from the heroic or the traditional sacred personalities, they all too often trivialize the importance of the stories for our own spiritual behavior. The use of sibling rivalry to explain Ya'akov and Eisav, or Yoseph and his brothers, or of wifely jealousy to explain the expulsion of Hagar minimizes the religious and national significance of these acts. Without such a significance the stories of a long-forgotten past seem of little interest or relevance for the moral or religious development of people today. In their place, we are left with psychological insights, inspirations for family counseling, or self-improvement.

At the other end of the spectrum, we have the creation of demigods, plaster of paris saints who cannot be conceived of as doing anything wrong. This creates a human class existing somewhere between people and God, something that most authorities would regard as being close to idolatry. Even if this is not so, the removal of human weaknesses and temptations also makes the stories devoid of any spiritual, religious, or moral significance. After all, we ordinary people cannot be called to account for our actions, nor can we be expected to emulate the biblical people, because they are so spiritual and so purified, far beyond our levels.

Traditional scholarship has always largely viewed the biblical personalities as people—men and women with parents, wives or husbands, siblings, and children. The text is rife with detailed genealogical data and with specific geographic sites regarding the heroes of its stories. Sarah and Rachel are beautiful; the eyes of Leah are weak. Some of the personalities, like the Patriarchs, are rich; others, like Saul, are taken from the plow to become kings and prophets. It is a gamut of social and economic classes. For me, personally, the real-life dimensions of the biblical heroes have been emphasized by the fact that Moshe, the savior, prophet of prophets, who ascends to Heaven to bring down the Law and speaks to God face to face, has a speech impediment (*Shmot* 4:10).

However, these are not ordinary people. Prophecy does not descend on vagabonds searching the byways for a revelation, nor is it the result of sudden ecstasy achieved by simple or ignorant people. Before Moshe and Aharon go to Pharaoh, the text repeats their genealogy to impress upon us that their lineage was equal to their mission (Hirsch, *Shmot* 6:14–27). Avraham is not a wandering Bedouin sheik but the friend of God (*Shmot Rabbah* 27:1) and a "prince of God" (*Bereishit* 23:6); whole chapters of the Bible are devoted to the sole purpose of describing his relationship and that of his descendants to the spiritual and religious descendants of Adam (Abarbanel, Introduction to *Shmot*). It would seem, therefore, that all the actions of these biblical personalities need to be seen in a perspective that achieves an equilibrium between sanctity and the imperfection that is human.

Sometimes this perspective will claim that the actions are considered wrong only out of consideration for the spiritual greatness of the people concerned; in regard to ordinary people, there would have been nothing wrong. At the time of *Merivah*, when Moshe smites the rock to draw water, he calls the Israelites "sons of rebels" (*Bamidbar* 20:10), thus insulting God's chosen people. The *midrash* teaches that for this one sin, "You punished the Man" (Ps. 39); the man being Moshe as it is written "and the Man, Moshe, was very humble" (beyond all the men on the face of the earth [Num. 12:1]). Because of his great humility, Moshe's rebuke of the people for the slight to his honor when they questioned his ability to draw water from the rock became a major fault. In other cases where he rebuked them to persuade them to repent or to warn them of their future behavior, there was no reflection on his humility and therefore no error (*Midrash Devarim Rabbah* 2).

Sometimes the perspective is that these acts were indeed sins. So the Ramban argues that Avraham sinned when he sent Hagar away and when he said Sarah was his sister. Abarbanel is a minority opinion when he writes in regard to the section in *Shabbat* quoted below, "then I am in error." Hirsch claims that the biblical figures are not meant to serve as role models, because Jews have only the Almighty as their role model.

Sometimes the perspective claims that the act was not actual adultery, theft, or bribery but was considered so by the text either because that's the way it was publicly perceived or because it was an abuse of the power of the people involved. "Why was the sanctuary at Shilo destroyed [the *mishkan* from the desert was established at Shilo some 10 km. northeast of Jerusalem from the entry into the Land until the time of Samuel]? Because of adultery and because of the insult to the sacrifices. [Both of these causes refer to the actions of the sons of Eli, the High Priest, under whose tutelage Samuel the Prophet grew up.] Shall we say that they committed adultery (1 Sam. 2:22)? No. However, they did not wish to sacrifice the doves and pigeons that women brought after birth, as here the portion of the priests was minute. Instead, they delayed the women, waiting for more substantial offerings of oxen and sheep from which their share would be greater" (*Talmud Bavli*, *Yoma* 9a). Because they delayed the return of the women to their homes and husbands or because of the immodesty of the crowds of women in front of the *Mishkan*, the text describes their actions as though they were adultery. R. Yitzchok Alfasi (the *Rif*, North Africa, eleventh century, a classical talmudic commentator) links this adultery to verses 13–16 in the same chapter, which describe how the priests insisted on taking the choice cuts of the sacrifices before they had been ritually concluded. The *Rif* says that their lust for meat, even at the expense of exploiting their communal position, was the corruption that led the text to describe their delay of the women's offerings as adultery.

The story of the sons of Eli is retold elsewhere in the Talmud: "One who says that Reuven sinned [with Bilhah] is in error, one who says the sons of Eli sinned is in error, one who says David sinned [with Bat-Sheva] is in error, etc." (*Shabbat*). All too often this version is seen as an attempt to free these personalities from criticism. However, care should be taken to remember the word "sin" used in the above quote. This is not merely a synonym of wrong or evil, but something very different and identifiable. Nowhere is anybody saying that the people in this list did right; indeed, in all cases they were punished. They did not, however, sin, and that distinction is important. For example, Reuven did not commit a forbidden sexual act with his father's wife, an act that would have entailed, even before Sinai, a death penalty. Instead he moved his father's bed from Bilhah's tent as an act of protest because now that Rachel was dead, Leah, his mother, was the rightful wife. Abarbanel ascribes his motive to Reuven's concern that Ya'akov would have another son who would reduce his share of the Promised Land. Others see his act as compulsive and irresponsible whatever the motive, that is, behavior not consistent with the traits required for kingship or priesthood. Irrespective of our understanding of the action or the motive, the text describes this as "he lay with Bilhah." Reuven was punished not by death, for a sin, but by loss of the kingship, priesthood, and double portion of land that should have accrued to him as the firstborn son. Because he did not sin, the text says "and the sons of Ya'akov were twelve."

MIKETZ

The Interpretation Is the Lord's

And he (Ya'akov) sent him (Yoseph) from the Valley of Hebron.
—*Bereishit 37:14*

And Yoseph settled his father and brethren in the Land of Egypt.
—*Bereishit 47:11*

There are ten chapters from the day Ya'akov sent Yoseph to see after the well-being of his brothers until the settlement in Egypt. Ten chapters of the Torah are devoted to the events leading to the descent of the House of Israel to Egypt. Ten chapters describe the conflict of the sons of Ya'akov, the sale of Yoseph, Yoseph in the house of Potiphar, Yoseph in prison, Yehuda and Tamar, Pharaoh's dreams, Yoseph's regency, the famine, the brothers come to Egypt, Yoseph withholds recognition, imprisonment of Shimon, Binyamin comes to Egypt, the goblet of Yoseph, Yoseph reveals himself, Yoseph sends wagons for Ya'akov, and finally seventy souls come to Egypt. This is a story replete with digressions, repetition, and much detail; a departure from the usual stark and almost spartan biblical style. In reality, however, there are two stories being told, one of human emotions, accident, trials and successes, but also another, that of the unfolding of the Divine Plan, for the implementation of the covenant with Abraham. The players in the one story see only the visible, personal, and human plots, but in reality, these are only the props and the costumes of Divine Intervention. In this respect, these chapters can perhaps serve us to see the same twin stories of the visible or natural events and the Divine Plan, both in our personal affairs as well as national or international developments.

"For I know the thoughts that I think toward you" (Jer. 29:11)—to give you a future and a hope, said R. Shmuel the son of Nachman. "The tribes were busy with the selling of Yoseph, Yoseph was busy with his sackcloth and his fasting [his suffering and trials in Egypt], Reuven was busy with his sackcloth and fasting [over the incident with Bilhah and his failure to return Yoseph to his father], Ya'akov was involved with his fasting and sackcloth [for the loss of Yoseph], Yehuda went to look for a wife [these are the normal or human stages in our story but]; God was busy too. He was creating the light of the King Messiah" (*Midrash Bereishit Rabbah* 85:1).

"And Ya'akov loved Yoseph because he was a *ben zekkunim* [usually translated as a son of his old age but more correctly as a wise son—*zakken* being the usual form for wisdom] and he made him a coat of many colors [the *midrash* sees this as] a cloak of kingship. The brothers saw all this and Yoseph's dreams as a repetition of the exclusionary nature familiar from the stories of Abraham and Yitzchak. Abraham sent Ishmael and the sons of the concubines away, destined to greatness and wealth, but not part of the Abrahamic covenant, which is restricted to Yitzchak. Yitzchak loved Eisav and Rifkah loved Ya'akov, and they did not share in the Abrahamic covenant. Eisav is given his inheritance in Har Seir but is excluded from the Covenant that devolves on Ya'akov alone. Was this pattern now to be repeated here among the sons of Ya'akov, so that the Covenant would be restricted to Yoseph? Knowing that kingship was the inheritance of Yehuda and fearing the dissolution of the 12 tribes, they judged Yoseph as a rebel" (Abarbanel, *Bereishit* 37).

Ya'akov loved Yoseph because he was the son of Rachel, the loved wife, or because he was the wisest of the brothers. Whatever the cause, he sent Yoseph to seek the welfare of the brothers, supervising their flocks in Schechem. He saw this as a normal procedure, unaware of the tragic results of the dreams because of the preference shown to Yoseph. The text mentions the valley of Hebron as being the place from which Ya'akov sent Yoseph. Hebron, however, is not in a valley. This led the *midrash* to teach that the sending of Yoseph was in reality only a way of fulfilling the depth (*emek*—deep) of the Covenant with Abraham who had lived in Hebron—that his descendants would be enslaved in a foreign land. Ya'akov's simple instructions in effect, if unwittingly, set in motion the fulfillment of this Covenant. From this our Sages taught a *halakhah*, "A person should never discriminate between his children. After all, because of two *selaim* worth of pure wool for the coat of Yoseph, the other brothers hated him and as a result [events moved beyond their behavior and] our forefathers went down to Egypt" (*Talmud Bavli, Shabbat*, 10b; see also *Mishneh Torah, Nachlaot*, Chapter 6, *Halakhah* 13).

Yoseph in Egypt sees his dreams evaporating as one tragedy after another befalls him. Instead of his coat, his beloved father, and the acknowledgment of his brothers, he is sold from hand to hand, tempted by Potiphar's wife, and imprisoned. How to see beyond the physical and visible events to recognize a Divine Purpose? After explaining the dream of the chief butler, he asks him to remember him when he is returned to Pharaoh's favor. "But the chief butler did not remember Yoseph and forgot him" (*Bereishit* 40:32). For his dependence on human agency, Yoseph was imprisoned for another two years (*Rashi*). However, despite this Yoseph remained "Yoseph HaTzaddik," steadfast in his faith in Divine Providence seeing into the seemingly acidental chain of events, the unfolding of His plan. Despite the dangers involved, he is careful to stress his origins and his family connection. He tells the cupbearer that he was stolen from the Land of Hebrews. The wife of Potiphar speaks of the Hebrew slave that her husband had bought to mock them. It is the cloak of the Hebrews that she tears and offers as evidence of Yoseph's crime. The *midrash* tells that for this he was rewarded by having his coffin brought to Eretz Yisrael when the people leave Egypt. Moses, who asked to enter Eretz Yisrael as Yoseph had done, was told, "He did not hide his identity as you did, the daughters of Yitro said, 'An Egyptian saved us.'" The

MIKETZ 61

Shem MiShmuel teaches that Yoseph understood the message of his dreams as being that if the brothers would subject themsleves to his temporary kingship they would be able to live out the terms of the Covenant in the Land of Israel. Alternatively, they would suffer exile, in addition to oppression and suffering. When he reveals himself to his brothers, he says, "Do not despair and let it not be wrong in your eyes that you sold me [to be brought] here. It was to preserve life that God sent me before you [not only the lives of the Egyptians and others but] to preserve for you a remnant in the land and keep it alive for your great salvation [reference to the future Exodus]" (*Bereishit* 45:5–7).

Only Yehuda seems to have been busy with things that have no apparent relationship to the sale of Yoseph. Deposed by his brothers for his role in that sale (*Talmud Bavli, Sotah* 13b), Yehuda goes to find a wife, marries, has three sons, and marries off Er, his firstborn and then later Onan to Tamar. Both prevent her conceiving, not wishing to mar her beauty through childbirth, and both suffer death as a Divine Punishment for it. Later, Tamar, as an act of *chesed* inveighs Yehuda to have a sexual relationship with her from which are born Zerach and Peretz (*Bereishit* 38). Peretz is the ancestor of Jesse and Jesse is the father of David, the Anointed One, the ancestor of the King Messiah.

Each of the players in our story saw only their perspective of it and acted according to their human merits or demerits. They enjoy free will throughout and bear personal responsibilities for their choices. Yet all their actions, together with seemingly isolated acts or accidental happenings, become woven into God's plan. Ya'akov sends Yoseph to the brothers, knowing of their relationship and of his dreams, yet as a father sees all his sons, the foundation of the House of Israel. Midianites and Ishmaelites "chance" by and Yoseph is brought to Egypt. The temptations of Potiphar's wife are punishment for Yoseph playing with his hair and bearing stories about the moral behavior of his brothers. Yehuda brings Yoseph's coat to his father saying "*Haker na*—Recognize" and measure for measure, is shown to be guilty when Tamar says to Yehuda, "*Haker na* the staff and signet ring and know by whom I am pregnant." Ya'akov is separated from Yitzchak for twenty years and so Yoseph, his beloved son, is separated for twenty years. By accident, Pharaoh is displeased with his chief butler and chief baker. They share Yoseph's prison and dream dreams, only so that Yoseph may be elevated to the regency through Pharaoh's dream. Every act and every particular always runs on two parallel paths: the human story and the workings of Divine Providence.

These two parallel paths not only are a constant theme in the *Tanach*, but even in our national history. Empires rise and fall for economic or geopolitical reasons, obvious and identifiable. At the same time, Israel finds new havens from expulsion or persecution. Certain cultural and social conditions develop owing to political and population changes, and they permit a flourishing of Torah study, scholarship, and Jewish thought: Spain and Italy in the late middle ages and the United States in our own times. "For My thoughts are not your thoughts and your ways are not Mine. Even as the Heavens are elevated above the Earth so are My thoughts and ways from yours . . . . So My words will not return to Me empty [without being fulfilled]" (Isa. 55:8–11). The Divine thoughts and ways are not simply superior but exist on an entirely different plane or dimension, beyond human knowledge, intellect, or measure.

Perhaps this is why these *parshiot* are always read during Chanukah. The Greeks did not destroy the Temple as did Nebuchadnezzar and the Romans. They did not destroy the Temple service. They only made the oil impure, thus perverting the faith. Oil is the symbol of knowledge and of wisdom, and they simply wanted to make this Jewish knowledge impure. How? They said, "Only that which we can see, count or understand with our human intelligence is true and exists. In our world view, only accidents and human actions exist, while you, Israel teaches that there is a knowledge beyond this, a knowledge revealed by a Divine Torah." Therefore, they said, Israel must declare, "We have no share in this revealed Torah" (*Shem Mishmuel, Chanukah*).

VAYIGASH

Two Sons of Rachel and Leah

Part of Ya'akov's message to his brother Eisav was "I have an ox and a donkey" (*Bereishit* 32:6). For the *Midrash* Rabbah on this verse, the ox refers to the priest anointed for war (Deut. 20), understood by the rabbis to refer to Pinchas but alternatively to the Messiah, the son of Yoseph as in the Mosaic blessing, "the first born of his bullock shall have glory" (Num. 33:17), and the donkey to the king Messiah, son of David, as it is written, "the poor man riding on a donkey" (Zech. 9:9). The Sages ascribed different tasks to each of those Messiahs, with that of Yoseph as preceding the son of David, that is, two different stages of redemption. The *Zohar* sees the whole story of the brothers as a forerunner or as a prophecy of the future redemptions of Israel. Of special relevance here is the role of the two kings, Yehuda and Yoseph, whose struggle is described at the beginning of our *parsha*.

Maimonides speaks of one Messiah, who will reestablish the Davidic dynasty, build the Temple, gather in the exiles of Israel, and implement all the Torah laws in their entirety (*Mishneh Torah, Hilkhot Melachim,* Chapter 11, *Halakhah* 1). In this, Maimonides is following the opinion of Shmuel that there is no difference between the Messianic period and our own lives, except for the freedom of Israel from the domination of the nations (*Talmud Bavli, Berachot* 34a).

There are, however, many authorities who see the Redemption as occurring in two stages. The first period only as *Atchalta DeGeulah*, the beginning of the natural redemption to be followed by the radical changes in nature and miracles such as those of the vision of Isaiah (2:2–4; 11:1–9), of the final redemption. The first stage is that of the son of Yoseph, but the full redemption is that of the son of David (*Kol HaTor*, Chapter 2, see also introduction of *Rav Kasher*). So there is a redemption that deals with physical or ordinary actions and there is a final redemption dealing with the spiritual. Each of these Messiahs is replicated in the different roles and spiritual characteristics of Yoseph and Yehuda throughout the *parshiot* of *VaYeishev*, *Miketz*, and *VaYigash*.

Yoseph's whole character and the stories associated with him represent a worship of God and an expression of His Will through the mundane and natural wherein the Divine, so to speak, is concealed and not clearly revealed. Yehuda is that worship and application where the spiritual and the godlike are made obvious and manifest for all to see.

"Yoseph, who sanctified God's name in private and in secrecy merited having one letter (*He*) of the Divine name added to his name (*Yehoseph*, Ps. 91:1). In contrast, Yehuda, who sanctified His name in public contains all of the four letters of the Divine name" (*Talmud Bavli, Sota* 10b). Yehuda admits his error with Tamar publicly, and his descendant, Nachshon, is the first to jump into the Red Sea. David's whole greatness lies in his ability to see his own unworthiness and to make public confession of his sin and repentance. This marks the special power that enables man to elevate to the Heavens and spiritualize even the materialism and mundane world in which we live. This is the strength to sanctify and to integrate with the Divine, the seemingly secular and unholy. The kingship of Yehuda is, as it were, a chariot for the kingdom of heaven, it is an expression of man's yearning and desire rooted in this physical world for Divinity and spirituality. Yoseph never revealed his spiritual greatness; always the Divine worship was hidden and in secret. His story is played out through dreams: his own, those of the officers of Pharaoh, and those of Pharaoh as well. His father kept the message of the second dream in the secrecy of his mind. *Rashi* explains that Yoseph cultivated and groomed his looks, whereas the *Zohar* teaches us that Yoseph in Egypt was careful to always be elegantly clothed. In these ways, all the spiritual greatness was covered and not revealed. Here the spirituality could easily be aligned and united with the *nistar*, the concealed and secret heavenly worlds.

So great spiritual treasures, insights, and influences are brought down to Earth from the hidden heights of Heaven. The power of this hidden spirituality is enhanced by being concealed even as is the evil that is hidden. So the descendants of Rachel (of Yoseph and Binyamin) are able to conquer Eisav and his descendants. Of them it is written "And Eisav said in his heart (hidden)," "and Haman said in his heart," while of her sons, we read, "and Jehoshua bin Nun [of the tribe of Ephraim] the disciple of Moshe, did not stir from the tent," and "Shaul [of the tribe of Binyamin and the first king of Israel] was hiding in the baggage" (Shmuel I 10:22), and "Mordechai [of the tribe of Binyamin] clothed himself in sackcloth . . . and Esther sent clothes to cover him" (Esther 4:1–4). Always the spirituality is hidden, clothed, or concealed as it is the weapon against the concealed evil of Eisav, Amalek, and the *sitra acher*.

Yoseph is Israel in Exile outside of its spiritual geographic entity, and Yehudah is Israel at Home in its Promised Land. In Exile, the Jew and the Torah are proscribed by persecution, by the ghetto or the Pale of settlement and imminent expulsions. Even when *Galut* is prosperous, kind, and stable, there is always the need to dissemble before alien cultures or powers. Yoseph is a Viceroy, yet he needs permission from Pharaoh to settle his brothers who are not free to move around Egypt as they wish. He needs to take an oath to bury his father in Hebron in order to persuade Pharaoh to let him go. He is known as *Tzafnat Paneach* because the gentile ruler gave him that name which is an identity different from the Hebrew known as Yoseph. Even his brothers do not recognize him. In prosperous Egypt, the long-lived exile of Babylon or the Golden Age of Spain, there is only partial Torah, even when teachers, scholars, and rabbis are blessedly prolific in all areas of Torah wisdom. The verse in *Devarim* 11:21, "in order that your days may be long in the Land that He promised to your fathers to give you even as the days of

Heaven on Earth," follow the laws of *Tephillin* and *Mezuzah*. Rashi queries this because they are not *mitzvot* dependent on the Land of Israel, and we are obligated to observe them everywhere. He answers, saying, "Here in Exile keep them as signs so that they will not be forgotten when you return to the Promised Land." However, not only do these *mitzvot* acquire a different meaning when practiced in the Holy Land, but there are many *mitzvot* of war and peace, economic and social life, government, and environment, which we are unable to observe solely as Jews outside Eretz Yisrael. These, a whole portion of Torah, are missing.

> It is in this way that we must understand why the two Messiahs are necessary, Yeshayahu tells us that Zion shall be redeemed in Justice and her prisoners in Charity. These are human attributes and part of our spiritual striving. However, for as long as Israel lies in the dust of exile and persecution, it is not possible for us to even bestir ourselves. So first will come the Messiah, son of Yoseph. He will bring down from the heavenly heights light and spiritual strength. Then when we are able to rise and our strength is restored, we will be able to raise up and spiritualize our actions so that Justice and Charity will reign. This is the role of the son of David. (*Shem MiShmuel, VaYigash*)

Yoseph and Yehuda are mirrored in the redemption of Purim and of Pesach. Purim is a redemption in which the acts of God are hidden in a byzantium maze of intrigue and turnabout. The players are a wise man, a beautiful queen, a stupid or erratic king, and an overambitious or paranoic vizier, but the name of God is not recorded. In Pesach, God reveals Himself throughout from the revelation to Moses at the burning bush, through the signs and wonders, to the plagues and miracles. We repetitively hear, "in order that Egypt shall know that I am God" or "in order that Israel shall know" or "in order that you shall tell your children"—knowledge, awareness, and public proclamation of His intervention in nature and history. Purim and Pesach are reflected even in the natural order. Purim is in Adar, the last month of winter, with the stirrings and pulsing of the sap that began to rise in the previous month of Shevat, but is still latent and hidden. Always Pesach is the festival of spring when the flowers and leaves burst into bloom—nature reflecting the two types of redemption.

In our own time, the Pesach-Purim aspect of redemption engages us. The Talmud teaches that there may be miraculous redemption, publicly revealed and acknowledged, as in Pesach [Yehuda] or a redemption like the *ayelet hashachar*, the slow natural transition from darkness through dawn to daylight of Purim [Yoseph; *Talmud Bavli Sanhedrin* 98a). To many, the state of Israel, with the hidden hand of God acting through human actions of war, settlement, and diplomacy, is the fulfillment of *ayelet hashachar*. Everything, according to this view, first formulated by Avraham HaCohen Kook, from the French Revolution through Napoleon, the Great War, and the Holocaust, is a step in this dawn. They broke up the European empires and stirred nationalism, including that of the Jews. Even the assimilation and anti-Semitism of this period are seen as steps in the Redemption. The Great Wars and the breakup of the Turkish Empire led to the nations of the world recognizing the right of the Jews to a national home in Palestine and finally the UN decision of statehood. Here was removed the halakhic ban against revolting against the nations and settling in Israel because this had acquired the acceptance of the nations. Jewish immigration, settlement, and industry-agriculture had caused the desert to bloom for Israel, some of the signs of the Redemption. "For others the Land does not give of its beauty only for Israel."

The daily *Amidah* progresses logically from the Ingathering of the Exiles, through the restoration of independent judiciary and political leadership, the failure of enemies to destroy us, and then the rebuilding of Jerusalem and finally the Davidic Kingship.

At the individual level, too, there is a Yoseph-Yehuda redemption through *Shabbat*. Filled with the cares, toil, and struggle of the weekdays, mankind would not be able to rise to the religious heights of this day. However, the *Zohar* ascribes the *mussaf* of *Shabbat* to Yoseph, the seventh of the righteous ones (Abraham, Isaac . . .), and it is his form of redemption that brings blessing and spirituality down from Heaven on *Shabbat* Eve. Then through the *kiddush*, festive meals, Torah study, and

Shabbat songs, we are able to elevate ourselves, our families, and our homes to the redemption of *Shabbat*.

The two Messiahs do not remain separate. "Take a stick and write on it 'for Judah' . . . another stick and write on it 'for Yoseph' . . . and join them . . . and they become one" (*Yechezkel* 37:16–17). The first stage of Redemption described by Maimonides and the spiritual and miraculousness of the final Redemption will be merged.

VAYECHI

Sur Mirah–Asei Tov

"As Ephraim and as Menashe" (Gen. 48:20). Throughout the Jewish world, it is customary for parents to bless their children on the Eve of *Shabbat* by saying to the boys, "May God make you as Ephraim and Menashe," and to the girls, "As Sarah, Rivka, Rachel, and Leah." The use of the matriarchs as a form of blessing on our children seems natural. But what is so special about Ephraim and Menashe that they should be singled out rather than, for example, the Patriarchs, as the symbol of parents blessing their children?

The whole *Parshat VaYechi* deals with just that. Ya'akov, the last of the Patriarchs, blesses his sons, describes their spiritual abilities and shortcomings, and thinks of what will befall them in the future. Yitzchak blesses Ya'akov. Moshe, before his death, blesses the Tribes of Israel, giving different insights and different perspectives to that of Ya'akov but in essence doing exactly the same thing, providing a blessing that is not a promise of material things or power, but a spiritual bequest. Indeed, for hundreds of years, Jews have done the same, following the patterns of their fathers. Great scholars and ordinary men wrote ethical wills, which, in effect, are the same as, in principle, that which Ya'akov gave to his sons. We regard it as natural that people should will their material goods to their children, but sometimes overlook the fact that we have also spiritual essence, whether it be our learning, our piety, or even simply, our life experience and wisdom. Shimshon Raphael Hirsch points out that the Hebrew word *nachala* (inheritance) has the same roots as the word for river (*nachal*) and in effect, these wills, both material and spiritual, are a flowing of the wealth in its widest sense from one generation down to another generation.

Indeed, Maimonides codifies that from a Torah perspective, there is a halakhic right of people to bequeath their wealth to their children, and this not only applies to Jews but also to non-Jews.

If the ethical will is a common feature in Jewish tradition, nevertheless, the specialty or particular attributes of Ephraim and Menashe still need to be examined. They are not the sons of Ya'akov, but grandsons, the sons of Yoseph, who were born and brought up in Egypt. They are strangers to the covenant, to the experience of the Tribes before they came down to Egypt, and are the prototype of generations of Jews raised in exile, in a non-Jewish environment, who nevertheless, because of their loyalty to their family, to their nation, and to the great wisdom inherent in Judaism, continue the tradition, and, therefore, they are symbols of this continuation.

When Ya'akov blesses Ephraim and Menashe, he hands over to Yoseph the double portion of the inheritance in the Land of Israel that should have belonged to Reuven, the firstborn. In the allocation of the Land of Israel among the tribes, the Tribe of Levi received no portion, thus leaving eleven tribes. Yet, the Land of Israel was divided into twelve portions, no portion to Yoseph, but two portions in the form of the allocation to Ephraim and Menashe.

It is possible to view the additional bequest to Yoseph as a mark of affection to Rachel whose sons thereby inherit three portions. Without it, Rachel would have been equal to Bilhah or Zilpah, whose sons each received two portions. Ya'akov's love for Rachel could not allow this (Hirsch), but there seems to be a far more important lesson and an additional message.

Reuven was the firstborn. The *Targum Onkelos*, the Aramaic translation-commentary on the Torah, translates the third verse in Chapter 49 as referring to the threefold inheritance that should have accrued to Reuven: priesthood, kingship, and two portions in the Land of Israel. Not only were the two portions taken away from Reuven, but the kingship, too, was handed to the Tribe of Judah and the priesthood to the Tribe of Levi.

To be a firstborn is an opportunity. It requires one's ability to use that opportunity and to achieve the spiritual level and action of a firstborn in order for one to receive these benefits. Reuven lacked that ability and therefore forfeited the rights of the firstborn. This is a pattern that flows through the whole of Torah. There is not a single major leader who is the firstborn in his family. Not only is this true among the sons of Ya'akov, but Moshe is the youngest one in his family, David is the youngest one in his family, and Gideon makes a point of stating that he is unable to save the Jews from Midian in the Book of Judges, because his father's clan is the smallest clan in the Tribe of Menashe, and he is the youngest son in his family. Indeed, the Prophet Amos points out that it is not because the Jews were the strongest or most powerful or most numerous of the Nations, but in keeping with this pattern, because of their smallness, because of their lack of significance, that God chose them. It was only because of the love He had for their forefathers. A pattern repeated in our *parsha* with regard to Ephraim and Menashe; even though Menashe was the firstborn, Ya'akov placed Ephraim first in the blessing.

Ya'akov's preferring Ephraim to Menashe in the sequence of the blessing was not done out of ignorance, even as he told Yoseph, "I know my son, that Ephraim is the younger one." Many commentaries have been advanced as to why Ya'akov changed the order in his blessing. There does not seem to be any defect or default on the part of Menashe, whereby we could justify the exchange and therefore the explanations take different forms.

There are some commentators who say that Ya'akov foresaw that Menashe would be a larger and more powerful tribe. This is enhanced by the division of Menashe into half a Tribe which lived in Trans-Jordan and half a Tribe which lived on the West Bank of the Jordan. Others teach that he foresaw the fact that the half Trans-Jordanian Tribe was exiled before the Tribe of Ephraim. The *Shem MiShmuel Sokochow* advances a philosophical reason for this change. The verse tells us "*Sur mira v'aseh tov*"—Leave evil and do good—and this is a constant challenge because one has to know which one to choose first. The question of the priority, of the sequence, is important. It's not possible to do two things at the same time, and therefore we have to choose what will be our priority.

This is the disagreement between Ya'akov and Yoseph. And it is shown in the names of the two sons. Menashe was named by Yoseph, as he puts it, "*Ki nishani*"—because the Lord made me forget the suffering of my past. In other words, parallel to leaving aside evil, leaving aside the wrong things. Ephraim was so called because "He made me fruitful in a strange land." This is a positive optimism, this is the first of doing good, of *aseh tov*. Yoseph held that the natural order was that at first a person should separate himself from the evil in the world, from his wrong deeds, and then go on to doing good. And Ya'akov held that first came the doing of the good. And therefore, he placed Ephraim before Menashe.

Not only is this ideological or philosophical approach used to explain the action of Ya'akov but it is also used by the same Chassidic source to explain some halakhic differences between *Beit Hillel* and *Beit Shammai*. In modern times, there is a tendency to examine the texts and to conceive Hillel and Shammai as two radically different personalities. Hillel is the kind, accommodating, understanding, peace-loving, outgoing personality; Shammai is the legalist, insisting on definitions, on the absolute letter of the law, and of things being exactly the way they are supposed to be. There is even an attempt to talk about different professions, with Shammai as the engineer, the architect. Everything has to be exact, in place, and one step leads to the other. People are different, and it's no doubt that this not only is true of Shammai but of all the other great teachers and halakhists in Judaism. Each had their own personality, and each had their own likes and dislikes, weaknesses and strengths. However, the attempt to then take a jump and deduce that the halakhic decisions of these two people, or of any other halakhic authorities are the results of those differences means that in effect what we have is not halakhah, no legal system, but simply the outcome of psychological analysis.

It is possible to show that all the major differences in halakhah between *Beit Hillel* and *Beit Shammai* are the result of an emphasis on different aspects of Jewish thought. For example, the Talmud tells us of a discussion regarding the order of the lighting of candles on Chanukah. *Beit Shammai* taught that on the first night one lit eight candles, and each night one less was lit so that on the last night only one candle was lit. *Beit Hillel* reversed the order, starting on the first night with one candle and ending with eight. There are many explanations for this, almost all of which are of halakhic nature. It is possible, however, to relate this discussion to our issue about *aseh tov, sur mira*, Ephraim, and Menashe.

Both Hillel and Shammai agree that there is *aseh tov* and *sur mirah*. People have to do both things. The ultimate aim is to live a life in which one desists from doing wrong and one also does right. One desists from doing that which is forbidden and also does that which one needs to do. The question is one of priorities. So *Beit Shammai* say that to do good before one desists from evil makes for hypocrisy and distortion, and, therefore, a person must separate himself from evil and then come to the next stage. The initial act of separating oneself out from doing evil requires tremendous power and energy and has a great cost. Afterward, the process becomes easier. And, therefore, on the first night of Chanukah we light eight candles; that's the maximum. And each day it gets easier, so on each day it's necessary to light one candle less. *Beit Hillel* held the view that indeed it would be preferable to desist immediately from wrongdoing and then go on to doing good. However, people are not built that way, so that this is impossible, and is far beyond the power of people. Therefore, what one first has to do is to do good, to do one just act, one act of mercy, to do another act of kindness. And the first acts are few, they are meager, they are sometimes petty. And then they gain in strength until a person grows so that he is doing so much good, so much of the right thing, that it is now possible to go on to desist from evil. So on the first night there is one candle, and on the second night there are two candles. And as Chassidic thought likes to teach, a little light chases away a lot of darkness, therefore *aseh tov*. And the Chanukah lights ascend in number, until on the last night there are eight candles. The law is like *Beit Hillel*, and in all those cases where the law is like *Beit Hillel*, *Beit Shammai*, despite their ideological difference, obeyed this law. So that all lights lit on Chanukah follow the ascending order of *Beit Hillel*. However, the Talmud tells us that at the End of Days, the law will be like *Beit Shammai*. Then it will be possible for *sur mira* to precede *aseh tov*.

Ephraim precedes Menashe, and Ya'akov sees in his vision so Israel will bless their sons saying, "May He make you as Ephraim and Menashe," putting *aseh tov first*.

SONG OF THE NATION

SHMOT—

INTRODUCTION

Don Yitzchak Abarbanel—Fifteenth-Century Spain

Abarbanel finds four reasons for the distinctiveness of *Shmot* and the separation between it and the first book of the Torah, the Book of *Bereishit*.

1) *Bereishit* contains the stories of great and righteous individuals; the Book of *Shmot* is the story of the Jewish Nation. In the first book, we are told of the actions of great spiritual people from Adam to Noach, Shem, Ever, Avraham, Yitzchak, and Ya'akov, and their sons. It is, perhaps, pertinent to point out that of these individuals all those coming before Avraham were not Jewish and were not part of the intrinsic Jewish spiritual inheritance. The movement to the second book is, therefore, actually the movement from the specific knowledge of a universal monotheism which all of those preceding Avraham had, and the creation of the Abrahamic Nation. The Book of *Shmot*, therefore, deals with their exile in Egypt and their redemption, the granting of the Torah and of the building of the *Mishkan* so that God would rest in the midst of this Abrahamic Nation.

2) Before describing the story of the Abrahamic Israelite Nation, the Torah wanted to tell us that this people were not the result of the

accidental migration of different tribes or the integration of individuals, either through conquest or through conversion into a national group. So, too, the national group was not the result of some gradual spiritual grouping, nor the result of disciples. The Book of *Bereishit* comes to tell of the *yichus* of this nation, describing its being descended from holy stock: Adam, and then through Shet, son of Adam, but not through Cain nor through Hevel, both of whom have spiritual shortcomings. Then down through the son of Noach, Shem, but not through Yafet nor through Cham, even though they, too, were the sons of Noach, the saint who was saved when the rest of humanity was destroyed. From the sons of Shem, the family tree descends through Ever until Avraham was born to this spiritual aristocracy. However, the Israelite nation procedes, not through all the sons of Avraham but only through Yitzchak, neither through all the sons of Yitzchak but only through the descendants of his son Ya'akov. And here all this spiritual inheritance becomes resolved into his twelve sons from which spring this Israelite nation, even as Rabbi Yehuda HaLevi explains in his book *The Kuzari*.

3) The first book is the Book of our *Avot*, the story of creation and all the generations. The ten generations from Adam down to Noach occupy only one *parsha*. So, too, the ten generations from Noach to Avraham are included in a second *parsha*. All these generations were only a preparation for the emergence of the *Avot*. And then *Bereishit* is divided, three *parshiyot* to Avraham, one *parsha* to Yitzchak, three *parshiyot* to Ya'akov because he is the father of the Twelve Tribes of Israel, and then three *parshiyot* devoted to the story of the Tribes themselves. Like *Bereishit*, the Book of *Shmot* has twelve chapters, but those twelve chapters are devoted to the actions of Moshe, so *Sefer Bereishit* with its twelve *parshiyot* is the Book of *Avot*, and the Book of *Shmot* is the book of Moshe who spiritually is considered among the mystics to be the equivalent of the *Avot* and the *Sh'vatim*.

4) The Book of *Bereishit* is, so to speak, the book of the reasons for the exile to Egypt and the redemption which forms the story of the Book of *Shmot*. So in *Bereishit* we are taught of the appearance of Avraham,

INTRODUCTION

of God's command for him to leave his homeland and his father's house, to go to Eretz Yisrael, to the Promised Land, and of the Covenant of the Pieces where the Lord promised Avraham that his sons would inherit this Land with its definite boundaries, but that they first would be subject to servitude in a strange land and then they would be redeemed and brought back here, and also the actions of the sons of Ya'akov, the sale of Yoseph, and the resultant descent into Egypt in fulfillment of that covenant. Following this book is the Book of *Shmot* in which exile itself and the redemption are mentioned following this introduction. The Book of *Shmot* is, therefore, the beginning of all four books in which the hero is actually the Jewish Nation—not individuals but rather the whole nation, men, women, and children. The spiritual greatness of individuals mentioned in the Book of *Bereishit* in Judaism now finds its embodiment in the religious life of a nation. As Shimshon Raphael Hirsch points out in his commentary to the first chapter of our book, at first the revelation, the emphasis, and the religiosity were on the treetops; from now on, all these are down on earth among everyday people and families. For that reason the opening verse of our book, "*V'eylah Shmot*—And these are the names," to tell us of the fathers and the mothers and the children who came down, these seventy souls, not names of princes or of prophets but the seventy souls who came down to Egypt and were, so to speak, the foundation blocks on which this nation, this *Mamlechet Kohanim*, this nation of priests and holy people, was to be created.

SHMOT

Exile and Redemption

And they treated us badly, afflicted us and imposed hard labor upon us.
—*Devarim 26:6*

The mystics saw in the exile and redemption of Egypt the prototype of all the future Jewish exiles, suffering, and redemption. However, even one who does not have a mystical approach or appreciation also sees clearly many similarities and common features between the story of that first exile and the long course of Jewish history. It is possible, it seems, to distinguish two main trends in the commentaries throughout the ages regarding the causes of this oppression. Neither of the two trends that we will discuss are aimed at combating anti-Semitism nor minimizing it. They are both concerned only with a proper understanding of the verses in the Torah. Perhaps we ourselves may be able to see in these two trends answers to the pattern of persecution, exile, and pogrom that feature so largely in the hundreds of years of Jewish history. One such trend sees the actions of the persecutor as flowing from his own interests, history, or sociopolitical factors. The other will seem to ignore the perpetrator and to concentrate primarily on the weaknesses, faults, and sins of the Jews themselves, which led to the pattern of persecution. It is quite possible for both trends to be seen simultaneously. However, our discussion will attempt to separate them so that the issues will be made clearer and meaningful for our own times.

Anti-Semitism

If we analyze the verses that Pharaoh speaks to his people, we find that there is no crime, no fault, and no shortcoming attached to the Jews themselves. Nowhere does Pharaoh say that the Jews commit crimes, that the Jews are immoral, or that the Jews are a cause of national trouble. Throughout, it is the existence of the Jew per se that is distasteful, or, as Pharaoh puts it, "Because the Jews were fruitful and multiplied and they increased and the land was filled with them." It was due to their mere physical existence and their numbers which caused this hatred of the Jew. So, too, the talmudic story of the Emperor Hadrian typifies this approach. These make any self-analysis by the Jews as to their role in causing persecution important only if it leads to their own improvement and their own understanding; after all, the perpetrator will hate them irrespective of what they do. As the Emperor Hadrian rode in his chariot, a Jew standing along the road bowed and greeted the emperor as befits his station and status. The Roman emperor ordered the Jew to be whipped for his insolence and for having the temerity, a defiled and despicable Jew, to greet the ruler of the world. A few days later, having heard this story, a Jew did not bow nor greet the emperor as he rode past to the city. The emperor ordered him whipped for his insulting behavior toward Rome and its king. His officers said, "Emperor, last week you beat a Jew for bowing to you, now you beat a Jew for not bowing." "Don't you understand," came the reply, "I will beat them, the reason is irrelevant."

This hatred all too often becomes translated into various forms of persecution. Although describing ancient history, the stages of Jewish enslavement in Egypt sound startling familiar to us. "A new king arose in Egypt who knew not Joseph" (*Shmot* 1:8). *Rashi* comments here the second of two of the talmudic explanations for the use of "new king" in this verse This king ignored, or chose to forget, the benefits that Joseph had brought to Egypt by saving them during the years of drought. How often have the Jewish contributions to various societies and civilizations in economic, cultural, and social aspects been forgotten almost in the twinkling of an eye? Ibn Ezra follows the second talmudic view, namely, that the king actually belonged to a new dynasty or perhaps a foreign conqueror. This idea is favored by many general scholars who have suggested that the enslavement followed the overthrow of the Hyksos by an ethnic Egyptian Pharaoh. These shepherd kings, they believed, were the Pharaohs who had befriended Joseph. How many times in the long Jewish history have changes of government or conquest by a foreign power resulted in the persecution, expulsion, or enslavement of Jews?

Irrespective of the source of this new Jewish policy, we should note that the text makes it quite clear that the initiative for the persecution came from the top. It was not the result of a petition by the ordinary citizens or agitation by the average Egyptian, that led to the enslavement. Rather it was a calculated instigation by the rulers or the ruler of Egypt that sought ways and means to enlist the rest of the population in this policy. Throughout the various waves of our subsequent enslavement and discrimination, we have often witnessed a similar process, whereby the religious, political, or economic leadership and classes of a particular society spearheaded hatred and oppression. Sometimes this was to provide a scapegoat intended to divert the attention of the population away from the excesses and failures of the rulers. Other times it was meant to achieve some political, religious, or economic advantage. In almost all cases, by and large, the source was that of the rulers.

Pharaoh, like many of the later ruling classes whose actions were patterned whether knowingly or unknowingly on those discussed in our *parsha*, did not call for an open destruction of the Jews. He called for a policy of dealing wisely with them, and he used numerous schemes to slowly introduce hatred of the Jews as normal and acceptable policy. The text tells us that the initiative came from the king, but ultimately all the Egyptians joined in the oppression. In verse 13, we read: "And the Egyptians made the Children of Israel to serve with rigor and they made their lives bitter with hard service wherein they made them serve with rigor," whereas in previous verses the subject is Pharaoh himself. Similar patterns have been repeated down to our own days. True hatred and true persecution, even when it started at the top of society, inevitably became the common behavior of the men and women and children of that society. Not only Pharaoh bears responsibility, but so do his people.

One is not guilty of interjecting experiences of later generations to see that the Egyptian policies followed a pattern emulated over the centuries. At first they used treasury officials to afflict them with a burden primarily of taxation, and special levies—all discriminatory and arbitrary. They were aimed at punishing the Jews, as one high official in the British Mandate in Palestine said: "In their pockets, where it hurts." Not only taxes were used, but also what in economic terms has exactly the same effect. Special legislation affected the Jew by restricting where one may live, what professions may be followed, what goods may be produced, and at what places they may be sold. If these were not actually done in Egypt, nevertheless the pattern set up there of economic oppression was usually the first step adopted in following centuries.

From here followed the hard work and the enslavement of verse 13. The Jews were to be separated from the rest of the population even as slaves are. In this new status, the Jew was made inferior to everybody else in Egypt, giving the most exploited and miserable Egyptian at the bottom of the strict economic and political hierarchy that existed somebody who was weaker, lower, and more despised than he (Rashi, Exod. 12:29). In different ages following the same pattern, we were put into ghettoes, made to wear special clothes, made to wear special badges, forbidden to employ non-Jews or to engage in social contact or anything that might break down the barriers between the slave Jew and the rest of society.

In verse 14, the Egyptians enslaved the Jews *b'farech*, sometimes translated as "with rigor," preferably translated as "overburdening harshness." The rabbis have used various illustrations of what this *farech* was. Some said they made the Jews do unnecessary work, that is, one Jew dug a pit and the other one filled it. Pitom and Ramses, the cities that the Jews built, were built on shifting sands, so the Jews built, and the towns became ruins and the Jews built again. Others saw in this a reflection on the type of work given, that of men given to women and that of women given to men. Others referring to the two parts of that word *feh rach*, with a soft mouth, that the Egyptians enticed the Jews by telling them was their national duty, this was their contribution to society. Almost all these rabbinic versions show how the Egyptians took away from the Jews laboring there, any sense of achievement, any sense of the accomplishment that usually accompanies work. The slaves were to be denied even the satisfaction of knowing that their work was a contribution and that their forced labor was beneficial to somebody.

In this way, in addition to the hard work of the previous verse, now came the removal of any dignity, of any purpose in life, which was indeed the ultimate harshness. When all this failed, Pharaoh gave an instruction that every male born in Egypt was to be thrown into the Nile. By and large, our commentators all see this as being an injunction aimed against the Children of Israel. However, the *Sforno* points out that it says "every son who is born you will throw into the water." This refers to non-Jews as well. All too often in world history what started out as acts of anti-Semitism, acts of persecution only of the Jew, became acts of oppression and exploitation of the non-Jewish public as well. Whether we would like to see this only as an anti-Jewish injunction or as a general one, by getting the Egyptians to participate in this act, Pharaoh made them blatantly and openly partners in the anti-Jewish policy of his government.

One may well ask that if Pharaoh and the Egyptians did not like the Jews, didn't want them, then why didn't they just expel them? Furthermore, Pharaoh was worried, as we read in verse 10, that they would join up with an enemy and leave. If we read the verse carefully, we notice that Pharaoh's fear was not that they would leave Egypt. His fear was that as they multiplied they would leave Goshen and then they would come and take over the rest of the country. This is a fear often repeated in later generations. This small, almost marginal, group seems so powerful, so rich, so competent that they would ultimately take over the host country. In effect, Pharaoh was saying, "Now the Jews own everything, they control everything, and they multiply rapidly so that soon they will not be content to live only in Goshen, but they will take over the rest of the country." So, too, the reference to an enemy in that same verse is also a pattern, in that every time a nation was involved in war with another nation both sides accused the Jew of being in alliance with the enemy. So the nineteenth-century Germans and French saw their Jews as a fifth column and as traitors. In Poland, the Polish nationalists in the First World War saw the Jews as siding with the Germans, and the Germans saw the Jews as allies of the Poles. Earlier, in the fifteenth and sixteenth centuries, the Jews were thought of siding with the Turks and the Mongols or on the other side of the fence, with the Christians. Moreover, very often, the cry went up, "The Jew does not serve in the army and the Jew does not fulfill his patriotic duty." Pharaoh was simply exemplifying a similar policy by telling the Egyptians that if war would come, the Jews could not be relied on.

Responsibility of the Jew?

These are all steps in an anti-Semitic policy formed by Pharaoh without any blame being attached to the Jew. However, our commentators also attributed some blame to the Jews. This blame was not in regard to their actions toward the Egyptians, nor for their degradation, nor for any complicity in the anti-Semitic process. Rather, it is the spiritual action of the Jew, unrelated to Pharaoh or to the Egyptians, that lies behind this trend of thought. The rabbis tell us that the Jews had sunk to a level where they were exactly like the Egyptians and almost completely assimilated. They grew their hair like the Egyptians, they worshiped idols like the Egyptians, they did not circumcize their children. The Jews had reached the thirty-ninth level of impurity and had the Lord left them in Egypt a little longer they would have disappeared altogether.

Others, like *Abarbanel*, went even further. They saw in verse 7, "they were fruitful and had numerous births and increased and were exceedingly strong and the earth was full of them," a criticism of the Jews.

Usually, this verse is used to explain that each birth was a multiple one—six children as there are six words for multiplying. Alternatively, as we read in the *Pesach Hagadah*, the Jews were *m'tzuyanim*. They were capable, and they were of the most advanced in every field. *Abarbanel* says that the Jews were everywhere. They were forsaking the ghetto in Goshen with a particular Jewish lifestyle, and filling the theaters and the bathhouses; they were leaders of commerce and leaders of industry. In no way was *Abarbanel* or any similar commentaries making the Jews accomplices in their own destruction, nor was he excusing the Egyptians. He was simply doing what was done throughout the Torah, making Jewish spiritual misbehavior the cause of their suffering, or their religiosity and observance of God's law the cause of their protection and redemption. Perhaps there is an echo here of what we read in *Devarim*, Chapter 11, verse 5. "We remember the fish we ate in *Mitzrayim* at no cost, the cucumbers, the melons, the leeks, the onions and the garlic." And the rabbis asked, "How do you eat for nothing?" Either they stole or they ate without *mitzvot*; there were no restrictions, there were no dietary laws, there was no halakhah, His law.

This pattern is paralleled by a ruling of the *Smag* (*Sefer Mitzvah Gadol*) by Rabbi Moshe Coucy, who commented on the law of returning lost articles. After he discusses the biblical obligation to do so, he makes the following comment. "How come this exile of *Edom* in which we live today is so prolonged?" (And he found the answer in the ethical-spiritual behavior of the Jews.) "When the Jew did not deal according to halakhah and according to Jewish teaching in his economic affairs with the non-Jew, they went to God and said, 'This people steals and lies and defrauds and You as the Lord of Justice cannot redeem them,' and the Lord, Whose name is Justice, has to unwillingly agree. However, when the Jews will behave in this respect as Jews, then the same nations will go to God saying, 'This nation, such a pious, such an honest, such a kindly, just nation, they deserve to be redeemed,' and the Lord of Justice will redeem us."

VAEIRAH

Ten Plagues

And these are the ten plagues that God smote Egypt.
—Pesach Hagadah

The ten plagues that God set on Egypt before the redemption must not be seen as simply proving that the God of Israel is more powerful than the forces of nature or the idols that men have made of those same forces. Rather, they must be seen as showing us that in fact no forces, either in nature or in the physical world or in the spiritual world, have any power other than that given to them by God. To attribute independence, even if they are relatively weak, to any other force rather than that of God is defined by Maimonides as idolatry. The forces of nature that are defeated, so to speak, by the ten plagues are in fact made to behave contrary to their very nature, showing that they do not have any real independent existence. So, the frog who is the weakest and most mild of the creatures, it does not even have any teeth, is turned, by the God who made him, into an embarrassment, an annoyance, and a pressure on Egypt. And so, throughout the plagues. Parallel to that is the fact that the plagues operated only in Egypt and not in Goshen where the Jews lived. The geographic bounds placed on the transformation of these natural forces also serves to show the lack of any individual unGod–derived or unGod–controlled existence. An illustration of these teachings is shown when Daniel's three disciples were thrown by Nebuchadnezzar into the flaming furnace. The angel of water asked God to let him go down to extinguish the fire, whereas the angel of fire was sent down. If the former would have been sent then this would be a natural event, simply showing that the God of Israel is more powerful than the God of Babylon, because water puts out fire. However, for fire to put out fire demonstrates that there are no free or independent properties in nature since the fire behaves exactly the way the Lord who created it desires.

In *Shmot* 5:2, Pharaoh denied the three basic princples of Jewish monotheism, and the plagues came to show the whole world, for all generations, the fallacy of his denial. He denied the existence of God: "I know not God." He denied that there is divine knowledge of all human actions and subsequent reward and punishment: "Who is God." He denied that the God of Israel forms, re-creates, and alters the physical nature of the whole Creation, according to His Will: "Who is God that I should listen to Him" (Abarbanel). Ten times the Torah repeats that it is the knowledge of these truths that is the purpose of the plagues. "In order that [Egypt; Pharaoh and Israel] should know that I am the Lord."

Various commentators have ascribed different ideas or motives to the plagues. In every case the order of the plagues is not a haphazard one but represents a logical and consistent behavioral pattern. There were commentators, like Abarbanel, who saw the plagues as a means of weakening Egypt, physically and politically. Pharaoh had said, "Who is God that I should hearken to His voice, I do not know God. And therefore, I will not send out the House of Israel" (*Shmot* 5:3). He had also said that the Nile, the source of Egypt's wealth and power, belonged to him, so that he was actually the source of this wealth. Therefore, it was necessary to teach Israel, Pharaoh, and the world that all power and all wealth has its source in God. So the plagues destroyed, in gradual stages, all the wealth and might of Egypt. Like some well-rehearsed military plan the plagues came first to cause inconvenience and to sow fear as in the case of the plagues of blood, frogs, and lice. Later, it led to bodily sores, and to the destruction of the wealth of its cattle and its herds.

Then came the locusts who ate the crops and the hail that destroyed everything left over. The population is imprisoned during the three days of darkness in which no man was able to move around. Finally comes the destruction of the firstborn, that which represents the whole future and the whole promise of Egypt.

Samson Raphael Hirsch sees in the sequence of the plagues a reaffirmation of each of the stages of the exile foretold in the *Brit Bein HaBeytarim*. First there was *geirut*, being strangers, then there was *avdut*, servitude, and then there was *inuy*, suffering. If we divide the first nine plagues into three equal groups, we find in each group of plagues this escalating order of oppression.

In each group, the Egyptians are first made to feel strange in their own land. The natural order whereby they lived before, the laws to which they were accustomed and the pattern of their daily lives, were disrupted by a new order in each plague. Being a stranger does not always mean being subject to physical persecution or to economic impoverishment, but it does always mean being apart. Being separate from the legal, social, and political life of the host society, the stranger is always at a disadvantage in any changed conditions. So, in the first plague in each group of three: blood, the beasts, and the hail, the Egyptians were made to feel strangers in their own land before the changed physical patterns of their lives. In the second group, the Egyptians were taught the meaning of enslavement: The slave may be well treated, even be a member of the same society, yet he is powerless, denied freedom of movement, of livelihood, and of political action. In the plagues of frogs, of murrain, and of locusts, the Egyptians were powerless to do anything about the disaster which came upon them, just as slaves are. Nevertheless, they were able to do something. They dug holes around the Nile to get water, and they were able to defend themselves against the beasts and the hail by bringing their flocks into the sheds. They were subject to the evils of the plagues, but they were able to protect themselves just as strangers are often able to protect themselves against the actions of the host society. Finally, the third aspect of the exile, namely the suffering, comes out in the third of each group: the lice, the boils, and the plague of darkness.

The magicians were unable to bring forth lice, and they could not even stand before Moshe because of the boils. The darkness was so heavy the Egyptians were unable to move, even unable to get up from their seats. The plague of firstborn combined in it all three aspects of strangeness, enslavement, and persecution.

This parallels the changes that occurred in the hardening of Pharaoh's heart. First we are told, "And Pharaoh hardened his heart," this was an act of free will, and then "God hardened his heart." This was a punishment. We learn an important truism for our own personal behavior in this. A person does an action for which he is liable to punishment by a human court. Meanwhile he does *teshuva*, he repents, and this repentance squares, so to speak, his accounting with God Who sees and ascertains the validity and truth of His penance. Human courts, however, are unable to do so, and, therefore, the courts will impose the punishment on the man even though he has repented. Without repentance, of course, the obligation toward God will remain even after the punishment inflicted by a court.

Menachem Mendel of Kotsk saw the ability of Pharaoh to withstand the onslaught posed by the plagues on his physical and his spiritual strength, a model for our own behavior. In the plague of the firstborn, the text says that at midnight there was a great cry in Egypt, and that Pharaoh woke up. *Rashi* comments, "from his bed." "What difference does it make to us where Pharaoh went to sleep, why should *Rashi* see it significant enough to state that he went to sleep in his bed?" asked the *Kotsker*. "Because," the *Kotsker* said, "this is the power, the strength, the ability of Pharaoh to persevere in his own way." Egypt is in ruins, nine plagues have come, and each one of them has sapped the power of Egypt. Now there is to be a tenth one, that of the firstborn. Pharaoh is king of Egypt. He has responsibility for the welfare of his society, and Pharaoh has a firstborn son. He is himself a firstborn son. And yet, instead of accepting God's rule, instead of cowering before the power of the Almighty, Pharaoh goes to sleep in bed as usual, paying no regard to the power or the threat of the last of the plagues. "This should be," said

Menachem Mendel, "the way Jews perform their own spiritual and religious tasks."

It was quite possible for God to take Israel out of Egypt by sending only one plague. This would have made sense if the purpose of the plagues was to punish or destroy Egypt. However, instead of one plague, there were ten, giving Egypt a chance to repent, as indeed many of them did, leaving Egypt together with the Israelites or giving them vessels of gold and silver when they left. Always the gate of *t'shuva* is open. However, there cannot be evasion of responsibility. Unlimited Divine Mercy would permit injustice creating greater evil than the original act. So, *S'forno* sees the destruction of the firstborn as the punishment, and the destruction at the Red Sea is seen by almost all the commentators as the final punishment.

The number ten has many parallels in our religious thinking. In ten sayings, the world was created, ten times God's word was used to created a world out of nothing: ten generations between Adam and Noach, ten generations between Noach and Avraham, ten plagues in Egypt, ten commandments at Sinai. The *Admor* of Sokochochaw saw a connection between all of these, showing that there had to be ten plagues, neither more nor less. Between Adam and Noach each generation destroyed one-tenth of that world created by ten sayings. Then came the flood and the world was destroyed and re-created. This was repeated in the ten generations between Noach and Avraham, each generation destroying, as it were, a tenth of God's creation. This time, however, the world was able to continue through the greatness of Avraham, the friend of God, and the father of the House of Israel. After Avraham, the evil of the world became concentrated in Egypt. Egypt was not just a powerful nation, the bread basket of the world, the center of a huge empire. Over the generations evil, in the spiritual term, was collated from all over the world to come to rest in the idolatry of Egypt, in which every creature, every manifestation of nature, even some of the vilest and most degenerate forms of animal life, insects, beetles, mice, snakes, rats, were all worshiped as part of the pantheon. Sexual immorality of the world came to be concentrated in Egypt, where Pharaoh would marry his sister and where Pharaoh agreed with Avraham that indeed his life was in danger; men could be killed for their wives. And the greatness of Egypt was built on the backs of slaves. Millions of men died to construct the canal, to raise the stones of a tomb for Pharaoh, or to construct and operate the irrigation that made Egypt possible. A hierarchy of status, economic power, and political expression enslaved even the Egyptians themselves, so that bloodshed and cruelty and the denial of the divinity of man flowed from all of the world to find its culmination in Egypt. In Egypt was destroyed God's world, created by ten sayings, and, therefore, Egypt had to receive ten plagues.

We are taught in the *Zohar* that for each plague that the Egyptians had a redemption came to the Jews. When there was darkness in Egypt, there was light for the Jews; when there was no water in Egypt, in Goshen the Jews drank water; when hail fell, it did not fall in Goshen nor did the locust eat of the crop of Israel. So, too, in the spiritual sense, each plague that came to punish or to destroy that which had caused the destruction of part of God's world gave to the Jews a spiritual revelation, enabling them to construct a world according to God's will. So not only were there ten plagues, but at Sinai we received ten commandments.

BO

To Walk in the Way

It should have said "Go to Pharaoh," but the text says "Come to Pharaoh" because it is impossible to go away from God.
—Rashi

Said Menachem Mendel of Kotsk, "God took Moshe by the hand as a father takes a child and said to him, 'Come, together we will go to Pharaoh.'" Indeed, parallel to that, God gave us His hand, His law, to enable us to walk through the challenges and triumphs of life. This law, halakhah, literally, "to walk," is a uniquely Jewish contribution, enabling people to tread a spiritual path through the everyday actions and mundane acts that constitute the lives of ordinary people. The ramifications of the *mitzvot*, of the laws and obligations and rights that make up this halakhic pathway, are extremely widespread so that they cover every facet of human activity, not only ritual, prayer, and religious acts, but also those related to the way we earn and spend our money, the type of criminal and commercial legal system we establish, and the rights and obligations of the state vis-à-vis its individual citizens including kosher and non-kosher war.

Almost all the signposts and guidelines of this halakhic pathway are demonstrated in one way or another in the Exodus from Egypt or flow from all that surrounds it. This is neither surprising nor fanciful. The purpose of the plagues was to demonstrate and to popularize "knowledge of the Lord." The exile in Egypt cleansed and purified Israel, spiritually and morally, a veritable smelting pot or refinery. The Exodus permitted the receiving the Torah at Sinai and the settlement in that Land for which this Torah was intended. So the first mitzvah, the sanctification of the New Moon and ordering the calendar, was given to Israel just prior to the Exodus, and the halakhic pathway continues from here. The most obvious example of this is the annual Seder and seven days of Pesach, the abstinence from leavened bread, and the eating of matzot. "And this day shall be for you a memorial and you will celebrate it, a Festival to the Lord, for all generations, an immutable law" (*Shmot* 12:14).

However, as the commentator *HaEmek Davar* points out, the observance of the Passover, the telling of the story of the Exodus on an annual basis, is insufficient for making this a part of our psychic, national, and individual memory. One only has to observe how in other cultures and other nations events that have occurred much more recently than the almost four thousand-year-old Exodus, are rapidly forgotten to appreciate this. So, many other acts are added by the Torah to keep this memory alive. It is like the case of a father who tells his child a story to illustrate an important moral lesson, and then reminds him of it every day. When the year comes around and the anniversary of the first telling recurs, the story is told in full. So, in addition to the annual Seder and Pesach, we have the memorial of the Exodus in every act of Jewish ritual: the circumcision, the marriage ceremony, every week the *kiddush* on *Shabbat* and, of course, all the other festivals. It seems that this, too, is insufficient, and therefore, the *Rambam* codifies that it is a positive mitzvah to remember the going out of Egypt everyday. Thus, the allusion to the Exodus in the *K'riyat Shema* we recite daily. The tefillin on our arms and head, the *tzitzit* in our clothes, and the *mezuzot* on our doorposts are constant reminders of this very same fact.

Of the four biblical paragraphs that are enclosed in our tefillin, two of them are taken from our *parsha* and clearly link the tefillin to the Exodus from Egypt. At first we read that, "You should bind them for signs on your hand and for a memorial between your eyes that the Torah of God shall be on your mouth, or in your mouth, because with a strong hand you were taken out of Egypt" (*Shmot* 13:10). Later we read, "They shall be for a sign and for frontlets between your eyes because with by strength of hand God took you out of Egypt" (verse 16). By binding the tefillin on our hand, we subject our strength to obsrving the Divine Will. That is why we also put tefillin on the stronger hand: right for a left-handed person, left for a right-handed one. The *Netziv* of Volozhin, and later Rav Kook, both saw in the use of the strong hand in these verses, the strength of hand, not only a reference to the punishment of Pharaoh, but far more importantly, evidence that the Exodus took place against the will of the Jews and that they were forced to leave the house of bondage. These memorials are important in keeping in our memory that which our minds would like to forget, through the numerous precepts.

The *Shabbat* before Pesach is called *Shabbat HaGadol* because the tenth of Nissan, the day the Jews took the Paschal lamb, fell on *Shabbat*. Even though the lamb was an idol for the Egyptians, there was a great miracle and no harm came to Israel (*Tur*). However, the tenth of Nissan does not always fall on *Shabbat*, so why do we continue to call it *Shabbat HaGadol*? "This is," said the *Shem MiShmuel*,

> because this miracle came to Israel as a result of its bravery and devotion shown by performing God's commandments despite the danger. The miracles vouchered to Israel prior to this are "the strong hand," like the hand or rope one extends to a drowning man; *chesed*, assistance given to somebody who is helpless. However, here Israel performed an act so the miracle was granted in justice, not in mercy [earned as it were]. At the Red Sea, too, Israel saw the "great hand," because they had acted to perform God's commandments.

So, too, the tefillin are meant to direct our thoughts and actions; the head and the arm.

The *Ramban* links the Exodus from Egypt and the commandments regarding the memorizing of such an act with the spiritual effect that these self-same precepts have. The Exodus is the most striking proof, for the *Ramban*, that the world has a Lord, a Creator, Who is All-knowing, Who is constantly re-creating, Who provides for all His creatures and is All-powerful. All the *mitzvot* related to the Exodus are a constant reminder for ourselves and our children and children's children of that which our eyes witnessed and saw at the going out of Egypt. When we affix a *mezuzah* to our door, put tefillin on our hands and forehead, remember the Exodus on *Shabbat* and the festivals and on all the other occasions in our lives, we are acknowledging God as the Creator of the world. We are acknowledging His providence and express our appreciation for the unlimited kindness in bringing us out from slavery to freedom.

However, there not only are ancient or revealed miracles to be remembered. The lessons of the Exodus have a meaning also at a more personal and mundane level. The message contained in the comments of the *Ramban* help us to understand the hidden miracles which occur to us every day. These are the ways in which the kindness and bounty of God the Creator are given to all His creatures, so that there is neither chance nor accident, neither at the public nor at the private levels. It is in view of this that the significance of the Exodus from Egypt has not been restricted to those *mitzvot* and rituals that we have mentioned. Indeed, there is a whole range of ethical and moral aspects of human life in the world of business, and in the field of human relations which are constantly linked in the Torah to the going out of Egypt. The spiritual and ethical teachings of the Ten Commandments are prefaced with the acknowledgment that they flow from the God Who took us out of Egypt. We were strangers in a foreign land. Experienced in and familiar with the feeling of hopelessness, exploitation, and alienation, which are the lot of the strangers, the Torah said we should not oppress the stranger, both in word and in action, but also in the provision of one legal system for native born and stranger alike. The mandatory resting of servants and animals on *Shabbat* is in the Decalogue in *Devarim*, linked to the Exodus. Such linkage is not a function of ethnic memory but of the teachings inherent in the Exodus, so the Torah tells us that the basis for the injunction against the interest-bearing loan is because God took us out of Egypt. So, too, one who lacks faith that He will provide for him even if he loses money by lending interest-free is lacking in belief in the God of the Exodus. The whole concept of just weights and measures, which come to prevent fraud and exploitation in daily business dealings, is linked in the Torah to the God that took us out of Egypt. The Sages explain this linkage as flowing from the fact that the whole purpose of going out of Egypt was to keep this and similar *mitzvot*. Alternatively, in line with the reasoning of the *Ramban* explained earlier, they taught that He Who was able to distinguish between the firstborn and the nonfirstborn, a fact of great secrecy and personal intimacy between husband and wife, will surely know and therefore punish one who perverts his weights and measures in secret. God's knowledge not only extends to the firstborn, but also to all the white-collar crimes primarily conducted only in secrecy and privacy. This linkage is natural and consistent. Rav Kook writes that the basic purpose of the Exodus is to fight the egoism and cruelty involved in the human struggle for existence, which subjects other people to exploitation and even to the depths of slavery. Because this egoism is so strong, it has to be fought until the natural profane instincts of people are conquered, so that the light of His holy sparks may penetrate. So we require the holy acts of placing tefillin on the arm and head to make possible this process of consecration of or transformation of the basic earthly drives into a power for just living and holiness.

The Exodus from Egypt constituted the subjection of the profane and most gross elements of human existence to holiness. Therefore, the holiness of the letters of the tefillin, which embrace the twin strands of deed and thought (arm and head), will manifest the triumph of the sacred over the profane. These tefillin are referred to as *totaphot*, which is understood by our rabbis to mean a sign of glory. For that reason, many persecutors of the Jews have looked for ways and means to demean the Jew while he was wearing his tefillin. In the recent holocaust years, Jews were forced to clean toilets or to sweep streets attired in their crowns of glory of *tallit* and tefillin. For that reason, the tefillin are not worn on the morning of *Tisha B'Av* when the splendor and glory of God's temple was destroyed. The rabbis tell us that just as we wear tefillin, so does God wear tefillin. And in the tefillin of God is written, "Who is like Your people, Israel, one chosen nation." In our tefillin it is written God is One. Our tefillin reflect His Glory and His tefillin reflect the glory of Israel who serve Him. This parallels the fact that the Torah calls the festival of the Exodus, *Chag HaMatzot*. This is a memorial to the greatness of Israel who in their absolute faith were prepared to leave Egypt without adequate provisions beyond their matzah dough, dependent on Divine Providence. To us it is known as *Chag HaPesach*, the time He had mercy on our homes. (This is in accordance with the *Targum* who translates *Pasach* not as "passed over" but "had mercy," *Matzah*—the glory of Israel, and Pesach, His Glory. And Levi Yitzchak of Berditchev, the chassidic arch-type of the lover of Jews, stood up in the synagogue one day and said, "When a man's tefillin fall on the ground he is required to pick them up and kiss them and restore them to their glory. God, Your tefillin lie in the dust. I order You to handle Your tefillin the way Your law instructs us.")

BESHALACH

Generation of the Wilderness

Israel, after the Exodus and its miracles, stands on the banks of the Red Sea, faced with the pursuit of Pharaoh, and asks, "Is the Lord in our midst or not?" (*Shmot* 17:7). So, too, all of us are not really convinced that our needs are assured, yet "He Who created our days, created their sustenance." Rabbi Eliezer the Modaite used to say, "Whoever has enough for the needs of today and yet asks 'what shall I eat tomorrow,' shows a lack of faith, as it is written: 'That I may prove him whether he will walk in My law'" (*Midrash Rabbah*, *Shmot* 42).

This *sedra*, the first of the saga of freedom, is replete with mumbling and complaints. Indeed, throughout the Torah we are amazed at the number of times that the Jews complained, queried, and showed signs of rebellion. It is common thought to ascribe this weakness to the many years of enslavement, the existence of a slave mentality, and the inability to handle their political and national freedom. This approach, common to *Rashi*, the *Rambam*, and other commentators, has a very strong kernel of truth. However, there is another approach, an approach that is more appropriate for our own needs. It comes to teach important spiritual and religious ideas that are relevant today to our own free society. This is the approach of the *Ramban* and the chassidic commentators who saw every complaint and every grumble as an expression of a religious error or a spiritual doubt, rather than merely the effect of enslavement.

The Jews who left Egypt are called by the talmudic sages a *"dor de'ah,"* a generation of great knowledge. They were found worthy to see great miracles, such as no other generation before or after them. The visible power and glory of God witnessed in Egypt was clearly granted to them. "The miracles that even a maidservant saw on the Red Sea, the great prophet Yechezkel ben Buzi did not merit." The whole nation stood before Sinai and was worthy to hear the Divine Voice. Therefore, for these commentators, the shortcomings of the Israelites in the desert had to be of a far more serious and spiritual nature.

If we will look at the complaints of the Israelites in this *parsha*, whether it is the question of the shortage of water, the bitterness of the water, or the lack of food, we will see how all of them revolve around the *Midrash* quoted at the beginning. We will see that the problem facing the Israelites was the problem that is inherent in the human condition, and which affects every act of ours, whether it is in economics, politics, or even in family relationships. This is the fear of uncertainty, the lack of knowledge as to what will be tomorrow. How does one cope with the unexpected events and uncertain future which of assuredly lie in the path of people, both at the individual and collective level? If everyone knew with certainty that they would have enough money or enough health and enough family ties and affection throughout their lives, there would be no point and no incentive to lie, cheat, or steal to protect themselves against this uncertainty. Of course, there are legitimate methods, such as insurance, investment, and the fostering of human relations. Nevertheless, because this uncertainty is such a permanent part of the human condition and the fear thereof so powerful, as often as not, we also seek immoral and illegal ways to protect ourselves. It is a lack of faith in God's ability or will to supply all our needs that makes us fear this uncertainty and seek even illegal ways to protect ourselves. One who deals in faith is often understood as referring to one who is honest in his business. But it would seem that to the rabbis, the ethical behavior always flows from the belief, the faith, that God supplies all our needs, and that it is unnecessary to fear the uncertainty.

"And they came to Marah and they could not drink of the water because it was bitter, and the people complained to Moshe saying 'What will we drink?' And Moshe prayed to God, and He showed him a tree which he cast into the water and made it sweet. And there he placed before them statutes and ordinances" (*Shmot* 15:23–25). The *Talmud Bavli*, *Sanhedrin* 56b, teaches us that at Marah the Jews were given the statute of *Shabbat* and the social-civil laws, the *chukkim* and the *mishpatim*. The *Shabbat* came to teach the Jews that just as God provided for them by transforming the bitter water into sweet, so, too, every *Shabbat*, even though they broke the cycle of economic endeavor and the increase of their material assets, nevertheless He would provide for them in the weekdays to come. So, too, in *shmiltah*, the Sabbatical year, the Jews asked, "What will we eat in the seventh and eighth year if we do not work and plow and sow and reap in the seventh one?" And God promised that his bounty would be so great, enough to cover them and to satisfy their economic wants. So the *Shabbat* and the Sabbatical year are examples of statutes came to teach the Jew that his faith in God the Provider would protect him against uncertainty. But even the *mishpatim*, the civil ordinances, came to teach the same lesson. The civil and commercial code of Judaism limits our economic profits, but also limits our economic gain by obligating us to assist others. By preventing us from benefiting at the expense of others, we should, however, have no fear that if we adhere to these laws and accept these limitations, God will not provide enough for us and our families.

So the *mechilta* on *Shmot* teaches us regarding verse 26 in this chapter, "And do that which is straight and honest in His eyes," that everybody, whose commercial activities and whose business is conducted with this faith in God the Provider will be highly regarded by everybody and it will be as though he observed the whole Torah.

Some two weeks later the House of Israel came to the wilderness of sin, between the Springs of Refidim and Mt. Sinai. And here the people complained to Moshe and to Aharon saying, "It would have been better for us to die in Egypt at the hand of God when we sat by the fleshpots, when we did eat bread to the full" (*Shmot* 16:4). The *Midrashim* show two different aspects of their complaints. In the *mechilta*, Rabbi Eliezer the Modait said that the Jews were slaves to the king in Egypt and therefore splurged themselves on the royal bounty, helping themselves to the best of everything that there was. The *Midrash Rabbah*, playing on the words "when we sat by the fleshpots" but not when we ate of the fleshpots, denies the validity of their complaints. They sat next to the pots while the Egyptians ate of the meat and of the best products, letting the Jews eat only bread while tantalizing them with the aromas and the anticipation with which the Egyptians taskmasters ate. In either case they had brought an idealized, exaggerated picture of the past, very often in the manner of poor people who describe their relationship with the rich and the mighty to impress us. However, in Egypt they were slaves; they had no responsibility for their own destiny, their economic and social lives. Even though the taskmaster beat them and persecuted them, nevertheless, he fed them to keep their strength up. Now, however, they were free men, and they faced the uncertainty of where the next meal would come from, and this was their complaint. This is the same fear of uncertainty and of the future that modern man in all societies faces and looks to solve. Some solutions are legal and moral, through the role of government and planned economies, through business acumen, or through savings, or a mixture of all three of them. *Rashi*, commenting on the *Talmud Bavli*, *Yoma* 75a, points out that their complaint was on a full stomach; actually they had flocks and herds. They were shepherds in Egypt, they lived with plenty of meat. They could have sacrificed this asset and eaten it. However, they didn't want to touch their capital, they did not want to decrease their economic stake. They wanted to satisfy the everyday needs from some additional source of income. This was the basis of their complaint. So, too, we see men and women who have net equities which neither they nor their children can ever use up, and yet they busy themselves increasing their economic stake, constantly trying to have more. This is a repetition of what our fathers did in the desert. This repetition is highlighted by the action of the Israelites with regard to the manna.

"And God said, I have heard the complaint of the Children of Israel. Speak to them saying that in the evening you will eat meat and in the morning you will have your full of bread and you will know that I am the Lord God" (*Shmot* 16:11–12). However, this gift of the satisfaction of economic wants from Heaven was meant by the Torah to come as a test of the ability of the Jew to recognize God's providence and subject himself to the restriction that comes from the same Provider. And our fathers were told that six days a week they would gather the *man*, but that they could only gather a certain amount—an amount that was enough only for one day. The next day they would again have to be dependent on God's bounty. The uncertainty and the fear of the future would have to be subject to this faith. And, of course, our fathers, like us, were unable to do that, and, therefore, on the very second day they went out and they gathered more than they needed. The Divine answer was swift and certain: worms and mold.

The *Ramban* sees the Jews coming through with flying colors from this test. Commenting in *Devarim* 8:2, he explains that it was a great test for the Jews to have no other alternative, to go into the great desert, the wilderness, only with this promise of manna that came down from heaven. Knowing that they were totally dependent on Him, nevertheless, every day they continued to wander in loyal obedience to the command of God. He could have led them through the cities, in which they would have had access to other sources of livelihood, but put them to this test because by following in the wilderness and trusting to His daily provision, they would show that they kept faith with Him. *S'forno*, however, sees this as an important moral challenge. The daily demonstration of God's providence by the bread and flesh descending from heaven freed the Jews from the cares and pain of having to earn a livelihood. Furthermore, they now had leisure because the economic tasks were nonexistent. Would they be able to have this carefree life and yet subject themselves to the moral and ethical disciplines of God? This is a parallel with the modern society of plenty, whereby to earn and create wealth we require, as in no other time in history, far less effort and time. So, too, the challenge to use our leisure and the earning of wealth in a moral and ethical way, has become greater than in any other period of history. *Ibn Ezra* is far more judgmental. He comments that every day the Jews were dependent on God for satisfaction of their daily needs. Every day the Jews were faced anew with evidence that all wealth comes from God. It is this dependence on God to which the Jews objected. This is why they went out to collect more than they needed. This is why they went out to see on *Shabbat*, perhaps Moshe made a mistake. This is why in Num. 11:6 they complained about the lack of alternatives: "All we have is the manna to look forward to." They wished to free themselves from their dependence on God for their daily bread.

God-given wealth comes with strings attached. If God is indeed the source of all wealth, then this wealth may not be earned by immoral or by unethical methods. If God is indeed the source of all wealth, then it has more than one purpose. Part of that wealth is meant to satisfy the needs of ourselves and our families. Part of that God-given wealth, however, is also meant to be shared with others. This sharing takes two forms in Judaism: *chesed* and *tzedakah*. *Chesed*, acts of righteousness, are those acts which we do for people to whom we have no legal obligation and to people who may be undeserving of it. But acts of righteousness are left to our own discretion, they flow from our feelings of pity, from our feelings of love for others, from our feelings of social responsibility. However, when we do not have such feelings, or when we feel that we have done enough, then we free ourselves from acts of mercy, acts of *chesed*. That is why Judaism also has *tzedakah*. *Tzedakah* comes from *tzedek*, justice, which coerces us to share our wealth. God-given wealth is meant to also serve social purposes, whether we desire it, and whether we feel that the cause is justified or not, so that in Judaism we always have had philanthropy alongside taxation, voluntary giving but also enforced social responsibility.

The illusion that our wealth is created by our own efforts or luck or foresight, rather than something given to us by God militates against such enforced social responsibility. This illusion makes us feel that we have absolute rights over our property but also that if we share some of it with others perhaps we will not have enough for our own needs. This is a major factor in the clamor for water at Refidim which follows the story of the manna. Regarding the manna, when they had a dual portion on Friday, they nevertheless went out on the Sabbath, assuming that their efforts would yield them food just as it had on the six days previously. So, too, with the water. The text should have been written: "The people had no water," but rather it states, "There was no water for the people to drink" (17:1). They had water in their vessels but there was no water supply. The text implies that the people were not thirsty at all but that they only said they had no water to drink. What they lacked was a continuous supply of water, making them dependent on God. However, if they had wished to ration themselves they would have had enough.

This inability to limit themselves was in fact what led to their grumbling about the water (*HaEmek Davar, K'tav V'abbalah*). The idea that God is the source of all wealth and that we are required to have a faith that He will supply all our needs is not meant to stunt the economic development of society, nor is it meant to prevent the enjoyment of the material goods received from God, nor to place fear and trembling in our everyday actions. On the contrary, this faith frees us from the fear of uncertainty. It ennobles man's economic actions so that he becomes a partner in God by achieving the satisfaction of material wants through normal and natural means. Mankind becomes, as it were, an imitator in the creation of economic wealth, of the God Whose providence provides it for them. The Jewish concept of God's power in the economy is a cheering one. Humanity, despite its weaknesses, shortcomings, and frailty, is able by its own efforts to gain a share in the creativeness of God. This power gives meaning and protection to our humble existence. We appreciate that the great, distant God Creator takes pleasure in knowing that His creatures are satisfied. In contrast to this, the self-made man who believes that manna does not come from heaven but only comes from his own efforts, or that water does not stream miraculously at God's command, or that the One Providence sweetens those things which are bitter, can never believe in a God, as Eliezer HaModai said: "One who cannot have faith in that which came to me today, will also be given to me tomorrow, he does not have faith in God at all."

YITRO

Ten Commandments

Face to face did God speak to you on the mountain.
—Devarim 5:4

Is it indeed feasible to imagine that hundreds of thousands of men, women, and children stood before *Har Sinai* and heard the actual words of God? Is it conceivable that all these people with their various religious and spiritual levels, even including the unborn souls of all the generations, were worthy of this highest form of prophecy, to hear God speak face to face with them? For Maimonides, who understood prophecy to be only available to people of a certain spiritual, physical, and mental level, and even that only in the form of dreams at night or visions, this is a particularly problematic issue. Only Moses was able to hear God face to face, and, therefore, Maimonides holds that the people heard only part of the Ten Commandments, and even that in a voice that they were unable to understand (*Moreh Nevuchim*, Part II, Chapter 32). Likewise, the *Ramban*, Nachmanides, also sought to solve this problem by arguing that the first two commandments, that is, those relating to idolatry and to the unity of God, were heard and understood. For the other eight, the people actually heard the voice but did not understand them. It seems that both these opinions, like that of Rabbi Yehoshua ben Levi in the

Midrash, are based on the verses in which the people asked that God should not speak to them, because they feared to die after seeing God visibly, but rather that Moshe should speak to God for them. However, in that same *Midrash*, the rabbis, that is, the majority, hold that all the commandments were spoken by God visibly and understood by each and every individual standing at *Sinai*. This is the opinion of *Ibn Ezra*, *Abarbanel*, and all the mystical interpreters and commentators. From this it follows that the Ten Commandments were given not through a prophet but directly by God Himself, that it was a code of behavior for the national group of Israel and not merely for the individual, and that it was engraved on stone, separate from the rest of the Torah, written in a book.

Irrespective of which of these opinions we would like to hold, the Ten Commandments have always formed a centerpiece of Jewish tradition and Jewish worship. There is almost no synagogue in the world that does not have the Ten Commandments embroidered or engraved within its walls. There was indeed a short period during the Byzantium times, in which synagogues were decorated with signs of the zodiac, with the *lulav* and *etrog*, with the menorah, and so on, but it seems that architecturally this was only a passing phase and the Ten Commandments took pride of place. In the Temple days, the Ten Commandments were recited each day after the Morning Sacrifice. This was only stopped because of the conception held by the heretics, primarily the Jewish Christians, that this was the whole Torah, that it was enough to be a "Ten Commandments Jew." Indeed, this misconception exists in many places even to this day. To wean us away from this misconception, the rabbis decreed that the Ten Commandments should not be repeated each day in the Morning Service as had been the custom since the destruction of the Temple. However, this does not mean that they accepted the marginalization or removal of the Ten Commandments from our daily lives.

Maimonides conceived of Thirteen Principles of Faith in which the Jew is obliged to believe (Commentary on the *Mishnah*, *Sanhedrin*, Chapter *Chelek*). These Thirteen Principles are usually included in the prayer book, and it's customary to recite them after the daily prayers. A close examination will show how they are derived from the Ten Commandments: "I am the Lord Your God," in the First Commandment corresponds to the basic principle of belief in the existence of God. Because the second principle is that of the unity, this corresponds to: "You shall not have other gods before Me." The third principle, that God has no corporeal form nor attributes, is to be learned from "You shall not make a statue or picture of any of the things in creation." The commandment concerning *Shabbat* in which we learn that six days did God make heaven and earth would correspond to Maimonides' principle that God existed before all creation. For us to love and keep His commandments, which is the next of the principles, we may glean from God's promise to extend *chesed* to those who love and worship Him. The sixth and seventh of the principles refer to prophecy in general, and the specific nature of the prophecy of Moshe. This we understand from the nature of the whole revelation of *Sinai*, where it is specifically quoted in the text: "This day we saw that God speaks to mankind and they may live." The eternal nature of the Torah is contained in the promise that God does show mercy to untold generations. The belief in Divine Revelation, which is the ninth principle of Maimonides, is contained in the verses: "Because they heard the voice of the Living God speaking and you have seen that from the heavens God spoke to you." God's knowing what people do and His reward and punishment for those actions form the tenth and the eleventh principles of Maimonides and they exist in the commandment, "For I am the Lord Your God, a zealous God, Who visits the sins of the fathers and extends the acts of righteousness." It is in those acts of righteousness for untold generations that *Abarbanel* includes the last two principles of Maimonides with regard to the Messiah and the ultimate resurrection of the dead.

Far more widespread and probably of greater importance to us in our daily lives is the teaching that the Ten Commandments represent chapter headings of all the religious obligations and duties that fall on the Jew. Textually, this is supported by the first verse of *Mishpatim* which reads: "And these are the judgments that you will place before them"

(*Shmot* 21:2). The *vav* of this verse is understood to be a link between the revelation at *Sinai* and the social, economic, and religious injunctions contained in these chapters, so that the rabbis taught: "Just as these, the Ten Commandments, were given at *Sinai*, so these, the following laws, were given at *Sinai*." There is thus a conceptual relationship that each of the Ten Commandments corresponds to groups of laws in these chapters, so that the 613 *mitzvot* as extensions, or implementations, of the covenant between God and the Jews sealed by these Ten Commandments (*Sa'adiah Gaon*; *Abarbanel*).

The poet-philosopher, Yehudah HaLevi, explained to the king of the Khazars, the nation that converted to Judaism en masse in the thirteenth century, that the Ten Commandments start off by mentioning God as the Redeemer from Egypt rather than the Creator of Heaven and Earth, because this covenant is that of a special relationship between the Jews and God. Simcha Bunim of Pchischa asked his student Menachem Mendel of Kotzk from where he drew his basis for the existence of God and his belief in Him. The reply was that in accordance with the *Rambam*, we see the greatness of Creation, the orderliness of the world about us, and all the physical laws that operate in that world, and thereby we understand that there must be a Creator. "That is very well for all peoples," said Simcha Bunim, "but we Jews derive our knowledge, our worship of God, from the Exodus of Egypt which marks a Divine relationship only with the Jews."

It is easy to see in the first four of the commandments the basis for many 'religious' halakhot regarding the Oneness of God, the worship, fear, and love of Him, all the obligations of *Shabbat*, Pesach, and other festivals. Indeed, the *Midrash* tells us that when God offered the Torah to the nations of the world, and they heard the first commandments, they said, "He is like any other king, like any other god. Everything He rules is for His own greatness, for His worship, for the ritual and religious laws acknowledging His existence." However, when the rest of the commandments were told to them, they said, "Oh, these later ones justify the former ones."

It is convenient and common for us to separate the commandments and all the laws which flow from them into those between Man and God, represented by the first five, and the laws between Man and Man, starting with "Thou shalt not kill." Indeed, this separation has always been the source of much distortion about Judaism, even creating a religious split personality. Sometimes the emphasis is on the relationship between Man and God, and the other tablets are ignored. However, as often as not, the emphasis is on the morality, ethical behavior, and social responsibility shown by the later commandments. Here, too, the unity of Torah is destroyed because the other tablet is ignored. It can be shown that despite the many rabbinical references to these two terms, between Man and Man, and Man and God, what is particular and specific to Judaism is its recognition of the unity of these two terms. The commandments starting with "Thou shalt not kill," "Thou shalt not steal, . . . commit adultery, . . . shall not bear false witness, and . . . shall not covet" are also a summary of laws. The laws of murder include the laws forbidding the selling of men as slaves whereby we deny them their freedom—a form of murder, and the question of the punishment to be dealt out to accidental killing. Theft, robbery, fraud, coercion, misrepresentation, exploitation, all these laws gather together under "Thou shalt not steal." Not only normal adultery is forbidden but even all forms of sexual deviation, incest, and lack of respect for the partner in marriage. Bearing false witness not only means a witness with false testimony but even one creating a false impression. There is a talmudic story of one who was owed a sum of money, but he had only one witness, whereas Judaism requires two. So he wanted one of his students to come along to court and simply stand there but say nothing, so that he would not really be a false witness. However, the other party would think that he actually had two witnesses and cede the case. "Thou shalt not covet"—coveting, explains Maimonides, leads to seeking forms of coercion and theft, to achieve a standard of living, or something somebody else has, when other methods legal or moral fail to do so.

However, Moses did not receive one tablet, he received two. If we separate the two tablets we permit a distinction between a Judaism of religious experience and ritual and ethnicism and a Judaism of morality, ethics, and justice. There is a danger that one may say that the social and civil legislation has nothing specifically Jewish about it. They thereby become part of the common human morality. Maimonides, and the *Sefer HaChinuch*, and many others indeed argue that these *mishpatim* are laws that the human mind would have understood on its own. If the Torah would not have taught us them, human intelligence would have formulated similar laws. To which *Abarbanel* caustically replies, "If this is indeed so, then why did the Torah bother to tell us these things? It would have been enough to tell us those five commandments which our brains could not envisage." It is interesting at this stage to point out that honoring one's father and mother is seen as a mitzvah between Man and God because there are three partners in every human being, the mother, the father, and God. Respect for each of these parties is interdependent. This commandment seems, however, to serve as a bridge between the two tablets. At *Marah*, the Jews received *chukim*, ordinances that seem to have no human explanation or of which the human understanding is limited (*Shmot* 15:15, *Rashi*). One of those is, according to the Talmud, honoring your father and your mother. I have seen this commandment, therefore, as a transition to the five following commandments, *bein Adam leChavero*. Like them, it comes to enforce a pattern of living contrary to human nature. In the natural world, the old and the sick leave the herd to make place for the young and the healthy. We had societies like Sparta, which got rid of its maimed and its weak and its old people. The concept of redundant people, of disposable people, is neither an ancient one nor a modern one. It simply follows the natural antagonism, created by competition for scarce economic resources. Over the burdens on the younger generations imposed by their parents comes the Torah to enforce behavior that is contrary to nature. There is no commandment to love one's parents, nor is there a commandment to honor one's parents when they deserve it. Rather there is a *chok*, an ordinance by a God-given morality to honor parents, per se.

So, too, the commandments against murder and theft, adultery, and coveting go beyond human wisdom to present a *chok*. This Divine Morality demands normative restraint of the human urge to take that which is not theirs, to want something that belongs to others, to destroy those who stand in their way, and to commit sins of the body against other people. *Abarbanel* argues that there are two differences between the social, moral, and ethical laws in the commandments and those created by the human intelligence.

They were given by God, and, therefore, any infringement of murder, theft, and so on, becomes religious crimes. They become antireligious acts, just as any transgressions of the Sabbath or idolatry. They are simply forbidden because God forbade them. Therefore, the damage done to the other party, or the degree of the other party's acquiescence and consent are marginal from a moral view. So, there are no victimless crimes in Judaism. The perpetrator is a victim of his own crime; he transgresses a God given law.

The second difference is that the Divine Wisdom of the Torah extended the humanly conceived ideas of ethics and morality. Society can envisage the case of a man killing another man; this is murder and forbidden by every society. However, attitudes to accidental or unpremeditated killing, euthanasia, class warfare, and ethnic cleansing differ from society to society. So, too, does the denial of human freedom, shaming others, or desecrating the human nobility inherent in the image of God. In Judaism, these are acts of murder. The punishment will vary from case to case, nevertheless they all flow from "Thou shall not kill." This Torah expansiveness applies also to "Thou shalt not steal." This does not mean only the forcible extraction of somebody else's property or of thievery by stealth. Any action whereby another's property is damaged, through my actions or transferred to me as a result of oppression, or deceit, are violations of "Thou shalt not steal." So the Divine Wisdom extended these injunctions between people far beyond that of the human morality.

Although *Shabbat* and idolatry, taking the Lord's name in vain, and all their derivatives are laws between man and God and so too are the derivatives and expositions of all the second group of commandments, nevertheless, there is a basic religious difference between them. Those between Man and God can be achieved by simple penance, or every year

Yom Kippur erases them. The second group cannot be atoned for unless restitution is made, unless the injured party has been appeased, and the damage redressed. At the same time, the mere paying of compensation, the mere returning of the stolen article, or the mere restitution of the status quo are not enough to achieve atonement. There has to be spiritual *t'shuva*, spiritual shame and spiritual compensation, because not only other human beings, but God, so to speak, was damaged.

Even within these social-religious commandments there is a difference. The *Shulchan Aruch* tells us that the punishment for false weights and measures is greater than that of sexual immorality. The *Ramban* says that this is because the latter is an offense against God, whereas the former transgresses both against God and humanity. One of the chassidic masters said that if God had not enjoined us against sexual immorality, human logic could have made it permissible in those cases where no physical or mental damage, as of consenting adults, and so on. However, the *Meirat Einayim*, a commentary on the *Shulchan Aruch*, writes that the reason why false weights and measures have this greater punishment is because sexual immorality can be atoned for by *t'shuva*. However, monetary crimes require greater penance. Restitution must be made and this is difficult when many people are involved. False weights, but also stock fraud and pyramid schemes, often involve so many thousands of people, that the perpetrators have no Torah or any other way in which to repent. It is true that all the codes prescibe the giving of charity and performing of righteous deeds. However, this is only of an inferior form of *t'shuvah*. Since we have a person who has no way to achieve proper atonement, the punishment is therefore greater.

MISHPATIM

You Shall Not Take Interest

It is symptomatic of Judaism that the very first Divine Injunctions after the awe-inspiring revelation at Sinai relate to social and economic issues. This is both a rational and an ideological consequence of the proximity of these laws to that covenant. From this proximity, the talmudic Sages derived that the seat of the High Court, the Supreme halakhic authority, had to be on the Temple Mount, in the courtyard of the Temple, both being expressions of holiness and Divine Worship. For ordinary men and women, this proximity is expressed by many rabbinic dictums. "One who wishes to be a devoutly religious person should be scrupulous in observing the laws of *nezikin*, Judaism's civil and tort law" (*Baba Kama* 30a). The first question one is asked by the Heavenly Court is, "Were your commerce and your business affairs conducted in faith?" The following questions refer to setting aside time for Torah study and yearning for redemption. This triangle of Judgmental questions reflects the integration of the altar and the negation of idolatry with which *Yitro* concludes and the laws of *Mishpatim*.

These laws could have begun with those of private property or the protection of human life. They could have expressed, as does the Code of Hammurabi, the rights of the various classes that make up the hierarchy of society or presented the liberties and economic rights that are the monopoly of citizens as did Athens. These laws, however, are a Divine Code for fulfilling the verse "and your brother shall live with you" (*VaYikrah* 25:36). They begin with the rights of the weakest and most defenseless members of society, the Hebrew bondsman indentured by the courts to compensate the person whose goods he stole, or self-indentured to save himself from hunger.

The moneylender and banker are perhaps the most pervasive of all the characterizations of the Jew, both by Jews and gentiles alike. Literature, folklore, and history books not only refer to Shylock but also to Isaac of York, the Oppenheimers, the Rothschilds, and the financial agents of European nobility, merchants, and kings. It is fitting, therefore, to devote ourselves to the laws of interest and moneylending in *Mishpatim*: "And your brother shall live with you."

The role of credit and interest, as well as the relationships between borrower and lender, have figured in all social and religious movements. Judaism, however, presents an intrinsically different perspective, one rooted in its attitude to wealth and economic activity. Such activity is permitted; indeed, it is the only way that the material needs of people can be satisfied. However, this legitimacy is tempered and restrained by the knowledge that God is the source of all wealth. This source predicates a certain pattern of behavior in the creation and use of wealth; the Torah's treatment of interest is part of that pattern. Capital in the form of real estate, draught animals (comparable to the modern forms of transport and machinery), and movable goods may be legitimately hired in return for rent. However, with regard to capital in the form of money—loan capital or credit, the Torah, in various texts, forbids Jews from taking interest, which in economic terms is no different from the halakhically permitted rent (*Shmot* 25:25–27; *VaYikrah* 25:36–38; and *Devarim* 23:19–20). This injunction does not seem to flow from any economic theory denying capital its legitimate profit, nor from any concept of the barrenness of money. Both are very powerful factors in establishing the antiusury of medieval Christianity and the antibanking attitudes of marxism and socialism.

Sefer HaChinuch (mitzvah 343) explains the injunction against interest as God's desire to purify Jewish spirituality. Hirsch comments that the wealth we receive from its divine source is not only meant to satisfy our own material needs but also to help others; earning a profit from the use of that portion of our wealth therefore is immoral. The fact that one is forbidden to take interest from Jews but may do so in regard to loans made to non-Jews strengthens the concept of interest as being legitimate but simply a restraint placed on Jews only, just as all our *mitzvot* go beyond those of Noachides. If taking interest is akin to fraud or robbery, it would be forbidden in Jewish/non-Jewish relationships, just as are all forms of theft or robbery. Indeed, even those authorities who either forbade making interest-bearing loans to non-Jews or permitted money lending only when all other economic functions were impossible, based their rulings not on the evil of interest but rather on the aspects of charity involved. Indeed, this is what the interest-free loan is all about: charity.

One who lives a whole life without taking interest does not fulfill all the Jewish obligations of wealth. These obligations require the active extension of interest-free loans. In the passage in *Mishpatim* (Exod. 22:25–27), the Hebrew word *im* is understood to mean "when," rather than "if." This is even more clearly stated in *Devarim* 15:7–8, where the obligation to lend money is unambiguous, a positive mitzvah and not only refraining from taking interest under the negative mitzvah. All the codes classify this obligation as a positive mitzvah, indeed as the highest form of charity (*Mishneh Torah, Hilkhot Matnat Aniyim*, Chapter 10, *Halakhah* 7; *Tur;* and *Shulchan Arukh, Yoreh Deah*, Section 249, Subsection 6). After all, the interest-free loan helps people break out of the poverty cycle or prevents them from becoming entrapped in it. Not only the poor are eligible for this form of charity, but so, too, are the rich in cases of temporary cash flow problems. The *Tur* in his ranking of charity further divides this premier group, making the establishment of a partnership preferable to the interest-free loan or employment; the shame of the poor increases as we move from one to the other, even though all of them are preferable to ordinary charity. These rulings should lay to rest the popular view that the interest-free loan was only an ancient financial instrument to tide farmers over until the harvest, or something that is restricted to financing consumer spending or family celebrations. The codes make it clear that it is one level of a Jewish banking system meant to fund normal business activity. In the mass immigration of the nineteenth and twentieth centuries, many of our parents and grandparents were unable to obtain credit or loans from the regular financial markets. Perhaps this was due in part to anti-Semitism, but that is an oversimplification. Lacking a record of financial performance, without assets that could secure the loans and as often as not, being strangers to the host ethnic or national groups, actually made our fathers bad credit risks for any responsible financial system. A similar situation exists today in the inner cities of most western countries and in the ranks of the unemployed. Unlike these societies, our fathers had access to communal and personal interest-free loans, and this helped many of them establish themselves economically in their new homes.

The use of two different terms for interest in VaYikrah 25:23, *neshech* and *tarbit*, forms the basis of the halakhic distinction between interest forbidden by the Mosaic code and that forbidden only by rabbinic law. *Neshech* is any form of loan—between two Jewish men or women—in which the lender receives payment for the loss of the alternative use of the money for the period of the loan. Not only is such payment forbidden, but the debtors can claim repayment in the *Bet Din* even if they originally agreed to pay this interest. This includes term loans, and according to many authorities, credit purchases of consumer goods, or funding of personal services or goods. The *tarbit* refers to payments to one party in the course of a business transaction; trade credit, investments by a nonactive partner, price increases, or currency fluctuations.

Although there is no recourse available to make *neshech* permissible, there does exist a legal form, *heter iska*, that comes to permit the relationship between the parties to a transaction involving *tarbit*. The authorities all insist that this is not a religious cameo but requires the existence of a real business transaction in which payment is made for risk, or for waiving management rights by the funder. For example, student loans may be regulated by a *heter iska* because the recipient is making an investment to obtain benefits and profits in the future from the studies—the creditor is funding such an investment (*Shoel u'Meishiv*, Vol. 3, Sec. 160). Because mortgage loans have many characteristics of *neshech*, there are authorities who require a special form of *heter iska* because the bond holder runs the risk of default and of declining real estate markets while the homeowners are investing in possible capital gains, hedging against inflation, and, at the simplest level, earning rent from the investment in their homes.

The emphasis on interest as an act of charity makes the interest rate irrelevant. In those cases where it is forbidden, anything above zero may not be taken, while in those cases regulated by the *heter iska*, we are not concerned with the rate of return, provided it is not shared equally by the active or inactive partners.

It has always been clear to the rabbis that the lender is helping the debtor by making credit available, indeed the *Torah Temimah* sees loans as concretizing the biblical verse: "And thy brother shall live with you"—a transaction that is to the benefit of both parties. We would all be economically worse off if capital and credit markets making funds available at interest did not exist. Indeed, a major problem in underdeveloped countries is the lack of such efficient markets, leading to stagnation or mafia-style usury. Despite understanding the economic benefits, the Torah instructed us to do acts of righteousness and lend our money interest free. So the *Admor* of Lubawitz, the *Ba'al HaTanya* writes that even though one cannot obtain rabbinic interest back in a *Bet Din*, yet God-fearing men should repay such money (*Shulchan Arukh Ba'al HaTanya, Hilchot Malveh u'Loveh*).

It would seem that for the same reason of righteousness, the injunction against *ribit* was accompanied by injunctions limiting the rights even of the lender of the interest-free loan. He could not dwell rent free in a house belonging to his debtor, have him teach his child for free, or even to expect a friendly greeting from a debtor, who, prior to the loan, was not accustomed to greeting him. These are all considered as interest by the rabbis (*Yoreh De'ah*, Section 16). Even the creditor's right to using the debtor's property as security for repayment of the loan was limited.

The millstone, or, for that matter, any article essential for the food of the debtor could not have a lien placed on it. A cloak or pillow could be taken as security, but the creditor had to return it at night or else "with what would he cover himself" (*Shmot* 22:27). Even those articles accepted as a lien required restraint on the part of the creditor. He could not just barge into the debtor's home or shop to examine the article whenever he wished. Everything had to be done to preserve the dignity of the debtor. One may not take a lien from a widow, whether rich or poor, because of the possibility of sexual harassment or of creating malicious gossip.

Because Torah justice is symmetrical, the rights of the creditor are clearly recognized. Repayment of a loan is considered an obligation just as extending it is. A debtor is not allowed to use the loan recklessly or in any way that would ultimately destroy the creditor's property, or deny the creditor payment when it becomes due or to delay payments.

What would the halakhic position be of the debtor who claims to be unable to repay the debt? Should one argue that because he is probably poorer than the creditor or that the same mercy that prompted the loan in the first place should be considered, both cases should lead to a waiving of the debt? All the codes rule that the *Bet Din* must search and discover whether there are any hidden assets or whether any claimed liens are not subterfuges to evade payment. Then the debtor's assets are sold, leaving only *tallit* and tefillin, weekday clothes, and food for a month. Any bankruptcy agreement whereby the debtor only pays a proportion of his debt is frowned on. In many communities, the debtor who does this was excommunicated until he repaid the debt. It is true that in these cases the debtor will be poor. However, to make the creditor directly responsible for the debtor's welfare simply because he granted a loan in the first place, distorts justice. Our modern economies are rife with examples of the immorality of enabling the debtor to maintain a previous lifestyle at the creditor's expense. At the same time, the debtor (or any workers made redundant as a result of the bankruptcy) is poor and needs to be provided for. This, however, is a communal obligation in which the creditor, as a member of the community, is obligated to participate.

Maimonides places the laws against interest in their rational position, among the laws of borrowing and lending. Both the *Tur* and the *Shulchan Arukh*, however, place the interest laws in *Yoreh De'ah*, that section of the Codes that deals with injunctions against idolatry, and the laws of what may or may not be eaten. Said Menachem Mendel of Kotzk, "This is because just as the food is not kosher, so too is the interest."

TERUMAH

To Dwell in Their Midst

Let them make Me a sanctuary that I may dwell in their midst.
—Shmot 25:8

"Heaven and the Heaven of Heavens cannot contain You: How much less this house that I have built" (1 Kings 8:27). So spoke Solomon at the consecration of the First Temple in Jerusalem. Yet mankind searches for a place, specific, known, and visible, where God can be found on earth. Even though wood, stone, fabric, or metal cannot really contain Him, Whose glory is eternal and fills the universe, nevertheless, God commanded Moses and Israel to erect a sanctuary so that He could dwell in the midst of their camp. He shrank Himself, as it were, not only for the *mishkan*, but even to speak to Moses from between the wings of the Cherubim. This Divine Merciful Act parallels His mercy when He created the world, providing space, as it were, for its inhabitants.

The *mishkan* followed them into the Promised Land, and there this Tabernacle became a Temple in Jerusalem. After its destruction in 586 B.C.E., it was replaced by one built by the returning exiles from Babylon. This, too, was destroyed and a long exile from Land and Temple began. Nevertheless, Maimonides codifies as law the obligation to erect a third temple, and there is no Jewish ritual ceremony or prayer service that does not contain a prayer for the fulfillment of this obligation.

All the commentators are divided into two schools as to the purpose and role of the *mishkan* and therefore of the Temple. This division flows from a textual problem. In our *parshah*, *Terumah*, we find the instructions regarding the construction of the Tabernacle. Then in the next *parshah* there follows the story of the Golden Calf. Only after that do we find the actual work and erection of the *mishkan* described, so that the Golden Calf incident is a buffer, as it were, between the two. *Rashi* and others, following a rabbinic principle that events are not always repeated in their strict chronological order, contends that actually first there occurred the sin of the Golden Calf and only then were they commanded to build the *mishkan*. *Ramban* maintains that the rabbinic principle only applies where there is a clear or logical reason for ignoring the time sequence. Because there is no such reason here, he and many other commentators hold that the commandments regarding the *mishkan* preceded the Golden Calf, even while the construction followed it.

The difference, however, is not simply of textual importance, but primarily of the purpose and role of the sanctuary in spiritual and religious life. According to those for whom the making of the Golden Calf preceded *Parshat Terumah*, the *mishkan* and, therefore, logically also the Temples, were solely a means of atoning for sin. The sanctuary is, therefore, primarily a part of the cleansing process of repentance. However, because according to the chronological sequence *Terumah* precedes the sin, *Ramban* and others teach that the *mishkan* has a purpose over and above atonement. For them, the primary purpose of the sanctuary is to be a meeting place between God and Israel, both as a collective and as individuals; of the Jewish God, as it were, shares of Himself to meet there with human beings. By making the Calf, Israel had disturbed this original concept meeting place; making atonement as an additional role for it.

It is this dual concept of the sanctuary—the meeting with God and the place of atonement—that became the mainstream of Jewish understanding. A concept enunciated by King Solomon at the dedication of the Temple: "Your eyes may be open toward this house night and day . . . to hear the prayer which Your servant shall pray toward this place and hearken to the supplication of Your servant and of Your people, Israel, when they shall pray toward this place . . . when they do sin against You . . . if they turn toward You, if they pray toward this place and confess Your name and turn from their sin . . . then hear You in heaven and forgive the sins of Your servants and Your people Israel."

This meeting place is not restricted to Jews. All people may have contact there, albeit in ways intrinsically different from the Jewish contact, which is obligatory, formalized, and of a special spiritual nature flowing from Israel as God's chosen people: "The stranger that is not of Your people, Israel, when he shall . . . and pray toward this house, hear You in heaven Your dwelling place and do according to all that the stranger calls to You for . . . that all the peoples of earth may know your name, to fear You as does Your people, Israel, that they may know that Your name is called upon this house that I have built."

"If they [Israel] sin against You . . . and You deliver them to the enemy, so that they carry Israel away captive unto the land of the enemy, far off or near . . . if they return to You . . . and pray toward their Land, which You gave to their fathers, the city which You have chosen [Jerusalem] and the house which I have built for Your name then hear their prayer . . . and forgive Your people . . . and give them compassion before (their captors) . . . for You did set them apart from all the peoples of the earth to be your inheritance" (1 Kings, Chapter 8).

The establishment of this meeting place with God is not an option for the Jews but rather an obligation. "It is a positive mitzvah to make a house for God" (*Midrash Sifri, Parshat Peah* writes rather "a house for the name of God") (*Mishneh Torah, Hilkhot Beit HaBechirah*, Chapter 1, Halakhah 1).

> This [the Temple, its sacrifices and its prayers] is only to prepare our hearts for His worship and . . . to spiritually finesse our bodies, because our bodies are spiritualized by our actions. These constant and manifold actions purify our hearts, clean them and refine them. He,

> God, wants our benefit and therefore, commanded us to prepare a meeting place [for our spiritual meeting with Him] that is pure and perfectly clean, to purify people's thoughts and perfect their hearts ... so by the refinement of our actions [through the Temple ritual] and the purification of our thoughts in the place we have established for Him, we will be able to merge with the Divine thought and spirit. (*Sefer HaChinuch, Mitzvah 95*)

The obligation to establish a meeting place is halakhically transferred to the synagogue of our own day, meant to fulfill the spiritual functions described above, that is, a *mikdash me'at*, a smaller sanctuary. This is one of the communal functions for which taxation may be imposed, over and beyond philanthropy. There was a half-shekel tax for the physical maintenance of the Temple and for the communal sacrifices. There was a similar tax system for synagogues and allied religious needs during the 2000 years of autonomous Jewish communities throughout the Jewish world. The existence of a House of God, Temple, or Synagogue, in the midst of a human society, makes the law of God and His spiritual guidance part and parcel of the everyday life of the people of that society. "For the Lord your God walks in the midst of your camp ... therefore shall your camp be Holy; that He see no unseemly thing in you and turn away from you" (Deut. 23:15).

It is not surprising, therefore, that this should be one of the three mitzvot to be implemented communally, upon Israel's entrance and conquest of the Holy Land. The Talmud lists them as, "to appoint a king, to eradicate the memory of Amalek, and to build the Temple" (*Talmud Bavli, Sanhedrin* 20a). Seemingly these three are unrelated, yet if we bear in mind their spiritual aspects, the connection becomes an integral one. The king is the unifier of the people, he is the heart of the nation and functions to fulfill the needs and welfare of society. The Temple is the place, chosen for the meeting of people and God, the place through which pass the prayers and spiritual aspirations of Israel and mankind. Amalek is the one who sneaks up on the marginal and weak, separating them from society. Amalek is the one who cools the spiritual fervor of the Jews for their God; a chassidic understanding based on the word *karcha*—to chance, but also to cool. Amalek is the one who denies God's power since he is the only nation who dares to attack Israel after witnessing the redemption from Egypt. Amalek, therefore, prevents the meeting between Israel and God and, therefore, must be destroyed before the Temple can be built. So, Saul is commanded to destroy Amalek before the Davidic dynasty and the Temple of Solomon can be established. The defeat of Haman comes on Purim before the rebuilding of the second Temple, and, so, through the extinction of Amalek, the King Messiah and the third Temple will be linked.

These three mitzvot, king, destruction of Amalek, and Temple, enable the Jews to draw on the intrinsic spirituality of the Land of Israel to enhance their own religious, moral, and spiritual growth. The *mishkan* in the desert is built of the products of the animal and vegetable kingdoms: wood, wool, flax, and leather. The sources of all these are alive, possess the ability to grow and to reproduce and respond to Divine and human care. After entering the Land, the Tabernacle at Shiloh had walls of stone with the tent of the *mishkan* as a covering—a blend of the animal and vegetable with the inanimate stone. Finally, Solomon's Temple was built completely of the inanimate stone. At first the Jews, in the desert without a king, achieved a spiritual level that was able to infuse only the living world with sanctity. Entrance into the Holy Land created a higher level that was able to release or reveal at least part of the sanctity of the inanimate objects. The addition of kingship meant a power of spirituality that could call forth holiness even from the stone and rock (*Shem MiShmuel*).

In the book of *Shmot* the injunction is for Israel to make an ark but later Moshe in *Devarim* is instructed to do so. "And they will make an ark" (*Shmot* 25:10): "and you shall make an ark for yourself" (*Devarim* 10:1). "Said Abba Chanan in the name of Rabbi Eliezer, 'When Israel does the bidding of God [and achieves holiness] the ark of the covenant is seen as their work. However, when they do not [so that the sanctuary has no effect on their behavior, spiritual or practical], then the ark is seen as the work of Moshe'" (*Talmud Bavli, Yomah* 3b).

In the same way, the rabbis explained the difference between the *keruvim* in the Tabernacle and those in Solomon's Temple. The former faced each other (*Shmot* 25:20), and in the latter they faced the Temple (3 Chron.). When the Jews followed God's Torah, the *keruvim* faced each other, but when they failed to do so, they turned away from each other to face the Temple (*Talmud Bavli, Baba Bathra* 99a; see *Rashbam*). When their social lives were in accordance with God's justice and charity, the people were related to one another. However, when the sanctuary was unable to influence their behavior, then they turned away from each other and were able to see only the building of the sanctuary.

TETZAVEH

Levels of Holiness

It is written a "*mikdash*"—a holy sanctuary—(*Shmot* 25:8) and not a "*mishkan*"—a tabernacle—that each person should sanctify themselves so that they can each become a seat for the Divine Presence. Then "I will dwell in their midst" inside each one of them. (*Siftei Kohen, Terumah*)

There are three degrees of holiness: The most elementary is achieved when a person separates themselves from forbidden things or actions. Then there is a higher level reached by sanctifying ourselves in those things that are permitted to us [by following Judaism's teachings, say with regard to the economic activity or sexual relationships that Torah permits us]. Yet the highest level is where all our actions are sanctified and done for the sake of heaven—"In all your ways you should know him" (*Mishlei* 3:6). Parallel to these are the three different levels of holiness of the Tabernacle: the holiness of the courtyard, the holiness of the *Ohel Mo'ed* and at its peak, the holiness of the Holy of Holies . . . . (*Shem MiShmuel, Terumah*)

It is in the light of these levels of holiness, we may relate the utensils, the altars, the *keyor*, the table, and the menorah which stood in the *mishkan*. Here I have primarily followed the ideas of Hirsch but have interwoven chassidic and other commentators. Our first contact with the *mishkan* was the *chatzer*—courtyard, which actually extended to all four sides. It was formed by white curtains of linen, held by silver hooks hung from pillars that stood on copper sockets. Here is the first level of holiness, the purification, the renunciation of the forbidden and the atonement. Here is negation of the material aspects of human nature in eating and drinking, sexual life, and commerce.

Here stood the altar on which sacrifices were offered; expressions of this negation are the *ashamot* for actual transgression; the *chatot* for the careless commission of sin through thoughtlessness or ignorance, a call in all cases for guarding oneself against spiritual stumbling in the future; and the *olah* for wrongdoing through laziness, through not doing that which is required, and through the negative mental sin of evil thoughts that divert our minds from the channels of truth. Just as practical energy needs to be harnessed to prevent wrong actions so, too, mental energy needs to be exploited to prevent the thought that is father to the deed. On the altar were also offered the *shalamim*—consciousness of the happiness, prosperity, and peace, physical and mental, granted by God. Unlike other sacrifices, not only the priests but also the owners ate of the *shlamim*. This is a physical expression of the moral and ethical perspectives that flow from recognition that God is the source of all our bounty; as such this Source requires certain codes of conduct regarding our wealth, abilities, and bodies.

The copper mirrors used by the women of Israel to beautify and preen themselves, they donated to the *mishkan*. At first, Moses refused to accept what to him seemed symbols of vanity. However, God saw in them the ability of the women to see their real beauty in their spiritual development, so these mirrors were used in making the basin for the priests to wash their hands and feet before performing their service in the Tabernacle (*Midrash Rabbah Shmot, Ki Tisah*). The *keyor*, the copper basin, was placed not in front of the altar, its logical place, but behind it, between the altar and the entrance to the sanctuary, to teach that purposeless entry into the courtyard is forbidden (*Talmud Bavli, Yomah* 5b

TETZAVEH

and *Sanhedrin* 83a). The priests were then required to make a deliberate detour of the altar to wash their hands, to impress upon them the importance of their worship. Menachem Mendel of Kotsk saw the ritual washing of the hands as the separation from forbidden actions even as Avraham washed the feet of his guests to rid them of the dust of idolatry. The *Maharal* explained that people then had such a negative concept of the religious value of mankind, that they were prepared to worship even the least valuable of things, the dust of the earth. Both consciousness of the value of mankind and the separation from forbidden actions are needed before the service of God may be undertaken.

The white forecourt of purification is only a preliminary level of holiness, an essential beginning of our pathway to the spiritual heights of the meeting place with God. Our odyssey moves to the *Ohel Mo'ed* with the menorah, the *Shulchan*, and the altar for incense. Both the *chatzer* and the *Ohel Mo'ed* had curtains in which two shades of red and a blue woolen thread were stitched onto the white linen background. Blue—the Godly, in conjunction with red—the animal and human activities of our actual lives. Neither bore the pattern of *charuvim*, to stress the human character that needs to be perfected, first in the separation from forbidden things (the *chatzer*) and now in the sanctification of those things permitted to us (the *Ohel Mo'ed*).

After the purifying sacrifice and surrender of the forecourt came the incense altar of the *Ohel Mo'ed*. The incense offering leaves no residue, all that remains is the pure spirituality, earned, as it were, by the separation from forbidden acts achieved in the forecourt. Just as the incense is completely vaporized, so, too, complete submission to God's law and wish is necessary before the material and intellectual activities of mankind can be sanctified through the table and the menorah. Chassidic masters taught that it is this spiritual dimension of the incense that predicates the recital of the incense preparation, both before the verses of praise and at the conclusion of the morning prayers (*Talmud Bavli, Keritot* 5a and *Yerushalmi, Yomah*, Chapter 4, Halakhah 4). Prayer is to begin and to end by being a pleasing odor before God. When we take with us this odor of submission and spirituality, then all our everyday actions can become sanctified through the teachings of the table and the menorah that stood behind the altar.

Food, material goods, financial assets, and wealth in all its forms are essential for the preservation and progress of human societies and, therefore, are perhaps the major forces determining our behavior, our social structures, and our histories, personal and collective. God created the world in a manner that all need to be provided for by human agency, effort, and skill. So the economic, agricultural, and technical efforts devoted to their creation are legitimate and part of the Divine Blueprint. However, the need for wealth is an unlimited one, neither age, nor gender nor abundance bring satiation. Of all our needs, wants, or desires, only of material wealth may it be said, "The less one has the more one wants, the more one has the more one wants." Because only one Adam was created and the world given to him for all his wants and needs, each of his descendants see the whole world as belonging to them. Unless this legitimate activity can be educated, guided, and made holy, evil, corruption, oppression, and war result.

It is this level of holiness that is provided by the table in the *Ohel Mo'ed* on which were placed each week, the twelve loaves, the *lechem hapanim*, bread and incense, nourishment and comfort. In *VaYikrah* 24:5, the repetition of instructions and care for these loaves occur after the festival cycle of the year, which recall the acts of God as founder and maintainer of the material nationality of Israel. They represent, therefore, the teaching that all our wealth has its source in God; this determines the way the wealth is earned and spent. The table was surrounded by a *zer* or golden band that formed, as it were, a framework, either holding the legs together or a rim around the top of the table. In either case, the *zer* comes to place the role of wealth creation in a proper perspective. Although it is legitimate, it is limited in time by the *Shabbat*, the festivals, and the sabbatical and jubilee years in which such activity is forbidden. It is also limited in time by the unlimited obligation to learn Torah that obviously restricts the amount of time left free to engage in economic or other activities. The *zer*, however, also places a conceptual restraint on economic activity by teaching an economics of enough. Only if this concept of enough exists is it possible to limit both the greed and the fear of economic uncertainty that fuel business immorality and social irresponsibility.

Although it is legitimate and commendable to seek out the most efficient moral forms of wealth creation, such activity is merely one aspect of life. "Not by bread alone lives man, but by My spirit." In the *Ohel Mo'ed*, there were also the seven-branched menorah and the Golden Altar for the incense. In the mystical tradition, olive oil is the symbol of knowledge, intelligence, and wisdom; it is this olive oil that is to be burned continuously in the menorah. Knowledge and understanding are only half of the meaning of light in a Jewish conception, because light also has an effect of movement, that is for progress and development. In the dark, everything is static and dormant; light awakens life and creativity. Our light here is the symbol of the spiritual retaining knowledge and action. Placed in the sanctuary, both of these become sanctified because "the beginning of wisdom is the fear of the Lord" (Ps. 111:10). Shmuel of Sochochow explains that our struggle with the Greeks on Chanukah was because of their contention that the human mind alone is sufficient as a basis for knowledge. We contend that it is the fear of God that provides the morality and truth of knowledge.

Of the Ark that stood in the Holy of Holies, it is written "and they shall make" (*Shmot* 25:10), something that is expected from the whole nation. This is appropriate because the whole task of making a sanctuary is concentrated in the Ark. *Aron* (Ark) is formed from *arah*, to prepare for eating, that is related to *harah*, to absorb the seed of life (conceive), making the Ark a container in which that which it receives is accepted permanently. The Tablets are of stone, the Ark is of wood, and it is Israel that develops and grows through them. This treelike growth, symbolized by the wood of which the Ark was made, flows from the Tablets that are one unit, the basic principles of our relationship to God and those of our relationship to others. So there are two *cheruvim*, facing each other with mutual consideration and regard for each other, yet at the same time their wings are spread upward to form a chariot or a home for the Glory of God on earth. If the wood is growth, then the gold that covers the Ark is the firmness and strength with which the nation follows the testimony placed in it. In this Torah the very being of the knowledge and of the nation's actions are sanctified to Heaven.

The utensils and furnishings of the *mishkan* are the teachings of the Torah to create such a people that God will dwell in their midst.

KI TISAH

Attributes of Mercy

"Then Moses supplicated before God." Not even forty days had passed since Israel had heard and accepted the commandments at Sinai, yet in the absence of Moshe they made an idol, a Golden Calf, and worshiped it. So God says to Moshe, "Go down [from Sinai] for your people have corrupted themselves."
—*Shmot 32:7*

Moshe said, 'Why are they my people?' 'When I sent you to take them out of Egypt,' God answered, 'I told you not to allow non-Israelites to join them. You, however, are humble and perfect, so you insisted that we are always required to accept penitents and seekers. I knew what the future held [that the mixed multitude would influence Israel to sin] and told you to refuse them. You insisted, and now they made an idol and say: "These are your [not our] god, Israel." So go down for your people have sinned.'" A few verses later in the same chapter, the Torah reads: "Now, therefore, do not hinder Me . . . that I may destroy them. Are we to understand that Moshe caught God by His cloak as one holds his fellow to prevent his actions? Rather, God in His mercy opened a path for Moshe [verse 10 should be translated as: 'if it were left unto Me'] and immediately Moshe in his love for Israel, supplicated God for forgiveness" (*Midrash Rabbah, Shmot* 42).

Not only did he plead for Israel's forgiveness but in reply to God's plan to destroy them and create a new chosen people out of Moshe, he offered his own life for their sake. "If now You will forgive their sin—if not blot me out, I pray, from Your book that You have written" (*Shmot* 32:32).

Forgiveness of the present sin, however, was not sufficient. Moshe threw down the Tablets of Stone, or allowed them to slip to the ground and be shattered. He let Himself be moved [by Moshe's prayer] to change His intent regarding the evil He had said He would do to His people (*Shmot* 32:14). After this, when Moshe descended he still held the Tablets, until he saw the Calf and the dances (32:19). Only then did he shatter the Tablets. *S'forno* teaches that it was not primarily the idolatry but rather the joy, enthusiasm, and dancing that caused Moshe's action. Idolatry is an error of the intellect and can be erased by teaching and learning. However, the great enthusiasm and joy of Israel showed that there had been a spiritual acceptance of idolatry that rendered them unworthy of the Commandments. Alternatively, the sexual abandon implied in the word *letzachek* (verse 6) often associated with sexual immorality, indicated to Moshe that sensuality rather than intellectual error lay behind the making of the Calf. The spiritual purification and religious education needed to eliminate corruption is far more difficult than intellectual errors; indeed, the former is often impossible. Idolatry had given birth to sexual immorality and this corruption of Israel's morality made them unworthy of the law, so he shattered the Tablets (Hirsch).

After the Tablets were shattered, the Calf destroyed, and all the idolators killed, Moshe was concerned with the fate that awaited Israel. So even after God forgave, Moshe had a further request. In his great *Ahavat Yisrael*, love of Israel, he wanted to obtain a promise even for the future. "And now . . . if I have found favor in Your sight, let me, I beseech You, have an understanding of the diversity and manifold aspects of Your way" (*Shmot* 33:13), that this people can be led in accordance with God's way and intention, despite their known fallibility, weaknesses, and sinful actions, it is necessary to have an insight into the unity of His diverse ways of *chesed* and justice. Moshe asks to know that despite the sin, there will always be the possibility of atonement and forgiveness.

A place was made in the cleft of the rock on Sinai where Moshe's plea was answered. God's goodness was revealed. "God remains always God, compassionate and gracious, slow to anger and full of mercy and truth. He exercises love even for the thousandth generation, forgiving crookedness, willful sin and careless wrongdoing, and He cleanses [from all of them]" (Verse 7). These are the thirteen attributes of God that He showed Moshe, the *tefillin* knot, as it were, at the back of His head, the attachment of God to His prophet and people. Rabbi Yochanan said, "Were it not written, it would be impossible [for us] to say it, [but] this verse teaches that He wrapped Himself [in a *tallit*] like a *chazan* and showed Moshe the order of [this] prayer. He said, 'Whenever Israel sins, let them perform before Me this order [of prayer] and I will forgive them,'" (*Talmud Bavli, Rosh HaShana* 17b).

Throughout the centuries, Jews have based their penitential prayers on these attributes, so much so that *Neilah*, the last of Yom Kippur services, is based primarily on them. After all is said and done, after the fasting, and the confessions, in reality we depend only on God's mercy for our atonement. This mercy is His attribute and characteristic, and because of this, He Himself taught this to Moshe: "You taught us to supplicate You with these 13 attributes [of mercy] . . . even as You answered them to the modest one [Moshe]" (Yom Kippur prayers).

Moshe's pleading for the people, despite his justified anger at their sin, has been seen throughout history as the essential quality for Jewish leaders. In reply to the angel's greeting, "The Lord be with you," Gideon asks why God has not now shown the same redemptive powers as He did in Egypt, but rather has delivered them into the hands of the enemy (Judg. 6:13). This call for God's mercy on an undeserving people is seen in text as a strength of Gideon's and marks him as a savior of the Jews from Midian.

However, there is more involved here than just the pleading for mercy. The thirteen attributes and the way they were taught to Moshe, show

God's infinite capacity for forgiveness and His constant tempering of justice with mercy. Leaders are called on to accept this and to attempt to emulate it, even in the face of justified anger. At the same time, wrongdoing, sin, and nonobservance of Torah are not to be met with tolerance nor with apathy. It should be remembered that the same Moshe who pleaded for Divine forgiveness, nevertheless, slew the Israelites who worshipped the Calf. Neither, however, are rebuke, judgment, and criticism to be performed in hate and anger. It is interesting to note that the praise of Israel's merits and greatness is contained in the songs of Bilaam, who came to curse but was made to bless. Moshe, the great lover of Israel, nevertheless utters two terrifying warnings of the results of their forsaking God's ways (*VaYikrah* 26:14–41 and *Devarim* 27:11–28:69). This is because to rebuke or to criticize one needs to love the person or persons being censured, otherwise the rebuke or criticism are simply expressions of one's hate rather than of sorrow and willingness to accept penitents. "We are commanded to turn people from their evil and to make them aware of their wrongdoing . . . . This should be done patiently and with soft words" (*Mishneh Torah, Hilkhot Deot*, Chapter 6, Halakhot 7–8). It is not for nothing that Jeremiah, whose whole prophecy was the prediction of dire and terrible destruction of the Kingdom of Judah, is the same prophet who, when his prophecy came true, composed the Book of Lamentations, his dirge and ode of sorrow upon this destruction. There is no trace of satisfaction at Judah receiving its just deserts or words of "I told you so." So God's forbearance of wrongdoing and willingness to forgive are repeated by prophets and rabbis, alongside their rebuke and criticism.

Gershonides, *Ralbag*, and *Abarbanel*, see Eliyahu's unwillingness to fit this mold as reason for the rebuke by God expressed in Kings I, Chapter 19. Eliyahu, seeing that the acceptance of "The Lord, He is God" by Israel at Mt. Carmel was short-lived and that Jezebel had enough public support to threaten his life, searched in vain for a prophecy as how to proceed now. So he made his way from Shomron to the wilderness. The angel fed him a cake and a cruise of water, and "he did eat and drink and then went in the strength of that meal, forty days and forty nights unto

KI TISAH

Horeb, the mount of the Lord" (8). There he came to what the use of the definite article in the text determines as "The Cave," namely, the known cave, the same one at which Moshe stood when the divine glory passed before him (*Shmot* 33:21–23). Here Eliyahu waited for a revelation, and the Word came to him asking what he was doing here in this Cave. Eliyahu answered that he had been zealous for the Lord, Israel had forsaken the covenant, and only he was left of all the prophets. "And the Lord passed by . . . a great and strong wind . . . but the Lord was not in the wind; and after the wind an earthquake but the Lord was not in the earthquake . . . and not in the fire . . . and a still small voice . . . . What do you do here Eliyahu" (11–13). Eliyahu repeated his answer to the first question. For *Ralbag*, the revelation questioned Eliyahu's right to be in the cave where Moshe had entreated for mercy for Israel, because Eliyahu had brought drought and suffering on the people instead of following the path of Moshe. He had used the power of the wind, the earthquake, and the fire rather than the still small voice of God's attribute of mercy. Now the mantle of prophecy was to pass to Elisha.

Jonah ben Amitai was the boy that Eliyahu brought back to life (1 Kings 17:17–24), and he became his disciple. He, too, was unable to emulate Moshe and to agree to God's great mercy and forgiveness. He even uses a paraphrase of the Divine Attributes taught to Moshe to explain why he objected to go to gentile Nineveh and bring the call to repentance. "Therefore, I fled to Tarshish for I knew that You are gracious and compassionate, long-suffering and abundant in mercy and repents of the evil" (Jon. 4:2). It is appropriate that this book with this Mosaic message should be read at the afternoon service on Yom Kippur.

He knew that this meant divine forgiveness even for the non-Jews of Nineveh if they would repent. According to Alshich, Jonah found this difficult because they were arch-enemies of Israel. Others have commented that the quick repentance of Nineveh was a rebuke to Israel, who, over the centuries, consistently refused to repent despite the many prophets sent to them. Irrespective of how we understand the Israel-Nineveh relationship, the Eliyahu-Jonah tradition is the antithesis of the thirteen divine attributes.

Moshe pleaded for Israel, even though he was aware of their sin and condemned it. He crushed the Golden Calf, added it to their water, and forced them to drink it. Then he called on the faithful to slay those who had worshiped the idol. This is justified punishment. Moshe, however, adds the leadership quality of mercy. He entreated God not to destroy Israel, rejected the offer of being the beginning of a new Chosen People, and asked for his own life to be destroyed rather than this sinful people. So we find that when he came down from Sinai with the second tablets and with God's forgiveness, his face shone with the Divine Presence (*Karan*; mistakenly understood by Michaelangelo to mean horns, hence the horns on his statue). This was his reward, *karnu p'nai Moshe*. Here, *karan* means shone and Moshe's face shone with the *shechinah*. This was his reward for the great love he had for his people, the ultimate role model for Jewish leadership.

VAYAKHEL

The Gift of Knowledge

Judaism does not see itself as a negation of human knowledge nor as an enemy of that which we can research and understand. On the contrary, this *sedrah* is one of many sources that show this ability and its related achievements to be a divine gift. "Has filled him [Betzalel] with the spirit of God in wisdom, in understanding and in knowledge" (Exod. 35:31).

> When the sun set on the first *Shabbat*, and the darkness began, Adam saw this as a sign of his punishment and trembled in fear. So the Holy One, blessed be He, showed him two flints and struck them so that sparks flew and there was light [fire] and Adam blessed it . . . .. Said Shmuel, we bless the lights [in the *havdalah ceremony*] *because this is the beginning* of the creation of light [for human use in contrast to the celestial light created on the first day of Creation, subsequently hidden because of human evil, until the Messianic period]. (*Bereishit Rabbah* 12:6)

This Divine sharing, as it were, of knowledge stands in stark contrast to pagan thought as exemplified, for example, by the Greek mythology in which the gods, jealous of mankind, refused to give them knowledge of fire and light. When these were stolen by Prometheus, and given to human beings, it was only at the cost of his punishment by the gods.

So the naming of the animals and the birds is only the first example of the wisdom granted to us. Adam in Eden had the wisdom and knowledge to name all the animals and birds in Creation. These names were not simply technical language, of itself a level of knowledge, but they symbolized the characteristics and nature of each type of creature as understood in the subjective view of the human mind. Among the blessings to be recited on various occasions is included, "Who has given of His knowledge to human beings," recited upon seeing an outstanding secular scholar. It not only is a mattter of thanksgiving, but a realization that the world was created in such a way that material wealth, social organization, and human progress depend on knowledge, in all its various disciplines and categories. Because the Creator provides us with all our needs, this knowledge, too, needed to be part of His divine plan. It is fitting, therefore, that this should be the first of the human requests made in the daily thrice repeated, *Shemoneh Esrei, Amidah*. We praise Him for granting insight and knowledge to frail mortals and ask for continued endowment. Without them, both our physical and spiritual existence would be the poorer, perhaps even impossible.

This legitimate and intrinsic part of human existence, however, includes a *yetzer harah*. This is usually translated as the evil inclination, but perhaps more correctly, it shoud be understood to mean the ability to do evil. This *yetzer* must not be seen as something external to God's creation, but for which education, guidance, and limits are provided by the Torah. Rather, for example, God Himself created the *yetzer* to steal, and then He gave man free will and the Torah knowledge to use it. However, He forbade stealing and therefore punishes the choice of people to steal (*Shem MiShmuel, Echad Mi Yodeah*, Passover *Hagadah*). Rashi comments on the verse in *Bereishit* 1:31, "Saw that it was very good." This is the *yetzer harah*; a *yetzer* essential to the development and existence of the world.

Hirsch views the story of the Tree of Knowledge in this light, seeing in the injunction against eating of its fruit not a Divine wish for mankind

VAYAKHEL

to be ignorant, illogical, or undeveloped but rather as the subjugation of our knowledge to His law and wisdom.

> It was animal wisdom which led the first human beings . . . and today it is this same animal wisdom which serves as midwife to every sin . . . animals are really like the Lord, knowing good and evil. They have innate instinct and this instinct is the will of God for them. Accordingly what they do is in accordance with this Divine Providence which rules within them . . . [and they have no alternative] in good and everything which is instinct keeps them back from doing is bad. Animals can do no wrong, they have only their one nature that they are to follow. (*Bereishit* V:1)

He goes on to argue that man is different because he has a choice to decide to do good and to refrain from evil. Furthermore, sensual enjoyment in all forms is a moral, free-willed act, so that we possess both sensuality and godliness within us. The Divine Voice speaks to us to tell us what is permitted and what is forbidden. Permitted and forbidden are perhaps more appropriate to Jewish teaching than concepts such as right or wrong, good or bad actions. With the revealed Torah but in free will, we may use our knowledge and our intellect to channel, educate, and purify our sensuality. Adam and Eve were not set in Eden to indulge their sensual nature in the delights and food of the Garden, but rather to use them in the service of God and His world. All the trees were permitted except that of Knowledge of Good and Evil, even though its fruit was tempting to the eye and good for food. When its fruit appealed to Adam and Eve, they perceived it as being good and, therefore, the Divine injunction forbidding eating it as bad. So, too, throughout the centuries, God's law of morality is presented as the enemy of all sensual enjoyment. However, in reality it is the Torah's limitations on human desires and knowledge that enables us to choose morality and justice in the pursuit and enjoyment of that which is permitted to us.

The Sages taught that if there is no wisdom, there can be no differentiation (between good and evil, between pure and impure, between permitted and forbidden (*Talmud Yerushalmi, Berachot*, Chapter 5, Halakhah 2). It is for this reason that the *havdalah* prayer, separating the *Shabbat* from the weekdays, was placed in the prayer for knowledge and wisdom.

"Give [wisdom] to a wise man and he will be yet wiser" (*Mishlei* 9:9). This refers to Betzalel. When Moshe told him to build the *Mishkan*, he asked, "What is the purpose of this meeting place?" Moshe answered, "That the Lord may fill it with His glory and teach Torah to Israel." To Betzalel's question as to where the Torah would be placed, Moshe replied that after the *Mishkan* was completed, they would make an Ark. "No," said Betzalel. "This is not fitting for the Torah. So first we will make an Ark and then the *Mishkan*." Therefore he merited that it should be called in his name, as it is written: "And Betzalel made the Ark" (*Shmot Rabbah* 3:2). "They disagreed as to the way of achieving the holiness, that is the whole purpose of mankind. Moshe first perfected his traits and his physical characteristics through his own spiritual and mental efforts, and then at eighty years of age was able to receive the revelation at the burning bush. He maintained, therefore, that first they should make the *Mishkan* [symbolizing our physical actions] and then the Ark that contains Torah wisdom. So man by his own efforts would arrive at spiritual peaks that would enable him to receive revelation. Betzalel, however, held that first the Ark had to be made so that we could use its knowledge to sanctify our actions. Betzalel's way became the preferred one bearing in mind that Moshe was of a spiritual dimension never achieved before or after. All other people required the Torah knowledge of the Ark before they could elevate and sanctify their everyday being" (*Shem MiShmuel*).

The *Chidushei HaRim*, founder of the Chassidic dynasty of Gur, relates how he read a *midrash* that said that Moshe taught his sons idolatry. In his anger over how could they even imagine that Moshe could do this, he threw the *midrash* from one end of the room to the other. His teacher, Menachem Mendel of Kotsk, explained this story as being parallel to the discusison of Moshe and Betzalel. When Yitro, his father-in-law, brought the sons to Moshe, he argued that their father should not educate them in an idological vacuum. Rather, he should expose them to all the philosophies, ideologies, and value systems in existence. This is the way that Avraham, Yitro, and even Moshe had been able to arrive at the belief in the One God and the falsehood of all the pagan systems. Moshe agreed, and the *midrash* links this with Menashe, the son of Moshe, who set up the idol of Michah (Judg. 17). The *Kotsker* explained that before the Revelation of Sinai, the way of Yitro was the only possible one, but now that Divine Wisdom has been shown to us, the previous way is fallible and false. That may create a deity that is a product of human knowledge and whose laws are only to be obeyed when they coincide with that knowledge. Before Sinai, the *midrash* tells us, the Patriarchs observed the whole Torah. This was an act of those whose observance is not commanded to them but the result of their own understanding . After Sinai, we observe Torah as we are commanded, so that we submerge our human wisdom to God's infinite word. "Those who [observe] because they are commanded to, are preferred to those [whose observance] does not flow from His commandments [the fruit of this knowledge]."

This way to spiritual, moral, and social perfection is exemplified by the roles of Shem and Yaphet, the ancestors of Judaic wisdom and Greek knowledge envisaged in Judaism. "God will open the mind [the feelings and intelligence] of Yaphet but will dwell in the tents of Shem" (*Bereishit* 9:7). Yaphet is the culture of aesthetics, philosophy, science, and law that raises people from the tyranny, the brutishness, the sensuality, and superstition of the savage and the primitive. This is a preparation for the mission of Shem, that is to teach mankind to live the whole of human life, social, spiritual, and moral, in such a way that God may dwell in their midst (Hirsch).

It is this issue of subjecting the knowledge of Yaphet to the Divine Wisdom revealed to Shem that was the source of the conflict between Hellenism and Judaism in the days of Chanukah and down the centuries until our own day. The Greeks argued that they could only accept that which could be observed objectively or that flowed from human understanding. Only that which could be verified by mankind's logic is acceptable. This latter became the standard of the European Enlightenment meant primarily to substitute human reason for the divinely revealed law, morality, and knowledge. This also is the basis of present-day humanist thought. No knowledge or wisdom exists beyond them, which makes them the sole arbiters of that which is moral, just, or true. These arbiters must ultimately reject any restrictions on needs, wants, and behavior beyond the parameters of this human knowledge and wisdom. Instead of pursuing a normatively good, just, or moral society, mankind seeks to minimize the damage done to the social fabric by the egoism, sexual appetites, and lust for political or economic power inherent in the human being. This is sought by various forms of social contract or legal systems. However, these develop or implement subjective, relative, and variable moral values rather than normative, consistent, and objective norms for human societies.

Although Judaism accepts the necessity, desirability, and power of human knowledge, it could not accept that this could be the sole or unlimited arbiter of good, morality, and justice. These concepts flowed from the Divine Wisdom revealed to mankind at Sinai. They come to purify, refine, and elevate human knowledge and wisdom so as to restrain and channel the desires, impulses, and needs of mankind. It was in contradiction to this that the Hellenists did not destroy the Temple oil, mystical symbol of knowledge, but rather sought to defile it. In this way, they proclaimed their negation of any limits on human knowledge and wisdom. The Maccabean revolt proclaimed that although such knowledge could create human morality, such morality was of necessity limited. It required Revealed Wisdom to enable mankind to achieve the most profound and pure forms of moral society.

PEKUDEI

Transparency

At first glance, we seem to be dealing in this *sedrah* with an inventory of all that went into the building of the *Mishkan*. However, our Sages saw in the repetition of something already dealt with in a previous text, the basis for the behavior of civil servants, trustees of public funds, and the administrators of such funds. It also became the ethical code of the autonomous Jewish communities throughout the centuries. With their own fiscal and legal systems, these communities were in fact ministates, so that these moral codes have significance for the citizens of the modern state, especially in view of the major role played by the government and its budget and economic policies.

Halakhah provides the legal framework for the protection of public funds against waste and fraud, but also for the implementation of an equitable fiscal system. Such a framework is of itself, however, insufficient to effectively prevent corruption. In addition, this requires spiritual and cultural norms that not only reject corruption but also create a social atmosphere which minimizes even the very appearance of unethical behavior. Such norms are provided by this *sedrah*.

At the outset, it is interesting to note the checks and balances provided by the division of functions in the raising of the funds for the *Mishkan* and their allocation. In Verse 21, Chapter 38, we read that Moshe [executive branch] commanded the raising of funds and determined their use. Ithamar the priest was the paymaster, whereas Betzalel and Ohaliav were the executors of all the work involved. Although this understanding of the verse by *Abarbanel* is extremely modern in its political conception, it is essentially a reflection of an ideal already expressed centuries earlier. The *midrash* teaches that although Moshe was in effect the sole trustee, he immediately associated others in the various functions involved. This was gleaned from the use of *Pukad* (commanded) rather than *Pakad* (supervised) in the verse to describe Moshe's function. This understanding of verse 21 became halakhically binding. "We do not appoint less than two trustees for raising public funds . . . [to prevent fraud. However, bearing in mind social and personal effects] the distribution is carried out by three since this is a matter of life and death" (*Shulchan Arukh*, *Yoreh Deah*, Section 256, Subsection 3).

Moshe, however, did not limit himself to the division of power that limits fraud but was also careful to render a full accounting of the money raised. This accounting was done even though God Himself had said, "Moshe, My servant, is different from all others, in the whole of My house is he trustworthy" (*Bamidbar* 12:7). "However, we read," said Rabbi Chana,

> When Moshe went to the Sanctuary, the people looked after him until he went into the Tent (*Shmot* 33:8), one said "See how fat is the neck, how powerful are the thighs of the son of Amram [Moshe; a sign of financial well-being]. He eats and drinks at the expense of the Jews and everything he has is from us." His fellow replied, "A person who controls the work of the *Mishkan* [collects the funds, appoints his nephew, Ithamar, as the paymaster and his great-nephew, Betzalel, as the contractor] is it a surprise that he should become wealthy?" When Moshe heard this immediately he rendered them an exact accounting. (*Midrash Tanchuma*; see also *Talmud Bavli*, *Kiddushin* 33b for a variant)

Even more impressive than Moshe's accountability is the very concept that the people could even suspect that the great prophet and lawgiver was perhaps guilty of some financial irregularity. It is difficult to conceive of such an idea ever being mooted, let alone considered legitimate, in other religious or spiritual movements regarding the founder. It seems a reinforcement of Judaism's teachings that susceptibility to error exists irrespective of the religious or spiritual status of a person.

Accountability is a function management, necessary but not sufficient to create a Torah culture of public office. This requires a conscious effort on the part of the office holder to avoid even the appearance of any abuse of position or power. Such avoidance limits the gossip, cynicism, and temptation for personal enrichment that all too often surround communal or political leaders. In the case of Moshe this is expressed in the story of the revolt of Korach (*Bamidbar* 17:15). There Moshe rejects the claims of misuse of his position, saying, 'Not one ass of their have I taken from them [to carry any load of mine, as when I brought my family from Midian. Perhaps the public service of taking Israel out of Egypt may have justified the use of public funds for their transport. Still Moshe paid for it himself] nor have I caused damage to any one of them.'

Centuries later, Samson and Shmuel reiterate this avoidance of the abuse of power. The blind Samson, shorn of his strength, stands between two pillars in the temple of Dagan in Gaza, the sport of thousands of Philistines. He prays for just one more demonstration of God's power; his cry, "Let my soul perish with the Philistines" is well known. Perhaps more relevant for future generations is the Talmud's understanding of the first verse of his prayer, "Lord, God, remember me and I pray of You strengthen me" (Judg. 16:28). "Said *Rav*, 'Remember to my credit the twenty years I [Samson] judged Israel and never once did I ask anybody to pass me my stave from one place to another [as a favor that could hardly be refused to one in Samson's position]'" (*Talmud Bavli*, *Sotah* 10a). So, too, Samuel, compared by the psalmist with Moshe and Aharon in holiness (Ps. 99:6) was careful to avoid any hint of exploitation of his exalted position as judge and prophet. He held the courts of law in circuits in various parts of the country so as to save all concerned from having to make their way to Beer Sheva where he lived. When his sons did not follow this practice but rather forced those seeking justice to trek to Beer Sheva, the rabbis taught that this was a form of bribery (*Talmud Bavli, Shabbat* 56a, based on *Samuel* I 7:16). After anointing Saul as Israel's first king, Samuel demands from the people publicly that they admit that in all the years of his leadership he had done them no harm. "Whose ox have I taken or whose ass have I taken or whom have I oppressed or from whose hand have I taken a ransom to blind my eyes [in judgment] and I will return it to them" (1 Sam. 12:3). The Sages understood this as referring to a form of leadership far beyond merely refraining from fraud and theft. They saw these actions as those of a leader who refused to benefit from his position or to exploit his office. So, "When I went to ask forgiveness for Israel (op. cit. 9) or when I was sent to anoint a king for them (op. cit. 17) I took my own sacrificial animals [for the performance of these public duties]. When I had to perform my judicial functions I did not follow the common practice and force Israel to come to me, but rather I [myself and at my own expense] wandered from place to place to grant judgment" (*Bamidbar Rabbah* 18:10).

> Said Rabbi Levy: Moshe said to the people, "During the wanderings in the desert I never asked anyone to carry my goods for me in their hands or on their donkeys. I carried my belongings, I loaded my own donkeys and I unloaded them." Said Rabbi Yochanan, the leader of the generation when serving the public should rather use his own property and wealth for that purpose as did Moshe rather than that of the public. (*Yalkut Shimoni, Korach* 12)

This long tradition of accountability, of not using one's position and authority for private benefit, and avoiding even the appearance of possible abuse is entrenched in halakhah.

> The overseers of the charity funds may not separate completely [to approach different individuals] for donations. Rather, they must keep each constantly in view. A trustee who found coins [or banknotes] in the public place [which legally would belong to the finder] or col-

lected payment [in a public place] on a loan he had extended, should not put them in his pocket but rather together with the charity he had collected. Then on his return home, he should take his money. Otherwise people would suspect that what he was putting in his pocket was some of the funds collected. So too he should count the charity money coin by coin, perhaps onlookers would suspect that he took some coins for himself . . . . If the trustees have to change the charity funds for another currency [a common problem before the emergence of a single national currency] or one denomination for another, they must do so through another person to avoid suspicion that they benefit from the transaction which could happen if they changed or sold the currency themselves. (*Tur, Hilkhot Tzedakah*, Section 257)

In his gloss to the same section, the *Rama* writes that to be clean before Israel and God, even the most scrupulous and pious of public officials need to render an accounting of the funds collected and distributed. Previously, he had written that the public are forbidden to give charity to overseers that are not trustworthy or cannot be relied on; this applies to the appointment of all public officials.

Bearing in mind the weakness of human beings, the power of greed, and our ability to rationalize our errors, it was necessary to prevent the temptations of public office. So the priest who collected the public donations entered the deposit area of the Temple, barefoot and dressed in a simple shift without sleeves or pockets. Similar care was exercised in preventing people who had a conflict of interest from taking part in decisions affecting the public purse, even if they were the most powerful people in the political hierarchy. The king and the high priest were not allowed to sit on the court that decided whether to declare a leap year to adjust the lunar year of our calendar to the solar cycle. Such a decision meant adding a thirteenth month so that Pesach would always be celebrated in the spring. The king, however, would want to avoid paying the additional civil service payroll and public expenses involved. The additional month of Adar added at the end of the winter moved Yom Kippur from late summer to fall. For the high priest this meant officiating barefoot, with only a thin linen shift on the cold stone floor and making his numerous immersions during the cold Jerusalem fall. Both of these officials had a conflict of interest and therefore were prevented from being part of the decision-making process.

The moral and ethical problems of the public sector bureaucracy and of the elected officials find expression in the treatment of the right of eminent domain. This enables them to appropriate private land as resources in the public interest. Eminent domain is clearly recognized in our sources and is the basis for many halakhic decisions. At the same time, however, the right of the king or government or local council to appropriate property is severely limited. Confiscated property, labor, or other services had to be paid for. The king was not allowed to accumulate gold and silver over and above the fiscal needs of defense or public works. So Rechavam faced a revolt supported by prophetic authority, not over the taxation needed for the public good but because of excessive taxation (1 Kings 12:3–18). There was even disapproval of the palaces raised by Solomon, his father, for the many wives and concubines. There are definitely no such rights of eminent domain when the appropriation is for the personal pleasure or profit of the legislator or official. World history is replete with examples of princes and nobles riding to hunt across the crops and fields of farmers and serfs or using forced labor for private services, all in the name of eminent domain. The modern state is not without its examples of appropriation of property for the benefits of the rulers. In the *Tanach*, however, when Ahab wished to obtain the vineyard of Naboth he could only do so after the murder of the owner under trumped up charges of treason and blasphemy (1 Kings 21). Seeking the halakhic validation for this seeming rejection of the accepted legal principle that a king may acquire land as he sees necessary, the rabbis held that because the vineyard was for Ahab's home in Jezreel not in the capital Shomron, it served no national or public purpose. In Jezreel, it was only to be used for the king's private pleasure and therefore the right of eminent domain did not apply. Naboth was determined to publicize this limitation on the king's rights and therefore refused to sell or exchange his vineyard. So also halakhically the right of the king or the state to tax was severely limited only to defense, those public services made mandatory by Torah such as Torah education and charity or such as approved by the majority of the citizens or their representatives (M. Tamari, *Challenge of Wealth* [Northvale, NJ: Jason Aronson, 1995]).

It seems that the public sector corruption that needs to be curbed does not flow only from greed for wealth or power. A chassid once told his teacher the following story of this type of corruption:

> When I first started to be responsible for the charity funds, I could not eat, sleep or study because of the terrible cries and the tears of the sick, the poor, the widows and the orphans. Later I found that with great effort I was able to at least eat and study, but still my sleep was constantly disturbed with dreams of their sorrows and pain. Now, however, I find that I can neither eat, sleep nor study with having heard and seen their trials and tribulations.

SONG OF HOLINESS

INTRODUCTION OF DAVID TZVI HOFFMAN

Based on the *Sefer HaMitzvot* of the *Ramban*

There are 247 *mitzvot* listed in *VaYikra*. This means that almost half of all the 613 *mitzvot* are contained in this book, justifying the last verse, "These are the *mitzvot* that HaShem commanded Moses to instruct the Children of Israel at Sinai" (*VaYikra* 27:34).

  There seems to be an additional reason for calling *VaYikra, Torat Cohanim*, beyond the fact that many of its laws relate to the sanctuary and the behavior of the priests. *VaYikra* details many of the ways that Israel may become a kingdom of priests, striving to cleave to God and to holiness. Actually there were two demands made of Israel at Sinai at the time of *Matan Torah*, "You shall be unto Me a kingdom of priests and a holy nation" (*Shmot* 19:6). Although each of these have a purpose of their own, nevertheless, the former is a means of achieving the second. In the role of priest, Israel seeks to cleave to Him so that He will dwell in our midst; but also so that we may achieve a divine level of holiness and a moral perfection both in our private and in our social or communal lives. Through these roles we may be filled, with a divine spirit; that, as explained in the *Kuzari* by Yehuda HaLevi, will bring us collectively and individually to the spiritual level of prophecy. Then we will be able to appear in the world scene as guides to all the nations of the world; veritable messengers of the Divine Will.

These two goals are reflected in the structure of *VaYikra*. The Tabernacle, *Mishkan*, was, as it were, to be a body within which the *Shechinah* resides. "They shall make Me a sanctuary and I will dwell in their midst" (*Shmot* 25:8). First Israel was commanded to perform all the laws detailing how this demand is to be realized. When this was done, the Divine Presence descended on the *Mishkan*. Now Israel was called to cleave to God in His sanctuary, by distancing themselves from everything that is rejected by the *Shechinah*. This is *Torat Cohanim* (Chapter 1–17). *Korbanot* is to draw close to God but also to correct any spiritual defects caused by sin. Then follow the laws of the priests and levites and their sanctification and duties. To ensure that the Divine Presence dwells in the midst of Israel, it is necessary to prevent all impurity, especially that of the body caused by eating forbidden (nonkosher) foods. Parallel to this all those who are *tamei* need to be separated from the Holy Camp. It is, however, impossible to correct, eradicate or expel every case of *tumah*, "His Glory dwells even in the midst of an impure Israel." Therefore, in His mercy, He granted us a Yom Kippur, to atone for all the spiritual impurity of our physical bodies (every sin defiles the sanctuary and causes the Divine Presence to depart).

With this ends the first part of *VaYikra*, *Torat Cohanim*, whose purpose is to teach Israel how to persevere their devotion to God, how to be a kingdom of priests.

The atonement of Yom Kippur is followed by the second part of *VaYikra* (Chapters 18–25), containing the injunctions for sanctifying life and the book of holiness [for creating a holy nation]. Family life, based on marriage, sexual behavior, social relations, and the fabric of communal life are all to be in accord with the dictates of *kedushah*. The sanctity of the priests and the unblemished sacrifices are an expression of this *kedushah*. Then there is the cycle of the festivals, *Shabbat*, *Shmittah*, and *Yovel* [sanctifying time and the ownership of wealth].

INTRODUCTION

[In its last pages *VaYikra* draws together *Torat Cohanim* and its portions of *kedushah*] into the covenant with Israel. In Chapter 26 we hear the positive results of obeying the *chukim* and the *mishpatim*, but also what the consequences are of disobeying them.

VAYIKRA

Korban—An Invitation

VaYikra, *and He, God, called to Moshe as one calls out to a friend.*

VaYikra, Leviticus, or even in its Hebrew version, *Torat Cohanim*, conjures up priestly duties, sacrifices, and ritual. Yet this *sedrah* and, indeed, the whole Book is dedicated to the path of holiness and purity. Traditional Jewish education started with children studying *VaYikra*, a fulfillment of the Midrashic saying, "Let those who are pure come and busy themselves with purity." Following the chapters dealing with the Sanctuary, it is logical for the Torah to teach ways of purification and sanctity of the priests or of the Sanctuary itself, but also of the people in whose midst the presence of God stood. This included the separation of that which is *Tahor* from that which is *Tameh*, rites of atonement and thanksgiving, communal and individual. *Tahor* and *Tameh*, insufficiently translated as pure or impure, exist in all the physical, social, and economic actions of people, so that those also form the scope and subject of *VaYikra*. There is *kashrut*, in food, sex, buying and selling, social responsibility, birth, death, religious ritual, and festival celebrations.

It seems that a proper perspective of the subject matter of this Book of Purity from the very beginning needs a clarification of two important concepts—*korban* in this *sedrah* and *tumah* in *Parshat Tazreah*. Usually *korban* is translated as sacrifice, denoting the idea of giving something belonging to one for the benefit of somebody else or of having to do without something that one values or desires. However, these ideas do not exist in the Hebrew word *korban* and are in complete contradiction to the concepts it comes to express. The alternative word often used, offering, likewise is inadequate to express the spiritual ideas embodied in *korban*. It always conjures up the idea of a gift in order to placate, find favor, or to obtain something in return by satisfying the one to whom it is given.

Grammatically, the root of *korban*, *karev*, means to approach or to draw closer, either physically or in a relationship. It can be a purely one-sided action as when one draws close to a place or a mutual experience between people, so, for example, within a social unit, *kerovim* are blood relations. The *makriv* bringing the *korban* intends to draw closer to God or to create a personal special relationship with Him. This is the whole ideology and purpose of the *korbanot*, neither the giving of gifts to placate the deity nor sacrificing something of value, rather part of the drawing closer to the Creator and the creating of a special relationship to Him.

This insight of Hirsch of the *korbanot* as a way to draw close to God is open to all people. The verse (*VaYikra* 1:2) of the instruction regarding the *korbanot* is made to the children of Israel, but continues "Any person of you"—this comes to include non-Jews (*Talmud Yerushalmi, Shekalim*, Chapter 1, Halakhah 4). "Non-Jews bring free will *korbanot* and those of their vows just like Jews" (*Talmud Bavli, Chullin* 13b). Not only is this path a way for men and women of all nations and creeds but Jews themselves provide a legacy of this as part of our ritual. The seventy public *korbanot* brought on *Sukkot* are on behalf of the Nations of the world. "If a non-Jew brings a *korban* and does not have the wine libation, this will be offered at the expense of the [Jewish] public" (*Mishnah, Shekalim*, Chapter 7, *Mishnah* 6). The final blessing of the supplicatory blessings in the daily *amidah* concludes in the Sephardic rite as "You hear the prayers of all mouths [everybody]." Solomon sees the Temple as the passageway for the prayers of all the nations (2 Kings 8:41–43), and Isaiah prophesied "their . . . offerings will find acceptance on My altar for My House will be called a House of Prayer for all the Nations" (56:7).

Rituals, external forms of worship, and religious hierarchies can become drained of their spiritual content, so that on a practical everyday level the religious, moral, and ethical dimensions are lessened or even lost. The rabbis of the *midrash* warned against this by referring to the word *Adam* in our verse. "Said R. Berachayah 'The Lord said to mankind, Your *korbanot* should be like that of Adam. Everything in the world was at his disposal and for his benefit and yet he did not offer anything stolen. So you too should bring only that which belongs to you, neither stolen nor earned through oppression'" (*VaYikra Rabbah* 4:7; also *Rashi, VaYikra* 1:2). One may wonder why of all the *mitzvot*, that injunction against robbery and financial oppression should have been singled out in this respect. After all, any mitzvah performed with stolen goods loses its validity and spiritual value. However, wealth is the very soul of a person, as the rabbis taught: "One who steals another's wealth it is as though he took his soul." It is not possible to draw close to God, the purpose of the *korban*, with something that belongs to another's soul (*Shem MiShmuel VaYikra*).

Berachayah's teaching in the above *midrash* simply reechoes the words of all the prophets against the false values, trivialization, and mechanical performance that can so easily and pervasively dislodge the moral and spiritual basis of the Temple service. Even though today we have neither a Temple nor *korbanot*, the prayer, external ceremonies, and rituals that form such an important part of our Jewish lives present the same religious problems as faced our ancestors. It seems that the only answer lies in the constant review and study of the symbolism, the ethical message, and spiritual wellsprings of this ritual. Perhaps the *korbanot* described—our *parsha* and the next one—may serve as an example of just this.

There are different types of *korbanot* mentioned that basically show two ways of drawing closer to God, one compulsory and the other voluntary; the former is in our *parshah* while the voluntary ones form the subject of the following *parsha*. The compulsory ones are the *Hat'at* (sin offering) and the *Asham* (guilt offering) through which atonement may be obtained.

The verses in Chapter 4 (2–3, 13–4, 22–23, 27) that enjoin the bringing of the *Hat'at* all describe cases where the sin was done through error, either through ignorance of the law where punishment for the act was *karet* (excision by God from Israel) or through negligence regarding a known law. Most of these cases refer to forbidden sexual relations. In all the cases, the question naturally arises: Why should negligence, ignorance, or carelessness require atonement?

For the *Ramban*, the reason is that there are no victimless crimes. Every sin, every wrong act, and every moral misdeed leave their marks on a person's soul even when done in error or carelessly. Atonement must be sought so that the soul of the inadvertent offender may have the opportunity to draw closer to God. That is why the term "soul" is used in our verse, to teach that the real essence of human personality, the mind and will, are affected. These are meant to guide and rule us; carelessness or ignorance mean misrule and lack of guidance, and, therefore, atonement is needed even if there is no intent to do wrong. Alternatively, atonement is needed because the hallmark of human beings is their intelligence and knowledge. Sins of omission have elements of commission in them when we are careless with the responsibility that these hallmarks call for.

Naturally, the greater the social, religious, or intellectual status of the person, the greater their responsibility and, therefore, the less reason there is to permit carelessness or indiscretion. The Torah describes a descending order of people liable to bring *Hata'ot*: the anointed priest, the congregation, understood by our Sages to refer to the highest legal authority, the ruler and only then the ordinary person.

Performing a conscious act by taking rams and troubling oneself to bring them to the Temple and performing the whole ritual will, according to the *Sepher HaChinuch*, impress on one's soul the extent of the wrong one has done and so one will take measures to avoid it in future. This is never achieved by simply saying that one regrets the unintended action. However, in sins committed intentionally, mere symbolic actions are insufficient; these require far more than bringing a *korban* as is clear from the *Korban Asham* (guilt offering; Mitzvah 95).

There are two types of *Asham* (Chapter 5:14–19): one as an atonement for the misuse of holy things, and the other for causing damage or violating the rights of other people and their property. Regarding the second group, we read

> If any person sin and commit a trespass against the Lord [Said Rabbi Akiva: When one repudiates one's agreements or one's obligations, this is a trespass against the Lord Who is always the third party to a contract or transaction (Sifre)] and deal falsely with another in a matter of deposit [trust money used for the personal benefit of the guardian] or of [denying] a pledge [or a loan received] or of robbery [taking by force something that belongs to another as distinct from theft, the taking of another's property by stealth] or has oppressed another [Said Rabbi Chisda: Repetitively saying to your neighbor, i.e., a creditor, go and come back tomorrow and I'll pay you; this is oppression (*Baba Metzia* 111a); withholding payment of wages, or the deliberate withholding of a recognized debt] or have found a lost article and dealt falsely therewith [either not publicized that the article has been found or refused to return it to its legal owner]. (*VaYikrah* 5:21–22)

In such cases the guilty person had to pay back the default and only then is he able to bring the *Korban Asham*. It is not possible to achieve atonement before rectifying the damage "for offenses against our Maker, Yom Kippur atones, however, for those against other people, Yom Kippur does not atone unless one has first [rectified the damage and] appeased the injured party" (*Mishnah Yoma*, Chapter 6, Mishnah 9).

There is an even more fascinating and moral dimension to those sins for which *Asham* is required for atonement. In all the examples described, one who admits his guilt is liable in addition to the *korban*, also to pay to the injured party a fine of twenty percent of the value of the wages, loan, deposit, or found article witheld. However, in the case where Reuven took an oath in court falsely denying any wrongdoing and then Shimon, the injured party, appears with witnesses to the sin, Reuven is only liable to repay the wage, loan, deposit, or found article. Because there has been no remorse, only discovery of the guilt, Reuven has actually done nothing. Therefore, Torah does not allow him atonement, neither through the *Asham* nor through the twenty-percent fine.

TZAV

Law and Religiosity

One hears it often said that Judaism is not a spiritual religion but solely a legal framework. This is believed, all too often, both by Jews and by others. Nevertheless, it is simply one of the many myths surrounding Judaism, which in reality is an exquisite balance between spirituality and law, between personal initiative and mandatory behavior. What greater legal personality can one imagine than Yoseph Karo, author of the *Shulchan Arukh* Codex. Yet the same Karo speaks to angels and is a leading kabbalist, just as was Elijah, *Gaon* of Vilna, the father of modern Jewish legalism and the arch-enemy of Chassidism, the mystical movement of modern times. Moses Maimonides, arch-rationalist and codifier of the most wide-ranging Jewish codex, constantly interweaves in his *Mishneh Torah* ethical and spiritual insights. There is the law and there is *lifnim m'shurat hadin*, beyond the letter; there is halakhah, the legal road, and there is *aggadah*, homiletics and spirituality, and there is justice and there is mercy.

This balance is also found in the *korbanot*. There are the *Asham* and *Hat'at*, guilt and sin offerings, but there are also *Shlomim*, peace offerings, and *Olah*, elevated offerings. The first two are mandatory and part of the process of atonement, whereas the latter two are free will expressions of the spiritual joy in God and thanksgiving for His Divine Providence. The *Ramban* writes that if a person feels filled with love for God he should enshrine it in a mitzvah to fulfill the verse "that ye awake not and stir up not the love till it please" (Song of Songs 2:6). Menachem Mendel of Kotzk taught that when the gates of love in Heaven are opened it brings love between Israel and their Father in Heaven and between each one of them and the other. It is in this light that these free will offerings should be seen.

Shimon bar Yochai taught, "The *Olah* is only brought for evil thoughts." Said Rabbi Levi, "This is explicit in the verse '*HaOlah* [that which cometh] into your mind, shall not be . . . to worship wood and stone' (Yechezkel 20:32)" (*Midrash Rabba VaYikra* 7:3; see also Job 1:4). "The *Olah* atones for non-fulfillment of positive *mitzvot* [someone forgot to give charity or to put on *tefillin*] or for a negative mitzvah related to a positive one [the injunction against closing one's hands not to give charity] both errors only in thinking" (*Talmud Bavli, Yoma* 36a). This is consistent with seeing the *Olah* not as it is usually translated "burnt offering" because it is consumed by fire. Rather, it refers to some form of desire for spiritual perfection, even seeking atonement for those thoughts that were never translated into actions. The *Olah*, to rise, symbolizes both the necessity and possibility of strength to rise higher in goodness and godliness. Our spiritual development is always upward, not forward.

Our Sages saw the word *tamim*, without blemish (*VaYikra* 1:3) to refer to the thoughts and desires of the one bringing the *korban*; the antidote to erroneous thoughts requires moral and ethical thinking. "The sinful thoughts are worse than sinful acts. These thoughts lead us to consider evil acts, legitimate or not wrong. [The thoughts are father to the deeds and so] they are actually more serious than the acts themselves" (*Mishneh Torah, Hikhot Deot,* Chap. 7; *Halakhah* 7). That is why, perhaps, the *Olah*, atonement for thoughts, is utterly consumed by fire, unlike the sin offering.

> One who sins against God actually sins against everybody in Israel since all Israel are guarantors for each other. However, in evil thinking

there is no mutual responsibility since this does not include those things unknown to anybody. Here the sin is therefore only to God and so the *Olah* is consumed by fire. In the sin offering, however, the priests, the representatives of the whole Jewish people, also have a share; this offering comes to atone for acts in which others were caused suffering or loss. (*Yalkut Yehuda, VaYikra* 1:23)

Obviously, thoughts do not only involve *mitzvot asei*, positive *mitzvot*. They are also the primary factor in all our actions. Beyond the question of the type of offering involved in atonement for these cases, it is clear that there is punishment for the sinful thought process. "You shall not covet" is the last of the Ten Commandments. It is the only one not explicitly connected to actions and so may seem to be protected against punishment.

One who covets [another's possession] . . . and exerts social pressure on the owner [who does not really want] to sell it, transgresses the commandment "You shall not covet" when he buys it, even though he pays him above market price. There is no corporal punishment since there was no illegal action . . . [but atonement required a *Korban Olah*] . . .. Lust leads to coveting, this [often] leads to theft. In those cases where the owner refuses to sell and if the owner tries to prevent the theft it may lead to murder. We can learn this from the story of Ahab and Naboth [King Ahab coveted the vineyard of Naboth who refused to sell it to him. Naboth was tried on a false charge of rebellion, killed and the vineyard transferred to the royal treasury (Kings I 21)]. (*Mishneh Torah, Hilkhot Gezeilah veAveidah*, Chapter 1, *Hilkhot* 9–11)

The *Olah* was a means of worship for Jews and gentiles. Adam, Cain, Noah, Jethro, and others brought *Olot* as did Israelites as well. However, the *shelomim*, peace offerings, seem to be an intrinsically Jewish worship; the revelation at Sinai provides an added dimension to a general concept. A burnt-offering, either wholly consumed or partially eaten by priests, as a form of worship, is easily comprehended. Not so one in which only a small part is offered, and the rest eaten by the individual or group bringing it, outside the sanctity of the Temple. *Zevah*, the term used in connection with or for *shelomim* is a general term for a meal usually eaten in a group. Communal eating is an important means of drawing the participants close to one another and to bringing peace or harmony to them. "*Shelomim* contains peace for all parties—blood and internal organs for the altar, part for the priests and the skin and meat for the owners" (*Sifra*). *Shelomim* is *shalom*, peace and *shalem*, perfect; brought out of a feeling of being in perfect harmony with life and oneself, close to God. In the *Olah*, we strive to raise our spiritual standards and the *Minchah* to demonstrate God as the source of material wealth and our joys. *Shelomim* signifies simply seeking for God, no petitions for anything, neither thanks for a special benefit. Only a state of mind of spiritual contentment arrived at by a joining with God or a striving to achieve a spiritual equilibrium through that joining. Not for nothing, the first *korban* enjoined on Israel was at the very establishment of the Nation, when the *Shelomim* of *Pesach* was sacrificed and eaten in individual homes in Egypt, a family meal of peace and harmony between a nation and its God, repeated every year at our *Seder* table.

Throughout *VaYikra* and *Tzav* the name of God, the attribute of mercy is used, never *Elohim*, the attribute of justice. Even the use of *Adam*, rather than *Ish*, is evidence of God's love as we see in its use as a term of endearment throughout the book of Yechezkel. Divine Mercy and Divine Love are expressed in the *korbanot* providing a way to draw closer to Him.

"The *Kadosh Baruch Hu* said to Yechezkel: '*Ben Adam*, son of kosher people, son of those who do acts of *chesed* and charity, son of those who are prepared to humble themselves or sacrifice themselves for the glory of Israel and of God.' So it is fitting to use *Adam* to describe one who comes before Him in repentance and brings an atonement for his sin" (*VaYikra Rabba* 2).

Instead of sacrificing our lives and our blood for all our evil actions and thoughts, we are allowed to achieve atonement inter alia, through the animals that are so similar to our basic instincts and bodily needs. No animal with any blemish, physical deformity, or defective internal organs can be used for *korbanot*. So, too, the sick, the old, or the lame are not acceptable. Indeed, the prophets protest it as hypocrisy and insulting, when the people bring unfit sacrifices, and they are accepted by the priests (Malachi and Hoshea). So, too, the Temple and its ritual are not meant for unhappy, depressed, or afflicted people. It is not a mecca for the blind, the lame, and the sick seeking miraculous healing or an escape through religion from their suffering. Rather, the sacrifices had to be unblemished, the priests without wound or mutilation, and the worshipers seeking a full, joyful, and complete life as part of a celebration of spiritual progress toward God. Hirsch points out that Judaism is not a religion for little children but rather one addressed to adults in full possession of mature physical and spiritual power, demanding their best and their strength (*Shmot* 30:14) and this is expressed in all the *korbanot*.

The first two *sedrah*s in *VaYikra* are full of the slaughtering of animals and birds, of the burning of offerings, and of the casting of blood upon the altar. They seem to be a license for blood lust and cruelty, an expression of a primitive religion. Yet we read "and no manner of blood shall you eat . . . any person that eats any blood, that person be cut off from his people" (*VaYikra* 7:26–27). The prohibition against the blood exists irrespective of whether the Temple exists or not, in all generations, in the Land of Israel and outside it. It is repeated numerous times in the Torah, and we continue to observe it in our own daily lives. The blood bears the *nefesh*, the life force, the whole ego, as it were, of the animal. These have no place neither in the *korbanot* nor in our food, otherwise they become part of our own ego and *nefesh*. In many societies, not all of them ancient, the use of the skins and horns of wild animals and the smearing of blood and fat on the bodies of warriors have been common. These are examples of a desire to identify with the life force and strength of these animals. Maimonides argues that cruelty and murder become part of a person who drinks and eats blood, just as the training of vicious dogs include feeding them raw meat with blood. Our kosher laws, through soaking and salt, remove the blood. However, there is a further dimension perhaps less well known but nevertheless of primary spiritual and educational importance. When the *shochet* starts his ritual slaughter of chickens, sheep, or cattle, he is required to first recite a blessing "Who has commanded us on *shechita.*" It is this that makes permissible what would otherwise be murder, even as we are prohibited to fish or hunt for sport. Then the first blood has to be sprinkled or dropped onto earth, covered with earth, and once again, "Who has commanded us to cover the blood." Animals may be slaughtered for food, their flesh may not be torn from them while they still live (even Noachides), their blood not eaten nor drunk but rather accorded dignity and respect.

> Such covering the blood hides our shame. It is the consciousness of shame that is the beginning of all moral improvement. The very nature of our ritual slaughter with the very specific and detailed rules and regulations [regarding the piety of the *shochet,* the careful examination of the knife, the care not to tear or to crush any of the blood vessels, etc.] create the understanding that one is not dealing with a helpless, unprotected object, but rather with a living soul. (A. I. HaCohen, Kook)

So the injunction against eating the blood and all those *halakhot* surrounding it "apply at all times and in all places, is obligatory on men and women" (*Sefer HaChinuch,* Mitzvah 148).

The perspective Judaism has to the *korbanot* may best be seen in the fact that they are only commanded to us after the giving of the Torah at Sinai. First are the laws of *Shabbat,* social relations and respect for parents (*Shmot* 15:25; see *Rashi* on that verse), then the Revelation at Sinai and only then the *korbanot.* It required the moral, ethical, and religious perspectives of these revelations to prepare Israel for the *korbanot.* Otherwise, they would have swept our fathers into the idolatry of the Egyptians and other nations.

SHEMINI

Limits of Spirituality and Ecstasy

The ever-present potential for prescribed prayer, ritual, and religious hierarchies to become degraded, mechanical, and even a veil for corrupt irreligious behavior not only is clear to us today but forms the basis of many chapters of our prophetic books. Jeremiah decries the people's belief that the mere physical existence of the Temple is sufficient to protect them from God's anger irrespective of their ethical and spiritual behavior. Yishayahu points out the bankruptcy of a nation that is meticulous in the sacrificial ritual, performed with hands covered with innocent blood, hearts full of deceit and envy, and minds scheming to oppress and defraud. Malachi upbraids the priests for teaching that the blind or the lame or the sick are appropriate sacrifices. Hosea sees the priests trading on the grief and pain of the worshipers. In our personal lives, aided by the repetitive set prayers and order of service, we too often slip easily into praying mechanically and by rote. For this very reason, our prayers are so structured as to allow greater spirituality in the primary and obligatory sections, by the preparatory psalms and prayers. The *Shema* and its *brachot*, the *Amidah*, *Hallel*, *Mussaf*, and reading of the Torah, achieve devotion and serious thought by such preparation. The mystics introduced the immersion in the *mikveh* for men to symbolically cleanse themselves before prayer while they and the later

Chassidic movement prayed while singing and dancing. We find the same search for an elevating experience during prayer in the prophets' use of song and musical instruments, even as the songs of the Levites were an integral part of the Temple service.

Less obvious but just as pernicious is the danger that the search for emotional expression, mystical motifs, and spiritual ecstasy in prayer may lead to otherwordliness, and so either a breakdown of the communal and social structure that is an integral part of Judaism or to a feel-good religion rather than the search for holiness. There are many examples in Jewish history of personalities and movements that were forced to leave Judaism because of exaggerated mysticism and spirituality. The circumstances surrounding the deaths of Nadav and Avihu, the sons of Aharon, described in our *sedrah*, have served our scholars as indications of just this danger.

Four times the Torah repeats the story of the death of Nadav and Avihu to impress on us that their only sin, the "foreign fire" that they offered, seems to refer to different aspects of this disequilibrium. The *midrash* (*VaYikra Rabba* 20) sees their refusal to marry and their lack of sons as the cause of their action. They saw celibacy as a means of achieving sanctity. Marriage and the sexual act are often seen to be major temptations, drawing men away from the most refined and spiritual worship of God. So many cults and spiritual movements have sought celibacy as an essential state for religious growth. Monastic movements, celibate founders and holy men, teaching of the evils of sex, all are expressions of theologies that could only envisage sanctity achieved through denial of and withdrawal from the realities of this world. Not so Judaism. The unmarried man is spiritually imperfect and flawed, so cannot serve as a judge because of the lack of merciful thoughts, and evades the very first of the commandments—be fruitful and multiply. He rejects the Divine Wisdom that sees in the married state the holy way of continuing the Creation and the Jewish nation. Ben Azzai, a Sage of the *Mishnah*, never married because his soul dedicated itself to Torah. Azzai was one of the few scholars who entered the *Pardes* (world of the highest insights into Torah). In the purity of his soul and the intensity of his love for God, he saw the *Shechinah* and died. A parallel to Nadav and Avihu's celibacy as a search for the ultimate religiosity.

"Strange fire which He had not commanded them" (*VaYikra* 10:1). Nadav and Avihu saw the miraculous fire that had descended from Heaven and that had accepted the offerings at the dedication of the *Mishkan*. In Solomon's Temple, too, a similar heavenly fire had descended in response to the king's prayer. They, however, desired more and wished to sacrifice something of their own, something that had sprung from an upsurge of religiosity and fervor. So they brought their own pans and an earthly fire from their homes. Excitedly they entered the sanctuary, without the prescribed priestly clothes, and without the obligatory washing of hands and feet. All of the service was a free expression of their own spiritual and religious feelings untrammeled by the Divine Code. Yet our Sages taught: "It is more meritorious to do that which one is commanded to do, than that which is not obligatory" (*Talmud Bavli, Kiddushin* 31a). Every blessing we recite before a ritualistic act expresses "Who had commanded us." Such acts need a personal understanding and an individual spirituality yet Judaism insists on them as part of a Divine Command. So public prayer, the festivals, *Shabbat* observance, kosher food, and religious symbolic acts are all part of a legal and obligatory framework. This framework extends beyond the religious acts to include marriage, social relations, and the earning and spending of money. Everything is that which we are commanded to do or to desist from. This creates a normative and obligatory morality independent from relativity, free from constant individual agonized decision making, and separate from changing social mores or standards. The fire that Nadav and Avihu brought was foreign to Judaism, and they were burnt by it.

The same *midrash* tells us: "The sons of Aharon only died because they decided *halakhah* in the presence of their teacher, Moshe . . . it is forbidden to decide *halakhah* unless one is 12 miles (the extent of the encampment in the desert) from one's leader." In our case, they decided to bring fire to the altar, a normal procedure, except on the eighth day when fire came down from Heaven, thus deciding a halakhah without consulting Moshe (*Sifra*). This is not the same as pointing out an error on the teacher's part nor as raising a new issue for halakhic decision. Neither is it like the meritorious act of their nephew, Pinchas, who, seeing Moshe and the elders unable to implement the law in the case of the public adultery of Zimri, stood up and did so in their stead. Irrespective as to whether Nadav and Avihu acted out of arrogance or out of genuine spiritual strength, their action is that of the *Zaken Mamreh*, the rebellious elder for whom there is a death penalty (*Mishneh Torah, Hilkhot Mamrim*, Chapter 3, *Halakhot* 4,5). It destroys the halakhic chain that goes back through history to the Revelation at Sinai. In effect it ultimately means that there is in reality no halakhic framework.

Nadav and Avihu were great people—God Himself says of them, "I will be sanctified by those that are close to Me" (*VaYikra* 10:3). What prompted the foreign fire they brought? How could they have made the spiritual errors they did? Shall we see the cause in a generational conflict or an arrogance or an ignorance?

"Wine and strong drink you shall not drink . . . when you go into the *Ohel Moed* so that you die not." This injunction to Aharon after the death of his two sons, teaches us that they performed their offering while they were drunk. However, the next verses speak of being able to "differentiate between the holy and the less holy, between the pure and the impure and to teach . . . the laws of God." We are not involved here in real drunkenness but rather in a slight diversion from the clear thought and undisturbed logic required of true Jewish worship. Their physical intoxication was a reflection of their religious ecstasy and spiritual drunkenness that led to such deviation.

This religious ecstasy and spiritual drunkenness flowed from the eighth day of the consecration of the *Mishkan*. Our Sages (*Talmud Bavli, Megillah* 10b) taught "that day there was rejoicing before God like on the day He created Heaven and Earth." The rejoicing at the Creation was possible because He also created *t'shuva*, without which the world could not exist. The building of the *Mishkan* allowed for the *t'shuva* on which the world depends and so the rejoicing was similar. "Adam asked Cain, what the course of his judgment was. 'I did *t'shuva* and achieved atonement,' answered Cain. 'This is the power of *t'shuva* and I was unaware' cried out Adam. Immediately he stood up and recited 'A psalm for the Sabbath day'" (Ps. 92; *Bereishit Rabbah*). The *Shabbat* for which this psalm is a thanksgiving, celebrates a creation made viable by the power of *t'shuva* so the joy of the eighth day was like the joy of Creation.

This number eight denotes a experience, or an achievement, or an obligation over and above the normal, rational, or material aspects of life and the world. This is in contrast to the number seven that represents the cycle of physical nature. So there are seven days of the week, six days of Creation, and the *Shabbat* of perfection of that creation. There are the seven years of the *shmittah*, a similar six-year cycle of agricultural production and economic endeavor, with its perfection in the Sabbatical year. There is the forty-nine-year cycle that culminates in the *Yovel* that restores spiritual and economic balance. Eight, however, is a number completely beyond these material-worldly cycles. At the personal level, "the alloted days of our lives are three-score and ten and if in vigor they reach eighty" (Ps. 90:8). *Abarbanel* explains that the years after seventy are all undeserved gifts. This he links to the fact that the seven days of *Sukkot*; with their *mitzvot* of *Sukkah* and the Four Species are followed by the separate festival of *Shemini Atzeret*, a day devoted only to thanksgiving and praise of God. Seven days a Jewish boy lives a mere physical and material life; similar to all other children. Then there is *Brit Milah* on the eighth day. This marks the covenant set in the flesh, to provide a sanctity and a spirituality to all the needs or actions of the flesh. The eighth day of inauguration of the *Mishkan* allowed Israel to see the glory of the Lord, and in their ecstasy and religious fervor at this revelation, they shouted and prostrated themselves. This nationwide ecstasy, this pervasive religious fervor, swept Nadav and Avihu upward so they brought a false fire.

When later Aharon lit the menorah, the text tells us he did as the Lord commanded (*Bamidbar* 8:3). *Rashi* comments that he did not deviate or change and this was to his credit: Asked the *Shem MiShmuel*,

> Is it remarkable that Aharon should not deviate or change from God's commandment? Yes indeed. As Levi Yitzchak of Berdichev said, "If

I would have been Aharon, in my ecstasy and the spiritual emotion of this great moment, the first lighting of the *Menorah*, I would have stumbled, perhaps spilt the oil, knocked over the cups of the *Menorah* . . . ." However, Aharon, in the religiosity of his mind and his intelligence was able to place ecstasy in its correct Torah perspective and do exactly as the Lord commanded. I have seen my grandfather, Menachem Mendel of Kotsk, pray on Yom Kippur, without motion, without movement, like a pillar of fire, the true ecstasy of the brain and mind.

TAZRIAH

Taharah and Tumah

Our Torah envisages our meeting the Creator not just in the precincts of the Sanctuary and its ritual. Such a meeting is not restricted to a specific priestly caste, important as these may be. Rather, a whole nation is to be drawn closer to God through the consistent separation between *Tahor* and *Tamei*, that which is pure and that which is impure; this separation is expressed in all the actions of the individuals but also in the sociopolitical structure. So the details of the construction of the *Mishkan*, the laws of its ritual, and of the *Cohanim* and *Levi'im* are a prelude to the wide-ranging laws of *Tahor* and *Tamei* that constitutes the rest of the Book of *VaYikrah*.

The Sages of the Talmud, the mystics, and the Chassidic masters stressed the relationship of *Tumah* to *metamtem*, meaning to block, to dull, to close, or to seal off. Everything that is *Tamei*, whether in food, or in bodily secretion and physical manifestation, or in social misconduct and immorality is *metamtem* the mind, the spiritual energy, and the hearts of people. As an antidote to this *timtum* came the laws of *Taharah*, of purity. "Rabbi Chananyah ben Akashya said: The Holy One, Blessed be He, wished to purify the people of Israel so He gave them Torah and *mitzvot* in abundant measure" (*Mishnah Makkot*, Chapter 3, *Mishnah* 16). "In all your actions you shall acknowledge Him" (*Mishlei* 3:5).

It is common wisdom today that people are what they eat and therefore purity starts with permitted and forbidden foods. This has nothing to do with considerations of health, as the species permitted to us are forbidden if they are diseased, died of natural causes, or are injured or defective. Perhaps, as Maimonides writes in "The Guide to the Perplexed," the forbidden foods are unhealthy, and, therefore, the Torah does not permit them. To this *Ramban* and most of the commentators objected, saying that this denigrates Torah to a minor treatise on medicine, come to cure ills that could be treated by drugs or medicines. Support for this objection to the health aspect may be found in the fact that the Noachide laws, which exclude all that which is intrinsically evil and present the basis for civilized society, do not forbid these foods. They are forbidden only to Jews, part of the extended Divine Guidance for creating a holy nation.

The Torah does not present reasons for why some species are permitted and others forbidden; the cloven hoof, chewing the cud, or the fins and scales in fish are not reasons, only signs. Throughout the centuries, scholars have presented various reasons. Most of them reflect the characteristics of the species concerned and their spiritual significance for us. The permitted species are all domesticated, having a relationship to mankind who cares for them and in return receives food from them, as well as clothing, labor, and shelter. They are all herbivorous, receiving their nourishment without bloodshed or cruelty. However, throughout, these same scholars understood that the real reason for differentiating between that which we may eat and that which we may not, is that Divine Wisdom has decreed thus. "One should not say it is impossible [to eat, for example, pork because it is unhealthy, revolting, unclean or any other reason] but rather it is truly possible [perhaps pleasant or healthy since it is eaten throughout the world]. Only, He forbids it" (*Safra Kedoshim*). It is this reason, teaching control and the submerging of lusts or desires, that provides the spiritual education and subconscious reflexes universally differentiating also between permitted and forbidden sexual acts, between kosher and nonkosher money, and between just social organization or power and injustice or oppression.

Shmuel of Sochochow taught that all the birds, fish, animals, and beasts are part of His Creation and have in them sparks of holiness. Yet, we need to learn that just as one can share in these sparks through eating of the permitted species, so, too, one can share in holiness by refraining from the forbidden species (*Shem MiShmuel, Shemimi*). There is a very common religious concept of achieving spiritual fulfillment through ways that add to growth—prayer, meditation, acts of mercy, and devotion to study. However, Shmuel of Sochochow teaches a unique characteristic of Judaism—that sanctity and fulfillment are also achieved through separation and negation. Our covenant with God is sealed by removing the foreskin of every male child. *Shabbat* is a day separated from the six days of creativity and action. We tithe our wealth since part of it is meant for the support of others. There are ways of increasing that wealth that are forbidden, just as there is forbidden food. In our marriage ceremony, some sexual acts that were forbidden now become permitted, and others still remain forbidden. There exists a constant balance in our spiritual growth between positive and negative acts, between the permitted and forbidden.

There is in our *sedrah* a further *Tahor-Tamei* dimension, one that relates to physically determined conditions that seem to dictate a loss of self-determination. These relate to childbirth, to menstruation, to issuing of human seed, to *metzorah*, and ultimately to death itself. In all of them, we lose our power of self-determination and of free will, thereby challenging the Torah's insistence on the moral freedom of mankind to choose. It would seem that Hirsch's view of all of them symbolizing loss of human moral freedom places these *Tahor-Tamei* laws in a proper perspective.

It is of great symbolic significance that "man is like the tree of the field" (*Devarim.* 20:19) and that these laws of *Tahor-Tamei* (*VaYikra* Chapter 12) start with "A woman has matured a human seed." Indeed, the word *tazriah* only appears in the Torah apart from our *sedrah*, in *Bereishit* 1:11–12, to describe the way plants and trees are propagated. The purely physical, almost mechanical process of the plant world related to fulfillment of a woman's noblest aspiration and ability significantly places the

TAZRIAH

Tumah solely in this realm. Although the child, once it is born, is morally a free agent, however, before then the origin and growth is unfree. The mother, especially during the pregnancy, is a part of the unfree process. So the separation after birth, the ritual immersion, and the sacrifice are all meant to mark the end of the loss of free will and the reentry into the Godlike world of moral freedom and responsibility. So, too, all the other forms of *Tumah* resulting from bodily emissions—*nidah, zav,* and *zavah*—reflect this same lack of free will and their purification, re-entry into free will. In his commentary, Hirsch sees the fact that the period of ritual separation—*mikveh*—for the birth of a girl is twice as long as that of a boy, as clearly showing this. The mother's state of impurity is interrupted in the case of the latter on the eighth day by the *brit milah*. Then the *nidah* continues for another thirty-three days before purification. However, with the birth of a girl, the *Tumah* period is a total of eighty days. Hirsch teaches that the *brit* commences the entry of the male child into free will, thus shortening the purification period.

The Chassidic masters explained the *Taharah-Tumah* of birth in a more mystical way. Menachem Mendel of Kotsk asked, "The keys of birth are only in His hands, not in the hands of angels or of messengers. How then can it be that this birth should cause *Tumah*?" To this the *Avnei Nezer* of Sochochow answered, "*Tumah* seeks consistently to attach itself wherever the *Kodesh* departs from, to fill the spiritual vacuum. So the *Zohar* explains the *Tumah* of a dead body as the major form of impurity, attaching itself to that from which the Divinity of Mankind has departed. So, after the child is born, *Tumah* seeks to replace the keys of life that God prevails over." In this vein, the *Kotsker* answered the query of the Chassidim as to why the Torah always describes cases in which something falls into a pure vessel or onto pure food. "This is because *Tamei* always seeks to find *Tahor* but *Tahor* never touches *Tamei*."

After a period of separation, and sometimes a sacrifice, all the cases of *Tumah* require ritual purification through water. In some cases, full immersion in living water is called for, in others only washing of the hands and feet. Springs and rivers, halakhically, do not acquire impurity even though some kinds of *Tumah* require that the food or object have been wet when the *Tamei* came in contact with it. Water in its pure state has neither taste nor color; all that it includes is water itself. Yet at the same time nothing living can exist without it. This purified, seemingly valueless element is essential for physical existence, and the thirst for it sustains all life. It is this that gives it the ability to purify and its integration into all the forms of *Taharah*. For that reason, Shlomo of Sochochow once told me that a *bracha* over water should only be said when one "lusts" after it in thirst; otherwise, one has no pleasure or profit from the water, thus removing its spiritual symbolism.

Water, however, possesses a further spiritual quality. The animals, birds, and human beings who live in the air or on the ground are not an integral part of those elements. Even when they are in their natural habitat and need it for their continued existence, nevertheless, life can continue even if they are temporarily separated from it. The birds who fly in the air are able to continue living even if they stand on the ground; indeed their nests, feeding, and mating are so. Animals and people are able to live even if they are treed or separated from the ground; only few of them live in the ground and even these emerge intermittently. Only those who live in the water cannot exist outside it. The fish can have no existence outside their element. It is not only the source of their food or a partial habitat but completely surrounds them so that fish and water are one, indivisible and indisputably linked. For the mystics, Torah is living water. Torah, pure and refined, is not only a temporary habitat but integrally part of every Jewish man and woman. Like the fish in water, they are able to immerse completely in it, and like the fish, they have no existence outside it. The ritual immersion in water or the washing of the hands, therefore, enables us to achieve purification through the Torah (*Shem MiShmuel*).

Netilat yadayim is usually translated as washing of the hands, yet *netilat* does not mean "to wash," but to raise up. So *netilat yadayim* before meals or in the priestly ritual or in the transition from *Tumah* to *Taharah* raises us and the acts we perform up to a higher stage of purity. The mystics and Chassidic masters taught that for that reason the hands should be raised up after the *netilat yadayim*.

METZORAH

Physical Ills and Social Immorality

It is common wisdom that in addition to having physical causes, illness also often results from mental ill health, tension, stress, and psychosomatic pressures. There is a special Torah perspective that sees *tzara'at* as a physical manifestation of antisocial behavior.

Tzara'at has usually been translated as leprosy, conjuring up a biblical parallel to leper colonies, the bell to warn others not to come close lest they become afflicted and severe quarantine. There are examples in the *Tanach* of this type of leprosy: Na'aman, the Syrian general, and the four lepers in 2 Kings 7. However, everything in our text militates against seeing the laws of *tzara'at* as relating to efforts at quarantine or hygienic treatments. In the case of the leprosy of the dwellings, the Torah prescribes that the affected house be cleared of all its utensils before the examination by the priest; sanitary measures to prevent contagion would surely have declared all the utensils unclean because of human contact. The Talmud (*Moed Katan* 7b) writes that no examination of a person, the house, or the clothes on which a leprous spot has appeared is to be made on the festivals, even though masses of people came to Jerusalem. This also applies to a bridegroom during the seven days of rejoicing. Fears of contagion should have made the expulsion of the leper mandatory from all cities and villages, yet this expulsion only applies to those cities, irrespective of their size, that were encompassed by walls at the time of Joshua's conquest; a *metzora'a* could therefore remain in any other city or village in the Land of Israel, even if at this time they are walled. Above all, none of the laws—examination, expulsion, or isolation—apply to a non-Jew, neither the clothes, the house, nor the person. All the types of leprosy are meant solely as a warning to people regarding their social conduct and as a call to repentance. "All four appearances of *nega'im* are only an altar for atonement" (*Talmud Bavli, Berachot* 5b).

For the Talmud in *Arachin* 15b, *metzora'a* is the short version of *motzi-ra*, one who spreads slander. So Moshe's (*Shmot* 4:1–6) hands were stricken with leprosy because he slandered Israel saying, "They will not believe me," even though later we read that when he told them of the imminent redemption, the people believed. So, too, Miriam was punished (by *tzara'at*) later for her evil talk against Moshe (*Bamidbar* 12:1–10). So severe is *lashon hara* that entry into the Promised Land was only denied when the spies slandered the Land, this despite the many other times the Israelites sinned. "See how *lashon hara* is more serious even than action [primarily because it spreads and multiplies a chain reaction of evil actions]. One who wrongly slanders his wife pays a fine of 100 *shekel* whereas one who forces an unmarried or unengaged woman, pays only 50 *shekel*." Perhaps the evil of all slander which repeats things that are true, lies in the fact that usually the slanderer has neither profit nor pleasure from the sin.

Further on, the same talmudic source in *Arachin* lists all the other antisocial actions that bring *tzara'at* of the body in their wake:

- Bloodshed—"and let there not fall from the house of Yoav [because he killed Abner, Saul's general] . . . that is a leper" (2 Sam. 3:29);
- False oaths—"and the *tzara'at* of Na'aman shall come on [Gechazi who took a false oath to get gifts from Na'aman]" (*Avot de Rabbi Nathan*, Chapter 9, referring to II Kings 5:26);
- Sexual immorality—"Plagued Pharaoh with *nega'im* because of Sarai" (*Bereishit* 12:17);

METZORAH

- Pride—"His [King Uzziyahu] heart was arrogant . . . and he went into the Temple to burn incense [a prerogative only of the *Cohanim*] and while he was angry with the priests [who tried to prevent him] leprosy rose on his forehead";
- Theft—"One who gathered wealth that is not really theirs [halakhic definition of theft] the priest will come and disperse all the goods and utensils that are in the house [that was plagued by *nega'im*]";
- Egoism/Selfishness—"and the owner of the house [plagued by *nega'im*]" (*VaYikra* 14:25). "Said R. Yishmael, One who seeks absolute ownership and does not wish to lend any of their possessions to others [pretending poverty] the *Kadosh Baruch Hu* exposes the wealth when all the contents of the house are removed and publicly displayed" (*Talmud Yoma* 11b).

The *Midrash Rabbah* adds its own list of antisocial actions as attitudes that bring *nega'im* as their punishment: a lying tongue, arrogant eyes, spilling of innocent blood, thoughts of violence, feet ready to run for evil purposes, spreading lies, quarrels between brothers, and giving false witness. In their usual fashion, the rabbis do not describe general social malaise or abstract moral exhortations but rather specify the human organs—eyes, ears, mouth, the hands, the heart, the feet—involved in the social acts that bring *nega'im*.

Yehuda HaLevi in the *Kuzari* relates the leprosy and the *nega'im* to the absence of the Divine Light as a result of the sins and evil listed by the rabbis. Just as when life departs all that is left is the dead body, changed in its whole appearance, so, too, the *nega'im* show the departure of Divinity, the Holy Image in which the perpetrator was created. It is this *tzelem elokim* that enables us to unite our minds, our bodies, and our souls in moral, spiritual, and just acts. The acts that cause the *nega'im* are the antithesis of these and flow from the absence of the Divine Presence, therefore, the person has to be isolated and separated from the body politic of Israel on which that presence rests. For the mystics, Rachel, Leah, Bilhah, and Zilpah, the mothers of the twelve tribes of Israel, are the antidote to the four *nega'im*, *seit* (intensely white), *sapachat* (shade of egg membrane or chalk), *baheret* (shiny white), and *tzara'at* (colorless). Rachel is the antidote to *baheret*, shiny white like snow. The snow is the severe spiritual coldness that prevents fervent and life-generating heavenly feelings from lighting up the hearts of Israel. Rachel, representing the fire and devotion of spiritual observance, strengthens them so that Israel may serve and worship with fervor and purity. It is this fervor that is symbolized by the Torah's repetition of words related to charity and acts of righteousness. "You shall surely [lit. open] your hand [to the poor]" (*Devarim* 15:11), "grant him generously [lit., grant]" (*Devarim* 15:14); the antidote to that which causes *nega'im*. It should be remembered that all the thirteen examples of social immorality are the subject of much of the lengthy confession *Al Chet* we recite on Yom Kippur.

The nature of these actions and thoughts is antisocial divisiveness and corrosion of interpersonal relations of husband-wife, family members, neighbors, and citizens. It is fitting, therefore, that seclusion and isolation from the family, community, and body politic should be the punishment. Yet the punishment of expulsion is only from those cities that are walled at the time of Joshua's conquest and thereby acquired the significance and status of the national camp as distinct from open villages and individual homesteads. However, it must be stressed the *metzora'a* is also banished from the Temple. Not only is society separated from the perpetrators, but there is also no place for them within the Divine Sanctuary or within the milieu of sanctity. It is fitting therefore that it is the priest, representative of that sanctuary and sanctity, that is to be the examiner, judge, and bearer of the declaration that such people are unworthy of the Nation and of the Holy Circle.

The *Shem MiShmuel* sees this role of the priests as flowing not merely from a role in the sanctuary nor from a social hierarchy, but rather it is intrinsic to the spiritual causes of the *tzara'at* and their atonement. All the social sins seen by the Talmud as causing *nega'im-tzara'at* are caused by a denigration of the intrinsic internal value of the individual harmed by those actions. The same actions and sins show the inner emptiness of the perpetrator and intensify, if possible, the lack of inner spirituality. This emptiness can only be discovered, and treated, by those who are the innermost spiritual center of Israel, the priests. Their service in the Divine Sanctuary, their knowledge of Torah, and their devotion to the internal harmony of the nation, demands that only they be involved in all the types of *nega'im*. "Be of the disciples of Aaron [the High Priest] loving peace and [actively] pursuing peace, loving [your fellow] creatures and bringing them closer to Torah" (*Avot*, Chapter 1, *Mishnah* 12).

Hirsch notes that the perspective of *nega'im* and *metzora'a* as symptoms of social strife, faults, and sins and a call for repentance of all of them is strengthened by the Torah's treatment of *nega'im* in clothing and the houses. Both of these attest to the social character of mankind, and they are the major expressions of group living and human association.

So their appearance must denote social and interpersonal faults far greater than those that cause *tzara'at* and *nega'im* of the body. The laws of *nega'im* in the clothing (*VaYikra* 13:47–59) are, therefore, far wider in range. Here even clothes owned by a Jew that originated in a non-Jew have to be examined, and all clothes with *nega'im* need to be sent out of all cities and even villages, not only the walled ones. Whereas when a bodily affliction remains unaltered after the second week of seclusion the person becomes pure, clothing in the same state must be burnt. Furthermore, the laws apply even when the thread is made into utensils or objects like sails of a ship. The *Shem MiShmuel* sees the atonement for the social faults and sins that are witnessed by *nega'im* of clothing, as necessitating the destruction of the clothing. Everything that is secret, internal, or given over to one's heart is always covered. The perpetrator of social crimes has removed internalized holiness from his personality and replaced it with impurity and evil. The clothing has covered up the hidden crimes and therefore needs to be unraveled, expelled, and destroyed. He continues to relate the three cases where *nega'im* occur—body, clothing, and houses—to the relevant *mitzvot*. The tefillin that adorn our bodies, the *tzitzit* that are in our clothes, and the *mezuzot* on our homes are constant reminders of our religious obligations that include our social responsibilities for the welfare of others, our ethical behavior regarding our wealth, and the ethical dimensions of our speech. They, therefore, serve as a spiritual protection against leprosy and the *nega'im* that come not primarily to punish, but rather to cause a consciousness of the slander, theft, murder, and other social sins in order to prevent them.

Our Sages saw pride and arrogance as the source of all these social errors and sins. Arrogant people are unable to sympathize with the needs of other people, or the harm they may be doing to those who, in their eyes, are imperfect or do not exist. Pride is all too often the parent of the egoism and selfishness that allows one to ignore the rights of others, and it is pride that predicates a lifestyle of "what's mine is mine and what's yours is mine" that our sages consider to be the mark of an evil person (*Avot*, Chapter 5, *Mishnah* 10). So in *Arachin* during the discussion of the cause of *tzara'at*, Rabbi Channa bar Chanana says, "What is the cure for slander? If the person is a scholar, devote yourself to Torah and if an ignoramus, become humble." In the purification of the afflicted house and of the leprosy, the priest needs to take the cedar wood, crimson thread, and hyssop; "let the person who became arrogant like the cedar humble himself like the thread and the hyssop" (*Rashi, VaYikra* 14:49).

ACHREI MOT

Repentance, Confession, and Atonement

The free will inherent in mankind predicates individual responsibility but also reward and punishment both human and Divine. Divine Mercy taught us of our ability to repent and change the course of our actions with the assurance that atonement follows. Repentance is not vouchsafed only to an elect nor is it far beyond the reach of ordinary, everyday men or women, Jew and gentile alike. It is not something purchased through indulgences nor can it be achieved through the efforts of others, or through faith alone. Rather, repentance is achievable by all people, without limitations of time and without considerations of the nature of the actions involved. T'shuva requires only, "the acknowledgment of the act, the admission that it is wrong, regret and the undertaking not to repeat it" (Maimonides, *Hilkhot T'shuvah*, Chapter 1, Halakhah 1). Ideally, t'shuvah should be a constant and ongoing spiritual process in our daily lives. In reality, it is rather a vacillating and fluctuating part of us, if at all. So Divine Wisdom provided a season replete with custom, prayer, and education to guide us to t'shuvah, the Days of Awe, Rosh Hashanah to Yom Kippur. In this season, it is always the *viduy*, the confession, that is the prerequisite for the t'shuvah defined by Maimonides.

Viduy is not an exercise in guilt nor a destructive litany of human weaknesses. There is no trawling in the murky depths of our thoughts and actions. Rather, *viduy* is a verbal expression of our ability to judge our actions and to accept responsibility for them. This liberation of our free will enables us to escape the depression of a spiritual morass from which we assumed we could never extricate ourselves. This *viduy* is the nucleus of the service of the high priest described in our *sedrah* and the essence of our own worship each Yom Kippur.

The *Cohen HaGadol*'s service is punctuated by his ritual immersions, paralleled by our own Yom Kippur eve immersions in the *mikvah* and conducted while dressed in a simple white shift, just as we wear the white *kittel*. The usual priestly gold vestments are not worn, rejecting the symbol of the great national sin of the idolatry of the Golden Calf, even as we need to reject our own immoral or unethical actions during this day. His confession as described in our *parsha* sets the pattern for our own. First he confesses his own sins and those of his family, then those of the priests, Israel's religious leaders, and then a symbolic confession of those of the whole nation. So, too, our own *viduy* is couched in the plural, our own shortcomings, those of our neighbors that we perhaps could have helped to avoid and also those of our community. Judaism's mix of individual responsibility and communal identity in which private morality is insufficient and active participation in charity and social justice is essential.

There are actually two confessions, whose repetition forms the basis of our Yom Kippur repentance: one a short form of twenty-four words arranged alphabetically, and the other in which each letter is repeated to signify a certain misdeed or sin. They are said privately in silence and then communally. In the short version, all the sins refer to social and economic actions. "*Ashamnu*" are the sins for which we need to bring *asham* offerings, like the case in which one denies a debt, misuses trust money, or withholds a found article from its owner. We have betrayed "*bagadnu*" through shoddy workmanship, callous redundancy of long-standing employees, or the breaking of contracts, written or verbal, even when no financial loss occurs to the other parties. "*Gazalnu*," since we have robbed, taking by force anything belonging to someone else—withholding wages or pressuring others to agree to a transaction against their

ACHREI MOT

wishes or to their disadvantage. We have blasphemed, "*dibarnu Dofi*," by desecrating God's Name (*Chillul HaShem*). Fraud, theft, and tax evasion, when perpetrated by Jews are blasphemies that associate God and His people with the perpetrator. We have caused perversion, "*he'evinu*," every deviation from honesty and righteousness—is a perversion of God's creation. This may be seen from the use of the word abomination in regard to false weights and measures (*Devarim* 25:16), just as in regard to idolatry or sexual immorality throughout the Torah. We have encouraged lawlessness, "*veHirshanu*," by buying goods or services from firms that evade taxes, financial reporting regulations, or pollute the environment. So, too, each of the other confessions relate directly to our everyday *actions* in the buying or selling, hiring or firing, advertising or packaging, as employers or employees, as citizens or public officials, as consultants or professionals.

The long version too refers to at least eighteen sins regarding money or business transactions: "*Beimutz HaLev*"—by acting callously. We act callously and insensitively when we disregard or even turn our backs on the needs of the distressed and disadvantaged in our community—the poor, the old, the sick, the addicted, and the stranger. We act callously when we withhold the ten percent tithe that as Jews we are expected to allocate at least as a minimum from our earnings and income. But it is also *imutz halev* when we shame our staff or our peers in front of others as are all forms of harassment or bullying behavior of debtors, suppliers, or staff.

Chillul HaShem, desecration of God's name, is such a grievous sin that only limited *t'shuvah* is possible. The Talmud cites economic misbehavior as one of the most common forms of *Chillul HaShem*. Fraudulent bankruptcy, white-collar crime, tax evasion, or defrauding social security are obvious examples. The subsequent defamation of His Name is increased by the degree of Jewish identity, bearing, or communal status of the culprit.

This emphasis on economic immorality comes not to deny the importance of sexual or ritualistic misdeeds but is simply a reflection of the recognition in Judaism of the great potential for evil inherent in our search for wealth and material goods. Because this potential is so powerful, the confession, too, needs to emphasize our repentance in this sphere. In the days of the Temple, the sacrificial service and Yom Kippur brought atonement. Today, halakhic sources show Yom Kippur of itself brings atonement. However, this only apply applies to those acts between us and God. Those unethical and immoral deeds toward our neighbors, our partners in the marketplace and indeed to any people, require more than just the observance of Yom Kippur. No fasting, no confession, not even recognition of these sins can bring atonement. After all, not only God has been harmed by these acts but so have people, and they need to be placated. The only way that this can be done is by rectifying the damage or by returning that which was obtained fraudulently. Judaism's balance between Heaven and Earth requires, however, that sins against God inherent in our interpersonal economic sins also be atoned for, so that Yom Kippur and repentance and confession are still required. "These sins between man and man need to be confessed aloud but it is great arrogance to loudly confess our acts against God" (*Hilkhot T'shuvah*, Chapter 2, *Halakhah* 5).

For many years, it was difficult for me to understand the transition in the Torah readings on Yom Kippur morning from the portion of our *sedrah* describing the high priest's order of service, to the seemingly unrelated, almost irrational reading in the afternoon of the long list of sexual perversions forbidden to us. The *haftorah* at *Minchah* from the Book of Jonah, with its universal message of the ability of all peoples to repent and find atonement, only heightens the seemingly discordant note of injunctions against incest, adultery, homosexuality, and bestiality. These were part of the lifestyle of the Egyptians from whose slavery we had been redeemed but also of the people of Canaan, the Promised Land for the establishment of a Holy Nation. Understandably, we were enjoined for all time not to follow this lifestyle, but perhaps the Ten Commandments or the chapters of *Shema Yisrael* would have been more appropriate to this day of confession and atonement. Life experience and the passage of time, however, have made clearer the great moral wisdom of our Sages in prescribing the reading of the forbidden sexual perversions at *Minchah* toward the close of Yom Kippur.

For *Rashi*, "*Kedoshim tiheyu*"—You shall be holy—means separating oneself from sexual immorality (*VaYikra* 19:2). There cannot be a restraint on behavior in the marketplace, respect for other people's property or person, and the foregoing of some individual rights in the widespread social activities that make up life, alongside complete freedom in regard to our sexual appetites. Control, perspective, and spiritual striving predicated by our belief in a moral and just God, need to be learned and practiced in all spheres, because all together they constitute the whole of our individual and collective being.

It should be noted that the list of sexual relations read on Yom Kipppur does not include rape, physical coercion, or any form of sexual enticement. These represented a completely different set of acts dealt with by halakhah but not of the same dimension as those categorized in this reading. Here the acts are forbidden not because they involve damage or injury to one of the parties or because they are unwilling partners. The Torah does not see them as acts of deranged or physically or psychologically deformed people. Rather they must be seen as acts of consenting adults with an assumption of physical sexual pleasure. Outside of the three monotheistic religions, they have been viewed for thousands of years and in a wide variety of societies, as victimless activities, sometimes condoned or part of accepted sexual lifestyle. Nevertheless, the Torah forbade them all despite this normality, the mutual consent, and an apparent lack of victims. The absence of these assumptions would make the forbidden sex relations similar to viewing *kashrut* as a Divine Health Guide or the socioeconomic framework merely as the result of human wisdom. Rather, "neither shall you walk in their statutes [of the Egyptians and the people of Canaan]; My statutes, *chukim*, and My social laws, *mishpatim*, shall you keep to walk in; I am the Lord your God" (*VaYikra* 18:3–4).

The textual use of *chukim* and *mishpatim* is the clue to the Torah's expression of the forbidden sexual relations. These are *chukim*, Divine

Decrees forbidding some of that which human desire or logic may perhaps permit. They have the same source as the *mishpatim*, that also flow from Divine Wisdom and Divine Justice over and above the social parameters of human morality. *Chukim* and *mishpatim* are the moral balance of Judaism, and so the rabbis commented on the verse, "And the people of S'dom were exceedingly evil and sinful—evil of each other and sinful to God, sinful with their bodies and evil with their money" (*Talmud Bavli, Sanhedrin* 109a). It was not lost on the Sages that the Torah talks about the *chukim*—laws of Egypt and Canaan. In S'dom, sexual immorality and economic oppression—the antithesis of *chukim* and *mishpatim*—were enshrined in the legal system (*Talmud Shabbat* 31a). Judaism in contradiction calls the section of the Mishnaic Code that deals with social, commercial, and criminal law—*Seder Nezikin*—The Book of Redemption.

For transgressions of these *chukim* and *mishpatim*, Divine Mercy and Divine Justice provides for atonement through confession and *t'shuvah*. The Gates of *t'shuvah* never close and redemption-atonement always follows. The long confession, *Al Chet*, is divided into three sections. At the end of each section, during the communal recital, we repeat the verse, "And for all of them, God of Forgiveness, forgive us, pardon us, grant us atonement." It is because of our assurance that Divine forgiveness, pardon, and atonement follow our confession, that this verse is sung collectively and joyfully.

KEDOSHIM

To Be Holy

> *"People* [menshlichied] *holiness.*
> —Menachem Mendel of Kotsk

In this *sedrah*, Moshe is commanded to address the whole of the Jewish people as distinct from the priests or Levites spoken to in the previous ones. The Sages in *Torat Cohanim* taught that "because you shall be holy is the synopsis of the basic tenets of Judaism, so it had to be taught to all the men and women."

The envisaged holiness is not envisaged as the status of a defined class nor is it a goal for priests, prophets, or holy men, nor a condition limited to special times or places. Rather the call to holiness is addressed to all the people, as a constant framework for their everyday living at home, in the market or in the halls of government and social organization.

It should be noted that the Jewish people are not called upon to be pure, like the angels, that is one who is totally removed from the lusts, tensions, or turmoil of human beings. We are called upon to be holy, that is, to separate, sanctify, and elevate that which is permitted to us in food, sex, economic activity, and social relations. This holiness is not couched in the singular because what is envisaged is not numerous holy individuals but rather such individuals living and creating a holy congregation—community—nation.

Menachem Mendel of Kotsk pointed out, "You shall be holy" is not just a commandment or an obligation, it is also a Divine Promise that ordinary men and women can be holy. It would seem that our concepts of Judaism, family bonds, tradition, spiritual growth, marital relations, and attitudes toward happiness must be seen in the perspective of the opening verse, "You shall be holy," and its promise.

It is doubtful if there can be any concept, philosophy, or ideology more positive, more enobling, and more spiritually stimulating than this promise. It is a promise that does not require an intermediary, neither human nor godlike, nor does it require superhuman strengths or special spiritual tendencies. Rather, this holiness is promised to all and sundry; each and every individual is assured that by their own efforts and acts they can be holy.

What is this holiness and how is it to be achieved? The Torah repetitively insists that it may be achieved only by keeping the covenants, the decrees and social laws given by the Divine Wisdom and Divine Love. Over forty of such *mitzvot* are included in our *sedrah*, and they are almost equally balanced between the demands of ritual or religious law and the social legislation; balanced between duties and relationships with God and our duties to other people. So filial obedience lies alongside the observance of *Shabbat* and details of the sacrifices lie alongside the agricultural gifts to the poor and the stranger. "You shall not deal falsely with one another, nor shall you swear falsely by My name. . . . You shall not oppress your neighbor nor rob him . . . the wages of a hired servant shall not be returned by you." This is only part of a long list of social laws, culminating in, "You shall love your neighbor as yourself," but followed by the *chukim*, about *kelaim*, mixing diverse kinds of cattle or planting a mixture of seed and *sha'atnez*, the wearing of clothes made of two kinds of cloth; sexual immorality and idolatry are forbidden, just as are all these forms of injustice.

Throughout, the parameters of the way to holiness are such as may be fulfilled and achieved by everybody. "For this which I have commanded you this day, it is not too hard for you, nor is it far away from you. It is not in heaven that you should ask 'Who shall go up to heaven and bring it down to us?'... neither is it beyond the sea... but the word is very close to you... that you may do it" (*Devarim* 30:11–14). Nothing is demanded or forbidden that is beyond the ability and the free choice of ordinary people. There are no edicts and no expectations that demand a denial of human nature or are dependent on the eradication of human needs or wants. Rather, the way to holiness lies in the constant refinement and transformation of these same needs and wants.

Celibacy is not a way to holiness. Normative sex relations, family purity, and permitted sexual acts are the Torah way to sanctify what could be a purely physical or animalistic lust. Fasting and asceticism are not ways to holiness. Kosher foods, permitted combinations, and temporary abstinence come to make holy what could otherwise lead to gluttony or bodily impurity. So poverty is not a way to salvation or holiness. Rather, Rabbi Yehuda HaNassi, the redactor of the first codex of the Oral Law, the *Mishnah*, placed the Chapters of the Fathers, the repository of ethical and moral teachings of the Sages of the Mishnaic Period (until approximately 250 B.C.E.) in *Seder Nezikin*. *Nezikin*, literally damages, is in fact the order of the *Mishnah*, containing all rabbinic commercial, civil, and criminal law. Here in this law he saw the major challenge to holiness, because the lust and desire for wealth is probably the most powerful of all human needs and wants. "The sexual need—the more one feeds it the hungrier it becomes, the less one feeds it the easier it is satiated" (*Avot deRabbi Natan*, Chapter 4, Section 8). Not so money, the less one has the more one wants, the more one has the more one wants. "One who has a hundred *zuz* wants two hundred" (*Midrash Kohelet Rabbah* 1:34). There is never enough.

Creating and earning wealth is not forbidden, but

> You shall not steal, neither may you deal falsely nor lie to one another [regarding price, quality or ownership of the goods or services sold]. You shall not oppress [defined halakhically as coercing another to agree to a sale not to their advantage or against their will; to deny a loan

received or to misuse trust money] nor shall you rob him [there is nothing immoral nor unjust in the employer-employee relationship but the latter may not rob the former by not working diligently or using the firm's goods or services for private purposes while as to the former] the wages of a hired person shall not be kept by you overnight. (*VaYikra* 19:1–13)

There are in business relationships and activities transactions or acts that may be perfectly legal but yet harmful and immoral. Indeed, it may be that ethical behavior begins where the law ends. This is envisaged in verse 14—"You shall not curse the deaf nor put a stumbling block in the path of the blind." Because the deaf do not hear cursing, this causes them no anguish nor injury, but there is a moral injury to the one doing the cursing. The blind in this verse in contrast to the deaf, are not physically blind but rather the Sages understood this, as a reference to those "who blind themselves to the results of their actions." So one is not allowed to sell harmful goods or services, even if the law permits it, to one who willfully blinds themselves to the damage done to them. The sale of nonkosher meat to a Jew or the paraphernalia of idolatry to Jew and non-Jew alike are stumbling blocks in the path of the blind. Because one is not allowed to steal, buying stolen goods causes the thief to stumble by providing a market for the goods, making theft profitable. We are obligated to maintain our bodies in health and so the sale to others of cigarettes or drugs that are harmful would be forbidden, even where legal and desired by the buyer. Israel's armament industry, a major dollar earning industry, poses a serious halakhic problem because it is forbidden as part of the *lifnei iver*—the stumbling block—to sell weapons to non-Jews; the assumption is that self-defense is not the primary purpose, and a Noachide is enjoined against other forms of killing. These stumbling blocks make the person supplying or abetting any of them— a *mesayei leovrei aveirah*—an accomplice to those who perform acts forbidden to them. The fact that they are aware that these are forbidden or harmful and are even keen to perform them simply means they blind themselves to their spiritual role, and to this we are forbidden to be accomplices. So a Jewish borrower cannot waive the right to Torah's protection, saying he is willing to pay the interest; this is putting a stumbling block in the path of the Jewish creditor who is forbidden to take interest.

There is another perspective to *lifnei iver* totally unrelated to helping people harm themselves or failing to observe their religious obligations. This is an aspect that has much relevance for lawyers, accountants, consultants in all fields, and public sector officials. It is considered to be a stumbling block when one fails to reveal any conflicts of interest. Beyond conflicts of interest, *lifnei iver* would also seem to include financial reporting or legal contracts that although being truthful and equitable, are couched in such professional jargon and obscure language that they are unintelligible to all those who are blind, that is lack the specific skills and education.

That the paths to holiness are not in conflict with human nature nor require the negation of human needs and wants may be clearly seen from the rabbinic understanding of "You shall love your neighbor as yourself." Said Rabbi Akiva, "This verse (*VaYikra* 19:18) is a major principle in Torah" (*Talmud Yerushalmi, Nedarim,* Chapter 9, *Halakhah* 4). Yet the same rabbi ruled differently in the case of two people stranded in the desert with one possessing enough water to keep himself alive. Should they share it and both die? Should one believe that "no greater thing can a man do but give up his life for another" and give his water to the other person? "No," ruled Akiva, and this became halakhah. "Your own life takes precedence" (*Talmud Bavli, Baba Metzia* 62a). Any other demand lies beyond the power of human nature, which cannot allow people to love and care for others more than for themselves. That is why Hillel taught: "That which is distasteful to you, do not do to others. This is the whole Torah, now go and study in order to be able to understand and practice the Divine Purpose."

Hillel phrased his answer in the negative to the gentile who wished to learn the whole Torah while standing on one foot, because in the positive form, as written in the Torah, it lies beyond human power to fulfill.

> Rather the Torah commanded us that we should love [desire for] others all the goodness, merit, and success that we desire for ourselves. Whenever we wish others to have wealth, honor, and wisdom, still we do not wish them to be equal or to surpass us. Love your neighbor comes to teach that we should be able to eradicate this jealousy from our hearts and be able to find satisfaction that our neighbor achieves or has that which we wish for ourselves. (*Ramban*)

All too often, the Torah's commandment to love others as a guiding religious or spiritual goal is quoted incompletely. It is only part of the Jewish undertanding of the mainspring of interpersonal harmony, as the verse concludes, "as yourself; I am God." This duty does not flow from philanthropy, nor from self-sacrifice, nor from starry-eyed idealism, but simply from the fact that God created man and woman in His Divine Image and therefore it behooves them to respect this divinity in others and actively seek their welfare. It is interesting to note that one of the practical implications of "love your neighbor" is the obligation of the courts to make the sentence of capital punishment as painless and honorable as possible. The criminal deserving this punishment, nevertheless, is created in His image, and the crime does not abolish this divinity. So, too, the corpse of the criminal may not be allowed to hang exposed, but speedy burial is commanded; otherwise it would be an affront to God (Deut. 21:23).

Ben Azzai claimed that the verse in Gen. 5:1, "This is the book of the Chronicle of Mankind," is greater than the verse used by Rabbi Akiva. What will be the case, Ben Azzai could argue, if a person has no desire for honor, wealth, success, or wisdom? Does this mean that such a person may damage, undermine, or prevent others from achieving them? The verse in *Bereishit*, however, makes the welfare of others mandatory, irrespective of our own desires, aspirations, or achievements, simply because the other person is created in the Divine Image.

EMOR

The Balance of Material and Spiritual

Are people simply a battlefield between two conflicting worlds—the material and the spiritual-moral—or is there a possibility of living a life that is a consistent balance of these two incongruous worlds? It seems that the *Omer* and all that surrounds it, is a prototype for such living. This prototype does not constitute a truce between material and spiritual but rather represents a balance that integrates them into a viable unity.

"When you come unto the Land that I give to you [and attain thereby the national independence that comes with a People's possession of its own independent country] and you reap the harvest, you [collectively] shall bring an *Omer* [a dry measure of grain corresponding to the amount of food necessary for one day (*Shmot* 16:36)] of the first harvest [that is the very first cutting of the new grain of the current year]; to the priest [to the Tabernacle or Temple]" (*VaYikra* 23:10).

This *Omer* is not merely an expression of thanks for the new grain, nor is it a sacrifice to placate or to share with the Deity. Rather it is an acknowledgment that God is the real owner of the land or all that it produces, and also, ultimately, of all the wealth that we possess. It is the acknowledgment of the Divine source of all our material-physical goods that allows and fosters the spiritual material unity. In this unity, while the legal ownership of the wealth is recognized as being vested in the individual farmers, nevertheless, the real ownership is demonstrated by the limitations placed by Torah on these same farmers. No harvest is allowed before the reaping of the *Omer* and its presentation permits him nationwide harvest. Furthermore, and perhaps even more importantly, "and bread [of the five grains: wheat, barley, oats, rye, and spelt, that constitute the halakhic definition of bread] of roasted grain or green ears [of grain] you shall not eat until this self-same day, until you have brought the offering [of the *Omer*]." This verse comes to prevent us from eating, in any form, grain that is legally ours—an expression of our acceptance that He is the real owner. Acknowledgment is ratified, as it were, further on in our chapter, when the former is required to leave unharvested the corner, *peah*, of his field for the poor and the stranger. These are the landless ones, who normally would have to wait for handouts from landowners and the wealthy. However, in this nation that acknowledges through the *Omer* that even the legal owners of the land are only tenants, the *peah*, *leket*, and *shechichah* (gifts of the poor) actually belong to the poor and the strangers. Unlike other forms of philanthropy, the legal owner is unable to choose whom is preferable and, therefore, allowed to enter the field and the *peah*. The property rights of the owner revert to the Real Owner, Who bestowed these gifts to those in need. He also demands that in addition to philanthropy, all owners of wealth may be coerced halakhically to pay for the social costs of society. Such payment, like the *Omer*, is the liquidation of their debt to the Owner for the wealth He has bestowed on them and allowed them to earn through their labor. *Tzedakah*, charity, is rooted in *tzedek*, justice.

This justice is one of the ways in which the material and physical withal that we create and possess is transformed into something holy and seen spiritualized, over and above satisfying our prosaic, if essential, needs. It is a way that is part and parcel of the *Omer korban*, a *korban* of barley that is commonly food for animals, relative to wheat that is primarily for human consumption.

All the living creatures brought as *korbanot* are meant to transform all our lusts and desires for the material into part of the Divine worship.

So too, the *menachot*, the meal offerings that may be brought only from wheat, come to transform our ordinary human wisdom into divine wisdom. Since wheat is the symbol of wisdom, in the same way the *Omer*, brought of barley, comes to transform the physical-material into part of the Divine pattern. Animals by their nature subject themselves easily to their human masters and we too are required to humble ourselves and subject our wills to His will. Such humility, however, may also have adverse effects when directed to other factors, possibly bringing in its wake despair and depression.

Therefore, the *Omer* was waved by the priest in order to elevate the nature of humility and subjection so that it is devoted solely to our Divine worship. It is fitting, therefore, that the *Omer* was brought following the first day of Pesach which is a festival of God's love, shown through the redemption, and of our freedom. When we left Egypt our subjection to Pharaoh was transformed to our labor and obedience to God.

["And you shall count unto yourselves from the morrow of this *Shabbat*, from the day of brining the *Omer* of the waving seven complete *Shabbatot* it shall be" (*VaYikra* 23:15). This is *Sefirat Ha'Omer* recited every night between Pesach and Shavuot.] In reality it should be called the *Sefirah* of the *Lechem HaPanim*, the two wheaten loaves brought on Shavuot. After all, we count in anticipation of that festival and the Giving of the Torah, even as one counts toward a joyous event or a special potential occurrence. This counting comes to purify and transform the animal desires and needs symbolized by the barley, which is an animal food and should have come after the sanctifying process as is the case with all other purifying actions. However, since the human desire for material-physical needs and wants is so powerful, people are unable to begin the process unless we were first given the ability to connect ourselves through the *korbanot* of barley to the Divine Source" (*Shem MiShmuel, Haggadah shel Pesach, Sefirat Ha'Omer*).

Sukkot has an *Atzeret*, an eighth day which is, as it were, an opportunity to grasp and hold onto all the spiritual progress and insights of the festival that preceded it. Pesach does not have an actual eighth day of *Atzeret* similar to *Shemini Atzeret*. Yet, in fact, this is not so. Rather, the

Atzeret of Pesach is only delayed until Shavuot, known also as *Atzeret*, which is the culmination and completion of the Exodus, of the Revelations of Divine Power and of the public witnessing of this intervention in the affairs of nations and people. What separates and yet integrates Pesach and Shavuot are the forty-nine days of *Sefirat Ha'Omer*. This daily counting process marking our anticipation of *Matan Torah* and our realization that the Revelation of Sinai in fact is the purpose for all that transpired on Pesach. It was for this Revelation that we were redeemed, even as promised to Moshe at the burning bush, "When you take the people out of Egypt, you [collective] will serve God on this mountain" (*Shmot* 3:12). How many teachings, how many commandments, and how many spiritual lessons from the Torah given at Sinai on Shavuot are expressions of Pesach?—the Ten Commandments, "Who took you out of the land of Egypt from the house of bondage"; just weights, just scales and correct measures; "I am HaShem Who brought you out of the land of Egypt"; "You shall not defraud or oppress the stranger because you were strangers in the land of Egypt"; sexual morality enjoined as the antidote to the perversions, illicit relationships, and unlimited sexual appetites of Egypt. On Pesach our bodies were freed and our physical-material needs and wants released from the bondage of Pharaoh. It is true that only free men and women can worship God and practice His commandments, yet in order that this should not become license, spiritual anarchy, and a jungle of warring interests and conflicts, we received a Torah on Shavuot. So, we count from the barley *korban* of the *Omer* to the two wheaten breads of Shavuot.

This process does not depend on the existence of a Temple and its priests, but rather is a function of "this day," the specified date—the sixteenth day of Nissan. *Chadash*, the injunction against the eating of the new grain, flour, cake, bread, and so forth, before this date applies even today in the Land of Israel and according to many authorities, even outside its boundaries. The date, as it were, is that factor on which Divine permission to use the new agricultural wealth granted to us depends. So important is the date that if for any reason, whether climatic or because of the discrepancy between the Jewish lunar calendar and the solar year, that it was not definite that there would be sufficient barley for the *Omer*; then an additional month of Adar was added. Since, however, it was the spiritual perspective of the date of the owner's permission that is so crucial to our sanctification of our material-physical wealth, this calendar change exists whether there is a Temple or not.

The *Omer* has to be brought on the "morrow of this *Shabbat*," the day immediately following the first day of Pesach and our *Sefirat Ha'Omer* commences on this same date. It is from the Exodus from Egypt that the spiritual journey toward Sinai commences and from which we draw the ability to subjugate the physical to *kedushah*. So, it is essential that the *Omer* and the counting follow the end of that day. For that reason the halakhah, oral law, insisted against the Saducean view that saw "the morrow of the *Shabbat*" as referring to Sunday. This view would destroy the link between the exact date of leaving Egypt and the *Omer*, depending on which day of the week that day occurred. Furthermore, the Saducean view would mean that *Matan Torah* would not necessarily always be seven full weeks from the Exodus, thus destroying the relationship between the physical freedom and the achievement of spiritual freedom through *Matan Torah*.

Each and every one of us counts the *Sefirat Ha'Omer* as distinct from the national calculated forty-nine-year *Yovel* cycle that is the duty of the *Sanhedrin*, the National Representatives. Each and everyone thus creates, as it were, a new sabbatical cycle of seven weeks. The days before each regular *Shabbat* need to be a preparation for that *Shabbat* so that all our work and activities have to be conducted in a manner that will enable us to enter the *Shabbat* sanctity, unashamed and spiritually elevated. Following *Shabbat*, these same physical and material pursuits draw from its sanctity so that they can be dedicated to His service. As we start to count the separate sabbatical cycle following our exodus from Egypt, we understand that our freedom, prosperity, and possession of our Land are only beginnings. Then each part of this cycle purifies and sanctifies all our actions and desires so that, ultimately, we can achieve the homage to God and fulfillment of our service of Him that enables us freely to acquire that *Matan Torah*, toward which we are counting.

S. R. Hirsch sees a specific contribution of the forty-nine days of the *Sefirah* counting and their culmination in the fiftieth day. The former are a parallel to the seven-day cycle of the laws of *Tumah* and *Taharah* that culminate in the eighth day of purity. So there are seven weeks of purification and the fiftieth day that releases us from the lack of freedom symbolized by *Tumah* of the material needs and desires. *Yovel*, the Jubilee Year, created a fresh foundation for widespread freedom and justice in the Jewish State and so the fiftieth day of the *Sefirah* brings the moral freedom for achieving the integration of spiritual stature with material-physical well being.

This integration is part of the process seen by the *Sfat Emet* when he notes that the *kiddush* on the festivals refers to *Moadim leSimchah* [best translated perhaps as times for acknowledging gratitude, rather than times of rejoicing], since the influence of all the festivals permeates our actions throughout all the days of the year.

BEHAR

The World Is Built By *Chesed*

A major stumbling block in the path of holiness is power of the economic *yetzer hara*. This almost unlimited lust for material wealth, this legitimate need essential for the material functioning of the world, is all too often the source of great evil, immorality, and even bloodshed. Greed not only becomes a stimulant to economic activity but unfortunately often leads to business immorality and social oppression. In addition, fear of uncertainty regarding our economic future, the state of our individual health, and so on, not only leads to legitimate investment policies but also to unethical methods of securing our financial security. It is appropriate, therefore, that as *VaYikra* draws to a close, its path of holiness should be devoted to *mitzvot* that cleanse and purify greed and alleviate the fear of uncertainty—*Shmittah*, the Sabbatical Year, and *Yovel*, the Year of Jubilee.

The charity that the Torah repetitively demands from us comes to limit our greed, insisting that the wealth given us is intended both to provide our needs and wants but also to provide for the poor, the weak, the ill, the old, and the stranger. The Jewish farmer had to tithe the harvest and the increase of the flocks for them, and had to allow them to come and glean—*leket*, and to take the forgotten sheaves—*shikhacha*. In this way, Torah was teaching him that it is fit and proper to reduce the money available for his own needs and that of his family. To this day, these obligations remain part of modern Israeli agriculture. Furthermore, Jews who are not farmers tithe their incomes for charity either based on the biblical injunction or as a custom that has become enshrined in law. However, Torah's education to restricting greed is not limited to charity. The talmudical sage, Rava, decided in this way the claims of an employer against workers who had broken casks of wine in transit. The owner seized their cloaks as payment, and the court ruled he had to return them. "This is the law?" asked the owner. "Yes," said Rava, "as it is written, and you shall walk in good ways." When the workers who were poor claimed their wages, the court held that the owner had to pay them, even as it is written "and you will go in goodly ways." A later responsum ruled that even though halakhically it was not possible to prevent Shimon from opening a business in competition with the veteran business of Reuven, nevertheless, because the former was rich with few dependents, he, Shimon, was not to compete—*lifnim mishurat hadin* (*Tzemach Tzedeck, Choshen Mishpat*, Section 418, Subsection 111).

Both men and women are enjoined against taking interest from other Jews and are obliged to make interest-free loans to them. There is ample evidence that the halakhah sees nothing intrinsically evil in earning an income from our capital. One may receive rent from an investment in real estate or from the hiring of capital in the form of heavy machinery. However, interest from capital in the form of money is not allowed. "This comes to inculcate in us feelings of kindness and charity, and so refine and spiritually elevate us," writes the *Sefer HaChinuch* (*Mitzvah* 66). For Hirsch, it is to teach us that part of our wealth was given to us for the benefit of others, and, therefore, it is wrong for us to earn interest on that part of our divinely provided wealth.

Jewish charity in all its forms is not simply philanthropy nor is it left to our individual feelings of kindness and mercy. Like all other aspects of Torah life, these charitable acts are enforceable by the *bet din*. "When one does not pay the charitable taxes levied on them by the community, the courts may seize his property even on the eve of the *Shabbat*" (*Shulchan Arukh, Yoreh Deah*, Section 248, Subsections 1–2). The farmer who did not leave the unharvested corners of the field for the poor was punished by corporal punishment just as any person who did not perform a mitzvah. The courts have the power to force a lender to return interest on a loan even when the debtor agreed to pay it.

The courts also have the obligation to prevent us from acting according to the people of S'dom. S'dom not only was devoid of acts of charity but even legislated against them, making egoism and greed national virtues. This was the antithesis of Abraham, and, therefore, taught the sages, "People who do not do favors with their money, it is doubtful that they are descendants of our father, Abraham" (*Talmud Bavli, Pesachim* 112b–113a). One of the most telling of Jewish legal decisions, contrary to the acts of S'dom, is the teaching that make mandatory those acts where "one has a benefit and the other [the owner] suffers no loss" (*Talmud Bavli, Baba Kama* 31a). So, for example, when a person has a field that they would like to sell, the right of first refusal has to be given to those whose fields adjoin to it. Here the seller suffers no loss because the sale is made at market price, yet the buyer, even at that price, has benefits; economies of scale, extension of existing facilities, and so on. Simple and self-evident as this may seem, in real life the last person we would sell our property to is the neighbor who may have an additional benefit for free. So, too, many family-held corporations go public or disintegrate because the shareholders, as often as not family members, refuse to sell their stock privately because this will give the other shareholders a benefit of increased ownership. A sale to an outsider where the neighbor was not given the right of first refusal can be canceled in a *bet din*, because we legally force people to refrain from the actions of S'dom.

Charity and mercy refer to acts beyond our legal obligations. So, commenting on the verse "and do that which is right and good in the eyes of God" (*Devarim* 6:18), S.R. Hirsch writes, "we are not to obey merely the dictates of right and duty explicitly set forth in the Law, but we must let ourselves be guided by the goodness and right which are implicit in this Law . . . .. Where there is a higher positive and good purpose, one should be ready to forego even those rights to which the law entitles one." Throughout the centuries halakhic decisions have been made "beyond the letter of the law" to do "that which is right and good in the eyes of God."

In the *Shmittah* and Sabbatical Year, such righteous and goodly ways lead to the abeyance of the legal right of private ownership. Although the Torah recognizes private property rights and provides protection against fraud, theft, and damage, nevertheless, there is no absolute private property right. On every seventh year, the farmer is enjoined against working the land that is clearly legally his; the profits from that possession not only are also his but are freely available to his workers, to the stranger, the cattle, and the beasts. HaRav Kook writes that the Sabbatical Year is the cure for the social ills and the communal selfishness of the "weekday years" even as *Shabbat* is the cure for our spiritual weaknesses and errors.

It is not, however, only greed that causes social immorality and unethical business practice. Fear of uncertainty is a constant in the real world in which we live. There is political uncertainty, uncertainty regarding our future earning capacity and our future financial needs, and uncertainty regarding our health and that of members of our families. When legitimate means of protecting ourselves against uncertainty such as savings, insurance, or investment seem insufficient, people become aggressive in competition without regard to the effect on others. They will cut corners in their businesses or careers and often turn to fraud or embezzlement. Free market believers argue that market forces provide protection against uncertainty while planned economics come to iron out the disequilibrium in the market and to provide safety nets when problems arise. Our fathers in the desert had similar problems, "and if you shall ask 'What shall we eat in the seventh year since we may not sow nor harvest our crops?'" The Torah's answer to them and to all future generations is clear: "Then I will command My blessing upon you in the sixth year—and until the ninth year [after the harvest of the year following *Shmittah*] you shall eat of the old stores." It is this belief that "the eyes of all [creation] look expectantly to You and You gave them their food [needs] at the proper time" (Ps. 145:15), which enables us to face the uncertainties of life and to take the risks that are part of economic endeavor. *Shmittah* is the ultimate test of this faith in Divine Providence. It is this faith that enables farmers to leave their source of livelihood in the future to the blessing that will come in the sixth year.

As time passes, whether through greed or through the fear of uncertainty, social equilibrium is disturbed, there appear haves and have-nots, and economic injustice grows. There is accumulation of wealth alongside poverty and prosperity alongside oppression. Political systems are built to perpetuate the social divisions, and riot or revolution often become the weapons to rectify the injustice.

Every fifty years, the Torah comes to provide a basis to cure the injustice and the oppression. "The land shall not be sold in perpetuity for the land is Mine, you are only strangers and sojourners with Me" (*VaYikra* 25:23). This concept of the real ownership of wealth, the temporariness of our rights and the guardianship nature of these rights, all make the principles of the *Yovel* far more than the mere redistribution of wealth. This basis is expressed in the three *mitzvot* of *Yovel* mentioned in our *parshah*: the *shofar* at the end of Yom Kippur, the return of the original owners to their possessions, and the release of the slaves. Halakhically, it is not possible today to implement all the laws of *Yovel* in their entirety because this requires Jewish settlement in the whole of the Promised Land according to the original tribal allocation. However, because all of the ills it came to cure still remain with us, it would seem that the *mitzvot* of *Yovel* have a relevance in guiding our present-day social thinking and our search for economic justice.

Yovel is commonly translated as Jubilee, related to the fifty years of seven cycles of *Shmittah* and an additional *Shabbat*. However, the Hebrew root of the word has the connotation of bringing or returning something to its real owner, so Hirsch sees *Yovel* as a "homebringing." This view introduces restitution and regeneration to the concept of *Yovel*, in addition to the liberation of the slaves, actually indentured bondsmen, and the return of property. This correction of the economic and social imbalance not only gave the poor, the dispossessed, and the servants freedom, but also a new status in society that makes possible their reintegration into society. Such a "homebringing" starts with the sounding of the *shofar* at the conclusion of Yom Kippur. The Jewish proclamation of freedom throughout the land (*VaYikra* 25:10) was ushered in by the *Sanhedrin*, the High Court, serving as the representative of the whole nation. This made it part of public policy in addition to the obligations of the individuals during this year. This concept of two parallel obligations, one fueling personal and individual acts and the other an expression of the national policy, is reflected in the difference regarding the counting of the period involved in the *Omer* and that of the *Yovel*. Individuals count the *Omer*, the forty-nine days between the permission to eat of the new barley crop and the first fruits, of *Chag haKatzier*, and the festival of the *Bikkurim*, the forty-nine days between the physical redemption of *Pesach* to the spiritualism of the Revelation on *Shavuot*. However, the obligation to count the cycles to *Yovel* is couched in the singular, making it a duty of the national-social-religious-political representative. Yom Kippur is the Day of Atonement, and at the *Yovel* we sanctify the year of national atonement of inequality and social division.

The return envisaged in the *Yovel* is of the people to the land (verse 10) rather than the land to the people. The *Yovel* is the reestablishment of the social cohesion and community that existed at the dawn of our history with our entrance into the Promised Land. It made no difference whether the returnee was poor or rich so that *Yovel* should not be viewed simply as a redistribution of wealth. Rather it is the integration back into the body public that seems to be important. So, too, perhaps, in our own days, the financial arrangements for the unemployed, the old, the ill or other weaker members of society, important as they are, nevertheless require in addition a concern and attention for their psychological and cultural reentry into society. The slaves freed by the *Yovel* must not be confused with slavery as we understand it in other times or societies. In the Torah system, these were either thieves who could not indemnify owners for the goods stolen or the destitute who had no means of employment or income. If the period for which they had been indentured either voluntarily themselves or at the decision of the court infringed on *Yovel* they had to be freed. For them, *Yovel* symbolized the dignity, freedom, and social equilibrium that formed the basis of the Judaic social system. So Jer. 24:17 prophesied hunger, plague, and the ravages of war as the punishment of the Jewish society that did not release its slaves in the *Yovel*.

The *Yovel* precluded the sale of land substituting lease-holding; the price of such leases depending on the number of years remaining until *Yovel*. Human nature being what it is and the desire to earn profits being the basis of all economics, it is not surprising that the *Yovel* system should provide opportunities for sharp dealing and price gouging. Unscrupulous sellers or buyers could easily exploit the ignorance or the need of the other party to pay less for the lease than that dictated by the period until *Yovel*. This *ona'ah*, price gouging above or below the market price is halakhically forbidden. *Ona'ah* still applies today in buying or selling goods or services and the protection of the *bet din* can be claimed for price fraud or overcharging. A sale may be annulled or the price differential claimed depending on the circumstances. A similar moral problem exists with regard to *Shmittah*. Here as the end of the cycle draws close, creditors will be tempted to refrain from extending loans that would become canceled with the advent of *Shmittah*. Against this selfishness there is little that exhortation or calls to piety can achieve so Hillel in the last days of the second Temple came to protect borrowers and allow them to borrow money; the courts became trustees of the loan that would then not be canceled. This *prosbul*, remains a valid halakhic measure to this day.

Yovel is a macrosolution to problems of social disruption and economic disequilibrium, but it only comes every fifty years. Torah provides a microsolution in the interim period, that of the family redeemer. When the poor were forced to sell their primary source of income, their land, the Torah placed an obligation on their kinsfolk to redeem it from the buyer and return it to them. This not only gave the poor financial assistance but a livelihood, dignity, and a positive role in society. This is considered halakhically the highest form of charity. Rabbi Shimon ben Lakish taught: "Granting a loan to the poor [to start a business] is superior to giving charity [because the shame involved is greater (Rashi)] and creating a business partnership with the poor is superior to everything" (*Talmud Bavli, Shabbat* 63a).

All corrective measures built into the Judaic society structure—*Shmittah*, *Yovel*, and charity—flow from and in turn influence our *Yirat Shamayim* and religious aspirations. "We can know that our behavior is derived from pure and spiritual motives when our innate sense of what is right becomes more exalted as a consequence of its religious inspection. If the moral quality of the individual and the public response [to ethical challenges] is diminished by our religious observance then . . . our supposed piety is of no value" (Avraham Yitzhak HaCohen Kook).

BECHUKOTAI

That Which Brings National Prosperity, Peace, and Happiness

Ever since the dawn of history, people have searched for answers at to what ultimately brings national prosperity, peace, and success. In various philosophies, languages, and religious faiths, mankind has presented fate-accident, physical-natural forces or the ability of the rulers or leaders as the answer. There has been the "if only" school of history, that of economic determinism, or stories of kings and governments. For the Torah, the answer is clear: history is in reality the result either of national adherence to God's laws and commandments or of disobedience to them. This answer is given throughout the Torah in various forms, sometimes in greater clarity and sometimes less so. Twice in the *Chumash*, after the particulars and circumstances of these commandments have been amplified for the nation, the consequences of their actions are clearly spelled out in great and terrifying detail.

In our *sedrah*, the rebuke—*tokhacha*—concludes the *mitzvot* of the Book of Holiness. Later, in *parshat Ki Tavo* in the book of *Devarim*, Moshe's reviews of the Torah framework for the entry into the Promised Land concludes with an even longer *tokhacha*. Often translated as blessings and curses, the *tokhacha* is really neither. It is, however, a clear statement that spiritual and ethical behavior of a society have consequences that express themselves in economic well-being, in social harmony, and in national security. This is a message further reiterated vociferously and constantly throughout the prophetic books of the *Tanach*, and preached throughout the generations of Jewish teaching.

It is significant that the *tokhacha* in its various forms is always couched in the plural, emphasizing that it is not individual welfare that it deals with but with the national destiny. The first paragraph of the *Shma Yisrael* (*Devarim* 7:4–9), dealing with the acceptance of the unity of God and His Kingship, is throughout in the singular; these are religious concepts that devolve on each individual separately. However, the second paragraph concerning the acceptance of His *mitzvot* and the consequences is in the plural; these are expressed in the type of society created, its moral and ethical mores, and the degree to which Torah is the framework for all activity.

For non-Jewish societies, too, there are consequences to the communal behavior. This not only is apparent from the stories in *Bereishit* but also from the prophets. The Jewish prophets spoke of the sins of the nations and their resultant history even as they did in regard to the Jews. In the first chapter, Amos describes the evil actions of Damascus, Gaza (Philistines), Amon, and Moab, and the consequences of fire, war, and exile. In the same chapter, the prophet continues to enumerate the sins of the Northern Kingdom of Israel and that of Judah; in all these cases, the consequences are the same. The refusal of Jonah to fulfill his mission of offering the possibility to repent to the people of Nineveh is clearly retold. The fate of the generations of the Flood was only sealed when they became guilty of theft and robbery (forbidden to Noachides, *Talmud Bavli, Sanhedrein* 108b). S'dom was destroyed in punishment for being sinful in their monetary acts "as it is written (*Devarim* 23:21) and it will be a sin for you," referring to one who delays payment of an oath or withholds the wages of a worker (*Talmud Bavli, Sanhedrin* 109a).

God's justice is without favoritism and unbiased, so a similar yardstick applies to Jews. Jewish loss of political freedom and the resultant exile also flow from their negligence of Divine Commandments. "The First Temple was destroyed [586 B.C.E.] because they sinned in idolatry, sexual immorality, and murder. The Second Temple was destroyed [70 C.E.] even though they were pious and did none of these sins yet, because of the needless hatred among people; because they insisted on receiving all that was legally theirs [not willing to waive their rights as acts of charity or mercy]" (*Talmud Bavli, Baba Metzia* 30a).

The story of Eliyahu and his duel with the priests of the *Ba'al* on Mount Carmel serves well to illustrate this message of material welfare, or otherwise, always being only a consequence of religious-spiritual behavior: "And Eliyahu the Tishbite said to Ahab, 'As the Lord, the God of Israel, liveth, before whom I stand, there shall not be dew nor rain these years, but according to my word'" (Kings 17:1). In the last verse of the preceding chapter, we are told that Hiel of Beth El built Jericho; his firstborn died when he laid the foundations, and the rest of his sons died during the various stages of building until when he finished the gates of the city, his youngest son died. The rabbis explain Eliyahu's causing a drought, to be a response to the claim by Ahab that the deaths of the sons was only a coincidence, a quirk of fate. Ahab argued that they could not be caused by Hiel's contravening the edict of Joshua that threatened just that punishment for the rebuilding of Jericho. "After all," Ahab said, "Moshe, his master, foretold that rain in its season would be a punishment if we do not keep the Torah. I have worshipped all the idols in contradiction to the Torah and my people together with me. Yet the country is at peace, prosperous and awash in plenty caused by years of solid rain fall." For Ahab, who worshipped *Ba'al* and *Ashtarte*, male and female deities of his wife, Jezebel's, people, rain was, despite Moshe and the Torah, a matter of the course of nature, a manifestation of physical laws that have no relationships to observance or otherwise of God's laws. It was to prove otherwise that Eliyahu brought three years of drought. Then he gathered the prophets of *Ba'al*, the teachers of the lack of any connection between religious and moral behavior and prosperity, peace, or human achievements, on Mount Carmel. To the Jews, Eliyahu asks, "How long will you vacillate between God and *Ba'al*?" And he challenged the prophets to bring down fire—in other words to demonstrate what causes natural phenomena. The text in 1 Kings, Chapter 18, describes how Eliyahu, as though in a controlled scientific experiment, seeks to obviate any effect of chance or charlatanism, so making sure that only some Divine Power can bring down fire and by inference also rain or any other natural phenomena. The bullocks chosen for the sacrifice are identical. The priests of *Ba'al* have numerical superiority of four hundred to one with all the statistical advantages of large numbers. They are given all day to call on their god, including even midday with the chance of accidental combustion, a perennial factor in Israel's long hot summers. Then in the late afternoon, with a weak sun, Eliyahu surrounds his altar with a deep, wide trench that fills with water after the offering; the wood and the altar are all drenched. His short prayer is answered with fire that dries up the water, the dust, the altar, and the offering. The people acknowledge the Lord He is God, the Lord He is God, even as we do at the conclusion of Yom Kippur in acceptance of God's judgment of our actions and the consequences of that judgment.

Jewish thinkers throughout the centuries were struck by the fact that all the rewards and punishments for spiritual behavior are material and physical. Rain, crops, herds, harvests, war, peace, freedom, slavery, exile, or sojourn in the Promised Land, plague and pestilence or health and glorious old age. Where is the spiritual bliss, the heavenly rewards, and the eternal life of the soul? Many religions criticized Judaism's presentation of things material as rewards or punishments for human spiritual actions. For the *Ramban*, the emphasis on the material aspects is a stage beyond the belief in the immortality of the soul and its spiritual rewards that are a cardinal tenet of Judaism. "The existence of the soul and its relationship to God is a fact of nature so that it must of necessity return to He Who created it. At the same time, there are actions for which the punishment is *karet*, the soul being cut off. However, it is a special expression of God's mercy that there be material reward and punishment, and so the Torah stresses them." Maimonides sees the material and physical rewards as being the wherewithal necessary to enable people to perform the *mitzvot*. In keeping with this idea, it is interesting to note that in Judaism alone, the founders of the religion were all wealthy. After all, the *mitzvot* are difficult and sometimes impossible to be kept in illness, abject poverty, and constant warfare (*Hilkhot T'shuva*, Chapter 9, *Halakha* 1).

It would seem however, that perhaps the real reason for the Divine Reaction to religious behavior being couched in material rewards and punishments lies in the fact that the *tokhacha* is addressed in the plural to a community and to a nation. National prosperity, national security, and national harmony are the consequences of national morality, national piety, and national obedience to God's teachings. Just as the sin of Adam and Eve in Eden led to the worldwide disturbance of the ecological balance of Creation and the destruction of the harmony originally existing between all the species, so national and international observance of God's law will lead to the restoration of this balance and harmony.

God's mercy tempers the Divine Justice so the *tokhacha*, even when justified, is expressed in stages. At first evil and wrong are met with warnings calling for change. These are expressed by intermittent and temporary droughts, pestilence, or subservience to foreign rule as in the Books of Judges and Kings. However, when Israel acts *bekeri*, as though these are accidents-*mikreh*—or natural phenomena or geopolitical factors, then *bekeri* becomes substituted for Divine Providence and His constant caring. *Bekeri* is a state wherein their prayers, normally the expression of a mutual relationship with God, are no longer of any avail. Israel is thrust into the haphazard, into the turmoil of what appears to be accidents of history, all seemingly devoid of a Divine Plan. The "Face of the Lord" obviously present and in full control, is not longer visible to them. Now the basis of their wealth is destroyed, they become aliens in their own land, and finally there is exile. The Holy Land cannot tolerate unholy acts and vomits Israel out, like the body does to foreign substances. Here, as we have experienced in our long exile, Israel trembles, even though nobody attacks them. There is neither satisfaction with success nor trust in the present. There is darkness at noon, while in the morning Israel prays for the night, but in the night, they wish for the morning—all because of the danger and the fear.

In Jewish tradition, the rebuke, far from being vindictive, or cruel, is moral and charitable. Any alternative would reward national immorality, idolatry, and crime. There would be neither justice nor a Judge seen to be able to punish or reward. Avimelech, king of the Philistine, indignantly challenges Abraham for suspecting that a civilized, rational, and progressive society could kill a man for his wife (*Bereishit* 20:10). Judaism speaking through Abraham answers clearly, "There is not fear of the Lord in this place." It is this fear that creates a normative morality, a morality that exists even when society has other acceptable mores and a morality that exists even when the legal system is powerless to enforce it. The *tokhachot* are the detailed description of the consequences for a nation that has no such fear.

Even if it is sometimes difficult to accept, the *tokhachot* are really an expression of love, as the *Sefer HaChinuch* explains regarding our obligation to rebuke people who do wrong (*Mitzvah* 239). "This results in peace between people since the rebuke is done in private and in a pleasant way; one regrets their actions and the other forgives. However, where this is not done, the hatred and anger remain, to be expressed later in harmful ways. With regard to the evil ones, we see that Absalom did not speak to Amnon [over the incest with Tamar] but later murdered him (2 Sam. 13:22–31)." At the national level, we have numerous examples of where the failure of the leadership to rebuke the people led to war and destruction.

Why was Israel punished when the tribes (Judg. 20) went to fight against Benjamin after the rape of the concubine at Givah? Because the *Sanhedrin* and Pinchas, the High Priest, should have girded their loins . . . and gone to every city in Israel in order to teach Torah. But they did not do so but each one concerned himself with their own interests, occupations, and spiritual growth. . . . [This mistake of the *Sanhedrin* prepared the ground for moral decay that led to the rape] and therefore it is as though they killed the thousands who died in that war." (*Eliyahu Rabbah* 11)

So, too, in the story of Kamtzah and Bar Kamtzah, the leadership of Jerusalem sat at the party to which Kamtzah came uninvited and was chased away in disgrace. They did not rebuke Bar Kamtzah, and, there-

BECHUKOTAI

fore, they contributed to the destruction of Jerusalem when Kamtzah, in revenge, caused the Romans to intervene. It is only an uncaring society that does not recognize the individual's obligation to protest injury, evil, or oppression, and it is only a cruel deity who does not caution against the sins of believers and followers.

Yet the *tokhacha* promises that God will not utterly destroy Israel, even if this is justified. Always a remnant is left, and always there is the ultimate ingathering and return to the people, land, and God relationship.

Our rabbis taught that *im* at the beginning of the *tokhacha* must not be translated as "if" but rather "if only," God's fervent wish that Israel should keep Torah and enjoy the consequences of such behavior.

SONG OF THE WANDERINGS

INTRODUCTION TO BAMIDBAR

Ramban

This book presents the commandment regarding the *Ohel Moed*. It follows the laws of the *korbanot* and those of purity and impurity that appear in *VaYikra*. Now the Tabernacle in the desert is hedged around with restrictions just as was *Har Sinai* when His Glory rested thereon [at the revelation of *Matan Torah*]. There He commanded (*Shmot* 19:12), "And you shall set bounds to the people saying, 'Beware not to go up to the mountain nor even touch its border, whosoever touches the mountain shall surely be put to death.'" Regarding the *Mishkan* it is written (*Bamidbar* 1:51), "The stranger [nonpriests or nonlevites] that will draw close shall be put to death." Furthermore, in *Bamidbar* 4:20, we read, "but they shall not go in to see when the holy things are covered, lest they die." Similarly at Sinai, it is stated (*Shmot* 19:21), "Warn the people lest they break through towards God in order to see; many of them may perish." Here (in *Bamidbar*) He commanded, "You shall keep the charge of the Sanctuary . . . that there be no anger on the children of Israel" (Num. 18:5). Regarding Sinai, it is stated, "And the priests who come near to the Lord [to serve] shall think of their being sanctified otherwise God may send destruction among them" (*Shmot* 19:22).

The Tabernacle moving in the midst of the camp was a kind of Sinai, on which the Torah had been given—accompanying them on all their journeys—demanding behavior appropriate to His Presence but also assuring them of His Presence even in the midst of their impurity.

"The order of the encampments [according to the tribes], the distance between the people and the Tabernacle, only the priests being allowed to come near . . . all this to enhance the glory even as our sages said, 'The palace of the King surrounded by sentinels.'" This whole book is concerned with temporary enactments for their stay in the wilderness and also with the miracles performed for them. It tells how He began to deliver their enemies to them and how the Land of Israel is to be divided among the Tribes [after the entry and conquest].

BAMIDBAR

To Be Counted

Literally, the title of our *parshah* would read "in the desert," and, indeed, the whole of the book that this *parshah* introduces deals with the wanderings in the desert from the time of the Revelation. However, in non-Jewish literature it is known as Numbers, because of the census taken in this *parshah*. Usually a census is taken for fiscal purposes, military or defense needs, or to ascertain proper voter rolls. Although commentators such as Abarbanel did indeed see the biblical census as often performing a secular function, nevertheless, mainstream thinking is that they served additional spiritual purposes. In their perspective, the method of counting the people, the language determining just who was to be counted, and the circumstances pertaining to each census, provide religious and spiritual lessons for Jews throughout the ages even in our own days.

Each of the musterings of Israel in the desert occurs at a significant or traumatic period. First there is the statement of the seventy souls who come down to Egypt. No special method of counting is noted. It is almost a little footnote to history: an insignificant family that wandered down from Canaan to Egypt, the granary of the ancient world, ostensibly in search of food during a famine. Yet the biblical text is careful to count them, each one by name. Not a band of disciples, but rather an extended family built around twelve brothers, each one with his wife and children, and they were not a band of wandering shepherds, but rather the expression of a Divine Covenant, destined to be refined in slavery and oppression to emerge as a kingdom of priests. Of such importance is the entry of this family into history that the text repeats, years later, the roll call of names and recalls their exact number. To teach us, said the rabbis, that despite the pressure to conform to the host society, despite the blandishments of a powerful and civilized culture, and despite the weakness of their numbers, Reuven, Shimon, and Levi, and so on remained just that, maintaining their language, names, and distinctive dress. They continued to be counted as the sons of Israel, determining a pattern that their descendants were to follow over thousands of years. Each person numbered as part of a family with faith to follow their destiny to Sinai, to become a holy nation.

Six hundred thousand foot soldiers and their families left Egypt and encamped at the foot of Sinai. In contrast to all the other recordings of the encampments in the desert, here the text is written in the singular leading our rabbis to connect "all 600,000 foot soldiers and their families camped as one person, with one mission, one heart; whereas all the other encampments were marked by grumbling and contention" (*Mechilta*). However, they did not stand alone at Sinai. Moses in his farewell speech (*Devarim* 29:13–14) proclaims that even all the untold future generations of Jews were counted among the multitude that stood at Sinai, obligating them also to witness the Revelation of God's Law and to be partners to an eternal covenant. Yet, that Revelation was marred by the sin of the Golden Calf when Israel proclaimed "these are your gods, O Israel." Shocked by their own sin, the people repented and demonstrated this by the outpouring of free will offerings that they brought for the Sanctuary: a sanctuary that was to place Divine Presence in the midst of their camp, in the midst of their daily lives, with all the temptations and the pious deeds involved. The trauma of the sin, penance, and forgiveness was registered in a numbering of the people after the sin of the Calf. Here the Torah expresses clearly the concept of the individual, the community, and the Sanctuary.

There is no passive membership in the Jewish people or in Judaism and so any numbering cannot be expressed by officials making their rounds and collecting information. Rather, each individual is required to perform an act, required to ransom the soul, as it were, when being counted. In Chapter 30 of *Shmot*, Moses is commanded that the numbering of the people is to be through each individual paying an annual tax of half a shekel to the *Mishkan* (later to the Temple). This makes the Sanctuary, not a holy institution unrelated to the average person, but rather a religious nerve center dependent on the active participation of each individual. At the same time, the importance of each individual is demonstrated by the participation in the national holy endeavor. Poor and rich alike were obligated to give their half shekel, neither more nor less. Each person on their own is in reality only a half an entity; in marriage we unite two people to become a new unity, and so, in the census, two people, each half a shekel, half a soul, become one. This concept of individual fulfillment, through sharing or through bearing part of the social costs of the community, is characteristic of Jewish life in all centuries and in all countries.

The Torah does not allow this act of membership to become merely the fulfillment of a citizen's fiscal obligation. When giving the law to Moses, the text reads "this they shall give." "This," said the rabbis, refers to God actually pointing with a finger to a vision of a coin, a coin of fire, teaching us that the shekel was an obligation to be fulfilled with warmth, energy, and enthusiasm. Religion is often considered the realm of slaves, of the weak, of innocents, of the poor, and the dispossessed—all those with little if anything to lose by following a religion. However, giving the shekel, the act of membership in Judaism, is only for those over twenty years old. Only those with the vigor and power of adulthood, faced with the temptations and challenges of real life and the ability to manage them, are the basis of this holy community. This idea is a reflection of the ruling of Maimonides that prophecy is vouched only to those possessing physical vigor, wealth, and great intellectual powers (*Yesodei HaTorah*, Chapter 7, *Halakhah* 7).

All the half shekels received were used only for the *korbanot tzibbur*, the national offerings. Each year in Temple times, the collection and thereby census of the half shekel was made during the month of Adar, preceding the *Pesach* festival. For this reason, the portion from *parshat Ki Tisa*, describing the obligation of the half shekel is read in the synagogue on the *Shabbat* before *Rosh Chodesh Adar*. The use of the half shekel is an additional testimony to the national-communal character of Judaism predicating that the *korbanot*, the drawing close to God, was not an individual act but rather one whereby all the individuals in Israel coalesced into a communal personality. In the Tabernacle, the first half shekels were used for the silver sockets of the wooden poles that upheld the Sanctuary; a Sanctuary resting on the communal census.

Now in our *parshah* after completing the Sanctuary and being taught the *mitzvot* of holiness that make it possible for the Sanctuary to be a meeting place between people and God, Israel had to be counted as a prelude to their journey to the Promised Land. "Just as their faces are not the same so too their thoughts differ" (*Talmud Bavli, Berachot* 58a). Each individual has different strengths, talents, and ideas—each individual had to demonstrate his willingness to be counted and be considered a member of the army of the Lord. "Take the sum total of the whole congregation of the Children of Israel, in their families, in the house of their fathers . . . by their head count . . . everyone that goes out to battle" (*Bamidbar* 1:2–3).

Each individual has a specific expression and search for holiness and spirituality. These differences enrich and diversify the nation's march to holiness and need to be counted. Yet this is not enough as people do not exist only for or by themselves. Individualism without roots, devoid of mutual obligations and lacking a common past or future, can be barren and even destructive. So the individuals are counted by *mishpachot*—rooted in the Hebrew "to join oneself"—and as a gathered mass, in their families. The *mishpachot* are linked to *batim* (houses), descended from common ancestors, and according to their tribes, ultimately coalescing into the whole congregation. Families, tribes, and the nation have memories, personalities, and a future that is something more than the sum total of the individuals that constitute them. A *minyan* has a spirituality over and beyond the ten that constitute it; they are an *eidah*, a congregation. So there is a *K'lal Yisrael* of individuals, families, and congregations that may not be aware of each other, yet, throughout the centuries subscribing to a common faith are destined to find expression in a national society in a Promised Land. It is because of the wide differences between individuals that constitute *K'lal Yisrael*, the varying moral and ethical standards and wide gamut of knowledge and commitment, that there is a mitzvah to love everyone of Israel, *ahavat Yisrael*. It is a Chassidic custom to declare before prayers that one is about to take on oneself this mitzvah, making the prayers like the Sanctuary, more than an individual experience but rather that of *K'lal Yisrael*, by its families, *batei avot*, and its tribes.

These spiritual overtones and concepts inherent in the numbering by shekels seem to have been overlooked or violated by the census taken by King David; one that was punished by a severe plague in which seventy thousand died (2 Sam. 24:1–15). *Rashi*, the *Ramban*, and other commentators on *parshat Ki Tisa* teach that the census by *shekalim*, an atonement for the soul, minimized the jealousy and hatred on the part of the surrounding nations, following a public census that would trumpet the size and power of the people of Israel. The Talmud (*Berachot* 62b) saw this as the sin of David; lacking the atonement of the shekel, the census is not a blessing but a plague. "Rabbi Elazar said in the name of Rabbi Yose ben Zimra, Moses numbered Israel in the desert for a purpose, preparing the march from Sinai and later prior to the entry into the Land of Israel, and therefore they were blessed. David, however, numbered them without a purpose, there being no war or national objective in the offering, and therefore they were punished" (*Bamidbar Rabbah* 213b). Abarbanel sees the sin in the census of David as flowing from the senseless pride and arrogance that caused the king to count the people. Not war, not a national purpose, not even a fiscal need led to the census, but simply the pleasure of a ruler in the knowledge of his power and the size of his empire. Human history, Jewish and general, is replete with monuments, war and state policies, similarly based not only on the pride of the rulers but also of the nations relishing their economic power, numerical supremacy, and the size of their empires. Counting by the half shekel, with its message of the nature of each individual, rich or poor, its teaching of communal responsibility and identity, and the concept of giving a ransom for one's soul, would seem to minimize this arrogance and pride.

NASO

Ascetism is Holiness?

The history of the world and the development of civilizations reflects to a degree that is perhaps often overlooked, the way in which the conflict between materialism and spirituality has been adjudicated. There is and always has been a seemingly never-ending litany of evils flowing from or contributing to human physical appetites and needs—greed, envy, lust, war, oppression, crime. At the same time, speech, intelligence, sparks of holiness, and the image of God that resides in men and women militate against all of them and call out for their defeat. Individuals and nations, religions and philosophies have always been called on to show how it is possible to prevent being swept away by the materialism and physical, and more importantly, how spirituality and morality is to triumph over the evil that these bring.

Perhaps the most common solutions have been those that throughout the ages have sought to flee from the world and its temptations. The desert, monasteries, celibacy, asceticism, and communalization of economic resources have all been offered as panaceas for the spiritual challenge of the material and physical. The human body and its needs, as well as the physical wherewithal essential for existence in the real world, become sinful; humanity is guided instead to aspire to an otherworldly, ethereal future. Physical pleasures are denied completely by the spiritual elite or denigrated as necessary evils for inferior or weaker people.

All these systems, movements, and messages of escapism and asceticism as viable solutions to the spiritual-material and physical struggle are inconsistent with Judaism. Torah comes to place sex, food, property, aesthetics, and human relations all within a framework of permitted or forbidden actions, times, or individuals. Everything in God's world is created good and beautiful for mankind to use, enjoy, and benefit from. Yet nothing is unlimited so that we are able and obliged to sanctify ourselves with that which is permitted to us. At the same time, that which is forbidden can be denied by ordinary human beings, without destroying or deforming God's world. No limits or demands are placed by Torah that contradict human nature; they only come to purify and spiritualize that nature. "One who says what's mine is yours and yours is mine [destroying the concept of private property, and the individual economic motivation] is an *am ha'aretz* [not evil but ignorant because this is contrary to human nature and therefore not only not viable but often results in greater evil than that which the idea itself came to correct]" (*Avot*, Chapter 5, *Mishnah* 10). It is this balance between material and spiritual, between limitation and enjoyment, and between the physical human and the ability within that self-same physicality to become holy, within which the laws of the *Nazir* must be viewed.

> If one should say, "Because envy, lust, arrogance and similar pressures are evil and destroy people, I will separate myself from them and follow asceticism," and then refuses to eat meat or drink wine, remains celibate, does not want to live in a pleasant house and wear pleasant clothes, preferring sackcloth and coarse wool and other ascetic actions as do the gentile priests—this is a wrong way and it is forbidden to follow it. (*Mishneh Torah, Hilkhot Deot*, Chapter 3, Halakhah 1)

We see from the sin offering that the Nazirite has to bring, that asceticism is considered a sin. After all, everything that God created in His world is beautiful, pleasant, and beneficial to mankind. Whenever our physical senses use or enjoy the fruits or benefits of this creation, we bless He Who created them. So the Chassidic masters taught that one who refuses to enjoy them or rejects completely the human phys-ical needs, he is, so to speak, rejecting the gifts of the Creator, and here-in lies the sin. Recently, in a discussion regarding the law of *Orlah*, whereby fruit may not be eaten before the fourth year of a tree's life, a similar idea was expressed to me. Dwarf deciduous trees have been developed with a life span of about four years but bearing fruit already in the first year. Over and above the halakhic discussion as to whether *Orlah* applies, one authority pointed out, that if the fruit would be forbidden, we would be unable to partake of that which God gave to us.

The halakhic ruling of Maimonides previously quoted is rooted in the teachings of the Sages of the Talmud: "Rabbi Elazar *HaKappar* said [the verse in *Bamidbar* 6:11] 'And shall atone for his sin of his soul' [this refers to the *Nazir*] who denied wine to himself. How much more so does it apply to those who embrace asceticism; from this we learn that one who fasts [more than is required halakhically] is to be called sinful" (*Talmud Bavli, Nedarim* 10a). "It is forbidden to dwell in a city that does not have public baths or gardens. A person will be held liable [in future judgment] for those tasty things [and that are permitted by the Torah] that they did not eat" (*Talmud Yerushalmi, Kiddushin*, Chapter 4, *Halakhah* 12). The *Yerushalmi* also teaches, "Are those things [in food, sex, money, etc.] that Torah forbids not sufficiently severe for you, that you have to wish to forbid even those things that are permitted" (*Nedarim*, Chapter 9, *Halakhah* 1).

In accordance with these views opposing asceticism, there are even *mitzvot* which are temporarily in abeyance, in those cases where their observance entails bodily suffering or even physical discomfort. These include, for example, sitting in the *sukkah* during the rain or the tefillin in cases of severe headache.

A young chassid told his Master that to be pure and pious, he was always dressed in white, rolled half naked in the snow, slept on a straw pallet, and ate only bran and drank water. The *Admor* went to the window, pointed to the paddock and said, "See my white horse pursues the same path to piety."

Nevertheless, the Nazirite vows are a legitimate part of the *mitzvot*, and the Torah calls such men and women *kadosh*. *Nezer*, from the word that Nazirite is drawn, means crown, and the growth of unshorn locks is seen as a glory. "Said Rabbi Elazar, 'One who fasts is called holy [according to *Bamidbar* 6:5]. If such a person is considered holy even though his asceticism is limited, how much more holy are those who deny all pleasures and benefits to themselves'" (*Talmud Bavli, Ta'anit* 11a). The *Sifri* from the above verse, "[The *Nazir*] is holy to God," wishes to teach that this holiness refers to the actual body of the *Nazir*, thus making the person actually a being of holiness. However, there is no ascetic motivation in the institution of the *Nazir* nor are these vows an attempt to destroy human lusts or desires. Rather they are part of the search for the holiness to be expressed within these self-same desires.

Maimonides writes,

> One who takes an oath [like the *Nazir*] to provide a physical basis for spirituality or to improve their actions, is praiseworthy and pleasant. For example, a person who is gluttonous and vows to deny meat [symbol of extravagant eating] for a year or two or; one who is an alcoholic and vows to refrain from drinking for a long time [except for *kiddush* and *havdalah* that are obligatory] or permanently; those who have a passion to enrich themselves or are driven to pursue wealth [the Sages included in this category people who gamble, those who lend money at interest, and those who buy and sell the produce of the *Shmittah* year] and take an oath to refuse to accept gifts or to deceive through legal methods; so too the vain ones who take such pride in their physical beauty and [in order to learn humility] take the oath of *Nazir*; and all other similar cases [where one takes an oath to refrain from anything that may lead to nonperformance of *mitzvot* (*Shulchan Arukh, Yoreh Deah*, Section 203, Subsection 6)] whose purpose is to enhance the worship of God, these oaths are what the sages referred to (*Mishnah Avot*, Chapter 3, *Mishnah* 13) "oaths are a fence for restraint." (*Mishneh Torah, Haflah, Hilkhot Nedarim*, Chapter 13, *Halakhah* 23)

These rulings of Maimonides puts the *Nazir* in its perspective of an aid to improved religiosity and enhanced sanctity, without destroying Judaism's balance between materialism and spirituality.

The *Sefer HaChinuch* expresses this balance clearly:

> People are a creation of the merger of materialism and spirituality [lit., wisdom]. If it were not for the Divine Desire that the world should be developed through this merger, our souls would serve Him as do the angels. However, the Divine Desire requires us to pursue material interests otherwise there would be no existence for this world. Such pursuit must of necessity divert our strength and our efforts from Divine worship and from spirituality. Nevertheless, because of our spirituality, it is laudable that, whenever it is possible, we should restrict our material pursuits [both those for profit and for pleasure] and devote ourselves to the worship of our Creator. This without entirely neglecting the work of the house [material and physical existence] or destroying it, because the King—God desired this existence as well. (*Mitzvah* 374)

This paraphrase of the *Sefer HaChinuch*'s understanding of the ideology underlying the *Nazir*'s oath is a reaffirmation of the balance between material-physical life and the demands and possibilities of our spiritual religious characters. This is not a balance or compromise, but rather a statement of the integration that typifies the human being.

The confession accompanying the first fruit offering, *bikkurim*, expresses thanks for the economic bounty granted to the Jewish farmer. In its conclusion, however, the confession also restates this material-spiritual balance. For the Torah, economic wealth serves two purposes: the use of the owners of the wealth and their families, and also the benefit of the poor landless and economically weak. "[So] and you shall rejoice with all the good which your God has given to you and your family, you and the Levite and the stranger" (*Devarim* 25:11).

BEHA'ALOTCHA

Prayer in Trembling and Prayer in Joy

Prayer is a major focus of Jewish Divine Worship and is an expression of the relationship between human beings and God. Sometimes this worship is in fear and trembling at His awesomeness, and sometimes it is an expression of the Divinity that is in us as partners in His Creation. Sometimes prayer brings down holiness from Heaven, but at other times this holiness rises from the earth through prayer. Sometimes prayer is an expression of a spontaneous outpouring of religious ecstasy whereas at other times, this is a disciplined response based on the Divine Will and halakhic forms. There are periods in the history of both individuals and communities when prayer is a permanent factor; at other periods, study or actions take precedence, albeit without ever one of these negating the other as a way to God.

At the very beginning of our *parshah*, the injunction for Aharon, the high priest, to light the seven-branched menorah comes to put these issues into perspective. It is fitting that this perspective should come after the many chapters devoted to the building of the *Mishkan*, the clothes and duties of the Levites and the Cohanim and the *korbanot*. In this way, guidance is given to some basic aspects of that Divine Worship for which the *Mishkan* was built.

When Aharon, the head of the tribe of Levi, saw that all the other princes of Israel brought sacrifices at the dedication of the *Mishkan* except his tribe, he was dismayed. Perhaps this was a sign that he had not been forgiven for the sin of the Golden Calf, and, therefore, his tribe alone did not participate in the dedication. Said *HaKadosh Baruch Hu* to Moses, "Tell Aharon not to be dismayed or afraid. He is destined for greater things. The *korbanot* [as typified by the offerings of the princes] are dependent on the existence of the Temple [as is the incense offered by the priests]; both ceased with the destruction and the resultant exile, but the kindling of the lights are [to be observed] forever. So, too, the blessings [of Israel by the Cohanim] also are to be observed forever" (*Midrash Rabbah, Bamidbar,* Chapter 15).

Ramban links the candelabra to the lights of Chanukah that we kindle in honor of the rededication of the Temple by the Maccabees, the descendants of Aharon, the high priest. Others have taught that our *Midrash* refers to the *Shabbat* candles lit in our homes every week. The *Midrash* understood that Aharon was also promised that the priestly blessings would also survive the Temple. In the Sanctuary the blessings were not answered by "Amen," which is the usual response of a blessing that is appropriated by those who hear it and makes it as though they themselves had said it. So, Hirsch points out that these blessings (*Bamidbar* 6:26–28) went beyond those assembled at the Sanctuary and far beyond the Temple. They were meant to include all the nation, indeed, all humanity. *Yisah* (uplifted), *Yair* (light), and *Yevarechecha* (bless you), the three components of the priestly blessings, correspond to the ideas that the Sanctuary comes to teach. Material blessings and mental enlightenment are brought together under the will of God revealed for the uplifting of humanity. These ideas are expressed eternally through the priestly blessings included in our synagogue ritual. In our homes, every *Shabbat*, we bless our children with this same priestly blessing. Indeed, the lights and the blessings of Aharon live on even in exile and even after the destruction of the Sanctuary. They must have, therefore, implications relevant for the Divine Worship of all generations.

The *korbanot* of the *Nesi'im* were not the result of a halakhic obligation nor of a Divine Injunction, rather they were the expression of a religious experience at the erection of the House of the God Who dwelt in their midst. In their ecstasy, they sought for something spontaneous, something beyond the forms and requirements of the ritual of the *Mishkan*. Such spontaneity and individual expressiveness often leads to high forms of spirituality and are pleasing to God, so the *korbanot* were accepted. Similarly, at the redemption at the Red Sea, Israel was carried away by their religiosity and ecstasy so what was vouchsafed to an ordinary maidservant was not realized by the prophet Yechezkiel. So, unbidden, they sang praise to the Lord on the sea, and their freely expressed emotions are part of our daily prayers of praise. At the dedication of the *Mishkan*, Aharon was concerned that perhaps he was spiritually inferior or lacking a religious standard because he did not follow the spontaneity of the *Nesi'im*. However, our Sages taught that "one who does that which is commanded and obligatory is preferred to one who does acts for which there is no Divine commandment." The first person needs to conquer his *yetzer harah* to do those things with which he disagrees or to refrain from doing things he considers beneficial or pleasant. Therefore, the reward is greater (*Tosaphot Kiddushin* 31a).

There is a well-known halakhic dictum, that a person's agent is considered to be identical to the principal. So, taught the *Avnei Nezer*, one who fulfills Divine Commandments becomes identified with the source, while those religious forms or acts that one follows or performs from our own desires or spiritual goals are not really expressions of God's will, which is the purpose of Divine Worship. Furthermore, it is not always possible to induce ecstasy nor to maintain self-induced spirituality over long periods; there will therefore be periods or situations where we will be devoid of contact with the Divine. So, Aharon's lighting of the menorah, solely in accord with God's commandment, resulted in the lights of Chanukah and of *Shabbat* that persist long after the destruction of the Sanctuary and over long years of exile.

For the mystics, the *Nesi'im* are considered, as is the king, as being the heart of the people, whereas Aharon and the priests are the brain or the knowledge of Torah. Shall we then see this knowledge as being devoid of heart and the worship of the priests as devoid of ecstasy, spontaneity, or religiosity? No, rather only that Torah should guide the spontaneity and the mind balance the heart. So, see how the wick draws the oil to feed the flame. The Maccabees were able to turn the light of their loyalty to God to defeat the Greeks and reconsecrate His Temple. The menorah gives light to the day adding to spirituality, but in the night, it dispels the fear and despair that can lead to disillusion or even prevent Divine Worship. The priestly blessings of peace are reflected in the lights of *Shabbat*, that day that brings peace to both the physical struggle and the spiritual difficulties of the weekdays. In regard to the menorah, Aharon is commanded *leha'alot*, to raise up the light, a phrase that is never used in regard to any other of the priestly duties. Here the purpose is to raise up the spiritual consciousness of Israel. King Solomon in building the Temple made the windows so that the light flowed out toward the people: a parallel example of how wisdom and Torah light the way for Divine Worship.

Moses receives revelation in broad daylight and perhaps this refers to the written law revealed at Sinai. The lights of wisdom of the menorah may be compared with the oral law, the study of which shows how the written word is to be fulfilled. Judaism's insistence that this Torah study, one way of worshipping and drawing closer to God, is both open and obligatory for all people, is parallel in the talmudical decision that the lighting of the menorah is not considered a priestly function, but is acceptable even when performed by laymen (*Talmud Bavli, Yoma* 24b). So, too, ordinary average people kindle the lights of Chanukah and of *Shabbat* and bless their children with the priestly blessings.

Although the lights are the exception to the rule that all functions in the Temple are restricted to Cohanim, still even these have an important message for Divine Worship by laity. Normally, the high priest was clothed in blue, red, and gold garments when making *korbanot*. However, during the *Yom HaKippurim* service, he wore only white garments. The former colors were those of the *Heichal*, the Sanctuary, positive indicators of achieving an ideal physical and spiritual Jewish life. White, the color of purity was that of the forecourt to the *Mishkan*, the lowly and simple beginning of the spiritual, ethical, and moral development. This contrast is reflected in the talmudic discussion as to whether the *shofar* on Rosh Hashanah could be a simple straight ram's horn or curved and spiral (*Talmud Bavli, Rosh Hashanah* 26b). The *Shem MiShmuel* explained that there are two ways to worship, and this discussion is concerned with which of them is specific to Rosh Hashanah. It is possible to view people in their divinity, with all their spiritual and moral power having contact with God. There is, however, also all that is spiritually frail, negative, and ungodlike within us, far removed from God and almost unworthy of His attention. The former is symbolized by the simple straight *shofar*, suitable for all the days of the year. Here we approach God with all that is positive and noble in us. The curved and bent *shofar* is our humility, awe and trembling at the vast distance between our reality and the Throne of His Glory. On the day that he is proclaimed by us as King of the Universe, on the day of His judgment, and on this Day of Awe, this is the appropriate worship.

Mortal men and women can only even presume to approach He Who spoke and the World Was, only if mercy and kindness are vouchsafed from Heaven. The *shofar* of Rosh Hashanah is curved and bent, an entreaty from human beings with all their imperfections and weakness for just that Divine Mercy and Divine Kindness. However, cognizance of our mortality, weaknesses, and unholy behavior can bring us to depression, despair, and guilt, fertile ground for even greater evil and immorality because after all, everything is lost and beyond salvation. Therefore, it is essential to restore people to the sparks of divinity inherent in them and to the realization of their ability to achieve holiness and to restore the balance between our dual nature in order to enable us to worship and serve Him as He intended. So, first the *shofar* is sounded to call us to recognize our weakness and repent, and God in his Infinite Mercy accepts our prayers. Then during the *mussaf* prayer, the *shofar* is sounded in a second series. Now it is possible to use all that is positive, divine, and spiritual in us in His service.

SHELACH

Sanctifying His Name

If the purpose of mankind is to serve God, then the mission of the Jewish People is *Kiddush Hashem*, to sanctify His Name. This devolves at all times and under all conditions upon every Jewish individual man and woman, is expressed in the acts of the community and is demonstrated by the history of the Nation.

Twice during their wanderings in the desert Israel is threatened with destruction as punishment for a traumatic sin: the first time with the Golden Calf and later by refusing to enter the Promised Land because of the false report brought to them by the spies. Because Israel had rejected it as if it were the Land that came as part of the promise to the Patriarchs, Moses could not use the merits of Abraham, Isaac, and Jacob in pleading for forgiveness in the latter case as he did in the sin of the Golden Calf. In both cases, however, he could and did use the cause of *Kiddush HaShem*. "Now if you shall kill this people as one man, the nations which have heard of Your Fame will say 'Because He was unable to bring the People into the Land which He swore to give unto them therefore He has slain them in the Wilderness. And now I beg of You, let the power of the Lord be great . . . slow to anger, abundant in loving kindness, forgiving iniquity and transgression'" (*Bamidbar* 14:15–17). In *Shmot* (32:12), Moses had argued that if He would destroy Israel, the Egyptians would say that it was only evil intent against Israel that motivated all the Divine Miracles that accompanied the Exodus, and not Redemption.

What difference does it make what the Egyptians, Canaanites, or others think? Surely their opinion cannot be a motive for Divine Behavior. To these questions of the *Ramban*, he and other commentators concern themselves with the answer of *Kiddush HaShem*. In both cases, the Name would be desecrated, His universal power denied, and so would be awareness of His intervention in human history. Mankind would fall back into paganism, comparing the relative strengths of gods of Israel, Canaan, Egypt, and so on. Not destroying Israel, therefore, not only is out of *chesed* and benevolence, but a prevention of *Hillul HaShem*. The public perception of God's continuous miraculous protection of Israel, and the widespread evidence of His continuous kindness to us, make His Name great and sanctify Him in the eyes of all the nations.

In the same way the acts of individual Jews either desecrate His Name or contribute toward *Kiddush HaShem*. The eyes of the world identify each one of us both with Israel and its God, so that our behavior in all spheres and at all times never remains simply personal or individual, but represents both the nation and God Himself.

So, too, all the scholars rank *Kiddush HaShem* as a positive mitzvah, independent of sex, age, or time, and *Chillul HaShem* as a negative one (*Mishneh Torah, Hilkhot Yesodei HaTorah*, Chap. 5, Halakhah 1). *Chillul HaShem* is a sin for which *Tshuvah*, sacrifices, Yom Kippur, and even physical suffering do not atone. After all of these, only death brings atonement (*Sefer HaChinuch*, mitzvah 296).

"Neither shall you profane My Holy Name but I will be sanctified among the children of Israel" (*VaYikra* 22:32–33). Hirsch explains this verse as telling us that each time we refuse to devote so much as an impulse of our being, one iota of our aspirations, of His Holy Will, we profane His Holy Name, and our example becomes propaganda to demonstrate the impotence of the Name of God that rests upon us.

Not only Aharon and Moses remained outside the Promised Land, but indeed the whole present exile is prolonged because of *Hillul HaShem*.

"Rather they [the Jews] should sanctify themselves even in those

SHELACH

[economic and commercial] acts which are permitted to them, even as it is written "and the remnant of Israel shall neither do evil nor defraud in speech nor shall there be found deceit on their lips." [Then] when God redeems us, the nations will declare in justice does He redeem them since they are people of truth. However, if their dealings are false, then the nations will say "The Holy One Blessed be He deals unjustly in that He chooses thieves and deceivers [and so the Divine Name will decree a continuation of the exile" [*Semag Hilkhot Hashavat Aveidah*].

Abbaye says,

> the Name of Heaven should become beloved because of your actions [as when] a person learns Chumash and Mishnah and Talmud and he deals with people in gentleness [Rabbenu Chananael substitutes and he deals with people in the marketplace in justice] but someone who learns . . . but does not deal with people honestly in business and his relationships with people are not based on kindness [gentleness] then what will people say? Woe to so and so that he learned Torah! Woe to his father who taught him! Woe to his rabbi who taught him! . . . See how corrupted his actions are, see how ugly his ways are. (Talmud Bavli Yoma 86a)

The concept of *Hillul HaShem* is derived from the word *Hallal* (empty space). It is as though the guilty person shows, God forbid, that the space he stands in is a country devoid of Him (*Nefesh HaChaim Sha'ar* 3, Chap 8). Difficult as it is to comprehend perhaps, it is precisely "because you trespassed against Me in the midst of the Children of Israel . . . at the waters of the strife at Kadesh . . . because you did not sanctify Me in the midst of children of Israel" (*Devarim* 32:51) that Moses and Aharon were not allowed to enter the Promised Land, and the former died on Mount Nebo and the latter on Mount Hor. Many opinions and thoughts have been suggested as to what the trespass was in smiting the rock instead of talking to it to draw water. Because both would have been miraculous, there needed to be a special sanctification of His Name in the speech to the rock. "Moses and Aharon would have taught the people that in time of need for rain [or for that matter for any of their material needs] they should pray and their prayers will be answered. Such prayer and its results are as much evidence of God's power over nature and His benevolence as are the public miracles such as drawing water by smiting a rock" (*HaEmek Devar, Bamidbar* 20).

Not only is *Hillul HaShem* halakhically a negative precept, but throughout the centuries, the autonomous Jewish communities introduced legislation to prevent or minimize it and to punish infractions of such legislation. Two of the numerous such enactments can show the communal concern and spiritual negative of *Hillul HaShem*.

[Concerning those Jews involved in the trade of counterfeit coins . . . instead of "The remnant of Israel does no evil," they [the gentiles] say, "Where is the God of this nation [thus demeaning Him]? . . . anyone found engaged in such activities shall be punished by Heaven [and] it shall be forbidden for any Jew to marry his daughter, to give him lodging to call him to the Torah, or to allow him to fulfill any religious function" (*Synod of the German Communities*, Frankfurt 1603).

"If a bankrupt debtor should offer to make a settlement with the creditors [instead of paying them all in full] then a ban is to be pronounced against him [because of the resultant anti-Semitism and *Hillul HaShem*]. For a whole year . . . unfit to take an oath, not called to the Torah until all the debts are paid. The creditors may take away the [festive] clothes he has made for his wife [in addition to their halakhic right to] all personal possessions, any jewels and so on except for his tefillin, a bed, food for thirty days etc. [in order to prevent the debtor from enjoying his former standard of living at the expense of the creditors]" (Council of Four Lords, Lublin, March 1624, see Beer HaGolah, Choshen Mishpat, Section 97, subsection 21 for a halakhic support for such a ban).

The positive *mitzvot* of *Kiddush HaShem* is as obligating and as fundamental as avoiding *Hillul HaShem*.

"You shall love the Lord your God with all your heart, with all your soul, and with all your strength" (*Devarim* 6:5). "With all your strength" comments Rashi, "with all your possessions for there are those who love their wealth more than their lives." So *Kiddush HaShem*, the expression of this love, is shown through the acquisition of wealth. Shimon ben Shetach sent his disciples to Ashkelon to buy a donkey from an idolater. When they returned, they found a jewel in the halter. They rejoiced, seeing this as an act of Divine Providence rewarding their teacher. He, however, insisted that they return the jewel. When they did so, the idolater exclaimed, "Blessed be He the God of Shimon ben Shetach" (*Talmud Yerushalmi, Bava Metziah*, Chapter 6, *Halakha* 5).

"With all your soul," said Rabbi Akiva, "even if He demands your life." Halakhically, every time a Jew is killed simply for being a Jew, this is considered *Kiddush HaShem*. Rabbi Akiva himself died with the words of *Shema* on his lips, sanctifying God's Name with his life. Over the centuries, countless Jews have fulfilled this *Kiddush HaShem*. Life in Judaism is precious, and in many instances, preservation of life overrules religious observance. Yet there are circumstances where Torah takes precedence even over life. "The whole House of Israel [men and women] are commanded to sanctify God's Name [that is to sacrifice their lives for the sake of God's Torah and His teachings] (Torat Cohanim Emor) . . . For three mitzvot—idolatry, adultery, and murder—we are commanded to die rather than allow ourselves to be forced to transgress them. . . . During times of persecution, then this martyrdom applies even to any of the mitzvot [whereas normally we would be permitted to transgress any of them rather than be killed]" (*Mishneh Torah, Hilkhot Yesodei HaTorah*, Chapter 5, *Halakha* 1–3).

God Himself acts to prevent desecration of His Name as we have seen regarding the threat of destroying Israel at the sins of the Golden Calf and of the Spies. This is true also of *Kiddush HaShem*. When Israel is in exile, dispersed, downtrodden, and persecuted, the nations of the world question His power to redeem His Chosen People, perhaps even to question His very existence because of the lack of power. Subsequently, a concept may arise of a new Israel to supplant the Old or of a new God to replace that of the Old Testament. The Kuzari king questions the rabbi philosopher as to what God was if His chosen People were so dispersed and degraded.

Yechezkel describes how the redemption of Israel may come about, not as a result of their repentance, but solely to remove these doubts or blemishes and thereby bring *Kiddush Hashem*.

> And I scattered them among the nations and they were dispersed throughout the countries . . . and they profaned My Name; in that people said of them, "These are the people of the Lord and are gone forth out of His Land. . . . I do not this for sake of the House of Israel but for My Holy Name which you have profaned among the nations whither you came. And I will sanctify My Name . . . and the Nations shall know that I am the Lord . . . when I shall be sanctified in you before their eyes. For I will bring you from among the nations and gather you out of the countries and will bring you into your own country . . . a new heart also will I give you and a new spirit will I put within you . . . and you shall dwell in the Land that I gave to your fathers and you shall be my People and I will be your God." (Ezek. 36:19–28)

KORACH

For the Sake of Heaven

Any dispute that is for the Sake of Heaven will have a constructive outcome; but one that is not for the Sake of Heaven will not. What sort of dispute was for the Sake of Heaven? The dispute between Hillel and Shammai [Beit Hillel and Bet Shammai], and that which was not for the Sake of Heaven? This is the dispute of Korach and his whole congregation. (*Mishnah Avot*, Chapter 5, *Mishnah* 20)

Our opening *Mishnah* compared Korach and his congregation with the disagreement between Hillel and Shammai, the former group representing a conflict not for the sake of Heaven. What is there about the differences between Bet Hillel and Bet Shammai that make them "for the sake of Heaven"?

There was no personality clash as they dealt courteously and respectfully with each other; the rabbis' way of saying that they were prepared to accept the opinions of the other side. Indeed, we know that after the long discussion, the halakhah is that we follow Bet Hillel in all but six cases. So the students of Bet Shammai observed the decisions of Bet Hillel. This is not surprising because the issue was not a new Torah or two religious beliefs but only what is the halakhah; that is, how does the Oral Law teach us to observe that which is in the Written Law? Both

Hillel and Shammai observed the traditional way of examining the law and abided by the authoritative decisions.

Whereas our *Mishnah* describes a quarrel between Bet Hillel and Bet Shammai, it only mentions the congregation of Korach without pitting them against Moses. At first glance, it seems that their quarrel was actually with each other. Korach himself argued that in view of his family's seniority, he should be the high priest rather than Aharon. Datan and Aviram wanted the rights of the firstborn—kingship, priesthood, and two portions of the land—to be returned to their Tribe of Reuven. The 250 communal leaders wanted the priesthood returned to the firstborn of all tribes, an honor taken from them at the time of the Golden Calf. In reality, however, all of them were challenging the Law of Moses that had decreed all the things they were opposing. Their own internal differences are only possible and viable if they negate the divinity of that law and the religious concepts flowing from it.

In addition, Korach used a populist economic argument, presenting himself as a leader concerned with the welfare of ordinary citizens, in contrast to Moses, a representative of the greedy priestly caste. Korach said, "there was a widow who harvested a field of wheat, came Aharon and told her to leave the corner unharvested, to give Trumah to the priest, and a tithe to the Levites. When she ground it into flour and baked Aharon demanded his share—Challah. She sold the field, bought sheep, then Aharon insisted on getting his share of the firstborn and of the wool. She slaughtered the sheep, but Aharon had to get his share. So she declared it ownerless, *hefker*, so it all passed to Aharon" (*Bamidbar Rabba, Korach*).

Moses first clears himself of even the most secret and subconscious trace of self-interest or aggrandizement, let alone a nondivine source of the law. "I did not use a single donkey of theirs for my burdens" (verse 15). Even when he returned from Midian to serve Israel and redeem them, he used his own donkey to carry his wife and children. However, all the claims those announced and those of secret agendas really were attacks on the divinity of the Torah and of the Oral Law. The reaction of Moses clearly shows this. The same Moses who consistently asks for

KORACH

Divine Forgiveness for Israel and as consistently refuses any notion of his supplanting the people, here asks God for a special new creation that will destroy Korach and his congregations. However, in the same way as the Torah was Divinely revealed at Sinai, a special, unique, and miraculous occurrence, so, too, the detractors of that Law require a punishment that is unique, special, and miraculous, clearly, and obviously solely of Divine Action.

"What is written above [before the Korach incident]? And they shall make for themselves, tzitzit on the fringes of their garments" (*Bamidbar* 15:38). Said Korach to Moses, "Does a Tallit [garment] that is entirely blue [*techeilet*] require tzitzit?" "Yes" replied Moses. "The blueness of a whole garment does not absolve it from tzitzit but four fringes do?" mocked Korach. Korach continued, asking, "A house full of Torah is not a fulfillment of the Law but a single parsha [of the Torah in the *Mezuzah*] is? (See Moses) none of these laws were commanded to you, you have proclaimed them solely from your own heart [mind] (*Bamidbar Rabbah* 18)." The same midrash tells of Korach's claim that Moses had unnecessarily burdened us with many mitzvot, a burden more onerous than the slavery of Egypt.

This is the way that the rabbis understood the claim of Korach "that the whole nation is holy, why then do you [arrogantly] set yourselves [Moses and Aharon] over the Congregation of the Lord" (*Bamidbar* 16:3); a claim reiterated by Datan and Aviram (verse 13).

Punishment, deserved as it is, is insufficient to teach Israel a spiritual truth that there are *mitzvot*, that these *mitzvot* were revealed at Sinai to Moses and that they are eternal. A test was needed wherein religious ritual would be observed in contradiction to this law and God would judge. Why incense—*ketoret*—not sacrifice or some other form of test? The ketoret is the most spiritual of all the Temple services. A mixture of spices, its offering was totally evaporated; only its smell, indeterminate, vaporous, and invisible remained as part of the Divine Service. So, too, the motivation of all concerned was a spiritual one. The 250 communal leaders questioned the need for a priestly caste, irrespective of who the high priest was. Because all the people are holy, all can officiate, not needing any leader or intermediary. Indeed, throughout our history those who have questioned the authority of the Heavenly Torah or the Mosaic Law have always had a spiritual motivation. Some have argued like Korach, that *mitzvot*, practical and legislated actions are unnecessary; all that matters is the spiritual intent. Others like the 250 leaders questioned the role of the religious authorities given them by the halakhic process. Like all concerned in Korach and his congregation, they, too, ascribed many laws, customs, or concepts to the human wisdom or personal value structure of Moses, or in other generations, of the rabbis.

It is these spiritual considerations that led Maimonides to classify as *mitzvot* and as basic tenets of Judaism: "I believe with perfect faith that the prophecy of Moses our teacher was true; that the entire Torah now in our hands is the same one that was given to Moses . . . that this Torah will not be exchanged nor that there will be another Torah from the Creator (Thirteen Principles of Faith, Maimonides, commenting on the *Mishnah, Sanhedrin* Chapter 10).

The test of the *ketoret* was conducted clearly in contradiction to the written law but changed temporarily by the oral law. Usually only priests were allowed to offer incense; here Israelites were. The incense was offered in special pans sanctified for this purpose, whereas now ordinary pans were used. Usually incense could only be offered inside yet here the communal leaders were instructed by Moses to stand in front of the Ohel Moed. This is an example of the power of the Oral Mosaic Law that gives such power to the sages and to the Bet Din, one that may be used only within the parameters of that same Law. In answer to the test, all of the congregation were destroyed.

This has been true of all the debates in Jewish law or custom throughout the ages. The Sadducee and Pharisee controversy ended with only the latter remaining in Judaism; the former rejected the concept of the Oral Law. There is enough evidence to show that it was a similar rejection of halakhic process that led to the exclusion of Christians from the Jewish body. The differences between Ashkenazim and Sephardim were bridged when the Rama (R. Moshe Isserless) wrote his gloss on the Sepharadic Joseph Karo's *Shulchan Arukh* creating once again a unified halakhah. It is sometimes maintained that the Chassidic-Mithnagdim struggle was over rabbinic authority or halakhic rules. However, if this were true, then based on the past historical experience we should have today two different Judaisms. Yet both groups flow into each other today because of the common halakhic basis.

Indeed, since the Hillel and Shammai differences were only for the sake of Heaven, halakhic Judaism continues whereas Korach and his congregation no longer exist. At the same time, the spiritual fervor and religious aspirations of that congregation are recognized in our sources. "Rabbi Eliezer said, "[the congregation of Korach have a share in the world to come since] regarding them it is written (1 Sam. 2:6) 'The Lord kills and makes alive, He brings down to the grave and raises up'" (Talmud *Sanhedrin* 109b). Rashi comments that they kept the commandments, since the Torah writes, "All the congregation is holy." It is true that Rabbi Akiva disagrees because their rebellion against the halakhah was all embracing, but it seems that most of the sages agree with Rabbi Eliezer.

Mendachem Mendel of Kotzk queried as to why the pans of incense were used to cover the altar instead of being buried in disgrace. After all, they were signs of rebellion. "Their whole sin flowed from their pride and ambition," he explained, "in their case it led to sin but when devoted to Heaven [covering the altar] pride is a source of serving God."

"Rabba bar bar Chana said, Every thirty days . . . they cry out from Gehinnom, Moshe and his Torah are true" (*Sanhedrin* 110b).

CHUKKAT

Permitted and Forbidden War

Shalom, Peace, is one of the Divine Names. "Be of the disciples of Aharon, loving peace and pursuing peace" (*Avot*, Chapter 1, *Mishnah* 12). "He who sustains or saves even one person, it is as though he saved the whole world. Each person is a whole world since only one Adam was created" (*Mishneh Torah, Hilkhot Sanhedrin*, Chapter 12, *Halakhah* 3; see also *Avot de Rabbi Natan*, 31). "The ministering angels wished to sing songs of praise, but the Lord said to them, 'The works of My hands [the Egyptians] are drowning in the Red Sea and you wish to sing *Hallel*'" (*Talmud Bavli, Megillah* 6b). David was not allowed to build the Temple because of the blood he had shed and many battles he had fought (1 Chron. 22:7–10). These and other sources leave no doubt about Judaism's love for peace and abhorrence of war.

Yet human nature and the reality of our world are such that there is also strife, bloodshed, and war, and, therefore, there needs be a Judaic guide even to these aspects of life. Sometimes Divine Justice requires the physical destruction that comes through war but sometimes war is only the result of the free choice of humans for power, wealth, or murder. Halakhically we are obligated to physically defend ourselves against those who wish to destroy us, even if this is only possible through war. So there are the many sources related to war. "The Lord is a Man of War, the

Lord is His name" (*Shmot* 15:13). So "Blessed the Eternal, my refuge! Who instructs my hands for combat and my fingers for war" (Ps. 144:1). The balance between peace and war is maintained by the halakhic guidelines for permitted and forbidden war. These always predicate that the outcome is not determined by wise human strategy, by chance, or by efficient weaponry. Always, as David answered the taunts of Goliath about his stone and slingshot, always "the battle is the Lord's" (1 Sam. 18:17). This is not synonymous with the ever-present human desire for Him to be on our side, but rather an acknowledgment of His Power in determining our affairs.

Twice in our *parsha* Moshe sent peace emissaries—once from Kadesh to Edom and later from the banks of the Arnon to Sichon, king of the Emorites. "And when you will draw close to a city to do battle, first you will offer peace terms" (*Devarim* 20:10). This, the first of the *halakhot* of war, was observed by Moshe when he asked permission to pass through their territory or alongside their borders. Israel asked first for permission to move along the king's highway, the normal route of traffic and people, without causing damage (*Bamidbar* 20:17). When this was refused, they offered to use the less traveled and more difficult road that wound through the mountainous terrain of Seir, *bamesillah*. In all cases, they would pay for any water they used, a gesture of goodwill because they had their own plentiful source in the miraculous well of Miriam. When the peace probes are rejected both by Edom and Sichon, the effects are different. Israel departs from Edom but does battle with Sichon. In each case, the motive of the adversary is different, so the effect teaches important lessons regarding the kashruth of war.

Moshe enumerates to Edom, his brothers, descendants of Esau, the trials and travails of Israel in Egypt and the deliverance meant to lead them to the Promised Land. In the midrash, Moses explains that Israel has suffered on behalf of Esau, the exile and slavery required by the Abrahamic covenant for possession of the Land, and, therefore, his descendants should assist Israel in its passage (*Tanchuma*). Yet the request is actually an acknowledgment that the same Divine Source of Israel's Promised Land has allocated Mount Seir to Esau, and, therefore, their territory may not be traversed without permission. When that permission is not granted, Israel seeks an alternative path. "So we passed from our brothers the children of Esau . . . and passed on the way of Moav . . . and the Lord said . . . You shall not distress Moav and you shall not provoke war with them, for I shall not give you an inheritance from their land for to the children of Lot have I given it as an inheritance" (*Devarim* 2:8–9).

Not only does Divine intervention determine the rights of nations to their lands, but it is also shown in their history, even as it is demonstrated in the daily fortunes of Israel. "Even as the sons of Kushiim are you unto Me, Israel, says the Lord. Did I not take up Israel out of Egypt, the Philistines out of Kaphtor (Crete?) and Aram out of Kir" (Amos 9:7). The Divine Intervention is, however, not only rewarding but also evenly balanced with justice, so Amos speaks of punishment for disobeying His Law both for Israel and for the nations. "Thus," says the Lord, "for three sins of Moav and for four I will not forgive. For burning the bones of the king of Edom to lime. I will send fire into Moav and it shall consume the palaces . . . and I will destroy the judges from its midst and I will kill all her princes" (2:1–3). Then the prophet describes how the kingdoms of Israel (ten northern tribes) and of Judea (the remnants ruled by the House of David) will be destroyed by fire and sent into exile. The acknowledgment that there is Divine Justice and intervention in the affairs of all peoples in no way detracts or denies the eternal special relationship that exists between Him and His chosen people. On the contrary, this relationship is strengthened thereby, making into a reality that which may have been only ethnic arrogance. The existence of temporary Divine-human relationships makes the existence of a permanent special one feasible.

Divine Justice or intervention in the affairs of mankind determines whether Moshe and Israel may or may not make war. Because this justice predicates Edom's inheritance, there is no war when permission is refused, and Israel turns aside. Perhaps it was the inability of the king of Arad to understand that "the battle is the Lord's, which led him to attack Israel after they did not battle with Edom." The verse (21:1) tells that when he heard that Israel came by way of Hachorim, he fought against them. "What tidings did Arad hear? He heard that Aharon had died and that the clouds of glory had dispersed. He imagined therefore that permission had been granted to attack" (*Talmud Bavli, Rosh Hashanah* 3a). The supernatural protection had been removed, and now only normal, physical, or geopolitical factors applied. These made the attack possible ignoring the teaching, however, that Divine Intervention ultimately determines the results. For the *Shem MiShmuel*, the intrinsic holiness of the clouds of glory and of Aharon who was as it were the essence of Israel as he went on their behalf into the Holy of Holies, no longer existed; this made it possible for Arad (actually Amalek) to attack. The Jews took an oath to God when they went to battle, as expression of their innermost dedication and devotion to Him, as it were a substitute for Aharon, and therefore were able to prevail. Once again the outcome is determined by the Divine Scheme of things. Could there be an echo in Arad's separation of miraculous-religiosity from normal human activities in the story of *Mei Merivah*? That story of Moshe smiting the rock instead of drawing water by speaking to it precedes the delegations to Edom. When Israel would enter the Land of Israel, obvious and visible miracles would no longer bring them protection or wealth. Instead they would be able to pray and their prayers would be answered. It was this lesson, demonstrated by the injunction to speak to the rock, that Moshe failed to teach them, and, therefore, he did not sanctify God's Name (*HaEmek Davar*). A sanctification not only shown by miracles but even through the mundane and material affairs of mankind.

If this is the message of the peace overture to Edom, the one to the Emorites details the *halakhot* of a permitted warfare. It must be borne in mind that the Emorites were one of the seven nations living in Canaan, the Land promised to Israel in the Abrahamic covenant. The fulfillment of that covenant had been postponed for 400 years as the sin of the Emorite, that justified their expulsion was not complete before then (*Bereishit* 15:16). The Torah commanded that because of their sins they were to be destroyed; nevertheless, even here Moses sends a peace mission to Sichon.

So, too, we learn "Joshua sent three letters [to the Canaanites] before entering the Land. "Whoever wishes to flee, should flee." [The Girgashi feared God and fled. They were rewarded with a fine portion of land in Africa.] "Whoever wishes to make a peaceful settlement should make peace . . . Whoever wishes to do battle, shall do battle" (*Jer. Talmud. Shevi'it*, Chapter 6, *Halakha* 1). Maimonides codifies this as halakhah: "It is not permitted to wage a war against anybody in the world without offering a chance of a peace settlement, irrespective of whether it is a *milkhemet Hareshut* [a war fought to expand the boundaries] or a *milkhemet mitzvah* [against Amalek, or to conquer Eretz Yisrael from the seven nations or to protect the Jewish settlement there in the future]" (*Mishneh Torah, Hilkhot Melachim*, Chapter 6, *Halakha* 1). In *halakhah* 7 of the same chapter, Maimonides rules, "When a siege is placed around a city to conquer it, it may not be surrounded on all four sides, only on three of the sides. A place must be left for [those who wish] to flee and for all those who desire to escape with their lives." The *Ramban* considers this as one of the 613 *mitzvot* of the Torah but restricts it to a *milkhemet reshut*. However, mainstream scholarship sees the Rambam as ruling this even with regard to obligatory war because it is derived from the war against Midian (*Bamidbar* 31:7) which was a *milkhemet mitzvah*.

Ya'akov epitomized these teachings when he met Eisav. He prepared himself through prayer, he sent gifts to placate Eisav and earn his forgiveness and thereby create peace, but also prepared for war. "And Yaakov feared greatly and it distressed him—he was frightened that he would be killed in the battle and distressed that he might kill others in self defense" (*Rashi, Bereishit* 32:8).

To ensure that we remain within this framework, there are a number of ethical and halakhic parameters to the conduct of a permitted war.

"[The king or state authority] may not lead the nation [to fight] a *milkhemet reshut* unless the court of seventy-one [judges—*Sanhedrin*] approves" (*Hilkhot Melachim*, Chapter 5, *Halakhah* 2). The *Ramban* adds that even in a *Milkhemet mitzvah* it is necessary to consult the Urim and Tumim as oracles. Maimonides (Chapter 7, *Halakhah* 4) rules that for a *milkhemet*, mitzvah no permission is needed.

From these words of Maimonides, it seems that after the disbanding of the Sanhedrin, Jews are only allowed to fight defensive wars. These and other halakhic limitations on the conduct of permitted war are paralleled by positive injunctions that come to create a spiritual and ethical prototype of a soldier. This is essential to prevent the brutality of the soldier and the removal of humane and moral constraints from him. Among those released from the battle in a *milkhemet reshut* were "any man who is afraid or fainthearted" (*Devarim* 20:8). Said Rabbi Yossi, "This is one who is afraid of the sins of his past" (*Bavli Sota* 44a); only those who are pious and clear of sin are suitable to serve in the army. On Chanukah, we give praise for the victory of the pure over the impure, the righteous over the wicked, into the hands of those who study Torah. The *midrash* tells that Avraham took with him the scholars among his disciples to free Lot, Moshe told Yehoshua to choose pious men to fight Amalek and Gideon took only three hundred men who had not bowed before Baal in the war against Midian. Rabbinic sources found moral and legal problems in the destruction of Shechem by the sons of Jacob but also in the killing of the Egyptian by Moses. Irrespective of their solutions, the rabbinic dilemmas keep the ethical issues of killing an enemy before the mind of the Jewish warrior. These are traits that are prerequisites for the conduct of permitted war.

Important as they are, considerations of fairness, mercy, and humanness are not the sole foundation of the *halakhot* of war. Over and beyond them is the Divine Presence in the camp. "It is a positive commandment to establish latrines in the [army] camp . . . and for every single soldier to keep a trowel together with his weapons to cover his excrement. [Soldiers are required to] follow these practices at all times, irrespective of whether the Ark accompanies them or not, even as it is written '[He walks within your camp . . . therefore] your camp shall be Holy'" (*Mishneh Torah, Hillahot Melakhim*, Chap. 6, *Halakhot* 14–15). If this applies, rules Maimonides, even in the unsettled and dangerous conditions of warfare, how much more so in the regular and normal lives, so that concern for sewage and sanitation become halakhically a requirement of Jewish communal authority.

It is the subjection of the army and of the individual soldier to Divine Law and morality that is the basis for the just war. "Do the hands of Moshe [raised to Heaven] do battle [in the war against Amalek]? Rather when Israel subject their hearts to their Father in Heaven and turn their faces on High that they are victorious" (*Rosh Hashanah*, Chapter 3, *Mishnah* 1).

BALAK

To Achieve the Spiritual Potential

Prophecy, direct communion with the Divine, was granted at the outset, to all human creatures, not just to Israel. "There has arisen no prophet in Israel like Moshe (*Devarim* 34:10) but in the nations of the world there has arisen *Bilaam ben Beor*" (Sifri). The *Tanna Devei Eliyahu* mentions a long list of gentiles who were sent to prophesy—Eliphan, the Temanite; Job from the land of Uz; Be'Or, the father of Bilaam, and, finally, Bilaam himself. Otherwise the nations would have said, "We would have accepted Your Torah and kept Your commandments if You would have sent us a Moshe." In a similar vein, the rabbis taught that before the Revelation at Sinai, the Torah was offered to all the nations.

At a more mundane level, this idea that spiritual opportunities are widely offered is repeated in various forms throughout the Torah. The important issue in life, however, is whether these opportunities are fulfilled correctly, as we may see for example, in the challenge of the firstborn. *Reishit* (beginnings) are important in all things; Torah is *Reishit*, Israel is *Reishit*, even the eternal enemy Amalek is *Reishit* (Num. 24:20). So the firstborn is the child with the most spiritual opportunity, with the promise of leadership, and with the potential for creativity. Yet in the biblical stories, promise and potential are never realized in the firstborn. Reuven is the firstborn, yet kingship goes to Yehudah, priesthood to

Levi, and the double portion of the inherited Land goes to Yoseph. Moshe is not a firstborn. Gideon is the youngest in his father's house whose clan's share is the smallest in the half tribe of Mennasheh (Judg. 6:15), and David, the founder of Kingship, the least of the sons of Jesse. It is the use of revelation and of prophecy by the nations of the world, not the potential, that is the issue in our *parshah*.

Because they refused Torah, although prophecy was granted to gentiles, the effect was not to draw them closer to God but the contrary. "Just as He raised kings, sages, and prophets for Israel, so He did for the gentiles. He raised up Solomon who built His Temple, and He raised up Nebuchadnezzar who destroyed it and arrogated to himself the characteristics of the Most High. He gave David wealth, that was saved for His House; the wealth given to Haman was used to pave the way for the slaughter of a whole nation" (*Tanchuma Balak* 4).

This issue of the free choice of what is done with the potential for spiritual achievement is one that faces all people down throughout the centuries. It is perhaps in this light that we can benefit most from our story of Bilaam. At the outset, the differences between Bilaam and Moshe and all the Hebrew prophets need to be made clear.

In every story of Israel's prophets, the very first revelations are accompanied by attempts to evade the calling. For all of them prophecy is not a career nor is it something to be pursued. Rather it is forced on them. Moshe protests his unsuitability for prophecy, and this pattern is repeated throughout the Tanach. God Himself testifies that the man Moshe is extremely humble, more than any of the people who live on the face of the earth.

Moshe covers his face in his cloak at the Burning Bush. For the others fear and trembling, humility and awe, and the knowledge of human frailty are a prelude to hearing His voice. Bilaam, however, arrogantly accepts the designation of Balak as a seer and a prophet. He pursues the prophecy and introduces his words by relating his antecedents and his spiritual power—"says Bilaam the son of Be'or, the man whose eyes are open." Bilaam even tries to circumvent Divine Opposition to his mission.

BALAK

Bilaam prepares himself for prophecy through magical means, seven altars, seven bullocks, enchantments, and solitude. The prophets of Baal work themselves into ecstasy through dancing, shouting, and incisions into their flesh to make Baal send down fire (1 Kings 18:26–29). Throughout the ancient world, priests and prophets used divination, sorcery, and omens to induce their forecasts.

The Torah seeks to separate all these from Divine Revelation. Always the *Neviim* are careful to stress the real source of their prophecy: "The word of the Lord came unto Hosea . . . the word . . . came unto me saying (Jer. 1:4) . . . and repetitively we read verses like . . . and the Word . . . was upon him—and the spirit of the Lord filled him." At the same time, there is the specific injunction, "When you come to the Land . . . not according to the abominations of those nations . . . There shall not be found one who practices divinations, an astrologer, one who reads omens, a sorcerer or animal charmer [for the sake of discovering the future] . . . or one who consults the dead. You shall be wholehearted with the Lord your God [with perfect faith in His Knowledge and Plan]" (*Devarim* 18:9–13). Bilaam himself sees a blessing in the Jewish repudiation of sorcery "for there is no divination in Jacob and no sorcery in Israel. Even [though] it is said to Jacob and to Israel what He has [or will] do [through Revelation and Prophecy]" (Chapter 23:23).

The tribulations and troubles that come upon Israel and the world are not the curse of the prophets but simply Divine Announcement of the results of the evil deeds of people. Our prophets, throughout, warn and beseech the people to repent and avert punishment. Furthermore, they consistently express their sorrow when the punishment is imminent or actually occurs. Moshe pleads for forgiveness of Israel. Jeremiah, whose whole mission is to foretell the destruction of Jerusalem, authors the Lamentations when his prophecy comes true. This is true also regarding the fate of the gentile nations. Isaiah trembled over the sorrows of Moav (16:11) and Ezekiel wept over the fall of Tyre (Chapter 27). Jonah earns Divine Displeasure when he seeks to run away and avert the mission to Nineveh that leads to the gentiles' repentance.

Indeed, admonition and rebuke are the province only of the pious whose love for others is great and manifest enough for there to be not even an inkling of hate in their motivation. It is only a Moshe, the great lover of Israel, who is able on numerous occasions in the Bible to foretell what the consequences of disobeying the Torah will be. The addition of the nineteenth benediction to the daily amidah calls down Divine Rejection of the Jewish apostates and the falsifiers of Torah. It was authored by the *Mishnaic Tannah*. Shmuel HaKatan was chosen to author this prayer because he taught "do not rejoice in the downfall of your enemy" (*Avot* Chapter 4, *Mishnah* 24). Bilaam, however, is only prevented from cursing Israel, who have done neither him nor Balak harm, by Divine Intervention. Even more illustrative however is the fact that he is willing to suggest that Moav expose their own daughters to sexual immorality to further his destructive design on Israel.

It is tempting and easy to ascribe Bilaam's inability to achieve the spiritual potential given to him as a prophet, either to cynical exploitation of those who turn to him for guidance, or to a lust for power, or to simple anti-Semitism. However, this understanding of the Bilaam story would blind us to important spiritual messages regarding our own free will and our spiritual potential.

The three blessings of Israel by Bilaam relate to three distinct areas of life that represent a spiritual challenge to mankind, material strength, mental prowess, and the physical functions of the human body, each area pertinent to a place that Bilaam raised altars for his prophecy.

First he went to the heights of Baal from where he saw part of the Israelite camp (Chapter 22:41). Baal was the idol of material prosperity, whose sign was identical with the phallus, symbol of generative power (*Talmud Jerusalmi Avoda Zara*, Chapter 3, *Halakhah* 6). Baal's favor was essential for national prosperity and growth, and Balak sought to impede Israel's prosperity. However, they are a people whose greatness does not depend on natural forces nor on human ingenuity but rather Divine Providence, a nation that does not seek to impose its greatness on others nor is measured in its numerical or economic power. "Not because of your numbers . . . were you chosen for you are the fewest of all the peoples. Rather because of His love for you" (*Devarim* 7:7–8). When it enters its own Land, the miraculous water of Miriam's well, the manna from Heaven, all the protection of the clouds of Glory ceased. Now economic welfare both individual and national depends on normal human efforts. Yet these efforts are guided and operative within a Divinely Ordained Law and Morality. There is no Baal, only Divine Providence in accordance with human moral being. This is the concept that Balak feared, because it would become a model for the whole pagan world in which he lived (*Shem MiShmuel*).

From the heights of Baal, Balak took Bilaam to Sdei Tzofim, the Field of Seers. Perhaps a way could be found to harm Israel through its gifted ones, those possessed of mental and spiritual powers. Abarbanel explains that Israel's wisdom flows from Divine providence because they are zealous in His worship and law. He redeemed them from Egypt and loves them as a friend—using *rei'a*, friend, as the root of the *t'ruah* in verse 21. The spiritual powers and knowledge of Israel cannot be used against them because "there is no divination in Jacob and no sorcery in Israel. Even now it is said [Divine Revelation of Torah] to Jacob and to Israel what He has done." "This people rise up like a lion"; from the moment Jews awake they perform His commandments, prayer, *tallit*, and *tefillin*. This is a basis for their whole day, becoming sanctified thereby even as the lion cub learns to find prey. At the end of the day, they recite *Shma* and entrust their souls to His Hands (*Midrash Tanchuma*). This idea is enhanced by the *Shem MiShmuel*'s interpretation of verse 21. He relates, "He saw no iniquity, aven, in Yaakov" to the pure and ethical ways Jews earn their livelihood, even when they are Yaakov, persecuted and weak. *Amal*, literally, labor in Israel, he relates to the economic motivation of the Jews when they are categorized as Israel, as flowing from their need to give charity and study Torah.

It is because of their integration of holiness into all their everyday actions that they have no need of sorcery or divination to find their spiritual guidance. Indeed, there is a complete separation between the religious functionaries in Judaism and any of the rites of passage that otherwise may lead to any relationship of religion and "mysteries." Childbirth, marriage, and death are in all faiths and cultures, phenomena that call for the presence of the priest, Shaman, witch doctor, or, holy man. Yet in Judaism women in childbirth are in a state of impurity forbidden to contact with all men, even their own husbands; priests are forbidden contact with dead bodies and graveyards, and marriage does not require a rabbi or holy man to officiate.

It is feasible for people to relate holiness and spirituality to economics, material goods, religion, and power. It is more difficult to relate in this way to the human body and its physical needs and workings. These seem to be an animal part of the human being, something to be dispersed and separated from our spiritual souls. So Bilaam asked Balak to take him to the height of *Pe'or* that overlooks the Wasteland. Pe'or is a cult that turns the most animal side of human functions toward the gods. Its worship was through the human alimentary system, showing that we are only the equals of the animals. Decency, modesty, and sexual purity are mere dreams, irrelevant and unobtainable.

Here at the height of *Pe'or*, however, the cloud of sorcery disappears from the mind of Bilaam, so he lifts up his eyes and sees the whole encampment of Israel and its tribes. He saw their tents organized so that the entrances did not intrude on the privacy and modesty of their neighbors. They live not in *batim*, houses, but in *mishkenot*, tabernacles. Each generation flows into the next like the streams. "It is this seed which is at the abundant flow" (24:7). All human seed belongs to God and is sacred to Him without any of the coarseness of *Pe'or*. It is through their sanctification of their sexual family life that the Tents of Jacob and the Habitations of Israel achieve their goodness and their beauty. It is through the encampment of Israel according to family and tribes around the Divine Law that the eternity of the Jew is ensured.

So the *brit*, the holy covenant, is sealed in the male sexual organ, ensuring spiritual completion through the removal of part of man, introducing restraint, modesty, and limits to human hunger and passion. So there is a *bracha* thanking God for the perfect and harmonized workings of the human digestive system. So the *Rama* can write in his gloss on the first section of the Shulchan Arukh, "Even in the most private places, even in the most personal of our activities, we should know that there is One who sees, knows and judges all."

Like all people, Bilaam has the opportunity and the chance for spirituality, prophecy, and sanctity. The decision to misuse all these and not to be like Moshe and the Hebrew prophets flows from his own choice of different possible values. "Whoever has the following three traits is amongst the disciples of our Father Abraham, but one who has different traits is of the disciples of the wicked Bilaam. A good eye [*chesed* and kindness] a humble spirit and a meek soul, is of the disciples of Abraham. One who has an evil eye [jealous and stingy], an arrogant spirit, and a greedy soul, is of the disciples of Bilaam" (*Mishnah Avot*, Chapter 5, *Mishnah* 22).

PINCHAS

The Cycle of the Jewish Year

If we understand Korban, not as sacrifice but more correctly as "to draw close, *lehitkareiv*"—then the Jewish year is built around way stations, of meeting places in time, in which the nation is able to draw close to its God. There are two such meetings each day, morning and at the end of the day, *Shacharit* and *Minchah*, a weekly meeting on *Shabbat*, then the new month, the three pilgrimage festivals, Rosh Hashanah and Yom Kippur. Each station has its special *korbanot*, its special perspective of the constant drawing closer of Israel to its God. All these *korbanot* are communally funded, an expression of a national spiritual service over and above the personal religious relationships of the individual expressed through *korbanot* of thanksgiving, sin-offering, purification, and their ritual. It is fitting that the complete list of *korbanot* appears only here, at the end of the wanderings in the desert, just prior to the death of Moses and the national entry into its Promised Land. After the experience of miracles, Divine providence, and their own spiritual weaknesses, such detailed expression of the periodic facilitating of closeness to the Divine, is to provide a dimension filled until now by Moses.

The *Shem MiShmuel*, echoing rabbinic tradition, saw the following spiritual lessons from the sheep as a *korban*. Although only kosher animals are eligible for the divine service, they must be unblemished physically, a symbol of the inadmissibility of unethical actions, nonpermissible thoughts, and blemished lifestyles in our daily lives. Just as in the sanctification of our eating habits so, too, in our spiritual meetings, there are only the hunted and not the predator, only herbaceous but not carnivorous, only domesticated animals with a relationship to people and society but not those of the jungle or of the wild. So we are to be meek in our daily affairs, family oriented and not predatory. Sheep trust explicitly in their shepherd and follow him unquestioningly. So in the *korbanot* they come to teach us these self-same qualities, "as the sheep collectively have only one voice so too we have only one voice to our Father in Heaven." The ox is the draught animal, beast of burden, and primary mechanical tool. Hirsch stresses that always the ox is referred to in the *korbanot* as being in its prime neither a calf nor one unsuitable for work. So Judaism is not a religion for little children, nor for the aged and weak. Rather it is when we are in our physical prime, with our developed intellectual powers and accumulating economic wealth that the spiritual and ethical challenges are most powerful. Therefore, it is just at these times that the Torah's teachings and law are most needed. It is, however, also when the mission of making everything holy can be translated into reality.

The spiritual messages of the *korbanot* are not limited to the animals but include everything used to draw close to God. On Pesach, there is the wave offering of the *Omer* merely a measure of barley, yet one that allows us to eat of the new crop, restricting our use of our own legal property. The *Omer* is of barley, food usually given to animals, symbol of the physical and political freedom of Pesach. Seven weeks later, the offering is of fine wheat flour suitable for human consumption; it is symbol of the spirituality and religiosity of Shavuot Festival of Giving the Torah (*Shem miShmuel*). This Pesach-Shavuot relationship is entwined by Hirsch's insight that only on Shavuot is the use of leavened bread allowed on the altar. Bread as the symbol of prosperity and national well-being needs the Torah to place political and economic freedom in a correct perspective. On Sukkot, pure water is poured over the altar. Judgment for rain at this time is called for by the most simple and priceless element. So, too, the four species used to praise God are primarily common noncommercial varieties of plants.

Parshat Pinchas presents the most complete list of meeting times for spiritual and religious elevation mentioned in the Torah. Elsewhere Pesach, Shavuot, and Sukkot, the three pilgrimage festivals, are sometimes mentioned by themselves, or sometimes only together with *Shabbat*, or to include Rosh Hashanah and Yom Kippur. Only here the whole annual cycle of the Jewish spiritual odyssey appears. Actually, we can discern three distinct and separate cycles, touching and linked to each other, yet each with a distinct religious perspective. Rosh Chodesh and *Shabbat* may be seen as one cycle, Rosh Hashanah and Yom Kippur as another, and the Shalosh Regalim as another.

Pesach, Shavuot, and Sukkot are way stations in Jewish history. The Exodus from Egypt forms a national and spiritual experience that demonstrates the existence of God, Divine Intervention in all the affairs of mankind, and the dependence of all natural forces on Him. Shavuot is testimony to Revelation of Divine Spirit and Word to human beings. Divine Mercy and Kindness is constantly recalled by Sukkot with its memories of the sojourn in the desert.

These three festivals also represent a cycle of the agricultural year. Pesach is the beginning of the harvest, Shavuot of the First Fruits and the wheat harvest, and Sukkot that of the ingathering of the fruits, the beginning of autumn. Indeed, in modern times, much emphasis has been placed on the agricultural nature of this cycle. In the main, this has been an attempt to empty them of their religious significance by making nature festivals out of them. In truth, however, this cycle is antinature despite the agricultural natural connection. All these festivals come to demonstrate that nature has no power of its own, but operates solely as a reflection of the Divine Creator. The human role, too, in this cycle, is shown as one ultimately dependent on the will of that same Creator. On Shavuot, the first fruits that are brought as *bikkurim* require confession: one in which the Jewish farmer recalls the simple beginnings of Israel, slavery in Egypt, Divine Grace in the giving of the Land, and His bounty represented by the farmers' success. At the end of the agricultural year, the same farmer, while reviewing the full barns and silos, is required to leave home and live in the temporary sukkah. On Pesach, there is Judgment Day for the grain; on Shavuot on the fruits; and on Sukkot on the rain. Our prosperity is dependent on those judgments. It is not the physical process that creates rainfall, but "You are He who Causes the wind to blow and the rain to fall." Neither is the field and its produce the sole private property of the farmer. The poor, the stranger, and the Levite—the marginal and the weak members of society—have a share in this wealth, so the produce has to be tithed, forgotten sheaves, grapes, and olives left for the poor; and the corner of the field left unharvested for their benefit. Indeed in Lev. 23:22, these laws are inserted between Shavuot and Rosh Hashanah, between the satisfaction of the farmer in the first fruits, and the Day of Judgment.

These agriculturally oriented festivals are intricately linked to their national character. A non-Jew may not eat of the Paschal Lamb, nor may an uncircumcised Jew. The seventy nations participate as it were in the *korbanot* of Sukkot, but on Shemini Atzeret, *korbanot* are brought only for Israel. Each of the Festivals is celebrated with the blessing, "Who blesses His People Israel and the Appointed Seasons." Only from the seven species with which Eretz Yisrael is blessed (*Devarim* 8:8) may *bikkurim* be brought. Almost all of the tithing, and agricultural gifts, apply only to the Holy Land: *teluyot ba'aretz*. The festivals follow the seasons of the year in Eretz Yisrael. Pesach, Festival of Freedom, is always Chag HaAviv, Spring Festival; indeed, the whole purpose of the Jewish leap year is to adjust our lunar calendar to the solar system so as to ensure that Nissan is always spring. For our rabbis especially, HaCohen Kook and Hirsch, this maintains the relationship of a people entering the rebirth and spiritual renewal of freedom parallel to the outburst of new growth and energy in the plant world after the hibernation of winter.

It is true that the whole world and all its generations has been influenced and touched by these stations. Pesach's rejection of tyranny and its message of freedom for men and women created in God's image has found an echo in all those societies touched by the monotheistic religions. The Law of Sinai is enshrined in many legal and social systems, blending justice with mercy and morality with spirituality. On Sukkot, seventy *korbanot* were offered, symbolizing the nations of the world and bringing a message of peace and Divine Providence for all.

There is a second cycle, Rosh Hashanah and Yom Kippur. This is the cycle of Creation both of the world and of humanity, through which God is proclaimed King of the Universe, Judge of all Mankind, inscribing the nations of the world in the Books of Peace, Prosperity, and Life, according to their moral behavior tempered by His Mercy. The six days of Creation culminate on Rosh Hashanah with Adam created in His image. So the prayers of this day reiterate that there is a creator, that all and everything in His world depends on Him and acknowledges Him as king. The Aleinu prayer, now recited thrice daily, was originally only said on these three days; it is the coronation poem par excellence.

On this day, He holds all the souls in His Hands, reviews their actions, and dispenses justice. On Yom Kippur, His mercy is revealed when knowing the weakness of people and their ethical deficiencies, He accepts their repentance and grants atonement. They are prayers of Israel but they mark universal events and truths operative in all humanity and creatures of this world. Noah, the second father of mankind, is remembered on this day, and the story of the repentance of gentile Nineveh is the *haftorah* of Yom Kippur Minchah.

Rosh Hashanah is the date whereby we mark the passage of the years since the creation of the world; it is the New Year for the counting of the reign of kings and for dating legal and social documents. These are the records of the political, social, and economic life of people and the Divine Justice that results from them. It is the summation of the worldly activities of the year that through the spiritual accounting and repentance of Yom Kippur prepare the world for the near future. Yom Kippur is called Rosh Hashanah (Ezek. 40:1) and the Talmud in *Arachim* 12a explains this as a reference to the *Yovei*, Jubilee Year. On the Yom Kippur of that year, the Shofar is blown to proclaim freedom and return of land to the original owners; and the Rosh Hashanah prayers of Malchiot,

Zichronot, and Shofarot are recited. In that year, Yom Kippur thus resembles the end and beginning of each normal year.

This cosmic cycle comes in the autumn of the year, after the harvest of summer and before the hibernation of winter and is thus linked to the national-historical cycle through Sukkot.

> Farmers bring their produce into the granaries and storehouses after they have winnowed the grain and separated the fruits according to their qualities. This is the process that is completed on Sukkot. So, too, in the spiritual world, it is only after the Din of Rosh Hashanah and the spiritual cleansing of Yom Kippur that we can enter Sukkot festival of Rejoicing and of Divine Providence. (*Shem MiShmuel*)

So the national-agricultural cycle meets the universal creation oriented cycle.

There is however a third cycle—*Shabbat* and Rosh Chodesh. They witness a merging of the other two cycles. *Shabbat* is the memorial of the six days of Divine Creation, but yet is specific only to the Jew. Rosh Chodesh is the cycle of the moon, clear to all people and witnessed by the whole world, yet its celebration is specific to the calendar of Israel. In these days, the cosmic becomes a sign of Judaism, a witness of the special relationship between Israel and its God.

"[With the seventh day] He had ceased from all His creating work that . . . to continue shaping it" (*Bereishit* 2:3). So all creative work is forbidden to the Jew; anything created from nothing. Yet *imitatio dei*, human creation is a continuous process. One *Shabbat* is the end of the work and creativity of one week, a day that is pure thought and Torah and a review of the growth of that week. It is, however, even as was the first Divine *Shabbat*, a preparation for the six days approaching—a powerhouse as it were for the spiritual challenges of these material and physical days.

Although all the world, inanimate, plant, animal, and human, is created during these days "between Me and the Children of Israel it

[*Shabbat*] is a sign forever that in six days HaShem made Heaven and earth and on the seventh day He rested" (*Shmot* 31:17). So in the repetition of the decalogue, the reason for our observance of *Shabbat* differs from that in Exodus. To the creation of the world (*Shmot* 20:11) there is now added the memory of the slavery in, and the redemption from, Egypt (*Devarim* 5:14–15). Only the free can observe the spiritual and physical *Shabbat* and only those who are subject to the *Shabbat* are really free. So are linked the cosmic-universal creation to the particularist and national cycle of the Jew. The injunction against this work and the resultant enforced physical rest frees us from the slavery, drudgery, and dehumanization of the treadmill of our daily struggle for economic wealth or the enjoyment of that wealth. Furthermore, this weekly memorial of the Creation by the Divine Creator provides the knowledge that He is aware of all our actions, judges them, and provides us with all our needs. It is this knowledge that provides the normative, constant, and uncompromising morality that is Judaism.

The moon waxes and wanes in a seemingly mechanical process, the subject of immutable natural and physical laws. Yet the very first mitzvah commanded Israel was the injunction to declare, each month, the exact date of the new month and whether the year would be twelve or thirteen months. The execution of this mitzvah was given to the authority of the *Sanhedrin* in Jerusalem—more specifically to the *Nasi*. The ancient world, in many different countries, had exact and wide-ranging knowledge of astronomy and expressed it in its architecture and in scientific tables or writing. So, too, the Mishnah tells that the *Nasi*, Rabban Gamliel, had different models of the movements and changes of the moon and still witnesses were essential so that the mark of humans would be placed on creation. "This month shall be for you a beginning [a renewal] of new moons; for you, that the declaration of Rosh Chodesh was given to a [human] court" (*Talmud Bavli Rosh Hashanah* 22a–25b). Judaism comes to free mankind from the slavery of time by giving human agency the power to decide on the functioning of the calendar (*Sforno Shmot* 12:1). This freedom made it necessary for the decision of the court to be based on witnesses.

The power given to the Bet-din to decide on the changes in the calendar frees us also from the tyranny of the cycle of natural forces. However, by granting this power to the free choice of human courts, the Creator shows Himself to be free and uncontrolled as it were, by the laws of the physical world He created. Not only is mankind a partner in the creative process flowing from Divine Creation of the world, but the Jew, through Rosh Chodesh, determines his own dates of *Chag* and *Moed*, the appointed seasons for meeting and connecting with the Creator. In other faiths or religions, the holy days are either fixed and constant, as in Christianity, or fluctuate throughout the year, as in Islam. However, in Judaism, it is human agency that ensures that Pesach always falls in the spring, that Yom Kippur never falls on Friday or on Sunday, and that fast days, excepting Yom Kippur, are never observed on *Shabbat*. In our own day, Israel's Independence Day, Yom HaAtzmaut, is the only national day whose observance is moved so as not to desecrate the *Shabbat*. More important, perhaps, was the fierce debate that ensured as to whether it should always be on May 15 as in 1948, or on the 5th of Iyar, the Hebrew date in the same year. Jewish tradition won, and *Hey Iyar* is always Independence Day, irrespective of its position in the non-Jewish calendar of that year.

MATTOT

The Power of Speech

Said Rabbi Shimon bar Yochai, "The Master of the World should have created us with two mouths. With one mouth we would have prayed, studied Torah, and voiced the purest of thoughts, while with the other one we would lie, slander, and gossip. In this way at least we would preserve some purity of speech. However, He in His Wisdom foresaw, that both mouths would have been used badly; at least with only one mouth, our lies, slander, and gossip are restricted.'"

Bar Yochai captured here the quintessence of our dilemma regarding that gift of speech which is the hallmark of humans. Regarding the Creation of Adam and Eve, it is written "a living being" (*Bereishit* 2:7), however, Onkelos translates this rather as "a being that speaks." These are beings that are able to communicate with one another and are able to express their feelings and thoughts in song and speech. They have the ability to communicate words of wisdom and affection, and also to express feelings of spiritual yearning or of moral development. Human beings not only are able to communicate with each other, but they are also able to speak directly through prayer and study with the God who created them. However, their interpersonal communications may be those of hatred and evil. Their speech may express feelings of jealousy, envy, and greed. Whatever the choice, speech and the tongue are always powerful tools for crafting social, communal, and religious life—perhaps the most powerful of all the tools available to mankind.

The printed word, radio, television, and the Internet magnify this power and increase it dramatically. They not only extend our ability to communicate and express ourselves, they also often determine social behavior, establish the parameters of morality, and overpower the individual's own preferences. They are, however, just as subject to the dilemma posed by *Bar Yochai*—one to be determined by free human choice. The multiplier effect on communication, introduced by the extended mechanical and electronic forms of speech, of necessity, dramatically expand any conclusions we come to regarding a sanctification of speech.

The ability to make a vow is our *parsha*'s example of the sanctification of speech. Human beings, by their oaths, are able to extend sanctity to things or actions beyond the *kedushah* given by Torah. When somebody says that they will refrain from eating or drinking things permitted by Torah, or that they dedicate some of their property to the Temple and to charity, or perform social acts not obligatory by *halakhah*, they are expressing a certain degree of the divine. So, too, when in business or in a legal dispute someone takes an oath, he is attaching, as it were, the divine to his transactions or his evidence. When one's evidence is false or when one does not fulfill the oath in regard to the specific transaction, one is obviously negating this divinity.

Although we are usually manifestly aware of the positive powers of speech in all spheres of life, we tend, as often as not, to be less conscious of the potential for evil inherent in speech. Our sources, however, are replete both with praise for proper use of speech but also with rejection of perversion in speech. "Lord who shall dwell in Your Tabernacle . . . speak truth in his heart. One who has no slander on his tongue . . . nor taken up a reproach against his neighbor . . . one who does these things shall never be moved" (Ps. 15). "Come you children . . . I will teach you the fear of the Lord . . . keep your tongue from evil and your lips from speaking deceit" (Ps. 34:12–14). The Sages found it strange that although

David and his army were pious and saintly, nevertheless, they suffered many losses in their various military campaigns. Ahab and his people were idolaters and exceedingly evil, yet there was no loss of life in their wars. This anomaly was explained by the fact that there was gossip and slander in the Davidic camp, whereas brotherly love and social peace existed in the army of Ahab.

The plethora of similar verses and midrashim make Judaism's abhorrence of lying, slander—*rechilut*, and gossip—*lashon harah* perfectly clear.

"You shall not tell lies one against the other; and you shall not swear falsely by My Name for you [thus] profane the Name of your God" (*VaYikra* 19:11–12). In the Ten Commandments, we read, "Do not take upon yourselves the name of the Lord in vain"; perjury, therefore, is a denial of His power in deciding our fate. This not only applies to the judiciary but also to believing gossip. "Do not put your hand [lit. meaning your power or your word] with the wicked person to be a false witness." (Hirsch translates *ed chamas* in this verse as a witness committing an outrage. Our rabbis saw this as forbidding bearing witness together with an evil person even if the evidence is true.) "Keep distant from a word of falsehood [obligating us to make efforts not even to create a false impression]" (*Shmot* 23:1–7).

> "One who spreads gossip about his neighbor transgresses a negative mitzvah even as it is written 'You shall not be a gossipmonger amongst your people' (*VaYikra* 19:16). Even though there is no corporal punishment for this, nevertheless it is a grave sin. What is gossip? One who goes from one person to another saying "thus said so and so or this is what I have heard about such and such a person." Even if it is true, nevertheless this destroys the world. There is something even far more heinous than the gossiper and that is one who says things that denigrate or shame another person. Here too this is forbidden even though it is true. Such *lashon harah* is different from one who spreads false reports ... There are three acts for which one is punished in this world and one also loses one's portion in the world to come, idolatry, sexual immorality and bloodshed, but [speaking] *lashon harah* is equiva-

lent to them all. (*Mishneh Torah, Hilkhot De'ot*, Chapter 7, *Halakhot* 1–3)

The Chafetz Haim, in his classic work of that name dealing with *Lashon Harah*, writes that the speaker and the recipient also transgress the negative mitzvot of "You shall not accept false evidence" (*Shmot* 23:1), "You shall not take upon yourselves the name of the Lord in vain" (Ten Commandments), and "be exceedingly careful regarding leprosy to observe and carry out with great care," since this is understood by the rabbis to be the punishment for speaking *Lashon Harah* (Chafetz Haim Lavim).

Important and basic as these rulings are, the power of speech and of communication however, goes far beyond the interpersonal relations to influence and often to determine the moral parameters, social values, and religiosity of society. Because all these are the concern of Torah, speech must of necessity be viewed in the same light as the sexual drive, food, economic activity, and all the other powers and drives that we possess. This means that just as there are kosher food, kosher sex, and kosher money, there is kosher speech and nonkosher speech. Just as the public authorities and *batei din* supervise, judge, and enforce a pattern of behavior in other areas, so, too, a Jewish scheme of living would, of necessity, have to include speech and its derivatives within this scheme. So in a Torah any speech, written word, or electronic media that educate towards and integrate into our daily lives, Torah values and normative halakhic behavior are permitted. In the same way, when speech and its derivatives are used for forbidden goals, they, too, become forbidden.

Kosher speech not only is permitted but also enjoined on us. Full disclosure of relevant data is a halakhic requirement in business transactions; nondisclosure may lead to *mekach taut*, and to *ona'ah*. The former, nondisclosure of defects in goods or services permits cancellation of a sale, even when there is no fraudulent intent on the part of one of the parties. The *ona'ah* lays either of the parties to a transaction open to legal action for overcharging. "One who hears others plotting to harm another's property or person [hostile takeover?] is obligated to inform the potential victim." One who hears, views, or sees evil actions and does not protest is considered as though he himself performed them. So the prophets protested the behavior of kings, priests, and nobles whenever justified. Adonyah HaShiloni encouraged the rebellion against Rehavam, son of Solomon; Jeremiah suffered imprisonment for his objection to the country's foreign policy; and Amos was persecuted for his protests against the social injustice in the Kingdom of Israel.

At a more pervasive and relevant level, we are obligated to use speech to comfort mourners or those in suffering. Even if we cannot help with financial charity, still we are obligated to give advice where needed. Not only is there a mitzvah to study Torah but those who have knowledge are required to teach others. Menachem Mendel of Kotzk told of his concern that our fathers lived in the desert for forty years without the mitzvah of charity because all needs were met miraculously. "However," he said, "in one area they were not equal. So the knowledgeable taught the ignorant as charity."

The converses of this are the injunctions against speech that encourages people to disobey Torah and against advice that guides people to do that which is forbidden to them. These include those who say, "Let us go and worship the god of others [that is anything to which the powers of God are ascribed]" (*VaYikra* 13:7–19) and the prophet who falsely ascribes his words to a divine source or who changes that which he is commanded to speak. Putting a stumbling block in the path of the blind (*lifnei iver*) is forbidden (*VaYikra* 19:14). This is giving another person advice that is physically, morally, or spiritually to his disadvantage, as well as advice in which we have a hidden conflict of interest. That same verse forbids cursing or defaming a deaf person. Although this is forbidden even in regard to normal people, the text's use of a deaf person comes to forbid cursing another even if the other person does not hear it and therefore is neither hurt nor upset (*Mishneh Torah, Hilkhot Sanhedrin*, Chap. 26:1).

It is sometimes difficult for us to appreciate that the expression of ideas and the ease of communication are not granted to everybody equally and that there often exist situations where one's normal ability is restricted or nonexistent. This is often true in husband-wife and parent-child relations, but also in other levels of social communication. Such difficulties exist in all societies, and there are a variety of therapeutic methods to enhance communications skills and ease of expression. There is, however, a religious area where these same difficulties exist, so that prayer as a contact with God is not always as natural, easy, or spontaneous as we may imagine. Just as one needs education and guidance in social communication, so, too, one needs them in one's spiritual intercourse. Knowledge of the language or of content of our prayers or of the skills of Jewish prayer are a requisite of Jewish life. They are not, however, sufficient to ensure meaningful and spiritually satisfying prayer. Regular and daily prayer are a step forward in this direction, providing the possibility that at least on some occasions our souls are able to soar in their contact with the Divine. The alternative of sporadic and occasional prayer restricted only to moments of spiritual elation or material need seems often insufficient to enable us to pray even at these times. This is analogous to the difficulty to speak among children reared in isolation without hearing others talk. One can stand at the *Kotel* in Jerusalem and witness people's inability to pray, primarily because the experience is strange to them. The same has been observed in the trenches when soldiers, who have never prayed, find it difficult to do so in spite of the fact that "there are no atheists in foxholes."

Speech that is prayer requires spiritual and emotional preparation if it is not to be the mere mouthing of words, a sort of prayer-wheel. Early pietists and later scholars found that learning Torah was such a preparation. The mystics and the Chassidic movement of the *Baal Shem Tov* immersed themselves in a *mikveh*, spiritual cleansing before prayer. They also introduced singing, dancing, and bodily movement to move their prayers from physical action to the mystical union. "All my bones [limbs] say Lord who is like to You" (Ps. 35:30). The *nigun*, the tune, carries the words on its wings, but the tune without the words is even like the incense offered in the Temple.

A major impediment in prayer is our inability to negate our own importance and to humble ourselves before the Master of the Universe. It is very difficult to praise Him for the goodness and the mercies if we see ourselves and our abilities as the source of these same gifts. It is as equally difficult to ask for Divine assistance or guidance unless we really understand and believe that He is the source of everything. Although arrogance and the view of self can prevent meaningful prayer, so too can the opposite. Sometimes we feel so depressed and despondent that God seems so far removed or far too great to hear and reply to us. Kalanymus, the *Admor* of Psetzianah, taught in the last days of the Warsaw Ghetto revolt: "Chanah, standing before Eli, prayed silently without moving her lips. The High Priest, forgetting the law that prayer could be said silently, rebuked her, considering her to be drunk, and so unable to pray properly. 'No,' answered Chanah, 'I am a woman of bitter spirit.' And so are we here concluded the *Admor*" (*Aish Kodesh*).

But we have an assurance that He hears the voices of the orphan and the widow, of the poor and afflicted, and of the broken and persecuted. He hears the voice of Jonah even from the depths, even from the inside of the whale. The *Ba'al Shem Tov* taught that there are many ways to unite with God, but prayer is the most efficacious, being available to all. "There are many keys to many doors in the House of God, but the ax breaks them all." Menachem Mendel of Kotsk said, "There is nothing more perfect or more complete [for Divine worship] than the broken heart."

It is really undeserved kindness that enables us to use our speech in prayer. "O Lord open my lips and my mouth shall declare Your praise" (Ps. 51:7).

MAṢA'EI

National Reward and Punishment

The way a society reacts to crime and treats its criminals is a major expression of its moral and ethical principles. After all, crime represents a violation of the normal fabric of society, a crisis as it were, in moral thought. There is a Torah response to the treatment of criminals that commences with *parshat Mishpatim*, which outlines the basic principles of civil and social legislation. This legislation commences with the laws of the Hebrew bondsman and maidservant, the weakest and most vulnerable of Hebrew society, having lost their freedom, which could be considered a form of death. Our *parshah* provides details of those who cause the death of their fellowman, the greatest of all crimes, already mentioned in *Mishpatim*.

That legislation mandated the sale by the *bet din* of a male thief, unable otherwise to pay back that which he had stolen. Actually, there was no sale but rather a form of indentured servitude, the receipts of which were to compensate the victim. During the period of servitude, the wife and children of the thief had to be provided for. It is maintained that this is far more equitable than the incarceration practiced in almost all societies today for the crime of theft. The victim is compensated, the family of the thief is provided for, society does not have the cost of jails, and so on. Although this is true, nevertheless the thief is denied his freedom, the essential basis for human existence. The *eved ivri* was deprived of his freedom because he had deprived others of their very being. "With all your strength, with all your might; there are people for whom their wealth is more important than their lives" (*Rashi, Devarim* 6:5). People risk their lives to create wealth but also to protect it from others. "A poor man is considered as dead," said the rabbis. The *eved ivri* was denied his freedom, causing a little death, as it were. He had abused his spiritual freedom by being unable to use his free will correctly when he stole. If, after the period of his servitude, he said, "I love my master, my wife and my children, I shall not go free. . . . Then . . . to the doorpost or the door [of the court] and . . . shall bore his ear with the awl and he shall serve him forever" (*Shmot* 21:5–6). As a free man, he could be a servant of the Lord, yet he barters this freedom for the patronage of a human master and for a life with a slave and her children. His fathers had earned their freedom by placing the blood of their Pesach offering on their doorposts, signaling their free will acceptance of God. The ear that had heard at Sinai, "You shall not steal," actually heard nothing, so had rejected the spiritual freedom earned in Egypt. So the Talmud, *Kiddushin* 22b, taught that the piercing of the lobe of the ear was to be done at the doorpost. The *Shem miShmuel* points out that the only place in the Torah, apart from references to Avraham, where the term *ivri* is used, is in regard to the thief sold into servitude. Avraham is called *ivri* because he stood *meiever*, opposite or in contrast to, the rest of the world. The thief withdrew back over to the non-Abrahamic world; he had become an *ivri*, one who passed back over. By opting out of the status of freedom, the *eved ivri* agreed to serve his master forever. However, this unlimited option is denied to him, forcing him, even against his will, ultimately to go free. "The children of Israel are My servants" (*VaYikra* 25:55) and the rabbis commented not the servants of other servants. So when freedom is proclaimed by the *Shofar* of the *Yovel*, Jubilee Year, on Yom Kippur, the *eved ivri* has freedom thrust upon him. He returns to his community and real free family. From this verse in Leviticus, a halakhah was learned that a worker may unilaterally choose not to continue to be employed or to withhold his labor as in a strike. He would be halakhically liable for any loss or damage incurred but this freedom is his. Work contracts that obligate both sides for periods longer than five years present halakhic problems, implying as they do a permanent loss of freedom for the employee. Macroeconomic policies as under socialist economics that guarantee full permanent employment or lifelong tenure as in the Japanese corporate model would need to be examined in a Jewish perspective. They actually represent a trade-off whereby economic security is exchanged for limitations on personal free choice. This creates a form of economic feudalism, similar to the feudalism of the Middle Ages in Europe, when people traded their freedom of movement and of economic choice for the military protection of the lords, barons, and kings.

In *Mishpatim*, the framework of legislation began with the law of *eved ivri*, the thief who causes the small death of those whose property he steals. That framework continues with those who shed the blood of others including premeditated killing and deliberate murder but also those guilty of manslaughter, that is, unintentional murder or accidental killing. For the latter, our *parsha* provides the six cities of refuge in addition to the forty-two cities given to the Levites in lieu of their share of the Promised Land. In all these cities, the freedom of the unintentional killer is circumscribed, a parallel with indentured servitude of the *eved ivri*. The exile continued until the death of the incumbent High Priest.

At the dawn of the new postdeluge world, the Noachide covenant warned, "However your blood which belongs to your souls of man, of every man for that of his brother, I will demand the soul of man. Whoever sheds the blood of man by man shall his blood be shed; for in the Image of God He made man. And you shall be fruitful and multiply" (*Bereishit* 9:5–7).

Whether one smites another with an instrument of iron, however small, that can inflict fatal wounds, or wood or stone of a size and weight sufficient to be fatal, in a manner that experts determine are a direct cause of death, one is a murderer to be punished by death at human hands. It is true that Torah law requires that the murderer be warned by witnesses, who also bear witness to the murder. It is true that a *Sanhedrin* that used the death penalty was a bloody *Sanhedrin*. There is even no evidence of the death penalty being considered as an act of vengeance nor of deterrence. Nevertheless, one who destroyed the image of God, one who spilled the blood that is the essence of life, and one who destroyed all the future generations who would have come into existence had the dead person continued to live, forfeited his or her right to all of these. When Cain kills his brother Abel, the voice of his brother's blood calls out from the earth.

Now on the threshold of entering the Land that is the vehicle for the holy society and for the sanctified individual life, to be crafted by Torah, the Noachide covenant of the inviolable dignity of the *Tzelem* Elokim, the likeness of God that is in mankind is renewed. Now it is extended to provide an institution for atonement even for unpremeditated manslaughter, that is, the *arei miklat* (cities of refuge) as a fundamental condition for Israel's possession and enjoyment of the Promised Land. Exile to these cities is the punishment for one who kills by accident without malice and without intent. It is true that technically there was an accident (*Shmot* 21:13); nevertheless, somebody died, blood was spilled, and a *Tzelem* Elohim erased. Such traumatic events cannot go unremarked and unrequited. Just as good deeds are credited to pious people, so, too, bad ones flow, even if indirectly, from other bad deeds. Exile is the penance of one who causes an accidental manslaughter, but the guilt is not his alone. The high priest, representative of the spiritual striving and achievements of Israel, knows that somehow his stewardship was lacking if people are killed; the exile is linked therefore to his own life span. The rabbis tell us that his mother or wife brought special food to the exile to placate him and prolong the priest's life.

SONG OF THE HOLY COMMONWEALTH

DEVARIM

Introduction: S. R. Hirsch

Although Hirsch never actually wrote an introduction to the book of *Devarim* or any of the books of the Torah, I have taken the liberty of creating such an introduction based on his comments on the first *parshah* of this book. These comments express succinctly the character of the whole book and its purpose.

The Mishneh Torah as *Devarim* is called is not a survey of the people's history nor is it a repetition of the laws previously given. Rather it is a guide to the society this generation is about to create when, in the immediate future, it crosses the Jordan without Moshe, into the Promised Land. So the salient points of their history since leaving Egypt are reviewed. Revelation at Sinai, the rebellions in the desert, and the victories in Trans-Jordan all teach valuable lessons for the new situation, and so needed to be repeated: Laws such as those of government, warfare, and centralized worship not relevant to their wanderings, were essential for the new commonwealth they were creating. Now was an appropriate moment, therefore, and so they were taught for the first time or new perspectives added. All the *Shalosh Regalim* and their laws were revealed previously in the books of *Shmot* and *VaYikrah*, so that their basic concepts and ideas should be seen as part of the Torah. Now additional perspectives and added dimensions would reflect a settled and independent nation, so *Devarim* presents their nationalism to be woven into the existing framework. At the same time, *Shabbat*, Yom Kippur and Rosh Hashanah, and *Shemini Atzeret* are not mentioned because they flow primarily from the personal relationship of the individual to God and so their importance is not changed by the settlement in the Land. In the desert, all the physical needs of the people were provided for directly from Heaven. In the new situation in the Promised Land, they would have to satisfy their needs through natural methods. Class differences and inequalities would arise so the laws of charity and social responsibility needed to be expanded and clarified. An essential phase of marriage was missing in the wilderness because the normal aspects of life—property, social rights, and legal conditions—were missing. Now, however, the settled condition in the Land, the acquisition of wealth, and the social structure required rules and regulations considering the ethical and physiological elements of entering and dissolving marriage. Here are introduced the laws of *kiddushin* and divorce, *levirate* marriage and forbidden unions, such as forbidding marriage with Moav and Ammon or the children of an incestuous or adulterous relationship.

Basic concepts such as the Ten Commandments, *kashrut*, economic honesty, charity, and love and fear of God are repeated here. They continue to have the same force and importance as before; their repetition comes to reinforce their importance in the new national political entity in the Holy Land.

Indeed, the first eleven chapters of *Devarim* detail the fundamentals of Torah. Love and Fear of God, Divine Unity and Torah study, *tefillin*, *mezuzah*, *tzitzit*, grace after meals, and the indivisibility and immutability of Torah provide the individual with the guidance and teaching needed in the normal or natural way of living that will result by crossing the Jordan.

The generation that enters the Land is distinctly different from that which left Egypt. They had no direct experience of the Exodus nor of the rebellions in the desert. These and the spiritual lessons to be learned were detailed for them by Moshe, and then in the final chapters, the trials and tribulations they would face in the future are detailed.

Throughout the book, the speeches, admonitions, and historical stories reveal poignantly the depth of feeling and love with which Moshe clung to his people and their future happiness. Throughout the book, Moshe expresses his longing to give Israel his spirit and soul to guide them in the future.

DEVARIM

The Pursuit of Justice

The pursuit of justice and the establishment of a judiciary are not in Judaism merely a means of adjudicating disputes, protecting property, and maintaining civil rights, but rather an integral of the Divine Attributes. So on Rosh Hashanah, the coronation is of the Divine King of Justice while human judges bear the name of divinity, Elohim. At the very outset of human history, the Divine Covenant with mankind made the establishment of a just legal system and the accompanying judiciary a requisite for that covenant. It is appropriate, therefore, that the book of Devarim, the final Mosaic discourses prior to Israel entering its Promised Land, should at the very outset determine the characteristics of a holy judiciary and its legal structure.

There are two groups of characteristics needed to qualify for this judiciary. "You shall discern [by holy guidance] men of valor [of wealth according to Rashi, military leaders according to Abarbanel], God fearing men, people of truth and those who [literally hate money usually understood as] who are impervious to bribes" (*Shmot* 18:21). These four characteristics typify judges who have the spiritual and material powers to judge in truth and are able to withstand political, economic, or popular pressure to pervert justice. Our *parsha* adds another element that will ensure justice in all its forms. Moshe chooses people "who are distinguished, wise and well known" (*Devarim* 1:15). "Wise in the laws of the Torah and knowledgeable in the sciences of the mind," even as was Betzalel of whom it is written [in connection with the Mishkan], "He filled him with Godly spirit with wisdom insight and [scientific] knowledge" (*VaYikra* 35:31) (*Abarbanel*). "Well known," familiar with the tribes and communities, they worked with (*Rashi*) but were also popular and acceptable to the people (*Talmud Bavli Sanhedrin* 16b and *Sifri Devarim*).

A just and moral society requires more than just a judiciary. There is need for leaders in all walks of life, officials to enforce the law, and a sociopolitical establishment. So while Exodus is concerned with judges, our *parsha* introduced additional leadership factors. These two groups of leadership characteristics determine the type of people eligible to fill all the many and diversified elements that create a society. Moses appoints leaders of thousands, of hundreds, of fifties, and of tens, until each one thousand Israelites were guided by 131 people. The commentators saw a rational and functional reason for this relatively large number. There were military officers for each thousand soldiers, there were judges for each hundred people, teachers of Torah for each fifty, and police for each ten. There were enforcers of the court decisions and supervisors of the markets. *Abarbanel* sees an ascending order of judges according to the sums in dispute and a separation of courts for monetary matters, real estate, and for civil and criminal cases either requiring physical punishment or the death penalty. He sees the necessity for those who will supervise or create the municipal infrastructure or administer the social costs.

This wide-ranging and extensive civil service characterizes Jewish social and communal life throughout history. Not only do we have textual evidence relating to the days of the independent states of Judah and Israel, but there is similar documentary evidence in Jewish life in *Galut*. There were distinct Jewish communities throughout the world until the nineteenth century that constituted autonomous ministates. These obtained charters, allowing them their own judiciary and independent legal system but also a fiscal framework for funding the social costs. This framework funded the local council, tax assessors, and collectors; religious functionaries; and public officials necessary for the health, security, educational, charitable, and legal services required by the community and the services themselves. Furthermore, the public sector supervised market behavior, pricing, and restraints on trade and economic activity. The concept of a civil service, its functions, and the spiritual qualities required are all a natural and integral part of the characteristic of Judaism as a national-communal religion rather than simply an individual orientated one. However, emancipation and the secular character of the modern political state severely curtails this national-communal characteristic. This has served to transform Judaism so that religion becomes focused primarily on the personal choice of individuals for a pattern of ritual, spiritual, and ethical behavior that is distinctly different from Israel's mission to constitute itself as a Holy Nation.

The character of the judges and of the public officials, while of great importance, is of its own accord insufficient to ensure the just society envisioned by Judaism. In the same way as all other spiritual qualities or merits are integrated with legal forms, so, too, are the various functions of the judges and officials. As in many other halakhic instances, the forms are both negative and positive.

In four different passages in the Torah, judges are cautioned to always give impartial treatment to all parties concerned. Here in our *parsha* (Chapter 1, 16) this is demonstrated by "hear the cases between." "Said R. Hanina, this is an injunction to the judges against hearing the words of one litigant before the other has arrived. It is also an injunction to the litigant not to get the judge to hear his version before the other has arrived" (*Talmud Bavli, Sanhedrin* 7b). For the Or Hayyim the "hear" in our verse is to induce patience in the judge, to allow the introduction of new evidence, and to persist in the court session, until the truth is shown. "Between your brethren" teaches the same commentary on the Torah requires the judge to pay attention to all that takes place in the court between the parties but also to hear the case without any differentiation between the parties.

The major problem of impartiality arises when there are great differences between the litigants, one is rich and the other poor, one is accomplished and the other ignorant or a failure, one is well respected and the other a ne'er-do-well. Five times the Torah challenges the judge to be impervious to the social, economic, or political differences between the litigants, each time with a different nuance or emphasis that comes to present different scenarios. There is to be no favoritism in judgment—literally, "recognizing a face" (*Devarim* 1:17), and actually, to ignore the personalities involved. This was seen in the Talmud to apply not only to the litigants, but also to the appointment of judges. This same verse not only refers to the differences between the people involved but also to the relevant sums involved—small is as important as large. Often consideration is urged for the poor or the weak and mercy is urged even if it means a distortion of justice. Sometimes, however, this mercy corrupts, leading to greater injustice and oppression even than if the poor were made to bear the full extent of their actions. However, "in righteousness shall you judge your neighbor" (*VaYikra* 19:15). This concludes the verse that begins "You shall not favor the poor nor honor the great." The *Midrash* teaches that one should not rule in favor of the poor litigant where it is unjust, arguing that after all the rich have an obligation to support the poor anyway. Another *Midrash* (*Mechilta Shmot* 23:6) sees the poor not only as financially deprived but also those who are poor in *mitzvot* or disreputable.

Mercy and consideration for the poor even as respect for the rich and powerful are forms of bribery. More insidious and powerful, however, is the direct bribery of the judges. These blind the eyes of wise and corrupt the words of the righteous. Direct payments of money are perhaps the easiest to avoid but there are others far more pernicious and often even accepted behavior. There is bribery through the political support for the election of the judge, status-granting social invitations to the judges or their families; even substantial contributions to charities close to their hearts or that they actucontrol. All of these ultimately distort perception and justice. The Admor of Gur once was offered a bribe that he refused. Unknown to him, the litigant subsequently placed the money in the coat hanging in the master's study. All through the case, the *Admor* found his original conviction of the guilt of the giver of the bribe blurred, so that he sought various justifications. He recessed the case, and when he put on his coat, he found the bribe in its pocket. "Now I realize," he said, "exactly what was distorting my judgment." His descendant, the Avnei Nezer, showed the monetary bribe he'd been offered to his sons, and replied to their query, "Indeed that is the problem with the bribe: it looks like all other money."

Not only judges, however, are included in the prohibition of bribery. Modern international commerce and finance are often faced with the impossibility of operating in countries where bribery of government officials or even of corporate officers is normal business culture. Even in their home markets, businessmen find that political contributions, employment of the unqualified but well connected, and unrecorded payments or kickbacks ease their transactions and growth. Ordinary people, too, are tempted to avoid fines or jump the queue through the bribery of officials, civil servants, or staff members. In all these cases, the recipient of the bribe has some discretion or role in the decision-making process and therefore are in fact judges. So "not only judges are forbidden to take bribes [and the giver forbidden to give them] but so too all of the officials and those engaged in communal affairs" (*Arukh HaShulchan, Choshen Mishpat*, Section 9, subsection 1).

Although no favoritism or discrimination is allowed within the judicial process, nevertheless the balance in Judaism between justice and mercy finds an expression outside this process. We are urged to express our religiosity in being prepared to forego some of our legally recognized rights. Our Sages tell us that Jerusalem of the Second Temple was destroyed because the people all insisted on litigation to obtain their full rights. Maimonides describes the *Talmid Chacham*, Judaism's role model, as one who, inter alia, "keeps his obligations in commerce even where the law allows him to withdraw or retract . . . if others have obligations upon him he should deal mercifully, forgiving and extending credit" (*Mishneh Torah Hilkhot Deot*, Chapter 5, *Halakhah* 13). In cases where a debtor is unable to pay, the creditors will be urged to behave charitably and waive their rights. If they refuse, then the *bet din* has to search and find all the assets of the debtor and sell them; payment of loans is a mitzvah. This is even if the creditor is rich and the debtor poor. After the assets are sold and the debtor left only with his *tefillin*, weekday clothing and food, he and his family are poor. There is now a definite obligation on the community, including the creditors to provide him charity, even with the standard of living he had been accustomed to. This charity is in moral contradiction to modern bankruptcy law that allows the debtor to enjoy this standard of living or to continue to operate the firm, at the expense of the creditors

VE'ETCHANAN

Love of the One God

Sh'ma Yisrael, a central part of our daily prayers, a reaffirmation of the Ten Commandments revealed at Sinai (*Talmud Yerushalmi, Berachot*, Chapter 1, *Halakhah* 5), is included in the text of the *mezuzot* on our doorposts and of the *tefillin* we bind on our arms and heads. These are the last words the dying Jew recites after the deathbed confession. Generations of Jewish men, women, and children sanctified God's Name through martyrdom with *Sh'ma Yisrael* on their lips. Halakhically, Sh'ma may be recited in any language if the knowledge of Hebrew is insufficient, requires understanding and intent, *kavanah*, and may be said aloud so as to be audible to the worshiper (*Shulchan Arukh, Orech Chaim*, Section 61); this is fitting for a declaration that is the foundation of the personal and communal value structure we endeavor to create.

The knowledge of God, the Creator, His intervention in human affairs and His recurring mercy, were all seen by Israel in the redemption from Egypt, at the revelation at Sinai, and throughout the wonders and miracles during the wanderings in the desert. We need to repeat the Sh'ma to continuously hear the national memories of all these revelations and the traditions illustrated by them, as handed down from generation to generation. In this way, we are able to use the knowledge of God contained in the Sh'ma, so that ultimately, we, too, are able to see and witness in our everyday lives, in the workings of history, and in the magnificence of nature that which was revealed at the dawn of the formation of Israel.

It is this Israel, the united national-community-family entity that is the subject of *Sh'ma Yisrael*. It excludes Ishmael and Esau of the Abrahamic descendants, it is more than the sons of Jacob, and even transcends the house of Jacob. The subject bears the name Israel, no longer Ya'akov, the subservient one, nor the supplanter, but rather the one who prevails. This is the Israel who creates with the Divine blueprint, the social-political and national unit that serves to bring the world to recognition of the Unity of God. Maimonides explains that through the monotheistic religions, Israel's teachings, albeit in a fractured and distorted form, bring mankind to ultimately accept the unity, that currently only Israel proclaims.

This unity is the antithesis of the human perception of many different attributes of divinity—anger, mercy, wisdom, kindness, war, peace, judgment, and forgiveness. This perception creates many deities, spirits of natural phenomena, or energy forms, each one representing a different attribute or power. Our world thereby becomes perceived as a constant clash between Heaven and Earth, this world and the next world, the individual welfare and the good of society, and between materialism and spirituality. Men and women accordingly become aware that their own faults, and weaknesses mandate that they worship those manifestations rather than the One God. It is this awareness that Maimonides sees as the spiritual foundation for idolatry. *Sh'ma*, with its proclamation of the Unity of God, and therefore the Oneness, categorically denies the very existence of deities or semideities. "They symbolized You in many varied versions, yet You are a Unity containing all the allegories" (Hymn of Glory).

The categorical denial of any duality or multiplicity beyond God is the basis for morality and ethical behavior. God makes men and women in His image, whereby it is possible for them to live in imitatio Dei. We, however, create our idols and our gods in our own image. So in the ancient world the gods had all the jealousies, lusts, and sexual appetites of their creators, suitably magnified to godly proportions. Such gods and goddesses could hardly be a source for the moral and ethical behavior of their worshipers. Furthermore, the multiplicity of deities ultimately means a multiplicity of moralities. Perhaps this is exactly what the worshipers really wanted. Gods and goddesses, deities, spirits, and natural phenomena that only needed to be worshiped without imposing restraints and limitations on the lusts and appetites of their worshippers. Indeed, our Sages taught that being ashamed to indulge themselves sexually, people invented idols that would permit that which is forbidden by the morality of the One God.

This Oneness is not simply the containing of conflicting attributes within the Unity. Rather the Oneness is an intrinsic whole without any conflict. The Oneness is of *HaShem*, the God of Love, but also of *Elokim*, the God who dispenses Justice, not only *HaShem* is One and not only *Elokeinu* is one, but *HaShem Elokeinu* is One. Judgment even when it punishes us is of itself only a manifestation of this Love. The bad things that happen to us are not the machinations of a god of darkness, nor of meaningless chance nor of the inability of God to protect us. Rather there is only One, so we say *brachot* on all the goodness He grants us, but acknowledge Him also for that which is denied to us. On the receiving of good news we praise Him while on hearing bad tidings, we say, blessed be the Righteous Judge. When Israel left Egypt they had witnessed miracles and great redemption, yet the Torah tells us that only at the Red Sea did they believe in Him. Prior to that, God had only been a source of salvation and benefits; it does not require great belief to accept such a God. When they saw Pharaoh and the chariots pursuing them and cried out in their fear, then they acknowledged that this, too, came from Him, "and they believed in *HaShem* and His servant Moshe" (*Shmot* 14:31). A *mitnaged* was sent by the rabbis to examine the Torah scholarship of the Chassidic leader Elimelech of Lizensk, the *Noam Elimelech*. "Tell me," he asked, "What is the meaning of the talmudic dictum 'One is required to bless Him on the evil things that happen to a person, as on the good'?" (*Talmud Bavli, Brachot* 57a). The Admor referred him to his brother Reb Zusha, and there he repeated his question. "What's evil?" came the quiet reply.

The Oneness of God calls to us to be in harmony and as one with all that occurs in our lives. Our thoughts, feelings, and actions need to be joined to the Divine Unity. When we acknowledge that Unity and dedicate ourselves to that Oneness, these become of themselves joined into a unity. Despite the inner conflicts, the divergence of our ambitions, and the changes in our physical and economic condition, we become one through our love for Him. This is a love that forms a unity with fear. "Here is written love further on (verse 13): "You shall fear HaShem your God," "serve Him with love and serve Him with fear. Those who love will never forget that which the beloved asks of them and those who fear will not do what is forbidden to them" (*Rambam*, Commentary on the *Mishnah*, *Avot* Chapter 1, *Mishnah* 3).

"With all your heart" with both the Yetzer HaTov and the Yetzer HaRah (*Talmud Bavli*, *Berachot* 54a). Actually, there is no *yetzer*, feelings, impulse, or intention that is good or evil. There are only our abilities to do good or evil within our own free choice. This extends to all the human desires for material things—food, sex, property, and social power. Without our *yetzarim*, these desires would be met or satisfied solely out of instinct. As a result that which is distasteful or dangerous would be avoided instinctively, but there would be no moral choice. Furthermore, without human desires the world could not exist, develop, or prosper. Within the framework of "with all your heart," makes the satisfaction of all our needs, wants and desires, a service of God.

"With all your soul," continues the Talmud in *Berachot*, "means if even He demands your soul." Beyond the recognition that all that which happens to us, even that which we see as evil and harmful, has its source in the One, lies the ability even to sacrifice our lives. Human life is sacred, yet not at any cost. There are ideals, spiritual striving, and a value system that may sometimes have to take precedence over the sanctity of human life. Just as there is a mitzvah of "you shall live by them," Torah laws, so there is a mitzvah of Kiddush HaShem, "even if He demands your life." So, saving life is a means of observing *Shabbat* or of Yom Kippur, yet surrendering may be the answer to idolatry, sexual immorality, or murder. In times of religious persecution, even the simplest and least significant of the mitzvot may have precedence over life itself. Carefully monitored, yet clearly enunciated, we sanctify His Name both in our manner of living but also sometimes by giving up that life.

"With all your might—with all your possessions" (*Berachot* 54a). The Divine Plan for the world is that people's material and economic needs have to be satisfied through human effort. However, such needs easily become transformed into wants that by their nature are almost limitless. More than any of the other human drives or needs, the economic one is never satisfied—one has a hundred dinar then wants 200," taught the rabbis. Since here "more is always conceived as being better than less," driven by greed and envy, the legitimate economic drive also creates fraud, oppression, exploitation, strife, and war. It is the very power and persistence of the economic *yetzer* that makes love of God so essential for its restraint. "The verse has already commanded us "with all your soul," even at the cost of our lives. Why then is it necessary to command us with regard to our wealth? "This is because there are many people for whom their wealth is more precious even than their lives" (*Berachot* 61b).

"VeAhavta, and you shall love" not only is a commandment to love that which we cannot see but is also a promise that such love is possible. "When we study and understand His commandments, His teachings, and His acts, we may come closer to understanding Him and attain joy in Him, this constitutes love of Him . . . . We have already explained that this also obligates us to call upon all mankind to serve Him and have faith in Him. Just as in the case of someone human that one loves, one recounts their praises, enlarges on their merits, and calls other people to also love him, so too we call upon the foolish and ignorant to seek a knowledge of the truth that we already have acquired (*Sefer HaMitzvot, Rambam, Mitzvah* 2). "What is the right kind of love? . . . the very soul shall be bound by the love of God, ever enraptured by it, even as is the mind of one who, being lovesick, does not cease to languish after the beloved one . . . whether sitting or moving, eating or drinking . . . it is quite clear that the love of the Holy One Blessed Be He, cannot become grounded in the human heart until one is completely enraptured by it and forsakes all else" (*Mishneh Torah, Hilkhot T'Shuva*, Chapter 10, *Halakhot* 3 and 6). So the psalmist sings, "All my bones will say, Lord who is like unto You" (Ps. 35:10) and every *Shabbat* eve, we sing the Song of Songs, Israel's love poem with its God, and the mystic Alkharizi sang, "Beloved of my Soul, Yedid Nefesh . . . my soul is lovesick for Thee."

What does this love consist of? "If He grants us well-being—we will acknowledge the source of our well-being and thank Him; if there is affliction and suffering in our life, we will bear it, trust in Him even more [and know that this too is from Him] . . . 'You have starved me, left me naked in the darkness of the night but taught me Your strength and greatness. Though You burn me with fire, I shall only love more.' This is as it is written "You shall love God your God, with all your heart and with all your soul and with all your might" (*Hovat Halevavot*).

"This love means that the Name of Heaven shall become beloved through you . . . one should study Torah and Mishnah [written and oral laws], . . . and minister to Torah Scholars . . . All our business and commercial dealings should be conducted in faith in Him, [alternatively, honestly] and our interpersonal relations should be pleasant and truthful. What do people say? "See how proper and perfected are such a person's ways" . . . 'You are My servant Israel in whom I shall be glorified' (Isa. 49:3) (*Talmud Bavli, Yoma* 86a).

"We learn from our ancestors that our love of God is expressed by making Him beloved of all the creatures. It is written 'the souls they [Abraham and Sarah] had made in Horon' (*Bereishit* 12:5). If all the inhabitants of the world gathered together they would be unable, surely, to create even one soul? What then does it mean 'the souls they had made?' This teaches us that Abraham converted the men and Sarah converted the women and brought them under the wings of the Divine Presence . . . (*Sifri*).

EIKEV

The Yoke of *Mitzvot*

Is the love of God and the recognition of His Unity sufficient for motivating and monitoring human striving for the Divine, for His Justice and His Righteousness? If so, then the *Shema* of *Vaetchanan* could stand by itself as the foundation for spiritual life. Yet there is Parshat Eikev with its specifically Jewish teaching that life also requires practices and acts that are applications of the love of the Divine and of His Unity. Bereft of *mitzvot*, lacking any action orientation, and without integration with the daily normal activities of people, the love of the Divine easily remains mere pious sloganeering and ineffectual religiosity. So the acceptance of the yoke of Heaven is balanced by the yoke of *mitzvot*, and "You shall love the Lord your God" is followed in our prayerbooks by "If you hearken, [hearken, you hearken for emphasis] to My commandments that I command you today" (*Devarim* 11:13).

> These commandments were only given in order to purify people. After all, what difference does it make to the Almighty whether animals are slaughtered in the throat or through the neck? So we see that the whole purpose of the mitzvot is to sanctify human beings. (*Bereshit Rabbah*, 48)

Each of these 613 mitzvot serves either to provide truth or prevent falsehood, either to educate towards good attributes or to educate against evil, either to provide just social frameworks or to protect against injustice. (Maimonides, Guide to the Perplexed, part 3)

To achieve this purification and the sanctification, it is essential that each and everyone should study and learn. So we are commanded, "and teach them diligently to your children, to speak of them [to make these spiritual and intellectual truths so relevant and impressive that they become the essence of the whole outlook on life of the children and their behavior] when you sit in your house, when you walk on the road and when you lie down [to sleep] and rise up [in the morning]" (*Devarim* 11:19). Repeated three times daily in our prayers, this fundamental issue of Torah study is the cornerstone of Jewish behavior and continuity. In Egypt, religion was kept hidden behind the hieroglyphics known only to the priests. In the Middle Ages, Bibles were kept chained to the benches and preserved in Latin, making them unavailable to the public. In other religions, even to this day, religious knowledge consists of secrets revealed only to the select few. Yet for us, the halakhah determines that "everyone is commanded to study Torah whether he be rich or poor, old or young, sick or healthy" (*Shulchan Arukh, Yoreh De'ah*, Section 246, subsection 1).

Our Torah study is, in addition, the key to the observance of His commandments. "Rabbi Tarphon, Rabbi Jose the Galillean and Rabbi Akiva, were asked, 'What is greater, study or actions?' They all answered, 'study, since it leads one to [the appropriate] actions'"(*Talmud Bavli Kiddushin* 40b).

Such an action-oriented religion requires spiritual preparation and emotional emphasis, otherwise a purely mechanical and meaningless ritual may emerge. Even worse, such actions may cover beneath their cloak, immoral and un-Jewish behavior.

When one comes to perform a mitzvah one should not do so suddenly or hurriedly. "The pious used to prepare themselves for an hour before their prayers [in study and contemplation], and a further hour after the prayers in order to gather together the spiritual effects of their having prayed [to carry them with them in their daily activities]." (*Talmud Bavli Berachot* 30) Rather one should collect one's thoughts as to the proper way [not only ritually] to perform the mitzvot.... I myself have found that the mitzvot I have done without preparation I have not performed properly. (*Chayei Adam*)

Such preparation must of necessity include the social and moral effects of our observance of the *mitzvot*. Yisarel Salanter pointed out that those who rise early to say the penitential prayers, the *Slichot* of Rosh Hashanah and Yom Kippur, need to be careful that they do not incur other sins in the process. They may make a noise when they rise and dress themselves, thereby waking the rest of the household and even their neighbors. If these include the sick people or the small children they cause them sorrow and pain. In their haste, they throw their household waste into the street, damaging those in the public domain. If they find their place in the synagogue unprepared or some disorder there, they shout and scream at the *shamash*, thereby transgressing the laws of *loshon harah*, and they are guilty of shaming their fellows in public [akin to murder].

It is possible to perform *mitzvot* sullenly without conviction, without spiritual joy, and without subjecting ourselves to the God who commanded them. The Talmud (*Shabbat* 31a) teaches that "the Divine Presence [our attachment to which is the whole purpose of the *mitzvot*] does not rest where there is depression and sorrow [both of which are often the soil from which error springs] nor in indolence, nor in frivolity... but only where there is rejoicing in His *mitzvot*." The same source observes that those *mitzvot* like circumcision that Israel accepted upon itself with joy, saying "I rejoice over Your Words, like one who finds great treasures" (Ps. 119). They still observe in joy by celebrating with a festive meal. This is indeed the only mitzvah that guards, identifies, and obligates us wherever we are and at all periods of our lives. King David in his bath regretted that here he was denuded of all *mitzvot*, yet when he saw the sign of the brit, his spirits revived. In contrast, those *mitzvot* that were forced onto Israel, such as the laws of sexual immorality, "and Moses heard the people crying and complaining according to their families" (*Bamidbar* 15:23)— which refers to family purity—these they observe in strife and unwillingly. So, too, those *mitzvot* like *milah* and the refusal to accept idolatry, that the Jews have suffered martyrdom for, they continue to observe under all conditions, in all countries, and at all times. However, those *mitzvot* like *tefillin* that were not the subject of *kiddush hashem*, they observe fitfully and intermittently.

The *Shem MiShmuel* sees that *mitzvot* observed without the correct motivation or without joy and not in the correct spiritual framework require atonement. Obviously, such atonement differs from the atonement for nonobservance of *mitzvot* and for sins of commission and omission. During Rosh Hashanah and Yom Kippur, we cleanse our souls and divest ourselves of those sins between us and God. This is parallel to the actions of a farmer who sifts winnows and cleanses the grain and the fruit before bringing them into the granary or sheds. There are two kinds of refuse that need to be cleared. One, in the case of grain, is chaff and the other is straw. The former is refuse proper having no value and is often mixed with thorns, weeds, and burrs; the latter has a value of its own being useful in the barns and stables. It is only with regard to the grain that straw is considered valueless and refuse. So, too, with regard to atonement. There are sins of which we need to rid ourselves completely, like the chaff and that we do during the Days of Awe. However, all the mitzvot that were done improperly, resemble the straw. These we do not discard but need to be cleansed and repaired. This is done by using straw or branches of trees that also have a value yet relative to the fruit are refuse, as *schach* for our *sukkah*. By linking these *mitzvot* to the joy and gratitude expressed on Sukkot, we cleanse and atone for the way and the spirit in which we observed *mitzvot*.

The message of the yoke of the *mitzvot* is followed by the consequences of not observing them. Economic prosperity, material wealth, and the ability to enjoy their fruits—"and you shall eat and be satisfied"—are granted to us in accordance with our spiritual behavior. Drought, poverty, and exile are direct results of the rejection of *mitzvot*. "He will send in your midst attrition, confusion and worry. . . . Your heavens will be as iron and the earth will be as iron . . . your rain will be dust and dirt. . . . You will take abundant seed to plant in the field but you will harvest little for the locusts will devour it" (*Devarim* 28:20, 23, 38). These rewards and punishments are couched in the plural since they are the effects of the national-communal behavior; regarding individuals, each one reaps only the results of his or her behavior. Awareness of the results of the national-communal behavior is *Yirat Shamayim*—fear of Heaven. Some would see this fear either as fear of punishment for denying God's words or as a fear of His greatness (*Maimonides Guide to the Perplexed*, Part 3, Chapter 2). However, this would mean that we observe not because it is true and just but because we wish to escape Divine Wrath. Alternatively, the second form of fear is primarily not available to the average person but usually attained only by prophets, sages, or saints. Nevertheless, both these views of fear of Heaven are vital to our conduct. Fear of punishment, Divine or human, is in many cases essential to preserving a moral social fabric. For example, the difference between corruption and crime is that in the former case, society accepts and does not punish or reject immoral or criminal behavior so that it becomes pervasive and acceptable. Although ordinary people may not be able to fully grasp the nature of the Divine Greatness or its relevance for their own personal lives, nevertheless, they are able to strive toward an emulation of that greatness.

For Abarbanel the fear of Heaven is something different from that envisaged by Maimonides.

> For the love that He bore to our fathers, redeemed us from Egypt, gave us a Torah and granted us the Land of Israel as our inheritance and for all the mercies that He has done to us far beyond the rational order, miraculously and according to His own Will, we are obligated to love Him . . . because of this love a person needs to carefully avoid sin . . . acting contrary to His wishes and revealed Torah shows ingratitude

and a lack of appreciation for all the mercies and kindnesses granted to us as a people. So we have a duty to love the Lord our God and serve Him with that love, but simultaneously to fear transgressing His words and to guard them carefully . . . then His benevolence in the Creation and His constant Providence will be apparent to all mankind . . . . In His justice and mercy He grants blessings, prosperity and peace to those who fear Him . . . as it is written "O, fear the Lord, you who are sanctified to Him, for there is no deprivation for those who fear Him" (Ps. 34:10), and also "the Lord favors those who fear Him, who await upon His loving kindness" (Ps. 147:11). From these verses we see that those who fear God are those who are sanctified in their actions . . . fear of God in those who seek Him . . . . Fear and love of God flow from the same source and serve the same purpose . . . . Why then did the Torah create two separate mitzvot . . . the love is the positive acts and thoughts leading toward our clinging to God . . . while the fear is the negative, refraining from acts and thoughts that lead to disobeying His Torah and laws. (Arbarbanel, *Devarim*, Chapter 11)

Why should the national reward and punishment be described throughout the Torah, indeed throughout the Tanach in material terms? These are flocks and herds, rainfall in its needed times so as to be a blessing, fruit, the rewards of our economic endeavors, and the peace and serenity and security to enjoy all of them. We may see this as an expression of Judaism's spiritual concern and evaluation of the material benefits and pleasures granted to us. However, perhaps because the human lust and need for these material benefits and forms of wealth is almost insatiable, they constitute the major cause for ignoring His commandments and not fulfilling the *mitzvot*.

People only rebel against the Kodesh Baruch Hu when they are wealthy and satiated, even as it is written [in our *parsha*]. "Be careful lest you eat and are satiated, build good houses and dwell in them . . . your flocks and herds multiply and you increase your gold and your silver and all your wealth increases . . . So your hearts become haughty and then you forget God your God . . . or you may say in your heart: My own strength [wisdom or hard work] and the might of my own hand create all my wealth . . ." (*Devarim* 8:12–18). At the making of the Golden Calf it is written and the people sat down to eat and drink and then they rose up to behave wantonly. [Sforno explains that Moshe only threw down the tablets when he saw with what enjoyment and enthusiasm Israel worshipped the calf, thus signifying that they were unworthy of the Torah.] The generation of the Tower of Babel only rebelled because of their wealth and prosperity; "they found the valley of Shinar and they sat there" (*Bereishit* 11:2) this matter refers to eating and drinking as in the case of Israel and the Golden Calf. (*Sifri*)

This then is the challenge of wealth, to realize the real source of wealth and prosperity, a source that demands that the wealth be earned within the parameters of Divine Law and Divine Morality and that it be used only for the purposes for which it is granted, that is, to satisfy the needs of the owner but also "your brother shall live with you." This challenge can only be met if the basis is "wisdom is the fear of God."

RE'EH

Pesach Questions of the Four Sons

Pesach, its ritual, its significance for Jewish life, and its religious messages are repetitively mentioned in the Torah; our *parshah* being the final source. So, too, there is almost no Jewish ritual that does not contain a reference to the Exodus from Egypt; the *seder* night remains perhaps the last link even of the disappearing Jew with Judaism. Persecution and discrimination may create hidden Jews so our history is full of secret *sedarim* from the days of the Byzantium empire, through Yemen, through the marranos of the Inquisition, the Holocaust, and communist rule. If Judaism has a meaning and a relevance even in the tolerant and open societies in which we modern Jews find ourselves, it behooves us, therefore, to seek some of them in our understanding of *Pesach*.

Our slavery in Egypt was specifically aimed at Israel and is an intrinsic part of our specific national history. Still, as with other examples of anti-Semitism, it may well have been also an expression of a cruel and despotic political system. Hirsch postulates the possibility that Pharaoh wanted to compensate the oppressed Egyptians by creating a pariah class, more persecuted and more miserable than they were; one that they themselves could oppress. Indeed, we know from Egyptian records that Pharaoh was a despot, ruling over a highly stratified society of classes of limited freedom but all based on a large slave population.

Hirsch, commenting on *Shmot* 1:9–14, traces a pattern of oppression that repeated itself throughout Jewish history. First there was taxation, a price demanded from the foreigners for the right to live in the land, for the protection of the state against the local population or simply a source of income for the ruler. However, their status soon changed from exploited foreigners to slaves, no longer having any legal rights, people that any and every Egyptian could oppress and deal with as they wished. "They [the Egyptians] embittered their lives" (verse 14) in contrast to the previous situation "and they [Israel] built stone cities, Pittom and Ra'amses, for Pharaoh [a form or taxation]" (verse 11). Finally, the fiscal burden and slavery developed into spite and degradation. The suffering foretold to Abraham—*geirut* (strangers), *avdut* (slavery), and *inui* (embittered) came to pass; it was a threefold persecution paralleled in reverse order by the redemption. "I will bring you out from under the suffering of the Egyptians [*inui*], will deliver you from their slavery [*avdut*], and will redeem you [*geirut*]" (*Shmot* 6:6). Because the whole basis of the Egyptian persecution was *geirut*, God announces that He Himself is the champion of the stranger. The memory of this protection is enshrined in Jewish thought as part of the redemption from Egypt and in Jewish law where the rights of the stranger, to person and property, are emphasized and reiterated twenty-four times in the Torah.

This message of concern for the rights of the unprotected sectors of society, as important and moral as it is, is only part of *Pesach*; otherwise, it would only be a recipe for liberation and social responsibility, rather than part of the acceptance of Torah. So there is a fourth language of redemption—"and I will take you to Me for a People and I will be your God." At the revelation of the burning bush, Moshe is told that he will know of his divine mission when Israel will worship at Mount Sinai. Indeed this is the underlying teaching of *Pesach*. It is true that *Pesach* is evidence of God's intervention in the affairs of mankind, and of nature being an expression of His creation. However, this evidence is only shown by our fulfillment of His law. We express our freedom from the bonding of Egypt through our acceptance of servitude to God. This is a servitude expressed primarily through acts and actions, through deeds but also through refraining from deeds, through permissible and forbidden sex, food, clothing, business behavior, social relations, and communal organization. When we gather in our families on *Pesach*, discuss and retell the story of the exile in Egypt and our redemption, it is the enjoined actions that constitute the observance. Our fathers slaughtered the paschal lamb and put the blood on the doorposts as a sign; we affix *mezuzot* and bind tefillin as memorial signs. We, like them, actually eat the *matzot* as the bread of affliction but also as the bread of redemption, a redemption that came so swiftly that there was not time for the dough to leaven. We recite a set text repeated over thousands of years, a fulfillment of a Divine Commandment to tell our children of the Exodus on this specific night. Our houses are freed of leaven and our ownership of leaven is abrogated, which is the performance of age-old acts cleansing us of physical servitude and of spiritual fermentation.

This primacy of enjoined actions in Judaism is the essence of the questions and answers of the four sons of the *Haggadah*. These questions and answers that have been relevant to Jews throughout the centuries revolve around the very nature of Judaism as a religion observed through acts prescribed by Divine Law and obligatory on all Jewish individuals. It is true that there are as many views on the nature of the sons and their questions as there are commentators. It is true that the wise son seeks answers while of the evil son it is written, "when your sons will say unto you" (*Shmot* 12:26), saying, not questioning. Only one who has questions regarding their own physical and spiritual future seeks answers; for the others, all is irrelevant. It is significant that despite his antagonism, there is place even for the evil son in the *Haggadah* and so place for all our children at our *seder*.

Nevertheless, it seems that many of these and other views should be integrated into the view of the *Shem MiShmuel*, that it is the relevance of coerced and specific actions that is the issue.

For the wise son, this relevance is clear because he asks, "What are these *eidut* [testimonies] and *chukim* [statutes] and *mishpatim* [judgments] that the Lord our God commanded you?" (*Devarim* 6:20). *Eidut*—*matzah*, *maror*, and the paschal lamb that bear testimony to our exodus. The *chukim* that it is to be roasted whole, no bones broken and nothing left over. There are also the *mishpatim* that the non-Jewish stranger and the uncircumcised may not eat of it.

Throughout Jewish history, the Divine Promise to protect Israel, testified to by the *eidut*, has preserved us against persecutors and enemies. The *chukim* is to teach mankind the multifaceted and hidden wisdom of the Divine. "Why may no bones of the Passover lamb be allowed to be broken? So that the dogs may drag them about and the Egyptians be made to realize the nothingness and vanity of what they worshipped and so be put to shame and the Holy One be glorified" (*Zohar Bo* 41b).

Mishpatim, social laws, and judgments reflect the Exodus and *Pesach*. "You shall do no corruption in justice, in meteryard, in weight or in measure; just weights, a just *ephah* and a just *hin* [the rabbis saw the similarity between this and *hen*, yes, to teach that one's yes should be yes and the no, no] shall you have: I am the Lord your God Who brought you out of the land of Egypt. Therefore, shall you keep all My ordinances and all My judgements" (*VaYikra* 19:36–37). "Brought you out of Egypt"—for this purpose—"that you shall be honest in your actions" (*Rashi*). "I distinguished in Egypt between those who were first born and those who were not [the most secret and hidden knowledge. So] I am also certain to punish those who immerse their weights in salt to defraud thereby other people who are unaware of the fraud" (*Baba Metziah* 61b). The same talmudic source repeats this rejection of secret crimes in relation to the injunction against taking interest from other Jews. "Take no interest of him [*neshech*] referring to extra payment on loans—forbidden by Torah law] nor increase [*tarbit*—extra payments earned through trade or commerce forbidden by rabbinic law] but fear your God; that your brother may live with you. . . . I am the Lord Who brought you out of the land of Egypt to give you the Land of Canaan and to be your God" (*VaYikra* 25:35–38). Sometimes a person lusts after the interest, and it is extremely difficult to cleanse oneself of this lust. Therefore, we persuade ourselves that it is a legitimate act because the money would otherwise remain unemployed (if there was no interest-bearing loan). So the Torah had to state, "Be afraid of your God [Who knows all the secrets of the human mind]." Or, one pretends that the money belongs to a non-Jew in order to be able to lend it in an ostensibly legitimate way. This fraud is known only to the heart and thoughts of the lender. So the rabbis taught that one who lends money at interest denies the Exodus and the Divine Knowledge and Divine Justice that it exemplifies. In addition to the message of the impossibility of secret crimes, there is the social concept in *mishpatim* as the link between the freedom of the individual Jew and the Exodus. "For they are My servants whom I brought forth out of the land of Egypt; they shall not be sold as bondsmen" (*VaYikra* 25:42). From, this the rabbis learned that a worker may leave the employer at any time (if there is monetary damage this would have to be paid); because Jews have only one Master.

Just as there are *eidut*, *chukim*, and *mishpatim* relating to *Pesach* so too Judaism relates to all other aspects of life and society. Just as the wise son understands that those relating to *Pesach* are commanded by "our God," so, too, Judaism ascribes the same Divine Source to all the other forbidden and permitted acts.

Not so the wicked son. He does not deny the exile in Egypt nor the Exodus. He does not supress his hatred for Jewish servility or suffering. He does not express any desire to forget the story of Jewish history nor any objection to be reminded of that story. His question is, "What does all this service [of *Pesach*] signify to you?" (*Shmot* 12:26). He has no need for prescribed ritual, no need for a law mandating certain actions or forbidding others, and no need for a Divine Source either for the ritual or the law. For this son, his own intelligence, moral sense, and spiritual compass are sufficient, not only to keep alive the Exodus and its significance but even for achieving all the lofty ideals and teachings of Judaism. This is a Judaism without halakhah, without kosher or nonkosher food, sex, clothing, business, war, social relations and without prescribed ritual bearing witness to God's revelation in history and His kingship of the world. "What does all this *avodah* [Divine Worship] signify?" rejects the role of a Divinely revealed law, of a religion based on "do and don'ts" and of a culture fulfilling itself in manifold acts. The *Haggadah* tells us that he excludes himself from the *k'lal*, usually translated as the community or the common body of the nation, but in reality the *k'lal*—the rule that there are *eidut*, *chukim*, and *mishpatim* that the Lord our God commanded. Both the wise son and this one use the word "to you" so logically we should relate distancing oneself from the community to both of them. However, there is no mention of God by the evil son, and no details of the action-based nature of Torah. It is this *k'lal* that is referred to. "Blunt his teeth" comes the answer of the *Haggadah*, teaching that even if he would have been in Egypt he would not have been redeemed. Blunting of the teeth has been used in folklore to refer to knocking out the teeth so that the evil son could easily be identified at Judgement Day. However, the evil son sees all the people busy eating at the *seder* to mark the memorial of the Exodus and all it signifies. "What [sort] of service does this signify?" The Jewish service is expressed on this night through the mere act of eating of matzah, bitter herbs, and the paschal lamb and of refraining from leaven or even possessing it. His teeth are blunted because he cannot accept or perhaps comprehend such a service of a physical and coerced nature. Even if he would have been in Egypt, he would not have been redeemed.

The answer to the son who does not even know to ask is taken from the same verse as is the statement and answer of this son, It is because of this deed that the Lord did for me when I came out of Egypt. The answer the deed that is remembered only when matzah and bitter herbs are before us.

SHOFTIM

Kingship, Statehood, and Government

The relationships between the governed and the rulers lies at the heart of any social unit, primitive or sophisticated, simple village or clan, tribal or confederation, national or empire. These are relationships that have been recorded since the dawn of history yet whose relevancy and centrality continue to exist in our own days. Because they are so all encompassing, any social, religious, and political movement or philosophy must relate to them.

These relationships are expressed in economic terms primarily taxation, in physical terms primarily as the provision of security and defense, and in a hierarchy of rights and obligations in spiritual, social, and cultural spheres. Judaism's perspective is reflected in this *sedrah* and reiterated in the prophetic books of the Bible but also in the halakhic literature down to our own day. It is true that statehood was lost for the two thousand years between the destruction of the Second Temple and the rebirth of the State of Israel. Nevertheless, during this period there existed autonomous communities with the right to a judiciary and a fiscal system, making them, in effect, ministates, thus requiring a perspective on rulers and ruled. The existence of these mini-states within a non-Jewish political system meant that this perspective had to relate also to non-Jewish governments.

The basis of the system lies in two streams of political-social authority. There are the *shoftim* and *shotrim*, judges and officials, and then there are the kings and leaders, *melech vesarim*. These are courts for adjudicating between rival claims, for determining religious ritual, and for creating standards of morality in economic activity and social responsibility. For this, there are judges backed by the authority of Torah and the power given to them to implement its laws on an ad hoc basis. Alongside these *sanhedrin* and *batei din* lies the authority of the king and the representatives of the people—leaders of tens, of hundreds and thousands, classified halakhically as *b'nei hair*, people of the city. All authority is to be guided, restrained, and supervised, so that it may implement the Torah constitution and not override or distort it.

"Everything that is written regarding the king [in 1 Samuel 8] the king may do" (*Talmud Bavli, Sanhedrin* 20b). This dictum gave the king (state) the right to levy taxes in money, in kind and in labor, even as the prophet Samuel warned the people when they came to ask for a king. The king has the right of eminent domain, so that land may be appropriated for public use. Maimonides codifies the obligation of every citizen to fear, respect, and obey the king, whose appointment is one of the three *mitzvot* incumbent on Israel with its entry and settlement in the Land (*Mishneh Torah, Hilkhot Melachim*, Chapter 1, *Halakhah* 1; and Chapter 2, *Halakhah* 1). Authority is always seen as essential protection not only against political anarchy or foreign conquest but equally against spiritual corruption. It is not for nothing that the two earliest religious and moral corruptions—the graven image/idol of Michah (Judg. 17–18) and the gang rape at Gibeah with the resultant civil war (Judg. 19–21) are introduced by, "there was no king in Israel." Rabbi Chanina, the deputy *Kohen Gadol*, says, "Pray for the welfare of the government because if people do not fear it, a person would swallow his fellow alive" (*Avot*, Chapter 3, *Mishnah* 2). It seems that of all the commentators and authorities, it is only Abarbanel who presents a consistent antimonarchistic system based on the republics of Venice and Genoa of his time. Samuel said, "The law of the land [literally of the king] is the [halakhic] law" (*Talmud Bavli, Baba Kama* 113a). So in all monetary matters that do not contradict Torah and in areas necessary for public welfare, non-Jewish governments acquire halakhic status.

Parallel to the system of the king there are the *b'nei hair*, ruling either through their representatives, according to the *Rashbah*, or through a consensus of the citizens. It would seem that it is this concept of democratic representation of the citizens that is most pertinent to our time. Indeed, there are authorities such as *HaRav* Kook (*Mishpat Cohen* 148), and *HaRav* Ovadiah Yoseph, former chief rabbi of Israel (*Yachveh Da'at* Part 5, 5:63), who rule that in a democracy, the elected local and national authorities have the status of the king, in addition to the traditional rights of the *b'nei hair*, so that these two trends seem to merge. "The citizens of a town are able to force each other to participate in the cost of building a wall and gate for the town [defense], to build a synagogue, to purchase a Torah scroll and the books of the Bible . . . . This applies to all the needs of the town. . . . The decisions of the majority are binding [in those cases like funding the *mikvah*, charity, Torah education that are obligatory on all individuals, a minority may force the majority to act according to these obligations]" (*Shulchan Arukh, Choshen Misphat*, Section 163, subsections 1–3). In a separate discussion, the *Shulchan Arukh*, the *Tur*, and the *Rambam* extend these rights beyond taxation, based on the talmudic discussion that "the people of the city are permitted to regulate weights, prices and the wages of workers. They also have the right to punish those who do not carry out their regulations" (*Baba Bathra* 8b). So, too, all the authorities recognize the right of the citizens to prevent immoral Jews or those who constitute a danger to the community from settling in their town.

The legitimacy, in a Jewish perspective, of government either of the king or of the citizens does not prevent that perspective from seeing the possibility for corruption and evil, inherent in the right of one person to determine the lifestyle, welfare, and freedom of others. There however, is no difference between that perspective, than the potential for evil in all facets of life, even when they are legitimate. Here, too, the Torah came to place restrictions and to demand acts that would ensure the holiness of government.

The king was required to write two copies of the *Sefer* Torah, one to be placed in his treasury and the other to be carried with him wherever he went. They remind him constantly of his servitude to God's Law; because his power is greater than that of ordinary people, he requires an extra sign, over and above the normal ones of *milah*, tefillin, *tzitzit*, and so on. At the *Hakhel* ceremony in Jerusalem on *Sukkot* of the last year of the *shmittah* cycle, the king read from the *Mishneh Torah*, the Book of *Devarim* publicly in the Temple in Jerusalem (*Devarim* 31:10–13). He read from the beginning of the book until the first paragraph of the *Shema*, the second paragraph in *Ve'Etchanan*, and finally the verses of the two tithes—*ma'aser sheni* to be eaten in Jerusalem annually, except for *ma'aser ani* that is to be given to the poor in the third and sixth year. It is fitting that the king, symbol of government, should read these verses that deal with the Divine Covenant, our allegiance to Him, and reward and punishment. Thereby, the king's own power is put into a Torah perspective. Because he is also the heart of Israel, not only its ruler, the whole state becomes part of that perspective. Therefore, the whole nation, men, women, and children, assembled on the first day of *chol hamoed* to hear and to study Torah, so that they may conscientiously observe it.

The requirement that the king had to be of the people of Israel and not a foreigner is not simply an expression of nationalism. It reflects the concept of the Jewish people as a collective body, children of the Abrahamic family with a common historical experience, devoted to a spiritual mission of sanctification of life, both as individuals and as a society. The whole purpose of the king is to apply these concepts and to make them viable; it is this purpose that is demonstrated by the threefold limitations on him—wealth, wives, and horses.

Although there is a right of taxation, the king's wealth is limited, not only because of the well-known temptations of wealth "but also to prevent the abuse of the position for his own enrichment." This right was limited to the needs of the state: to meet the public sector payroll and build an infrastructure. Eminent domain was denied when, as in the story of Naboth, the king demanded a vineyard in Jezreel, in which not being the capital, he was only a private citizen (*Malbim* on 1 Kings Chapter 21).

For Hirsch, the limitation on the number of his wives was not because of the danger that they would turn him away from the spiritual role the king had to play in creating a kingdom of priests. Rather the text clearly states, "so that he does not turn his heart away," a corruption that simply flows from his own desires and appetites.

"It is forbidden [for any Jew] to return to Egypt to live . . .—in three places the Torah forbade this [*Devarim* 17:16; *Devarim* 28:68; *Shmot* 14:13. This make it a threefold transgression] . . . . However, it is permitted in order to trade or for commerce, it is only forbidden to dwell there [this would seem to apply only at the time when there is an independent Jewish state in *Eretz Yisrael* as shown in *Sukka* 51b regarding the settlement in Alexandria during the Second Temple period] . . . because the Egyptians are morally, religiously and ethically more corrupt than any other people" (*Mishneh Torah, Hilkhot Melachim*, Chapter 5, *Halakhah* 8). The king, by increasing his standing army and its chariots, would make Israel dependent on Egypt and expose them to its immorality according to the *Rambam*, and according to Hirsch, to a despotic and corrupt political system that is the antithesis of that of the Jewish Kingdom. Abarbanel sees this dependency as teaching the king and the people, that their military successes and physical security was a function of the foreign power supplying the war material, rather than acknowledging that the battle is the Lord's." It is these spiritual dangers that forbade the Egyptian sources to the king, even though trade is halakhically permitted.

As in the case of the king-state function, so, too, in the *b'nei hair* system, the Torah came to place spiritual, legal, and moral restraints, because there is no form of power that is not liable to the threat of corruption. At the first instance, they had to come from the tribe, clan, or community they represented, so that they may identify with the problems, needs, and potential of the citizens. So Moshe refused to sit on a chair, despite his age, during the war against Amalek, in order to share in the public travail. Elimelech was punished because he preferred to go to Moab, rather than meet his responsibility as a *parnass* during the famine (Ruth 1).

"You shall teach them the Laws and the Teachings and make known to them the way they shall walk and the work they shall do. But you shall choose from all the people capable and accomplished men, who fear the Lord, who hate profit [wealth]" (*Shmot* 18:20–21). These two suggestions of Jethro to Moshe reflect the above-mentioned limitations on the king. Here there is the need to study and know the laws and teachings, and for the king there is the presence of his Torah. Their fear of the Lord and their attitude to wealth parallel the warning against his turning away from God and the restraint on the king's wealth. So for the *b'nei hair*, too, the halakhah and spiritual values come to limit the power of the rulers. The communal records available over many centuries and countries tell of the scholars, pious men and people of accomplishment in the Jewish communal councils. These include for example the Synods of Spanish Jewry (until 1492), the councils of Franco-Germany from the time of *Rashi* until Frankfurt of the seventeenth century, the supranational *Va'ad* of the Four Lands of Eastern Europe—town councils of Poznan, Padua, and even that of Suggenheim—1756—in Germany with its twelve families.

However, of themselves, identification with the community and the moral-spiritual caliber of the officials are insufficient to prevent the corruption that flows from office. The moral problem is not fraud or crime; these are restrained by police action and the judiciary. Rather, there is the ever-present risk of abuse, of conflict of interest, and the sense of unlimited power. So, halakhically, the decisions of the councils are to be supervised by the rabbinical courts, so that taxation could not be confiscatory nor discriminatory and so that those social and religious costs mandated by halakhah could not be avoided. Furthermore, no decisions of the council could be contrary to Torah. So, zoning laws, economic competition, prices, and weights and measures, protecting the rights of refugees, the poor and weak, and funding education and security, all had to be within the halakhic guidelines and not solely by the interests or philosophies of the councilors.

Spiritual guidelines, too, facilitated the morality of the self-governing communities.

> The family of Avtinas refused to teach anybody the art of preparing the incense for the Temple service. When their approach to the *Sanhedrin* for an increase in wages was refused, they went on strike. After the priests from Alexandria were unable to make satisfactory incense, they were re-instituted with a doubling of wages. The rabbis cursed them, asking what prompted them to hold a whole nation to ransom and abuse their power. "We have a tradition in our family that this house [Temple] will be destroyed and perhaps one of those who learned from us would abuse the holiness of the incense." The daughters and wives of the house of Avtinas never wore perfume or scent, to ensure that nobody even could suspect that they themselves were abusing the power of their husbands. (*Talmud Bavli*, *Yoma* 38a)

KI TEITZEI

The Torah Spoke Only Regarding the Yetzer Harah

Are the natural human tendencies to do good or the power of our consciences, sufficient to create the parameters for moral lives? Is faith, either in humanistic values or in a deity, of itself enough to guide us in choices between good and evil or between right and wrong? Are acts in accordance with a normative and prescribed pattern of behavior the only or even the most desired moral guide? These and similar questions lie at the heart of religious and moral philosophies and movements throughout history. Perhaps the *Yefat To'ar*—beautiful captive of Chapter 21:10–14, may shed some perspective or guidance.

At the outset, Hirsch's comment on verse 10 should be noted. In his view, the treatment of the captive woman, comes to proclaim the sexual sanctity of every woman against male passion and to protect her from careless treatment or abuse. This is the introduction to the family laws dealt with here on the eve of Israel's entry to its Promised Land, just as the laws of marriage rights were introduced at Sinai by the proper treatment of the poorest of the poor, the *amah ivriyah* (*Shmot* 21:7–11). This aspect of *Yefat To'ar*, is in its essence similar to the Torah's prohibition of wanton destruction—*ba'al tashchit*—and the obligation to avoid indecent thoughts and immorality, all of which are framed initially in terms

KI TEITZEI

of the dehumanizing conditions of war, yet apply to even a greater degree in the course of normal life. In the midst of war, people see nothing wrong in purposeless destruction or the wanton abuse of nature, so it is in that frame of mind that the Torah details which trees may or may not be part of military action (*Devarim* 20:19). Army life is conducive to license, hygienic neglect, and to primitive sanitation, so here the Torah demands a pure and holy camp, not only free from physical uncleanness but also from spiritual license so that the Lord may dwell in its midst (*Devarim* 23:10–15). The fear, the imminent danger and the drudgery, and the callousness of war and army life create the spiritual conditions for rape, sexual immorality, and promiscuousness.

In the *Sifrei*, our sages taught that regarding the captive the Torah spoke only in response to the evil inclination. Rather than risk forbidding an action that may lead in the future to further spiritual evil and corruption, the Torah provides a safety valve, as it were for lust. The *Torah Temimah* queries this logic, because if we applied this to other *mitzvot*, there could never be any observance. Always we would claim that the evil impulse overpowered us, and, therefore, we should, like the captor of the *Yefat To'ar*, be permitted to do that which we desire. He stresses that from the text and from rabbinical teachings, *Yefat To'ar* must be perceived solely within the framework of the confusion of war, almost akin to *pikuach nefesh*, a life-saving situation. This idea is spelt out by the *Rambam* when he writes,

> When the advance guard enters the enemy's territory [where the search for kosher food entails a dangerous degree of risk] they may eat non-kosher food, pork, etc. if they are hungry and cannot find other food . . . .. So too such a soldier may cohabit with a gentile prisoner . . . however, then he may not just desert her. Rather he has to take her into his home . . . and may not cohabit with her again until [her conversion] and marriage [*Tosafot in Kiddushin* 22a and *Rashi* and *Ramban* on the *Chumash* mention, however, that no sexual relationship is permitted before conversion, etc., and marriage] . . . .. *Yefat To'ar* is not permitted except in the case of an [accidental] capture [as distinct

from a woman he saw before the battle and desired] . . . so too it is not permitted to take two captives [because it is not possible to lust after both simultaneously] nor may he give one to his father or brother [because this is not relevant to his own state of mind in the battle],
(*Mishneh Torah, Hilkhot Melakhim*, Chapter 8, *Halakhot* 1–3)

After the return from battle, the captive is granted a period of mourning for her parents or, according to Rabbi Akiva, for her former gods and homeland. This period is either thirty days, according to the *Yerushalmi*, or ninety days according to the *Talmud Bavli*, because of textual use of month and days in verse 13. During this period, her shaven head, long nails, and simple clothing are meant to test his love for her. Then conversion and marriage are permitted, but if he has no desire to marry her, she is set free. In such a case, she may not be held as a captive nor sold "because you have afflicted her."

The Talmud in *Sota* (44b) includes in the category of those who may not serve in war, one who interrupts his prayer with casual talk. This is an example of the rabbinic view of the soldiers of Israel as pious and holy men, a view that introduces an additional perspective to the whole concept of *Yefat To'ar*. The *Or HaChayim*, in his usual mystical approach, sees the piety and the holiness of these soldiers as the vehicle that permits them to perceive and redeem the holy souls that dwell in the enemy nations, gathering in the holy sparks of the convert. At the same time, it is these self-same soldiers that face the challenge of the *Yetzer HaRah* under conditions that are more stressful, ethically less clear-cut, and morally more complicated than their normal spiritual environment. So, too, all men and women under conditions of economic stress, of spiritual confusion or where there is little chance of being observed, face special spiritual challenges. In their everyday lives, natural morality and general social values are sufficient to practice their accepted spiritual teachings, distinguish between right and wrong, and maintain ethical forms of behavior. These often break down when they are faced with abnormal situations. So, the rabbis taught that a person only sins when *ruach shtut* enters, so upsetting the moral and religious equilibrium. Under these conditions of blurred sensitivity, of ethical indecision, and of spiritual tension, it is the mitzvot with their rigorous training over years of observance that helps to ensure normative conduct.

The Midrash tells that as Joseph bent to kiss Potiphar's wife, the face of his father appeared before him with all its spiritual connotations and then he fled. Another Midrash tells that the sight of the tzitzit in his garments prevented his sin, which is why she tore them, showing the Hebrew garment as a sign of his intentions.

The repetitive distinction between kosher and nonkosher food, between permitted and nonpermitted actions on Shabbat, and between wealth that needs to be given to charity and which may be used for personal needs or wants, create similar reactive responses. Thereby, ordinary people may, in spiritually stressful conditions, distinguish between kosher and nonkosher money, kosher and nonkosher sex, and kosher and nonkosher social acts. The observance of the mitzvot makes all of these automatic responses parallel to the military training that makes the soldiers reactions to fire, attack, or advance under fire automatic; without such training, it is doubtful that soldiers would ever fight under the danger of enemy guns.

The Shem MiShmuel sees the three mitzvot observed by the Yefat To'ar—shaving the head, care of her nails, and the weeping—as relevant to one who wishes to correct his ways. The hair refers to the intellect because the hair has its roots in the [literally, sweat of] the brain, the nails correspond to the body, and the mourning represents the soul's emotion. All three refer to the Tumah or impurity that leads to sins of mind, body, or soul. In the case of the ba'al teshuva, it is necessary to remove [shave] the evil beliefs and rationalizations of wrong behaviors, to cut or avoid luxuries that the body craves, and to turn the emotions towards the Holy One, thereby purifying the soul.

KI TAVO

Fruits of the Land

Throughout the Bible, there are scattered references to trees, fruits, and agriculture, from the Tree of Knowledge in Eden, through the *bikkurim* ceremony of the First Fruits mandated in our *parshah*, figuring in the prophetic visions and in the Psalms of David. Their destruction or their bounty on which humanity depends, reflect punishment or reward for the religious and ethical behavior of the nation (*VaYikra* 26:19–33; *Devarim* 11:13–17; 28:1–51). They serve as symbols of the blessings of pious and righteous individuals—"and he shall be like a tree planted by the steams of water that brings forth its fruit in its season and its leaves do not wither" (Ps. 1:3). They are a means of fulfilling social obligations like in the agricultural gifts to the poor and stranger or they are part of ritual praising God like the Four Species used in the *Sukkot Hallel*.

Although crops figure as part of the farmer's private property, their use and enjoyment is restricted and restrained so as to demonstrate the reality of Divine ownership. *Chadash*, the grain of the new harvest, may not be eaten in any form, by any individual, until the nation has brought a measure of the first barley (*Omer*) to be waved in obeisance before He Who grants sustenance to all (*VaYikra* 23:10–14). This idea at another level is represented by permission to use national sacrifices only after

KI TAVO

new crops in the wheat bread were offered on Shavuot. Ungathered stalks, forgotten sheaves, and unharvested grapes or olives automatically become the property of the poor and the *peah*, the corners of the field, are removed from the ownership of the farmer, who may not even decide to which poor they are to be given. Every seventh year, *Shmittah*, the land stays fallow and its products declared ownerless. Then in the Jubilee Year, *Yovel*, indentured servants are freed even against their will, and the land, basis of much of wealth, reverts to the original family-tribe distribution. *Shabbat* restores the spiritual equilibrium of the individual, and *Shmittah* and *Yovel* cleanse society of socioeconomic illness and corruption. When the farmer brings the first fruits of the year to the Temple, there is a confession that needs to be recited, a confession that clearly demonstrates publicly and succinctly that all agricultural bounty is the result not of human diligence nor of natural phenomena but solely of Divine Providence (*Devarim* 26:1–12).

This view, a spiritual connotation of trees, fruits, and crops, over and above their physical and material reality, is an expression of the religious and moral challenge that these and all other forms of wealth present. It is a view that echoes in "for man is the tree of the field" (*Devarim* 21:19) and led our Sages to point out that these are the only two species in Creation that have an *orlah*, that have an uncircumcised state in their lives. The *orlah* in man is the foreskin and is removed in every Jewish boy on the eighth day after birth as the sign of the Abrahamic Covenant. The removal of the foreskin as a sign on the sex organ integrates all sexual relationships into the pattern of holiness that is Judaism. So, too, there are uncircumcized lips that need to be cleansed and sanctified, and there are uncircumcized hearts that require that the *orlah* be removed. The *orlah* in trees are the first three years of existence during which the fruit is uncircumcised and may not be eaten. The fourth year is the circumcision, the *orlah* is removed in that year by taking the fruit to be eaten in the Temple in Jerusalem. Always *orlah* came from disobedience: Adam was born circumcized but disobeyed the one commandment given to him and so his descendants were born with *orlah*. The trees were commanded to "yield fruit after his own kind whose seed is in itself" (*Bereishit* 1:11). Fruit and tree were to have the same taste yet the trees disobeyed, yielding fruit of different taste—so there is *orlah*.

Bikkurim are brought only from the seven species that are the sign of the special blessings of the Promised Land—"wheat and barley and vines and fig trees and pomegranates; a land of oil olive and honey [date]" (*Devarim* 8:8). These species acquire special halakhic status, so that there is a special grace to be recited whenever they are eaten and they need to be eaten in accordance with their rank in this biblical verse. Not only is the Land blessed specially with these species, over and above all the other crops and fruits that grow there, but it is a Land "that drinks of the rain of Heaven [in contrast to Egypt that had to be irrigated by human labor. So] a Land which the Lord your God cares for; the eyes of the Lord . . . are always upon it from the beginning of the year even until the end of the year" (*Devarim* 11:10–12). It is indeed a Land flowing with milk and honey. Rabbi HaCohen Kook saw all these blessings of the Land also as spiritual characteristics; making it a sort of sanatorium for the ethical and religious ills of the people. Both milk and honey are permitted as kosher foods that have their origin paradoxically in forbidden sources. Milk is produced in the udder—a contradiction of the nonkosher mixture of meat and milk. Honey is secreted from the body of the impure bee. This is the land flowing with milk and honey—part of the process of transforming the forbidden into kosher.

Fruit and trees, human spiritual seeking, and the sanctification of material and physical wants and needs, became intricately woven in our sources. Each of the species present another facet of Jewish personality, individual and national.

"Noah began to be an *ish adamah* and he planted a vineyard" (*Bereishit* 9:20). Some saw *ish adamah* as negative—a cloddish man, earthbound and incapable of spiritual elevation. Others saw Noah as a partner in the Divine, an *ish adamah*, whose planting parallels creation "from the beginning of the making of the world, the Holy One, blessed be He, busied Himself only with planting, for it is said: 'planted a garden eastward in Eden.' So shall you busy yourselves only with planting at the beginning, as it is said, 'and when you shall come into the Land and you shall have planted all kinds of trees for food,'" (*Midrash VaYikrah Rabba* 25:3). The vine itself is a reflection of the challenge and opportunity inherent in our Sages' discussion of the *ish adamah*. "Wine makes glad the heart of man," yet "when wine enters, secrets emerge [uncontrollably]." The *midrash* tells that Satan brought fertilizer for the wine of Noah. He had mixed the blood of a lamb, a lion, a monkey, and a pig—the stages of human behavior when drinking wine: at first docile like a lamb, then aggressive like the lion, chattering like a monkey, finally rolling in their own filth. Yet Jewish ritual and living are interwoven with the grape and the wine. There is wine for every meal on *Shabbat* and Festival; there is the wine of the *brit* and of marriage, and there is the wine of *Havdallah*. There is no joy without wine, taught our Sages. Despite this, none of the satanic ingredients produce their appropriate reactions. This is only because of the link between the drinking and the *kiddush*. Remove this link and Jews react like everybody else.

"The tree of which Adam [and Eve] ate [Centuries of European art and literature notwithstanding, the apple seems to be resonant of the judgment of Paris in the *Iliad* rather than of Jewish origin. This origin saw the Tree of Knowledge either as wheat, the ability to taste of, which shows that a child has acquired knowledge or] ... says Rabbi Nechemiah: This was the fig, that wherewith they were spoilt they were also re-dressed. As it is said 'and they stitched a fig leaf'" (*Talmud Bavli, Berachot* 40a, also *Sanhedrin* 70a). However, God in His mercy clothed them with clothes of *Or*, said Rabbi Meir. "Not clothes of *or* (leather when spelt with an *ayin*) but clothes of light" (*Midrash Bereishit Rabbah*). Prophetic vision sees peace and tranquility when each sit beneath the shade of the vine and the fig (Kings 4:25; Michah 4:4; and Zechariah 3:10).

Perhaps this vision flows from a message of hope because "the vine and the fig shed their leaves and stand stark and dry [in winter—persecution], then revive and flourish and new leaves come forth" (*Pirkei de Rabbi Eliezer* 51). The vision also is reflected in the claims of future generations on the fruits (natural resources) of the present.

> Hadrian saw an old man of a hundred years planting a fig and asked, "Do you expect to see and eat the fruits of the tree you are planting?" Answered the old man, "Lord Emperor, I am planting now; if I live and eat the fruits, well and good, and if not, just as my fathers toiled for me [planting the seeds for future generations and husbanded natural resources accordingly] so too I toil for the generations that are to come."
> (*Tanchumah Kedoshim* 8; *Kohelet Rabbah* 2:23)

"A bell [of pure gold] and a pomegranate [of blue and purple and scarlet and twined linen] a bell and a pomegranate, round about the hem of the robe [of the High Priest] to serve in [the Sanctuary]" (*Shmot* 39:24–26). Chassidic masters saw the bells clanging to announce the entry of the priest as a sign of the confidence and pride needed to officiate, but of the muted pomegranate as the humility and frailty of humanity needed to prevent arrogance and idolatry. Pomegranates were filled with 613 seeds, like the *mitzvot*, commanded to us, or like the wisdom gathered from Torah study. "Even the transgressors of Israel are full of good deeds as is a pomegranate of seeds" (*Talmud Bavli, Eruvin* 19a). Rabbi Meir was a student of the *Acher*, the other one, Elisha ben Abuha, who became an apostate. Rabbi Meir ran alongside his donkey even though the *Acher* rode through the streets of Tiberias on *Shabbat*. "Meir," queried the sages, "he is an apostate." "I know," came the reply. "I ate of his seeds [of knowledge] and then cast away the rind [his apostasy, like the inedible skin of the pomegranate]" (*Talmud, Berachot* 37a).

The pomegranate flowered—"these are the children of Israel who sit and work at Torah and sit on rows after rows like the seeds of the pomegranate" (*Shir HaShirim Rabbah* 6:17).

"To see whether the vine flourished and the pomegranates budded" (*Shir HaShirim* 6:11) is the song of redemption read on *Pesach*, the Festival of Freedom, at the beginning of the spring when the dead vines and pomegranates bud and leaf.

Israel among the nations is like the olive among the trees. Just as oil and water do not mix but remain separate, even in the same vessel, so

Israel and the nations remain separate even when they dwell together. Just as the olive does not give up of its oil for the lamp nor for food unless it is crushed, cracked, and pressed, so, too, Israel does not realize its spiritual or moral potential unless it is persecuted. In the orchards all fruit trees resemble each other, not so the olive; where the trunk of each tree grows differently, so, too, each one of Israel differs from the others. "Why is the word Land written twice [in *Devarim* 8, separating the seven species into two groups] a Land of wheat . . . a Land of oil olive and of honey date? To tell you that the Temple depends on those two things [wheat, sign of knowledge and olive, sign of wisdom]" (*Talmud Yerushalami, Bikkurim*, Chapter 1, *Halakhah* 3). The olive tree, like wisdom, is never without its leaves, neither in summer nor in winter. Pure olive oil is used for the *ner tamid*, the perpetual lamp for which the windows were built in such a way that the light shone out of the Temple illuminating the world. The first drop of pure wisdom, free of lees, is what needs to be drawn by the wicks of effort toward the flame. Wisdom is "brethren dwelling together in unity. It is like the precious oil upon the head, coming down upon the beard; even Aaron's beard [the anointing oil poured upon the head of the High Priest]" (Psalms 133), lighting a light unto the nations (Isa. 42:7).

"The righteous shall flourish like the Palm . . . planted in the House of the Lord . . . They shall still bring forth fruit in old age; they shall be full of sap and richness" (Ps. 92:13–14). Like the righteous, nothing of the palm is without use; its fresh fruit is eaten immediately, and even when dried, lasts for many seasons, its leaves and wood for roofing, for shade or fiber. The palm puts forth a new leaf, month after month, whenever another grows old and withers, so the righteous bequeath their righteousness down the generations; a veritable "Tree of Life." Palm leaves are for rejoicing before the Lord (*VaYikra* 23:40), the palm in the Four Species signifies the spinal column, a symbol of human righteousness (*VaYikrah Rabbah* 30:13). Palm leaves are a symbol of Jewish peace and harmony (I Kings 6:29) even as are the righteous. "Soft dates which do not keep are exempt [from *peah*]" (*Talmud Yerushalmi, Peah* Chapter 1) "so too was it with Israel in the wilderness. Some [like fruit that can be kept safely] entered the Land, some [the soft, unlearned, boorish] did not" (*Bamidbar Rabbah* 3:1).

The apples are not one of the seven species, nor do they seem to be indigenous to the Land of Israel. Nevertheless they, too, represent spiritual ideas and acquired mystical symbolism. It is the apple dipped in honey on Rosh Hashanah that accompanies our prayers for a good and sweet year. The taste and smell of the apple are the breadth and depth of the Torah. Rabbi Akiva praises the righteous women of Israel for they went out in the apple groves of Egypt to give birth to the generation of the Redemption (*Talmud Bavli, Sotah* 11b). For our Sages, the children of Israel are likened in the Song of Songs to the apple, because just as this fruit forms before its leaves so, too, they forestalled "we shall hear" by "we shall perform." Furthermore, it only fruits finally in Sivan, in the month that the Torah was given. "All flee from the apple at *hamsin* time for it has no shade [the leave only appearing later] so did the nations flee on the day of the Revelation at Sinai, except for Israel" (*Shir HaShirim Rabbah* 2:3).

It is in the *Zohar* and the literature of the kabbalah that we can so clearly see the mystics association of the apple with Israel's spirituality.

Like an apple [tree] among the trees of the forest, so is my Beloved among the young men [sings Israel of its God]. (Song of Songs 2:3)

"How beloved is the *Knesset Yisrael* that she praises the Holy One thus! But why praise Him with [the metaphor of] the *tapuach* [apple]? Because the *tapuach* has all the three qualities [of a fruit]: color, subtle fragrance, and taste. [In the *Sefirot*, this refers to *Tifferet*, which harmonizes love and judgement, so that it contains healing for all.] Concerning Him it is written, "Heal me and I shall be healed." Through Him all judgments are healed and all illnesses are healed. Just as the *tapuach* contains healing for all . . . so too the Holy One is healing for all. Just as the *tapuach* contains all three colors, so also the Holy One has all three colors [a red peel on the outside and white flesh within corresponding to *Gevurah* and *Hesed* while it itself is green corresponding to *Tifferet* the harmony between the other two (*Matok Midvash*; *Zohar Achrei Mot*)." It is fitting that of Shimon bar Yochai personifying the *Zohar* and *Kabbalah* they sing: "Bar Yochai, You ascended the [trees] in the apple orchard, to gather many curative treasures. The secrets of the Torah [you pluck] like shoots and flowers. 'Let us make man' was said in reference to you (*Piyut Bar Yochai* on Lag B'Omer.)'"

NITZAVIM

Eternal Covenant

When the Israelites heard the hundred curses of our previous *parshah*, their faces blanched in fear (*Rashi, Devarim* 29:9). So, too, for us. We read and study our long history with its record of anti-Semitism, oppression, persecution, and exile, and are saddened and frightened. Throughout the ages, there have been marginal Jews who have sought to evade this record through assimilation; sometimes successfully but often not, as even quarter, thirds, and eighth-part Jews have been caught up in the national tragedies. Their fate is ultimately even worse as described in verse 17–20. Even as committed, identifiable, and proud Jews, we all too often worry our wounds until they become our guiding motives and references, even though they may have become festered. There easily develops an ideology of a nation fated to suffering, with the word Jew becoming synonymous with persecuted minorities. It thereby appears that we can only exist and maintain our Judaism when persecuted. So we fail to be inspired by the long periods of great spiritual creativity, intense religiosity, and social morality during the periods of physical safety and prosperity that actually overshadow the tragedies. Jewish life is not one long holocaust nor a constant *Tisha B'Av*. This is the real lesson of *Nitzavim*.

The Covenants between this Chosen People and their God have remained intact and are as operative as they were when they were made with Avraham, with Israel at Sinai, and with the generation about to enter *Eretz Yisrael*. The Chassidic masters noted that covenants and contracts are not primarily made between lovers or in cases of perfect relationships. Rather, they come to spell out obligations and rights of both parties, irrespective of their respective motivations or actions. Both Deity and people have a contract that even the sins and misdeeds of the People do not abrogate nor does the physical persecution that punishes these sins. The *Ba'al Shem Tov* separated the verse (*Devarim*) into: "*Anochi*, I am" [with you] even when "I hide My Face." "With our bodies we became His servants when He redeemed us from the slavery of Egypt, our wisdom became integrated with His when He gave us Torah at Sinai and our national structure became His vehicle for justice and social living, when He granted us the Promised Land" (Abarbanel). So after describing the desolation, poverty, and exile whereby Israel is punished, the Torah continues, "but despite this [desertion of His Law] even while they will be in the land of their enemies. . . . I have not despised them nor have I abhorred them nor will I utterly destroy them . . . I will remember the Covenant I made with their ancestors whom I brought out of the land of Egypt to be unto them a Lord." "These are the laws, the social laws and the teachings between Him and the Children of Israel . . . " (*VaYikra* 26:44–46).

The eternal nature of the Covenant is expressed by the textual construction of verses in our *parshah* and by the use of words that either appear seldom or nowhere else in the Torah. They all stress the unity and communal nature of the people. Men, women, and children are specifically mentioned in this Covenant as distinct from any of the other Covenants. All the social and political classes are pointedly included:

> Tribal leaders, elders, administrative officers, each and every man of Israel, small children, women, [even the most marginal classes, that of the] stranger [according to some authorities this includes only *Gerei Tzedek*, those who accept the Torah; according to others all those who observe the Noachide laws] hewers of wood and drawers of water [usually understood to refer to insincere converts like some Canaanites

according to *Rashi* or the Gibeonites (Jos. 9:3)] . . . not with you alone do I establish this covenant . . . but with whosoever is standing here today . . . [and even] with whosoever is not here with us today [all Jewish souls even in the distant future were present]. (*Devarim* 29:9–14)

It is this totality of peoplehood and social integrity that is involved in the eternal Covenant.

So the *Shem MiShmuel* understands the figure of speech pillar [*nitzav*] a solitary stone in the first verse of our *parshah*. This is used as distinct from an altar which is constructed from a number of different stones. The altar refers to a confederated unity of different groups, as, for example, where Eliyahu built one with twelve stones representing the Twelve Tribes of Israel. Our text uses the symbolism of a solitary stone to depict an integrated, homogenous, and single-minded unit, that is the party to this Covenant, sealed just prior to their crossing the Jordan into the Promised Land. In the desert, each tribe had its own specific position in the camp, its own flag, and its own place in the marching formation. It was only when they entered the Land of Israel that the tribes and clans intermingled to form a unity. The only other time this unity was achieved was at the Covenant at Sinai "and Israel camped [singular] opposite the mountain" as one single person with a single purpose (*Rashi, Shmot* 19:2). However, in contrast to these two examples of a unified national personality indicative of the *tzelem*, the Divine Image, the sojourn of Israel in the desert was fractured by quarreling, by contention and disunity. So too, at the Red Sea, the plural forms are used to denote their actions, leading the rabbis to talk of different camps and opinions as to what should be done. Regarding Egypt, however, the text (*Shmot* 14:10) reads: "Pharaoh drew near . . . behold Egypt journeying [singular]." It was this unity of the enemy that frightened Israel and that could only be counteracted by the unity of God. The *Shem MiShmuel* adds to his explanation the idea that in the Divine Promise of eternal protection the words "utterly destroy or obliterate" is used. In *VaYikra* 26:14, the law requiring the farmer to leave *peah*, a corner for the poor, the same word *lechaleh*

NITZAVIM

are used, rather than harvest or reap the corner. A people who do not utterly destroy their field but leave something for others will not be destroyed. Furthermore, he points out that *peah* is only available to the poor; at the end of the harvested field. This shows a people whose economic beginnings—ploughing, planting, and harvesting, all have a final aim, to be able to let others also have a benefit from their work.

For Abarbanel, the Covenant established in *Nitzavim* is not one based solely on history, ethnicity, or fear, but also on a superior wisdom and spiritual understanding. *Nitzavim* is used in the Torah to denote a readiness to argue, for example, "Dathan and Aviram stood up to argue at the entrance to their tents" (*Bamidbar* 16:27). So all the people, irrespective of class or status, were gathered at this Covenant, to give them a chance to argue out and discuss with Moshe their questions regarding the idols (ideologies and beliefs) of the nations they had encountered. Moshe would then be able to remove their doubts, and convince them of the truth of Torah. They will then be able to enter the Covenant in perfect faith.

Parshat Nitzavim is always read on the *Shabbat* before Rosh Hashanah. The coronation of the King of Kings requires us to have an understanding of our common destiny but also an undertaking to strive for the national cohesiveness of the *matzeva*, the single pillar.

The human body only operates when all its limbs and organs are a unity, becoming a living being that is more than the sum total of those limbs and organs. So, too, we acquire through cohesiveness and community, a spiritual dimension that is greater than the sum total of the religiosity and identification of the individuals that make up the Jewish nation. A circle has a point that is its center and around which it is constructed or drawn. So, too, the *tzelem Elokim* is the spiritual innermost point of the human beings created in His Image. *Shabbat* is the internality of the six days of the week, just as Israel is among the nations (*Shem MiShmuel*). Simcha Bunem of Psyicha explained that we were given many *mitzvot*, rather than only a few that could be observed more carefully and more successfully, so as to provide everybody with at least some *mitzvot* that only they would or could observe and practice fully with devotion. Menachem Mendel of Kotsk said, "You shall be holy"

(*VaYikra* 19:2) is written in the plural because it is only by our being an integral part of the Jewish people that ordinary men and women can become holy. It is these spiritual moral and religious meanings of our national identity and communal cohesiveness that enable us to face the Day of Judgement, so that the sole Judge becomes the sole King and His Name becomes One.

Parshat Nitzavim is followed by the mitzvah of *Hakhel*, a mitzvah that reiterates and reestablishes, as it were, periodically the Covenant. On the first day of *Chol HaMoed Sukkot*, the king read the Torah before the assembled nation. The language of *Hakhel* is as wide ranging as the opening of *Nitzavim*: "Gather together the people—the men, the women, the small children and your stranger within your gates [cities-village] so they will hear-learn-fear the Lord—and diligently observe and perform all the words of the Torah" (*Devarim* 31:12). This assembly of the entire nation in all its tribes, clans, and families, of all social, economic, and educational classes, was gathered immediately after the end of the *shmittah* year. Rabbi HaCohen Kook saw the *shmittah*, sabbatical year, as coming to cure Israel of the social dislocation, economic greed, and oppression of the six previous years, just as the *Shabbat* comes to cleanse us of the materalism and mundane of the days of the week. The *Hakhel* is the public demonstration of this spiritual and moral lesson of the *shmittah* year. It is the application of the innermost religiosity and cohesiveness of a people living according to a Divinely revealed Torah. When this message of the *matzevah* is weakened or threatened, then persecution and suffering occur, and the Covenant is shaded or overcast, even while it remains eternal. When the *matzevah* exists, it is central to our lives and stands upright in all its dignity, and then salvation comes.

The *Kli Yakar* adds that not only are all equal during *shmittah*, but on *Sukkot* each leaves their permanent homes, their permanent status, and the usual social divisions. This makes it a time for peace and unity. Salvation at the time of Purim was preceded by the Jews' action on Esther's instruction to Mordechai, "Go and gather in and assemble all the Jews" (*Esther* 4:15). Persecution and an exile that still continues was caused by the needless hatred of our forebears at the time of the Second Temple.

VAYELECH

The Hidden Face of God

A covenant promising an eternal relationship and continuous protection can lead to arrogance and to an assumption that whatever deeds are performed, they will not be punished. A chosen personality, whether an individual or a nation, may be misled into spiritual apathy and even to evil decisions, relying always on their special status. The special covenant of *Nitzavim* is hedged, therefore, between the terrible punishments detailed in *parshat Ki Tavo* and the clear announcement of *hester panim*, in *VaYelech* of the concealment of the Divine Presence, when Israel continues to sin. For the same reason, perhaps, this *parsha* is often read on *Shabbat Shuva*, between Rosh HaShanah, Day of Judgement, and Yom Kippur, the Day of Atonement.

    The *hester panim* of *VaYelech* is theologically complicated by the placement of verses 17–18 (*Devarim* 31) after the Jews have already repented, hardly an occasion for such Divine Concealment. Generally speaking, this should not pose a serious ethical or moral problem, because it is quite clear halakhically that *t'shuva* does not always mean that no punishment still occurs. Financial and economic crimes, for example, require the return of the fraudulently acquired wealth or compensation for the damage caused. Without these acts, the *t'shuva* is meaningless. The death penalty ordained by Torah for a number of crimes is to be imposed even if the perpetrator did *t'shuva* (the fact that today halakhically it is almost impossible for a *bet din* to impose such a penalty, does not erase this idea; it should also be remembered that halakhically a secular power may impose a death penalty in order to prevent violence and crime). Some sins can only be atoned for by pain, suffering, and sorrow Divinely imposed; this also even where *t'shuva* has been made. Without *t'shuva*, in all these cases, human and divine inflicted punishment would be even greater (*Mishneh Torah, Hilkhot T'shuva*, Chapter 1, *Halakhot* 3–4). Over and above these general observations regarding *t'shuva*, the two verses of *hester panim* in our *parsha* provide special insights.

"And many evils and tribulations will be visited on them [Israel] and they will say on that day, 'Is it not because my God is not in my midst that these evils have come upon me?'" (*Devarim* 31:17). In this verse, the people seemingly admit their guilt; because He has been removed from their midst, they are being punished. Yet almost all the commentators see this as being a defective *t'shuva* in ways that have important perspectives for our own behavior. Some rabbis saw their *t'shuva* as flowing only from the severity of the punishments and their fear of a similar fate in the future, or a *t'shuva* that was only verbal and superficial because they admit that He was not in their midst, or that they only comprehended intellectually that they had sinned but this was not translated into action. These inferior forms of *t'shuva* cause the Divine Presence to still be removed.

The *Chatam Sofer* sees in this verse that they only admitted to the sin of idolatry. They recognized that they had ceased to worship Him and had followed other gods. Nevertheless they still continued to do many evil and forbidden things, considering that because they had admitted to idolatry, all the rest would be forgiven. Because idolatry is seen by almost all the commentators as the meaning of verse 17, it needs to be remembered that this does not only refer to the making of images or statues of gods. Rather, giving any idea, person, force, or value structure the power, role, or oneness of God is idolatry. So here, even though they only said or thought that God was not in their midst, limiting and removing Him from their lives, they would be punished because idolatry,

VAYELECH

unlike other sins, is punishable even only for the thought process. So, Simcha Bunem of Pshischa taught that this was their sin, considering that there could be a stage or a situation when He was not in the midst of Israel, something no Jew ever has the right to feel or to think, irrespective of the nature of the situation. Indeed, none of the traditional sources understand *hester panim* as meaning the absence of God, His inability to prevent suffering and tragedy or the existence of another force that could somehow share some of this power. Even when the rabbis taught that when He releases forces of destruction, pain, and suffering these forces do not always distinguish between evil people and righteous ones, nevertheless, they never considered that such forces in any way were independent or a substitute for His solitary power, justice, and mercy. We are obligated to bless Him for the bad things that happen to us even as we are for the good things. In the early days of Chassidism, the *mitnagdim* sent a delegation to test the Torah knowledge of the Chassidic head, Dov Baer of Mezeritch, successor to the *Ba'al Shem Tov*. They presented him with this rabbinic dictum and asked for an explanation. He sent them with their question to Reb Zusha, who turned to them asking, "What's bad?"

Sforno sees verse 17 of our chapter as showing that the Jews did not immediately acknowledge that all their sufferings and persecutions were the result of their own actions. Instead, they sought remedies and solutions in the natural order of things—economic action, flight, armed resistance, or diplomacy—because in reality they considered the suffering and persecution to be rooted in natural, political, or physical phenomena. It is this consideration that the Torah describes as turning to other gods.

Hirsch notes that the text does not say that the evil that Israel has done is the cause of *hester panim*, but rather it is as it were "because He is not in my midst," that Israel has sinned. We complain that it is because of *hester panim* that the suffering comes on us rather than owing to our own actions. We wish to forget that the *hester panim*, the persecution and the suffering, come on us because "turned to other gods. . . . the special relation depends on complete devotion to Him. He never ceases

His special relationship to Israel . . . nevertheless no sin escapes His punishing attention and misfortune follows sins." The prophet Amos postulates this when he said, "Only you have I known of all the nations of the world and therefore I will visit upon you all of your sins" (3:2).

Rabbi HaCohen Kook, while accepting that persecution and exile came as a result of the nation's desertion of Torah, introduced a new dimension in the concept of *t'shuva*. *T'shuva* is usually translated as repentance but literally means return, so the national repentance comes as a result of its return to its Promised Land. For the nation not to return is an act of free will, prolonging the exile that originally came as a result of national sin and so being of itself, a new sin.

Kook makes a distinction between "and you shall return towards [*ad*] the Lord your God" (*Devarim* 30:3) and "you shall return unto [*el*] . . . the Lord your God" (30:10). Between these two verses lie seven verses describing how God will bring back the captivity, gather in Israel from among all the peoples He has dispersed them to (originally to punish them), and bring them back to the Land that our fathers possessed. When we have possessed it, we will listen to His voice and perform his commandments, and then we will return unto Him with all our heart and all our soul. In the *t'shuva* process of the individual first, there is the desire to repent, weak and flickering as it may be. This is strengthened until finally full *t'shuva* is achieved. In the nation, there arises a will to return to its homeland, to its intrinsic spirit, and to its own undistorted personality. This is the flickering of the desire to *t'shuva*, return towards—*ad*—that is rewarded by the Divine Ingathering of the exiles even from the furthest corners of the world. When the ingathered exiles repossess the Promised Land, God's bounty is showered on them. Fields that lay barren under foreign occupation and the deserts that existed while we were in exile, bloom and flourish as in *Devarim* 30:9, "will grant you abundance in all your handiwork, the fruit of your womb, the fruit of your animals, and the fruit of your Land for good, when the Lord will return to rejoice over you for your benefit even as He did."

Kook understands verse 6 which tells of the Divine circumcision of the hearts of the ingathered exiles as part of the spiritual effect that living in the Holy Land has on us. The sanctity of this Land enhances our religious potential, provides a stimulant to renewed and extended observance of Torah, and cleanses us of the spiritual confusion and distortions that exist outside its border. It is these effects that ultimately lead the nation to proper *t'shuva* where they return to *El*, unto God.

All the various commentaries and views on *hester panim* see the eternal covenant between Israel and God as providing for the continued existence of the Jewish People, irrespective of persecution and oppression, despite any of the sins of the people. We express this every year when we say at the *Seder*, "And it is this promise [of the Abrahamic covenant of Chosen People and Promised Land] that has stood by [protected] our fathers and ourselves, for not only one [enemy] has risen to destroy us but in every generation they have stood [gathered to] destroy us." The continued existence of a Jewish people, dispersed, oppressed, and persecuted over many centuries, is the evidence of Divine Intervention and Divine Guidance in world history. Seen in the perspective of *t'shuva* of Kook, the modern ingathering of the Jewish exiles in all is aspects and developments, is only the most dramatic phenomena of this concept in modern times.

It is as evidence of the eternal covenant that *Ha'azinu*, the farewell song of Moshe is written. Heaven and Earth, eternal and indestructible, not only are witness to the covenant but also symbols of this covenant. The *Shem MiShmuel* sees *Ha'azinu* as a document given to Israel that is to be produced whenever persecution threatens, a document signed as it were by God Himself. There is a talmudic story of a woman whose husband spent many years abroad on a caravan for trade, without any possibility for communication. Her neighbors mocked her and taunted her with his desertion. When her husband returned and expressed his astonishment that she was steadfast in her belief that he would return, she handed him a bundle of his letters to her before the marriage saying, "It was these that kept my faith alive."

Levi Yitzchak of Berdichev in his usual laconic style once put the whole issue of Divine Anger at the shortcomings and actions of the Jewish people in a special perspective. "If You, Master of the World, are so disgusted and disappointed with us after thousands of years, perhaps You should give another people a chance to be Chosen. See how happy You will be with the Russians, the Germans, the French or with any other nation!"

HA'AZINU

Stages of Redemption

This song is neither a song of praise for deliverance, as is the one Moshe and Israel sang at the Red Sea, nor is it one of prayer and supplication, as are the psalms of David, nor is it a dirge of national suffering, as are the lamentations of Jeremiah. This is the song of future redemption and the promise of an eternal covenant. Nachmanides and Abarbanel use the text of *Ha'azinu* to show that it cannot refer to the redemption from Babylon after the first exile. Rather, the description of the national redemptive process only fits that of the *Galut Edom*, that exile in which we have lived since the destruction of the Second Temple. Because Abarbanel sets out the discussion in a formal and detailed format, his commentary can serve as a perspective of the realization of the redemptive promise. It must be remembered that these are not a perspective of irrational mystics nor of messianic fixations, but rather one expressed by the majority of rabbinical commentators since Nachmanides and Abarbanel down to our own times. Modern Torah scholars are divided as to the exact application of these stages in redemption to our own times, but it seems that all are agreed that we live in an age when the footsteps of Messiah are clearly seen even as described in *Ha'azinu*. Nineteenth- and twentieth-century giants such as the *Chatam Sofer*, the *Netziv* of Volozhin, HaCohen

Kook, the *Chafetz Chaim,* and Elchanan Wasserman, all saw in our days a pattern of the final redemption.

The Napoleonic wars engendered a fierce debate in the Chassidic world, as to whether they were the Wars of *Gog* and *Magog* that herald the coming of messiah. A subsequent growth of nationalism in Europe stirred rabbinic leaders like Mohilver and Kalisher, to an involvement with the fledgling rebirth of political Jewish nationalism. International recognition as in the Balfour Declaration, the League of Nations Mandate, and the UN vote in 1947, of the rights of the Jews to create a national home-state in *Eretz Yisrael,* removed a halakhic obstacle to a rebuilt Zion that would otherwise constitute a revolt against the nations. Disparate as they were in many areas, both Kook and the *Chafetz Chaim* encouraged the study of *Kodshin,* those tractates dealing with temple service, and sought a preparation for their own personal roles as priests in that service.

The defeat of nazism and the collapse of the Soviet Union, both enemies and destroyers of Jews and Judaism, signaled Divine retribution to many. Israel as a sudden center of ingathered exiles, a flourishing Jewish society, and the establishment of an unprecedented Torah center, all seem to fit the thoughts seen by Nachmanides and Abarbanel in *Ha'azinu.*

There are seven tenets of our belief expressed in this song.

It is inevitable that the revenge [punishment] on Israel's enemies will be exacted. "I shall grip Justice in My Hand, repay vengeance on My enemies and bring retribution on those who hate Me . . . for He will avenge the blood of those who serve Him and visit retribution on His enemies . . . [peace will follow for] His People will bring atonement to His Land" (41–43). This principle was not implemented either in the period of the Second Temple (510 C.E.–70 C.E.) nor at any time [being left for the future at the end of the present exile].

There is a time limit to the exile that is fixed by His infinite wisdom. However, this limit has not been revealed to anyone. [The Talmud expresses an additional time for the end of the exile that reflects the *t'shuva* of the Jews.] This cannot refer to the end of the Babylonian exile because Jeremiah already foretold that it would only last for 70 years.

Redemption of Israel will occur after the people have expiated completely their sins and justice has been done. "For He will judge His People . . . when He sees that all their power is gone and no one is saved or helped" (36). So their situation will be one of utter degradation, and then justice will demand that they be redeemed. As the prophet said, Zion will be redeemed in justice and her prisoners through *tzedakah*. This does not refer to the Second Temple as then the exile was not in poverty and suffering but rather the honor and wealth in Babylon was greater than that to which they returned.

This exile will not end because of the merit of the Patriarchs even as the *Ramban* has written, but solely because of the glory of His Great Name "lest their persecutors misinterpret [their ability to oppress Israel] lest they say, 'Our hand is superior, it is not God Who has brought all this [destruction],'" (27–28) even as the prophet Yechezkiel (Chapter 20) prophesied, "and I will gather you [exiles] in from all the countries wherever you have been scattered and [thereby] I will be sanctified through you in the eyes of the nations . . . for My Name's Sake and I will for My Name's Sake not permit its desecration in the eyes of the nations [through the continued exile that seems to show My inability to save Israel]." Here redemption comes at its prescribed time without the Jews repenting. The *Rav* [Yehuda HaLevi] has explained this is because the Jewish nation bears witness to the Divine Name and proclaims the truth of His existence, so that the destruction of this nation will cause the desecration [the disappearance] of His Name throughout mankind.

The resurrection of the dead will occur close to the ingathering of the exiles, "See now that indeed I am He and there is no god with Me. I kill and bring back to life again, I have struck down [in death] and I will heal [bring back to life]" (39), and the angel said to Daniel, "and at that time all My people shall be delivered . . . and multitudes of those who sleep in the dust shall awake, some to everlasting life and some to shame and everlasting contempt" (Dan. 12:1–2).

The redemption and the atonement revealed in this song, *Ha'azinu*, is not dependent on our *t'shuva* nor on our listening to God's word nor on the observance of His commandments. *Ha'azinu* is a document that bears witness to evil and sins we have committed. He in justice brought on us, therefore, great anger, persecution, and punishment, still we were never totally destroyed nor our memory erased. Then He, Whose Name is Blessed, for the sanctification of His Great Name, and to prevent the desecration in the eyes of nations, will return and have mercy on us, will exact punishment on our enemies, will forgive our sins and will have mercy on us once again and will thereby hide our sins. So this song is a clear promise of the future redemption. "Great is this song that has relevance for the present and recollects the past; that has in it relevance for the future and for the world to come" (*Sifrei* 27).

"Every word of the Song has been fulfilled [as regards the past] and nothing of it will be negated. From everything that it bears witness to, regarding our inheritance of the Land, its fertility and its bounty that is part of its righteousness [but] also of our sins and transgressions that have been punished by the gentiles. These troubles, persecutions, and oppressions are part of our punishment and we have suffered them during the times of the First and Second Temples and during our exile. Since we have seen that all these things have been clearly witnessed in this Song, so it is fitting that we should faithfully and firmly believe that even so the redemption, the ingathering of the exiles and the punishment of the enemies will also come true. We shall believe and look forward to these words of redemption and salvation uttered by [Moshe] His prophet, the trusted one, never before was there a prophet like him nor shall there ever arise one like him" (*Abarbanel*).

VEZOT HABERACHA

Tribes, Months, and the Signs of the Zodiac

The Twelve Tribes of Jacob are the chariot or the foundation on which the People of Israel, in their past history, present experiences, and future ways, develop and exist. It is in this perspective that rabbinic thought, as expressed in mystical teachings, homiletic literature, and biblical commentary, views the sons of Jacob and therefore the blessings both of Ya'akov (*Bereishit* 4:9) and of Moshe in our *parshah*. Each tribe has a separate personality, name, and role in history. Therefore, each son has a special blessing that represents the personality and role. The geographical areas in which they settled became part of the personality and the role, not only in the spiritual or mystical sense but even in the historical and physical perspective. The tribes of Reuven, Gad, and half of Manasseh opted for the pasture lands of Transjordan originally because of their flocks, but soon they became separated from the nation, physically and spiritually. Ultimately they were the first tribes to be exiled. Ephraim, part of Manasseh and Issachar, lay in the fertile and prosperous center of *Eretz Yisrael*, exposed to the trade routes and to the resultant social and cultural influences of foreign nations, thereby becoming centers of idolatry and assimilation. Yehuda, Binyamin, and Shimon, because of physical conditions of semidesert, valleys, and relative isolation, were able to maintain a greater degree of religious and political independence. Interesting and important perhaps as these socioeconomic and political facts are, they pale, however, into insignificance before the spiritual qualities and religious characteristics specific to each of the sons of Ya'akov and to their descendants in their families, clans, and tribes. Twelve tribes, Twelve months of the year, and Twelve signs of the Zodiac, are interwoven in a tapestry of spirituality, personalities and religiosity; as described by the *Chassidic* Master, Shmuel of Sochochow.

According to the order of the encampment, the flags and the march in the desert, the first tribe is Yehuda (*Bamidbar* 10). Nissan is *Rosh Chodashim*, first of the months (*Shmot* 12:2), the month in which we were redeemed from Egypt and the month in which the future redemption will occur. This is the spring, the time of renewal in nature, and it is also the spring of natural redemption and renewal. *Pesach* is in Nissan, in which all the forces of nature and the developments of human history are shown to be subservient to His Crown and under His Kingship. Yehuda is first of the tribes and "the scepter shall not depart from Yehuda neither the lawgiver from between his feet" (*Bereishit* 49:10) and from Yehuda will come the Messiah of the future redemption. Yehuda is derived from *hodayah*, to give praise, because the Matriarch Leah was the first person to praise God for His Benevolence; she had given birth to three of the twelve Tribes of Israel. When she gave birth to a fourth son, she acknowledged His Chesed and called him Yehuda, from whom was descended David the King, whose whole being was one of praise and song to God. Nissan, whose sign is the lamb, is a fitting symbol of submission and humility, for our own behavior on the festival of freedom, when we acknowledge that only Divine Mercy redeemed us. It is also fitting for David, the archetype king who could humble himself as a worm before his Maker. Yehuda can acknowledge in humility the justice of Tamar's reproach, and submit to the consequences of his own guilt. So each person in Israel who wishes to purify themselves, should at the outset acquire these merits of truth, not to deceive themselves nor others. Through Nissan, all the months of the year submit and acknowledge the justice, power, and mercy of God.

Tammuz is the fourth month so it represents Reuven, who is the fourth of the Tribal flags. Tammuz (worshiped in ancient idolatry as the god of sex, heat, and summer) is linguistically derived from the Aramaic as "to heat the furnace" (Dan. 3:19) and describes the fiery nature of external desires and lusts. Its sign is the crab, one of the forbidden foods, whose eating increases desires and lusts; its root is evil, warmth. Reuven, however, repents and busied himself with sackcloth, prayer, and righteous actions, thereby achieving atonement that changes the results of his actions. (It may be noted that Shimon, whose actions at Shechem were cursed by Ya'akov, is not included in the blessings of Moshe, whereas Levi, his partner at Shechem, is. Levi repented by not being involved in the worship of the Golden Calf, and rallying to Moshe's call. Shimon, however, was represented by Zimri who persisted in the public sexual sin with the daughters of Moav.) This month of Tammuz witnessed the breach in the walls of Jerusalem in both the First and Second Temples, which preceded the destruction of both of them. As Reuven was able to change, so this month and the days until *Tisha B'Av* will be transformed from fast days and mourning, to joy and festivity. So the present period of national mourning between the seventeenth of Tammuz and *Tisha B'Av*, will be like *Chol HaMoed* of the festivals. Tammuz will be changed from the sin that led to the shame of exile, to a month of purity and sanctity that bring honor to Israel and its God.

According to the order of the flags, the month of MarCheshvan (literally, Mr. Cheshvan, primarily because of its bountiful rain) belongs to Manasseh. This is the eighth month, and Manasseh is the eighth tribe in the order of marching, following Ephraim who is the head of the third group (*Bamidbar* 10:22–23). These two tribes represent the double portion of Yoseph in the ranking of the tribes for purposes of inheritance of the Land. These two represent the concept of "leave off evil, *sur mirah*, and do good, *asei tov*," a concept that is pertinent and central to all our decisions and acts, both in the spiritual and the material aspects of life. Their names are evident of the concept. Of his firstborn, Manasseh, Yoseph says, "He has made me forget, *nashani*, all my suffering and my father's house"; the second son he called Ephraim because "he has caused me to be fruitful in the land of my affliction" (*Bereishit* 41:51–52). Yoseph thought that first we are obliged to leave behind our wrong actions and evil thoughts, *sur mirah*, and then only can we come to *asei tov*. First there is Manasseh and then Ephraim. Ya'akov created a new form of religious life by teaching that first one must, and is able to, do good, *asei tov*, and then one will be able to *sur mirah*. So when he blessed the sons, he replaced Ephraim first (*Bereishit* 48:13–20). Yoseph's priorities are extremely difficult to realize, and often disappointment and depression follow when people are unable to *sur mirah* first. This is also the basis for many of the halakhic differences between *Bet Hillel* and *Bet Shammai*; the former places *asei tov* first as a humanly achievable path, which later leads to *sur mirah*.

The two months, Tishrei and MarCheshvan, relate to Ephraim and Manasseh. Tishrei with its penitential prayers and repentance, with the many *mitzvot*, *Shofar*, Yom Kippur, *t'shuvah*, and *viduy*—repentance and confession, *Sukkah*, *lulav*, *aravah*, *nisuch hamayim*—libation of the water, *Simchat Torah*—rejoicing of the law, is the epitome of doing good; this is Ephraim. MarCheshvan that follows is *sur mirah*, the lifestyle that avoids subsequently unethical, irreligious, and evil actions.

The sign of MarCheshvan is the crab. The *Avnei Nezer* taught that even though the sign under which a person is born affects one (*Talmud Bavli*, *Shabbat* 146a), nevertheless, Jews have the spiritual power to rule over their natures. [The same source describes how meritorious deeds and religious stature, overpower the significance of the Zodiac signs. The birth of Yitschak is expressed by showing Avraham the stars, according to which he and Sarah were unable to have children, but that they are placed beyond the power of the horoscopes (*Bereishit* 15:5).] The *Shem MiShmuel* adds to his father's teaching that we are able to elevate the root of the *mazalot* and use it to enhance the sanctity of our religious life. The crab relates to the coldness and lack of emotion that lead to spiritual laziness and idleness. Jews use this for *sur mirah*, to be cold to evil and be lazy regarding inappropriate actions. Furthermore, the crab calls for a coolness to materialism and less enthusiasm to wealth creation, that are both necessary for *sur mirah*.

Of Asher, Ya'akov said, "His bread shall be fat and he shall yield royal dainties" (*Bereishit* 49:20), and to Asher he [Moshe] said, "Be blessed with children; let him be desired by his brothers and let him dip his foot in oil" (*Devarim* 33:24), all blessings of prosperity, economic success, and wealth. Asher, the eleventh of the flags, is the tribe of Shevat and the bucket, container, of water is its Zodiac sign. In this month, nature begins to flower, the fruit trees begin to bud, and there is renewal after the long dormant months of winter. *Tu BeShevat* is the New Year of the trees. This judgment day of their fruits was fixed on this date by Hillel, because the power of winter is weakened by then, and the fruit buds are already steadily growing and being strengthened (*Rosh Hashanah*, Chapter 1, *Mishnah* 1, see *Meiri*). However, all this promise of material prosperity symbolized by Asher and Shevat, must be seen in a correct perspective.

The purpose of food and indeed of all material wealth is to provide the physical sustenance of the human body and mind that could not exist without it. There is a taste to food that satisfies our hunger, a satisfaction that was given to us as a *chesed*, otherwise, we would be completely engrossed in our material concerns. It is this ability to limit our pursuit of materialism and curtail our labor that differentiates between eating and "the pour into me, *halitaini*" of Eisav, an expression that appears only once in the Torah (*Bereishit* 25:30). For Eisav there is no distinction between the secondary eating and economic activities and between the essential purposes of life, the social obligations, and the spiritual striving. Asher is the role model who is able to evaluate correctly all the preparatory activities of business, accumulation of wealth, and the enjoyment of physical things. Shevat is the first flowering and budding of nature, the first steps of a new economic cycle. Then there follows the four *parshiot*: *Shekalim* (our active participation in the national-spiritual service); *Zachor* (eradicating war against the holiness); *Parah* (purification from the *tumah* of death and its denial of free will); and *HaChodesh* (human mastery over time). In the midst of these four *parshiot* there are *Purim* (with its obligations of charity for the poor and the establishment of sound relations with our fellows, but also the knowledge of the miracles wrought in our normal everyday lives); now follow *Pesach*, the *Omer* (acknowledging the real source of our wealth); and the Revelation at Sinai on *Shavuot*. The days and months all ascending in the spirituality are needed for a correct perspective of wealth.

INDEX

Aba bar Kahane, R., 36
Abarbanel, 56–57, 77, 107, 108, 136, 146, 174, 263, 290–291, 316, 319, 345–346
   on anti-Semitism, 85–86
   and census taking, 225, 229
   and the covenant, 337
   and fear of heaven, 306–307
   and plagues visited on Egypt, 88–89
   and Ten Commandments, 111–112
Abba Chanan, 125
Abbaye, 243
Abel, 284
Abraham *See* Avraham
Absalom, 33, 218
Accountability, 146–149
Actions
   antisocial that bring *tzara'at*, 182–183
   evil, 278
   forbidden, 232
   human, 6–9, 15, 23
   in Judaism, 311
   permitted, 232
Adam
   and Cain, 173–174
   creation of, 7, 9–11, 130, 252, 270
   mitzvot given to, 16
   sin of, 7
Adam and Eve, 14
Admor
   of Gur, 293–294
   of Lubavitch, 41, 118

Admor *(continued)*
   of Psetzianah *See* Kalanymus
     of Sokochochaw, 91
Adultery, 56–57, 110–111, 190
Ahab, 150, 166, 215, 276
Aharon, 55, 174–175, 236–239, 242–243, 248
Akilos, the convert, 42–43
Akiva, R., 53, 162, 197–198, 245, 251, 303, 324, 332
Alfasi, R. Yitzchok *See Rif*, The
Alkharizi, 301
Alshich, 137
Amalek, 38–41, 124–125, 255, 319–320
Amnon, 218
Amos, 214, 254, 278, 342
Angels
   and controversy over creation of man, 9–10
Anti-Semitism, 80–85, 309, 334
   Jewish responsibility in, 85–86
Apples, 331–332
Arbitration, 54
Ark of the Covenant, 125, 131–132, 142
Arrogance, 186
Asceticism, 231–235
Asei tov, 351–352
Asham, 161–162, 164, 188
Ashamnu, 188
Asher, tribe of, 353
Ashkenazim, 250–251
Assimilation, 85, 334

Atchalta DeGeulah, 64
Atonement, 135, 167–168, 190, 192, 305, 348
   for social faults, 185
Aurelius, Marcus, 48
Avdut, 89
Avihu, 171–174
Avimelech, 4, 218
Avnei Nezer of Sochochow, 179, 238, 294, 352
Avraham
   and change of name, 20, 47
   and circumcision, 52
   and covenant, 35, 327
   as first Jew, 18
   as friend of God, 55
   God's promise to, 19–20, 79
   and Hagar, 56
   hospitality of, 32
   and Ishmael, 59
   and justice, 4
   and Sarah, 33–34, 56
   and Sodom, 29–30

B'nei hair, 316–317, 319–320
Ba'al HaTurim, 45, 118
Baal, 262–263
   prophets of, 261
Baal Shem Tov, 279–280, 335, 341
Baer of Mezeritch, 341
Bagadnu, 188
Balak, king of Moab, 23, 260, 262–264

INDEX

Banker, 115
Bankruptcy, 119, 295
Bar Kamtzah, 218–219
Bar Kapparah, 47
Batei din, 316
Beit Hillel, 72–74, 247, 352
   and sequence of creation, 6–8
   and *Shabbat*, 7
Beit Shammai, 72–74, 247, 352
   and sequence of creation, 6–7
   and *Shabbat*, 7
Bekeri, 217
Ben Azzai, 171, 198
Benjamin, Tribe of, 218
Be'Or, father of Bilaam, 259
Berachayah, R., 160
Bereishit, 3–4, 77–79
Berlin of Volozin, Naftali Zvi *See Neziv*
Bestiality, 190
Betzalel, 142, 146, 291
Bikkurim, 328
Bilaam, 259–265 *See Also* Bilam
   and Moshe, 260
Bilam, 3, 23
Bilhah, 183
Binyamin, 58
   tribe of, 349
Blasphemy, 189
Blessings
   of children, 69
   for food, 44
   of land of Israel, 328
   priestly, 237, 239

Blood
   eating of, 168
   of sacrifices, 169
Bloodshed, 182
Bribery, 293–294
Bunem of Psycha, R. Simcha, 10, 109, 337, 341
Business
   and competition, 206
   relationships, 196

Cain, 14, 173, 284
Calendar
   functioning of the, 272–273
   lunar, 18, 202–203
Capital punishment, 198
Celibacy, 171–172, 195
Census, 225–228
Chadash, 202
Chafetz Haim, 277, 346
Chag HaMatzot, 98
Chag HaPesach, 98
Chamas, 12–13
Chana, R., 146
Chana, Rabba bar bar, 251
Chanah, 280
Chananael, R., 243
Chananyah ben Akashya, R., 176
Chanina, R., 316
Channa bar Chanana, R., 186
Chanukah, 62, 73–74
   lights of, 237–239
Charity, 30, 116, 200, 205–207, 211–212, 295

Charity (*continued*)
  accountability for, 148–149, 151
  and interest, 118
  Jewish, 206
  and Noachides, 16
Chassidism, 164, 171, 346
Chatam Sofer, 22, 340, 345
Chesed, 29–30, 104, 205–212
  God's, 15, 43, 135, 242
Chidushei HaRim, 10, 142
Chillul HaShem, 189, 242–243
Chisda, R., 162
Chol HaMoed, 351
Christianity, 9
  Jewish, 107, 250
Chukim, 111, 191–192, 194, 312–314
Circumcision, 20, 52, 264, 304, 327
Cohen HaGadol, 188
Communal behavior
  consequences to, 213–217
Communication, 275, 277–279
  social, 279
  spiritual, 279
Confession, 187–190, 192
Corruption
  public sector, 151
  and Sodom, 29
Coucy, R. Moshe, 86
Covenant
  between God and Avraham, 19–20, 35, 38–39, 42, 59–60
  between God and Chosen People, 334–339, 343
  between God and Noah, 16
  eternal nature of, 335–336
  with mankind, 290
Coveting, 110–111, 166
Creation
  cycle of, 270, 272
  of man, 11
  sequence of, 5–7
  story of, 78
  of world, 7, 272–273
Crimes
  secret, 312–313
  societal reactions to, 281
  victimless in Judaism, 112, 161
  white collar, 97
Criminals
  treatment of, 281
Crops, 326–328
  use of, 326
Cycles
  National-agricultural, 271
  national-historical, 271

Daniel, 88, 347
David, 33, 252–253, 260, 276, 304–305, 350
  and Bat-Sheva, 57
  census taking of, 229
Death penalty, 284, 339–340
Depression, 304
Desert
  wanderings in the, 225, 241

Devarim, 287–290
Divine
  anger, 343–344
  attributes, 14, 137, 297–298
  creator, 272
  forgiveness, 50, 135–136
  image, 198
  intervention, 254–255, 262, 268
  justice, 8, 14, 135–136, 214–215, 217, 252, 254, 270
  kindness, 15, 240, 268
  mercy, 6, 8, 14–15, 133, 135–137, 187, 217, 240, 268
  name, 243–246
  plan, 58–59, 61–62
  promise, 194
  promise to protect Israel, 312
  providence, 262–263, 270, 327
  revelation, 108, 261, 263, 268
  sharing of knowledge, 139–140
  voice, 106–107, 141
  wisdom, 144
Drunkenness, 173
Duality
  of mankind, 9–10

Economic(s)
  of enough, 131
  greed, 45
  injustice, 209
  macro- policies, 283
  planned, 208
  uncertainty, 45
  and unethical behavior, 45–46
  yetzer, 300
Edom, 38, 254–255
Egoism, 183
Egypt
  idolatry of, 91–92
  and Jews return to, 319
  slavery in, 309
  ten plagues visited on, 87–89, 91–92, 94
  and those who went down to, 225–226
Eidut, 312–314
Eight, the number, 174
Eisav, 41, 50, 65, 253, 256, 353
  children of, 254
  traits of, 39–40
  and Ya'akov, 37–38
Elazar, R., 229, 234
Eli, 280
Eli, sons of, 56–57
Eliezer, 34–35
Eliezer, R., 20, 36, 42, 125, 251
Eliezer of Damascus, 19
Eliezer the Moabite, R., 99
Eliezer the Modait, R., 102
Elijah, 33
Elijah, *Gaon* of Vilna, 164
Elimelech, 320
Elimelech of Lizensk, 298
Eliphan the Temanite, 259
Elisha, 33, 137

Elisha ben Abuha, 330
Eliyahu, 136–137, 215–216
Eminent domain, Right of, 150
Ephraim, 69–74
   tribe of, 72, 349, 351–352
Eretz Yisrael
   creation of, 346
   mitzvot of, 22
   spirituality of, 21
Esau See Eisav
Esther, 65, 338
Ethical behavior, 196
Eved ivri, 282–283
Evil, 49, 51, 72–73, 299
   inclination, 323
   leaving off, 351
Exile in Egypt, 311
   as prototype of all Jewish exiles, 80
   reasons for, 78–79
Exodus from Egypt, 203, 268, 288, 298, 309, 312–313
   as being forced upon Jews, 95
   as demonstrating halakhic pathway, 93–94
   and Jewish relationship with God, 108
   lessons of the, 96
   purpose of, 97
   and receiving the Torah, 94
Ezekiel, 261
Expulsion, 184

Faith, 322
False oaths, 182
Fasting, 273
Festivals
   agricultural, 268–269
Firstborn, 71, 259
Flood, The, 12, 27
   generation of, 12–13, 15–16, 214
Forbidden, 141–142, 233, 311, 313, 325
   foods, 177–178
   sexual acts, 177, 190–191
Four Species, 174, 268, 331
Free market, 208
Free will, 61, 90, 140–141, 164–165, 178, 187–188, 195, 252, 260, 262, 275, 299
   loss of, 179
   offerings, 165
Freedom
   moral, 204
   physical, 203
   spiritual, 203

Gad, tribe of, 349
Gamliel, R., 272
Gazalnu, 188
Geirut, 89
Gershonides, 136
Gid HaNasheh, 51–52
Gideon, 135

INDEX

God
  chesed of, 15
  and creation of man, 5
  of Judiasm, 13
  thirteen attributes of, 135–137
  unity of, 297–299
Golden Calf, 14, 122, 133–134, 136, 138, 188, 226, 237, 241, 245, 248, 308, 351
Gomorra, 21, 27
Good, 49, 51, 72–73, 299, 351
Gossip, 276
Government, 315–321
Greed, 206, 208–209
Guilt
  offering, 161

Ha'azinu, 343, 345–346, 348
HaCodesh, 353
Hadrian, Emperor, 81, 329–330
Hagar, 19–20, 34
Haggadah, 311, 313–314
HaKadosh Baruch Hu, 3–4, 167, 183, 237, 307–308
HaKappar, R. Elazar, 233
Halakhah, 93, 145, 172–173, 316–317
HaLevi, R. Yehuda, 78, 109, 155
  and leprosy, 183
Haman, 37–38, 40–41, 65, 260
Hammurabi, Code of, 114–115
HaModai, Eliezer, 105

Hanina, R., 292
HaNassi, R. Yehuda, 195
HaShiloni, Adonyah, 278
Hat'at, 160–161, 164
Hayyim, 292
Heaven
  fear of, 306
  for the sake of, 247, 251
Hellenism, 143–144
Hester panim, 339–341, 343
Hiel of Beth El, 215
Hillel, 8, 72–73, 197, 211, 247–248, 251, 353
Hillul HaShem, 243–244
Hirsch, Samson Raphael, R., 22, 37, 45, 50–52, 56, 79, 127–128, 168, 178–179, 185, 204, 206–207, 209, 237, 242, 267, 269, 276, 287, 309–310, 319, 322, 341
  and inheritances, 70
  and *korbanot*, 159
  and plagues visited on Egypt, 89
  and story of Tree of Knowledge, 140–141
  and wealth, 116
Holiness
  in daily actions, 263
  degrees of, 127, 130
  of Jewish nation, 193–198
  paths to, 197, 205
  search for, 228

Holy of Holies, 131
Homosexuality, 190
Hosea, 170, 261
Hoshea bin Nun, 65 See Also Yehoshua
  and change of name, 48
Humanism, 144
Hyksos, 82

Ibn Ezra, 82, 103–104, 107
Idolatry, 34, 87, 134, 215, 297–298, 340
Illness, 181
Immorality, 26–28
  economic, 28, 189–190, 192
  sexual, 134, 182, 190, 192
  social, 184, 208
Incense, 129–130, 249
Incest, 190
Individualism, 228
Inheritance, 69–71
Interest
  and charity, 118
  laws of, 115–116, 120, 312–313
  student, 117–118
  terms for, 117–118
Inuy, 89
Isaac *See Also* Yitzchak
  and justice, 35
Isaiah, 159–160, 261
  vision of, 64
Ish adamah, 328
Ishmael, 20, 38

Israel
  allocation of land of, 70–71
  children of, 51
  and complaints in wilderness, 99–102, 104–105
  creation of nation, 77, 167
  demands made of at Sinai, 155–156
  in exile, 65–66, 334, 338, 342, 346–347–348
  future redemption of, 63–64, 345, 348, 350
  as kingdom of priests, 155–156, 176
  land of, 18, 21, 336
  and national history, 62
  in promised land, 65
  and separation from other nations, 330–331
  spirituality of the land of, 125
  state of, 67, 315, 319
  and unholy acts, 217
  yichus of nation of, 78
Israel *See* Ya'akov
Issachar, tribe of, 349
Ithamar, 146

Jeremiah, 136, 170, 261, 278
Jeshurun *See* Ya'akov
Jewish
  annual spiritual cycle, 268
  banking system, 117
  civil service in, 291–292

INDEX

communities and ethical codes of, 145
leap year, 269
legalism, 164
membership in the people, 226–227
mission of people, 241
nation, 337
national destiny, 214
national identity, 338
national morality, 217–219
nationalism, 346
pattern of oppression in history, 310, 334
people and holiness, 193–198
spiritual misbehavior, 86
stereotypes, 115
year, 266
Jezebel, 136
Joab, 33
Job, 259
Jochanan, R., 3
Jonah, 214, 261, 280
Jonah ben Amitai, 137
Jose the Galillean, R., 303
Joshua, 215, 256
Jubilee, Year of *See Yovel*
Judah, Tribe of, 71
Judaism, 168
    actions in, 311
    and asceticism, 231–235
    aspects of, 171–172, 267, 303–304
    beginning of, 18
    civil and tort law, 114
    and combination of materialism and spiritualism, 22–23, 215–217, 231, 235, 307
    conflict with Hellenism, 143–144
    and creation of a holy nation, 35, 79, 156
    and daily living, 36
    and dualism, 9–10
    and families, 31
    founders and wealth, 216–217
    God of, 13
    halakhic, 251
    and human knowledge, 139, 144
    justice in, 41, 290
    and materialism, 42–43
    membership in, 226–227
    myths surrounding, 164
    national-communal character of, 228, 292, 306
    and two tablets of Ten Commandments, 110–111
Judges, 290–292, 316
    and bribery, 293–294
    impartiality of, 292–293
    and justice, 293–294
    and mercy, 293–294
Judiciary, 291
    establishment of a, 290

Just, 3–4
Justice, 8, 14–15, 30, 54, 135–136, 138, 177, 200, 214–215, 293–294
  in Judaism, 41
  pursuit of, 290

K'lal Yisrael, 229
Kamtzah, 218–219
Kalanymus, 280
Kalisher, 346
Karo, Yosef, 15, 164, 250–251
Kashrut
  laws of, 168
  and sinews, 51
Kavanah, 296
Kedushah, 203
Ketoret, test of the, 250
Kiddush, 204
Kiddush Hashem, 241, 244–246
Kings, 316–318
  limitations on, 319–320
  wealth of, 318–319
Kli Yakar, 338
Knowledge
  divine sharing of, 139–140
  of Good and Evil, 141
  human, 139–141, 143–144
Kook, Avraham HaCohen, 67, 95, 208, 269, 317, 328, 338, 342–343, 346
  and purpose of the Exodus, 97

Korach, 247–251
  congregation of, 248–249, 251
  revolt of, 147
Korban, 266 See Also Korbanot
  sheep as a, 266–267
Korbanot, 156, 158–159, 164, 167–169, 200–201, 237–238
  laws of, 223
  of the Nesi'im, 237
  purpose of, 160
  of Sukkot, 269–270
  types of, 160–161
  tzibbur, 227–228
Kosher, 325
  foods, 195
Kotsker, The, 39, 143

Laban, 4, 48
Lashon harah, 276–277
Lavan See Laban
Law
  family, 322
  of marriage, 322
  Mosaic, 250, 270
Leaders, 316
Leadership
  and abuse of power, 148
  and conflict of interest, 149–150
  qualities of, 138, 291
Leah, 32, 55, 57, 183, 350

INDEX

Leprosy, 181, 183, 185–186
Levi, Tribe of, 70–71
Levi, R., 47, 165
Levy, R., 148
Levy, Isaac, 16
Lifnei iver, 196–197
Loans
    interest free, 116–117, 206–207
    payment of, 294–295
    and rights of debtor, 118–119
    and rights of lender of interest free, 118–119
Loew of Prague, R., See *Maharal*, The
Lot, 19
    and Sodom, 26–28
Love
    applications of, 302
    commandment to, 300–301
Lust, 323–324

Ma'aser ani, 318
Ma'aser sheni, 318
Maccabean revolt, 144
Maccabees, 239
Machpelah, Cave of, 32
Maharal, The, 25, 44, 129
Maimonides, 49, 87, 111, 164, 168, 187, 216, 227, 256–257, 294, 297, 316
    and coveting, 110

    and fear of heaven, 306–307
    and forbidden foods, 177
    and inheritances, 70
    and interest, 120
    and the messiah, 63
    and *mitzvot*, 250
    and *Nazir*, 233–235
    and Noachide Laws, 16
    and prophecy, 106
    and redemption, 68
    and Ten Commandments, 108
    and Third Temple, 121–122
    and Thirteen Principles of Faith, 107–108, 250
Malachi, 170
Malbim, R. Meir Leibush, 49
Man
    created in image of God, 5
Manasseh, tribe of, 349, 351–352
Manna, 102–105
Manslaughter, 283–284
Marah, 101, 111
MarCheshvan, 351–352
Martyrdom, 296
Matan Torah, 203
Matriarchs, 31–32
Meir, R., 14, 54, 329–330
Menashe, 69–74
Mendel of Kotsk, Menachem, 37, 90–91, 93, 109, 120, 129, 142, 165, 175, 179, 194, 251, 278, 280, 337–338

Menorah, 129, 131, 238–239
Mercy, 6, 8, 13–14, 30, 133, 135–138, 207, 293–294
Messiahs, 63–64, 66, 68, 345, 350
Metzora'a, 182, 184
Mezuzah, 96, 296, 311
Micah, 52
Michal, 33
Mikveh, 170–171, 179, 279
Minyan, 228–229
Miriam, 182
Mishkan See Tabernacle
Mishpachot, 228
Mishpatim, 312–314
Mitzvot, 93, 205, 216–217, 249–250, 325, 337
   613, 109, 303, 330
   consequences of not observing, 305–307
   and holiness, 194
   motivation for, 305
   performance of, 303–304
   purpose of, 302–303
   rejoicing in, 304–305
   related to the Exodus, 96
   and teaching to children, 303
   in *VaYikra*, 155
Moadim beSimchah, 204
Mohilver, 346
Money, 45
Moneylender, 115

Monotheism, 269–270, 297
   Jewish, 88, 143
   universal, 77
Morality, 217–218
Mordechai, 37, 65, 338
Moses *See* Moshe
Moshe, 22, 55, 78, 90, 93, 172–173, 182, 193, 213, 226, 237, 239, 253, 262, 288–289–291, 298, 308, 310, 319–320, 349
   and Bilaam, 260
   blessing of, 351
   and building of Tabernacle, 145–147
   and census taking, 227, 229
   and Korach, 248–250
   law of, 248
   and Marah, 101
   names of, 47–48
   and pleading for Israelites, 135–138, 241–243, 261
   and prophecy, 259
   and Promised Land, 242–243
   and smiting the rock, 56, 255
   and speaking to God, 106–107
   and tablets of Ten Commandments, 134
Murder
   deliberate, 283
   and eating of blood, 168

laws of, 110–112
premeditated, 283
and ritual slaughter, 169
Murderer, 283

Na'aman, 181–182
Naboth, 150, 166, 318
Nachmanides, 16, 21, 345–346
　See Also Ramban
Nachshon, 64
Nadav, 171–174
Names
　significance of, 47–48
Napoleonic wars, 346
Nasi See Rabban Gamliel
Nazir, Laws of the, 232–235
Nazirite, 232–234
Nebuchadnezar, 88, 260
Nechemiah, R., 329
Nega'im, 183, 185–186
Nesi'im, 237–239
Netilat yadayim, 180
Nezikin, laws of, 114
Neziv, The, 33–34, 95, 345
Ninevah, 137
Nissan, 350
Nitzavim, 337–339
Noachide
　covenant, 283–284
　laws, 16–17, 116, 177
Noah, 11, 16, 270, 328–329

Noam Elimelech See Elimelech of
　Lizensk
Nonkosher, 325

Oaths, 275
Offering
　burnt, 165–166
　free will, 165
　guilt, 161
　meal, 201
　national, 227–228
　peace, 164
　sin, 161–162, 166, 232
　unblemished nature of, 168
Officials, 316
Ohaliav, 146
Olah, 164–167
Olive tree, 331
Omer, 199–203, 210, 267, 354
　korban of the, 202
Ona'ah, 211
Onkelos, 274
Or HaChayim, 324
Orlah, Law of, 233, 327–328
Ovadiah, wife of, 33

Paganism, 9
Palm, 331
Parah, 353
Parents
　honoring, 111

Paschal Lamb, 269
Passover, 94
Patriarchs, The, 4
Pe'or, 264
Peace, 252–253
  emissaries, 253, 255
  settlement, 256
Peace offerings, 164
Peah, 200, 336–337
Perjury, 276
Permitted, 141–142, 233, 311, 313, 325
  foods, 177–178
  sexual acts, 177
Persecution
  Egyptian, 310
  of Jews, 80–83, 331, 334, 338, 341–343, 348
  pattern of, 80–81, 83–85, 310
  religious, 300
Pesach, 66–67, 94, 149, 201–203, 267–269, 273, 309–314, 330, 350, 354 *See Also* Passover
  Atzeret of, 201–202
Pharisee, 250
Philanthropy, 200, 206
Pinchas, 63
Pniel, 52
Pomegranates, 330
Poverty, 195

Power
  and abuse of, 147–148
  division of, 145–146
Prayer, 45, 171, 236–240, 279–280
  penitential, 135
  of praise, 238
  prescribed, 170
Pregnancy, 179
Pride, 183, 186
Priests
  role of, 184–185
Private property, 232
  rights, 208
Prometheus, 139–140
Promised Land, 22, 287
  generation entering the, 288
  inheritance of, 20–21, 259–260, 349–350
  refusal to enter, 241
  return to, 342–343
  settlement in the, 288
Prophecy, 259–260
  and gentiles, 259
Prophets, 261, 278
Prosbul, 211
Purim, 41, 338, 353
  redemption of, 66

Rachel, 55, 57, 59, 70, 183
  descendants of, 65

INDEX

Rahab, 33
Ralbag, 136–137
Rama, 149, 250, 264
Rambam, 94, 99, 109, 256, 299, 317, 319, 323
Ramban, 49, 56, 99–100, 106, 113, 165, 216, 229, 256, 347
   and candelabra, 237
   and the Exodus, 95–96
   and forbidden foods, 177
   and Golden Calf, 122
   and *Kiddush HaShem*, 242
   and manna, 103
   and miracles, 96–97
   and victimless crimes, 161
Rashbah, 317
Rashi, 29, 64–65, 81–82, 90, 99, 102, 174, 211–212, 229, 244–245, 251, 290–291, 312, 320
   and holiness, 181
   and *mitzvot* specific to *Eretz Yisrael*, 21, 66
   and *Shabbat*, 7
   and sin of Golden Calf, 122
   and social *mitzvot*, 41
   and *yetzer harah*, 140
Rav, 147, 347 *See Also* Yehuda HaLevi
Rava, 206
Rebellion
   of Jews in wilderness, 99
Rechavam, 150
Redemption
   final, 346
   of Israel, 63–68, 79–80, 311, 345–347–348
   language of, 310
   of Purim and Pesach, 66–67
   stages of, 345–348
Refidim, water at, 104–105
Reishit, 259
Repentance, 13–14, 90, 122, 137, 187–188, 190
Restitution, 113
Reuven, 70–71, 162–163, 259
   and Bilhah, 57, 59
   tribe of, 349, 351
Rif, The, 57
Righteous, 3–4
Ritual(s), 160, 170
   purification, 179–180
   slaughter of animals, 169
Rivkah, 31–32, 34–35, 37, 55
   and Yitzchak's blessing, 39
Rosh Chodashim, 350
Rosh Chodesh, 268, 271–273
Rosh Hashanah, 5, 44, 187, 240, 268–271, 288, 290, 305, 332, 337, 339
Ruth the Moabite, 19

S'dom *See* Sodom
S'forno, 103, 134, 308, 341
Sabbatical year, 101 *See Also* Shmittah
Sadducee, 250
Salanter, Yisarel, 304
Samson, 33, 147
Samuel, 147–148, 316 *See Also* Shmuel
Sanhedrin, 283–284, 316
Sarah, 19, 36, 55, 352
   and change of name, 47
   death of, 31
   hospitality of, 31–32
   and prophecy, 33–34
   as role model, 33
Saul, King, 33, 55, 65, 148
Schneersohn of Lubavitch, R. Menachem Mendel, 16
Second Temple, 347
   destruction of, 3–4
   generation of the, 3
Seder, 167, 343
Seder Nezikin, 192
Sefer HaChinuch, 111, 115–116, 218
Sefirat Ha'Omer, 202–203
Sephardim, 250
Sepher HaChinuch, 206
Serach bat Asher, 33
Seven, the number, 174

Sexuality immorality *See* Immorality, Sexual
Sfat Emet, 204
Sh'ma Yisrael, 296–297
   and national memories, 296–297
Shabbat, 7, 101, 174, 238–239, 268, 271–273, 288, 300, 327, 338
   and blessing children on eve of, 69
   and redemption, 67–68
Shabbat HaGadol, 95
Shabbat Shuva, 339
Shalosh Regalim, 268
Shalom, 252 *See Also* Peace
Shammai, 8, 72–73, 247–248, 251
Shavuot, 202, 267–269, 326–327, 354
   wheaten breads of, 202
Shekalim, 353
Shelomim See Shlomim
Shem, 143
Shem MiShmuel, 22–23, 61, 72, 95, 174, 184–185, 240, 255, 263, 266–267, 282, 305, 311, 325, 336, 343, 352
Shemini Atzert, 174, 269, 288
Shevat, 353

INDEX

Shimon, 58, 163, 351
  tribe of, 349
Shimon bar Yochai, R., 14, 20, 165, 274–275, 332–333
  and sequence of creation, 6, 8
Shimon ben Lakish, R., 211–212
Shimon ben Shetach, 245
Shlomim, 164, 166–167
Shlomo of Sochochow, 180
Shmiltah See Sabbatical year
Shmittah year, 44, 205, 208–209, 211–212, 327, 338
Shmot, 77–79, 287
Shmuel, 63 *See Also* Samuel
Shmuel, R., son of Nachman, 59
Shmuel Hakatan, 262
Shmuel of Sochochow, 48, 131, 178, 350
  and Eisav, 40
  and *Shabbat*, 6–7
Shoftim See Judges
Shotrim See Officials
Shulchan Aruch, 113, 120, 317
Sibling rivalry, 54
Sicarii, 3
Simlai, R., 15
Sins
  of actions, 165–166
  of biblical personalities, 56–57
  of business, 189
  economic, 190
  intentional, 161–162
  monetary, 26, 189
  offering for, 161–162, 166
  and *ruach shtut*, 324–325
  social, 184, 186
  of thought, 165–166
  unintentional, 161
Siserah, 33
Slander, 182, 186
Sodom, 19, 21, 25–27, 192, 207, 214
  crime of, 28
  destruction of, 30
Soldier, 325
  life of, 323
  prototype of a, 257
Solomon, King, 10, 33, 150, 159, 260
  and First Temple, 121–123, 239
Sorcery, 264
Soul, 161
Speech
  evil in, 275–276
  gift of, 274
  kosher, 277–278
  nonkosher, 277
  power of, 277
  and prayer, 279
  as tools, 275
  uses of, 278

Spirituality
  hidden, 65
Stranger
  rights of a, 310
Stumbling block, 196–197
Sukkot, 174, 201, 267–269, 271, 305, 338
  Atzeret of, 201
  korbanot brought on, 159
Sur mirah, 351–352
Synagogue, 124

T'shuva, 113, 173–174, 187, 192, 339–340, 342–343, 348
Tabernacle, 121, 126, 132, 142, 174
  altar of the, 128, 131
  building of the, 145, 236
  consecration of the, 173
  copper basin of the, 128–129
  courtyard of the, 128
  in the desert, 223–224
  levels of holiness of the, 127–128
  and the *Ohel Mo'ed*, 129–131, 173, 223, 250
  as place for the *Shechinah*, 156
  raising funds for the, 145–146
  ritual of the, 238
  role of the, 122
  at Shiloh, 125
Taharah
  laws of, 176, 204

Tahor, 158, 176, 178–179
Tamar, 64, 350
Tameh, 158
Tamei See Tumah
Tamim, 165
Tammuz, 351
Targum, The, 98
Targum Onkelos, 70–71
Tarphon, R., 303
Taxation, 151, 315, 317–318, 320
  half a shekel, 227–228, 230
Tefillin, 94–98, 296, 311
Temple
  first, 214–215
  obligation to establish, 123–125
  role of the, 122
  second, 3–4, 215, 347
  Solomon's, 126
  third, 125
Ten, 91–92
Ten Commandments, 96, 106–113, 166, 190, 202, 276, 296, 302
  two tablets of the, 110–111, 131
Ten martyrs, 54
Tephillin See Tefillin
Theft, 110–112, 183, 281–282
Thief
  sold into servitude, 281–282
Thirteen Principles of Faith, 107–108, 250

Tisha B'Av, 98, 351
Tishrei, 352
Tithing, 46–47, 205–206, 269
Tokhacha, 213–214, 217–219
Torah
    consequences of disobeying the, 262
    and the courts, 320–321
    knowledge, 142
    learning, 279
    as living water, 180
    and morality, 141–142
    offered to other nations, 109
    questioning of, 250
    refused by gentiles, 260
    study, 239, 301, 303
    unity of the, 110
    and wealth, 25
Torat Cohanim, 156–158
Tree of Knowledge, 329
Tree of Life, 331
Tribes
    of Jacob, 349–350
Tu BeShevat, 353
Tumah, 158, 176, 178–179
    of a dead body, 179
    laws of, 204
Tur, The, 116, 120, 317
Tzara'at, 181–182, 184–186
    laws of, 181
Tzedakah, 104, 200
Tzedek, 200
Tzellafonit, 33

Uncertainty
    fear of, 100–103, 105, 205, 208–209

VaYikra, 155–158, 168, 176, 287
Viduy, 187–188

War, 323–324
    defensive, 257
    forbidden, 252–253, 256
    halakhot of, 257
    just, 258
    obligatory, 256
    permitted, 252–253, 255–257
    and sanitation, 257
Washing, 129
    of hands, 180
Wasserman, Elchanan, 346
Water, 180
Wealth, 24, 43, 195, 308
    as coming from God, 44–45, 104, 115, 130, 199–200, 206, 209, 354
    lust for material, 205
    moral use of, 25, 51, 103–104
    need for, 130
    purposes of, 46, 235, 353
Wills, 69–70
    ethical, 70
Witness, 110
Women
    treatment of captive, 322, 324

Worlds
  material, 199
  spiritual-moral, 199

Yaakov Yoseph, R., 15
Ya'akov, 36, 41, 42–43, 52, 57, 349, 351–352–353
  and angel of Eisav, 49–50, 52
  and blessing of sons, 69–72, 74
  and change of name, 47–50
  and Eisav, 37–38, 48–49, 51, 63, 256
  and Laban, 4
  and the ladder, 44–45
  sons of, 53, 350
  and tithing, 46
  and Yoseph, 59–60
Yael, 33
Yaphet, 143
Yechezkel, 167, 246, 347
Yechezkel ben Buzi, 100
Yefat To'ar, 323–325
Yehoshua, 48
Yehoshua, R., 20
Yehoshua ben Levi, R., 106–107
Yehuda, R., son of R. Illai, 54
Yehudah, 59, 61, 259
  birth of, 32
  kingship of, 64
  and the messiah, 63–64
  and sale of Yoseph, 54
  and Tamar, 64
  tribe of, 350
Yehudah, R., 25–26
Yehuda HaNasi, R., 48
Yetzer harah, 24, 140, 238, 299
Yetzer HaTov, 299
Yirat Shamayim, 306
Yishayahu, 170
Yishmael, R., 183
Yisrael *See* Ya'akov
Yitzchak, 20, 31, 34–35, 38, 53
  and appeasement of Avimelech, 4
  and blessing of sons, 37, 39, 48
Yitzchak, R., 18
Yitzchak of Berditchev, Levi, 98, 174–175, 343
Yochanan, R., 135, 148
  and sequence of creation, 6, 8
Yom HaAtzmaut, 273
Yom Kippur, 44, 54, 113, 135, 137, 149–150, 156, 162, 187–188, 190–191, 210, 268, 270–271, 273, 282, 288, 300, 305, 339
Yose ben Zimra, R., 229
Yoseph, 52, 70, 325, 351–352
  and coat of many colors, 59
  and dreams, 61
  in Egypt, 58, 60, 65
  and the messiah, 63–64
  sale of, 53–54, 58–59
  and wife of Potiphar, 60
Yoseph, HaRav Ovadiah, 317
Yossi, R., 257
Yovel, 205, 209–212, 270, 282, 327 *See Also* Jubilee Year

INDEX

Zachor, 353
Zealots, 3
Zilpah, 183

Zimri, 173, 351
Zodiac signs, 352
Zusha, R., 299, 341

About the Author

Dr. Meir Tamari is currently the director of The Center for Business Ethics and Social Responsibility in Jerusalem. He was the chief economist in the office of the governor of the Bank of Israel and a lecturer on corporate finance at Bar Ilan University. Dr. Tamari has authored numerous books and articles on business ethics, risk evaluation, small firms, and corporate finance, including *Al Chet: Sins in the Marketplace* and *With All Your Possessions*. He serves as a scholar-in-residence on Jewish ethics in business and economics.